The Disney Afternoon

ADVENTURES

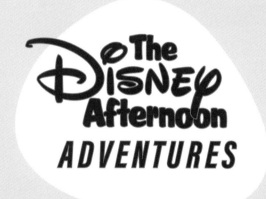

FANTAGRAPHICS BOOKS, INC.
7563 Lake City Way NE
Seattle WA 98115
(800) 657-1100

Visit us at fantagraphics.com.
Follow us on Twitter at @fantagraphics and
on Facebook at facebook.com/fantagraphics.

Publisher: GARY GROTH
Editor: DAVID GERSTEIN
Design: CHELSEA WIRTZ
Production: PAUL BARESH
and CHRISTINA HWANG
Associate Publisher: ERIC REYNOLDS

Thanks to Thomas Jensen, Lee Nordling, Erik Rosengarten, Ken Shue, and David Cody Weiss.

First printing: August 2021 • ISBN 978-1-68396-430-8
Printed in China • Library of Congress Control Number: 2020948306

The stories in this volume were originally created in English in the United States, except where noted, and were first published in the following magazines: "Just Us Justice Ducks" Parts 1 and 2 in American *Disney Cartoon Tales* #7, October 1992 (KJL 010 and KJL 011-1), "The Legend of Tummi, the Werebear" in Brazilian *Disney Mix* #4, May 1989 (S 88023), "A Goofy Movie" ("Dingo et Max," created in French) in French *Les classiques du dessin animé en bande dessinée* #18, July 1996 (E GN 96-06A), "A Beagle Badtime Story" in American *Disney Adventures* Vol. 4, No. 6, May 1994 (KJZ 145), "New Kid on the Dock" in American *Disney Adventures* Vol. 1, No. 7, May 1991 (KZ 3090), "The Legend of the Chaos God Part 1: Crystal Chaos" in American *Disney Adventures* Vol. 4, No. 9, July 1994 (KJZ 132), "The Legend of the Chaos God Part 2: To Half and Half Not" in American *Disney Adventures* Vol. 4, No. 12, September 1994 (KJZ 135) "The Legend of the Chaos God Part 3: Spookus Ex Machina" in American *Disney Adventures* Vol. 4, No. 13, October 1994 (KJZ 141), "The Legend of the Chaos God Part 4: Tow For Broke" in American *Disney Adventures* Vol. 5, No. 1, November 1994 (KJZ 144), "The Legend of the Chaos God Part 5: Reign and Thunder" in American *Disney Adventures* Vol. 5, No. 2, December 1994 (KJZ 148), "Raging Bull" in American *Disney Adventures* Vol. 4, No. 9, July 1994 (KJZ 153), "Mrs. Beakley's Secret Love" in American *Disney Adventures* Vol. 2, No. 6, April 1992 (KZ 3190).

Cover art by James Silvani • Color by Erika Terriquez
Title page art by John Blair Moore and Rick Hoover • Color by Gail Bailey and David Gerstein
Back cover Gummi Bears vignette by Daan Jippes • Color by David Gerstein

ALSO AVAILABLE
Walt Disney's Uncle Scrooge: Island in the Sky (Carl Barks)
Walt Disney's Donald Duck: Jumpin' Jupiter (Luciano Bottaro) (*Disney Masters* Vol. 16)
Walt Disney's Mickey Mouse: The Man From Altacraz (Romano Scarpa) (*Disney Masters* Vol. 17)
The Complete Life and Times of Scrooge McDuck Volumes 1 and 2 (Don Rosa)
Mickey All-Stars (40 international artists, including Giorgio Cavazzano and Mike Peraza)

FROM OUR NON-DISNEY CATALOG
Nuft and the Last Dragons: The Great Technowhiz (Freddy Milton)

DISNEP
DARKWING DUCK

JUST US JUSTICE DUCKS
AND OTHER STORIES

The DISNEP Afternoon
ADVENTURES

CONTENTS

The stories in this volume are presented here in their entirety as first created in 1989-1996.

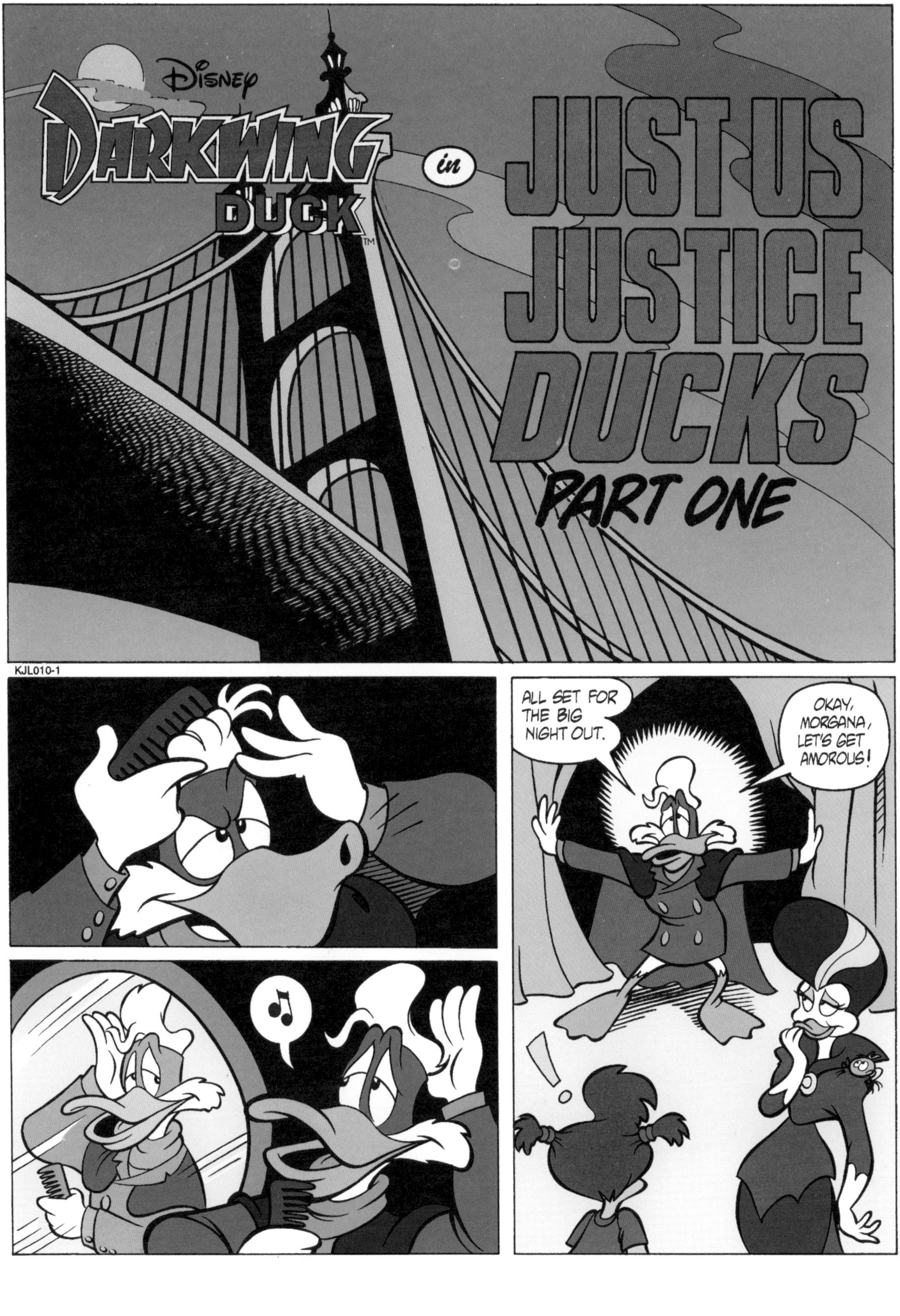
Disney
DARKWING DUCK
in
JUST US JUSTICE DUCKS
PART ONE
KJL010-1
ALL SET FOR THE BIG NIGHT OUT.
OKAY, MORGANA, LET'S GET AMOROUS!
!

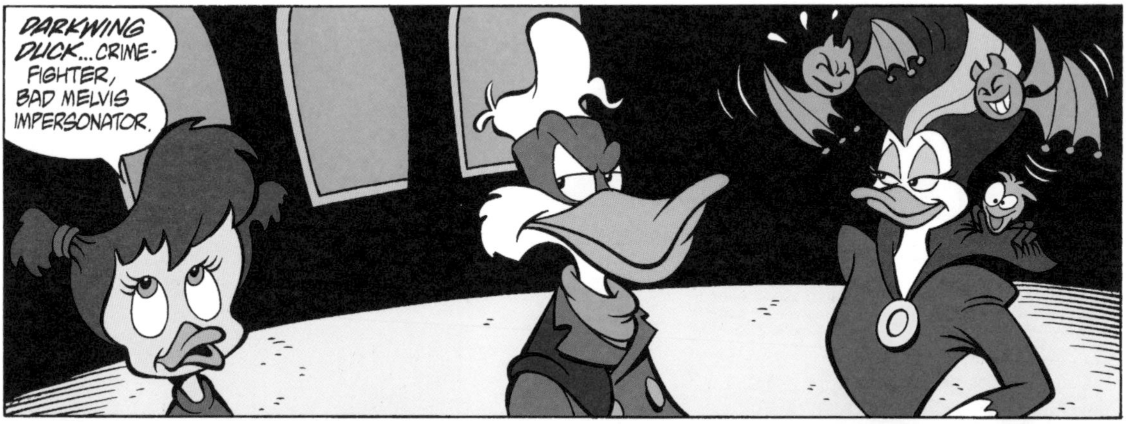
DARKWING DUCK... CRIME-FIGHTER, BAD MELVIS IMPERSONATOR.

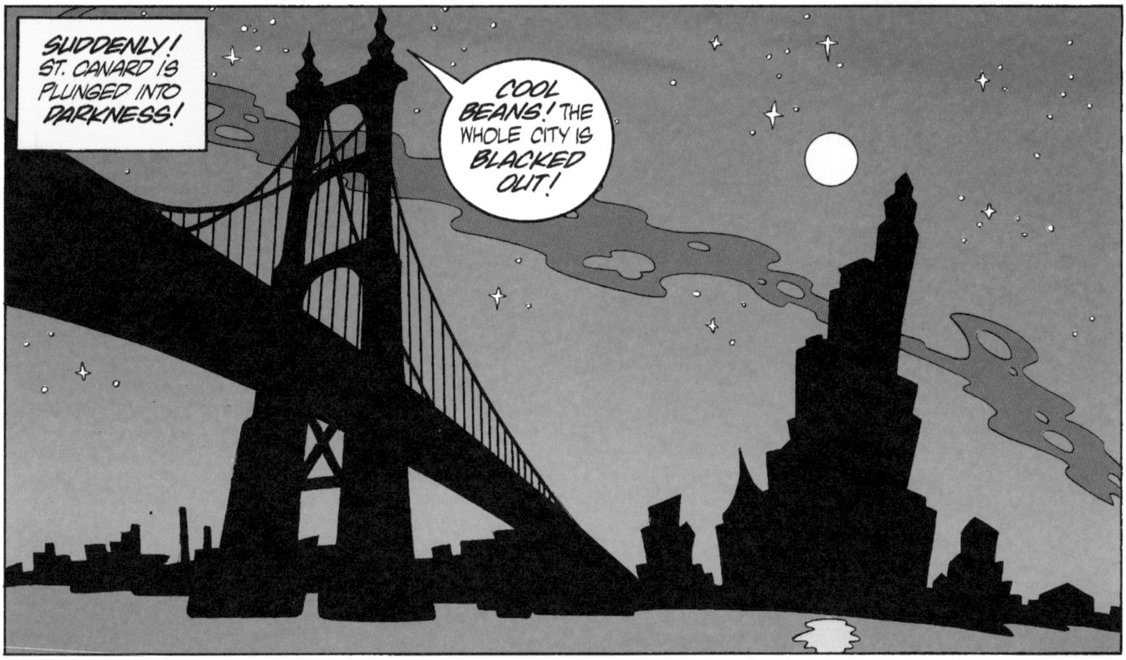
SUDDENLY! ST. CANARD IS PLUNGED INTO DARKNESS!
COOL BEANS! THE WHOLE CITY IS BLACKED OUT!

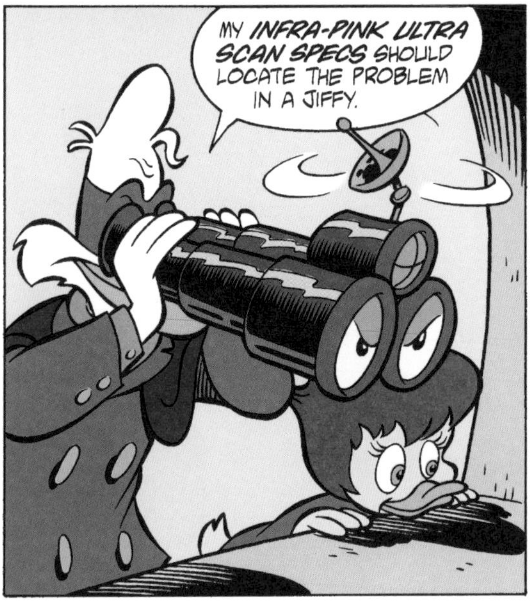
MY INFRA-PINK ULTRA SCAN SPECS SHOULD LOCATE THE PROBLEM IN A JIFFY.

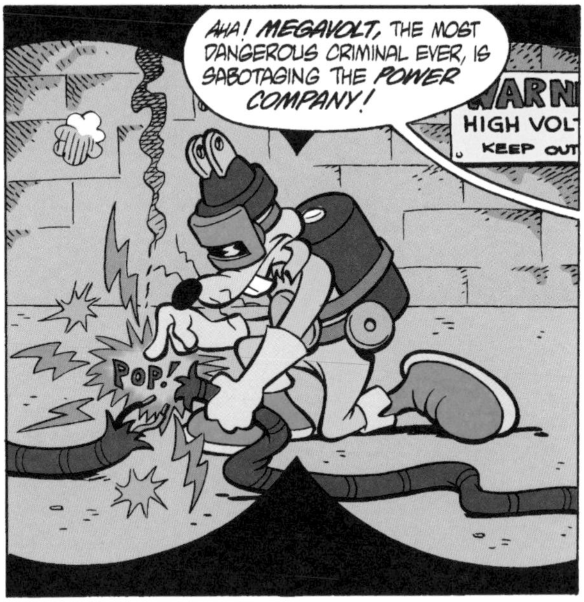
AHA! MEGAVOLT, THE MOST DANGEROUS CRIMINAL EVER, IS SABOTAGING THE POWER COMPANY!
HIGH VOLT
KEEP OUT
POP!

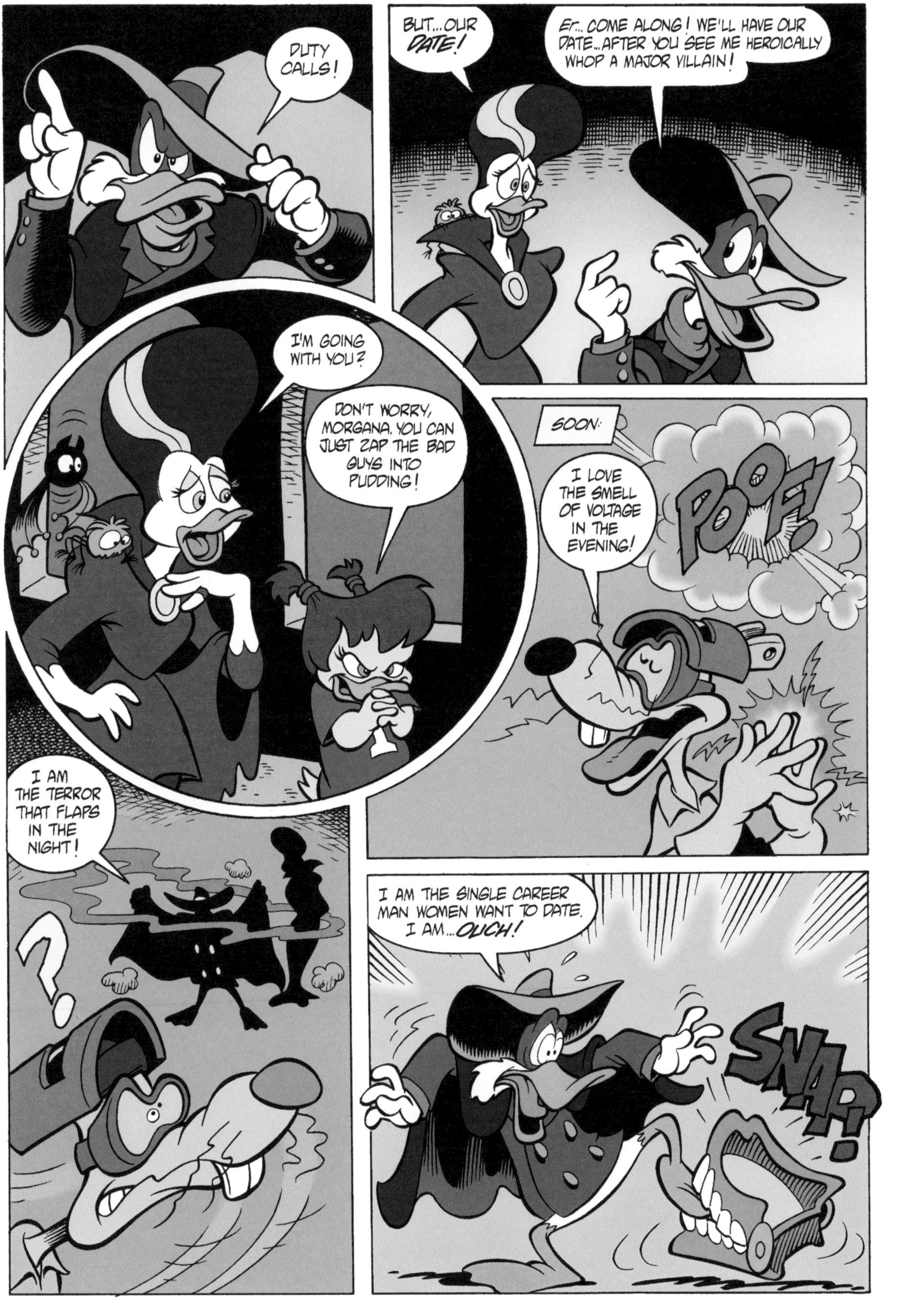
DUTY CALLS!
BUT...OUR DATE!
Er... COME ALONG! WE'LL HAVE OUR DATE...AFTER YOU SEE ME HEROICALLY WHOP A MAJOR VILLAIN!
I'M GOING WITH YOU?
DON'T WORRY, MORGANA. YOU CAN JUST ZAP THE BAD GUYS INTO PUDDING!
SOON:
I LOVE THE SMELL OF VOLTAGE IN THE EVENING!
POOF!
I AM THE TERROR THAT FLAPS IN THE NIGHT!
?
I AM THE SINGLE CAREER MAN WOMEN WANT TO DATE. I AM...OUCH!
SNAP!

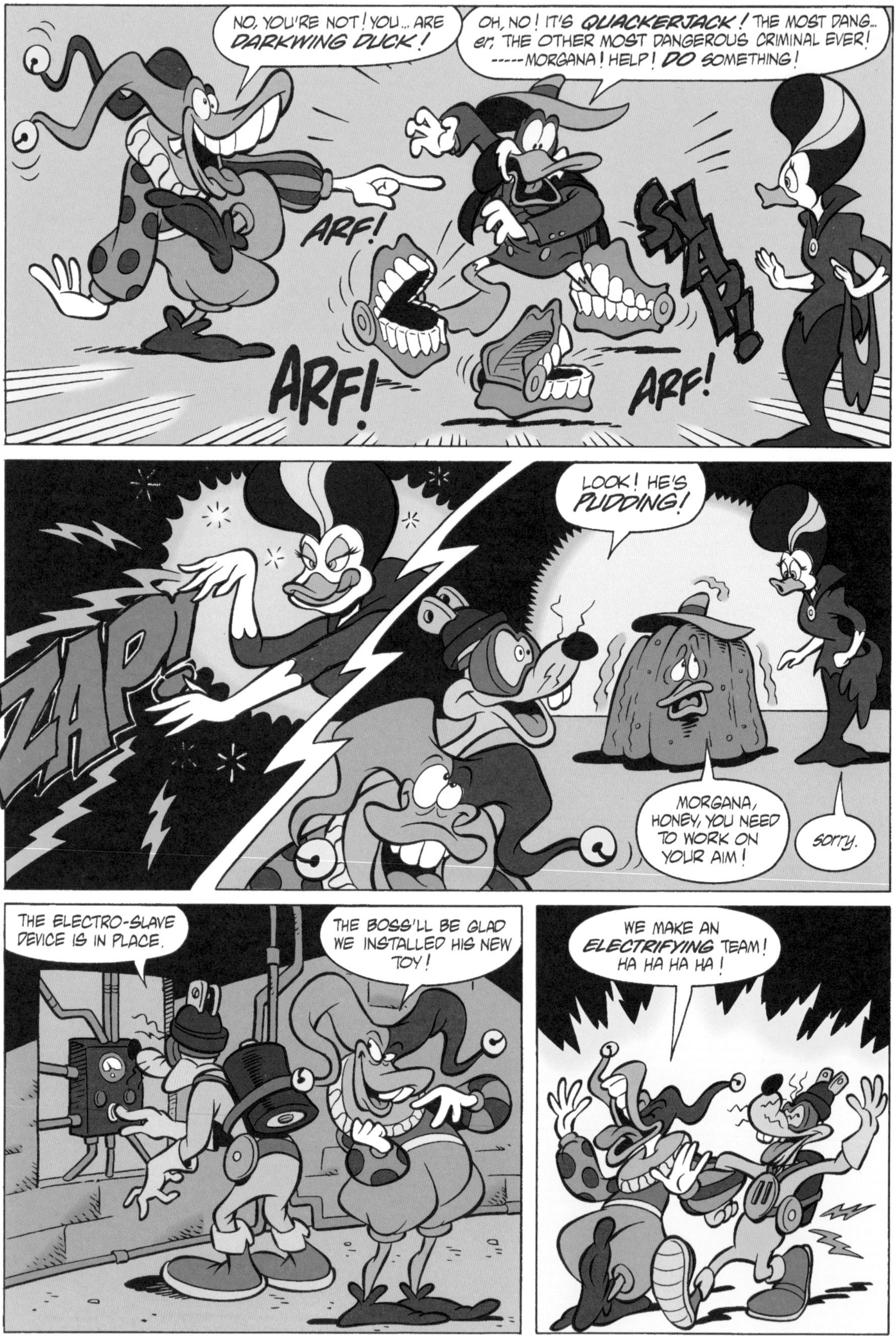
NO, YOU'RE NOT! YOU... ARE DARKWING DUCK!
OH, NO! IT'S QUACKERJACK! THE MOST DANG... er, THE OTHER MOST DANGEROUS CRIMINAL EVER! -----MORGANA! HELP! DO SOMETHING!
ARF!
SNAP!
ARF!
ARF!
ZAP!
LOOK! HE'S PUDDING!
MORGANA, HONEY, YOU NEED TO WORK ON YOUR AIM!
sorry.
THE ELECTRO-SLAVE DEVICE IS IN PLACE.
THE BOSS'LL BE GLAD WE INSTALLED HIS NEW TOY!
WE MAKE AN ELECTRIFYING TEAM! HA HA HA HA!

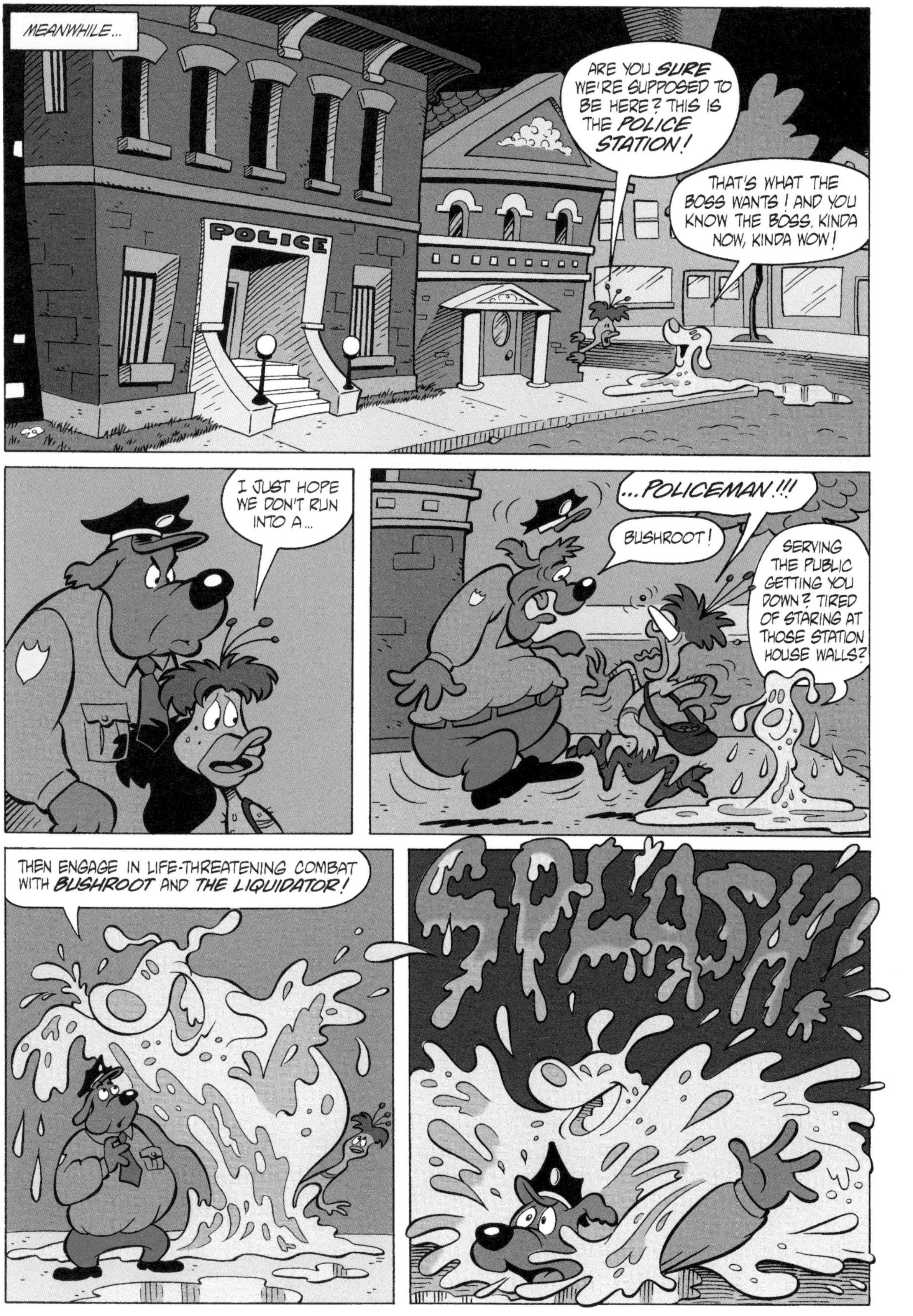
MEANWHILE...
ARE YOU SURE WE'RE SUPPOSED TO BE HERE? THIS IS THE POLICE STATION!
THAT'S WHAT THE BOSS WANTS! AND YOU KNOW THE BOSS. KINDA NOW, KINDA WOW!
POLICE
I JUST HOPE WE DON'T RUN INTO A...
...POLICEMAN!!!
BUSHROOT!
SERVING THE PUBLIC GETTING YOU DOWN? TIRED OF STARING AT THOSE STATION HOUSE WALLS?
THEN ENGAGE IN LIFE-THREATENING COMBAT WITH BUSHROOT AND THE LIQUIDATOR!
SPLASH!

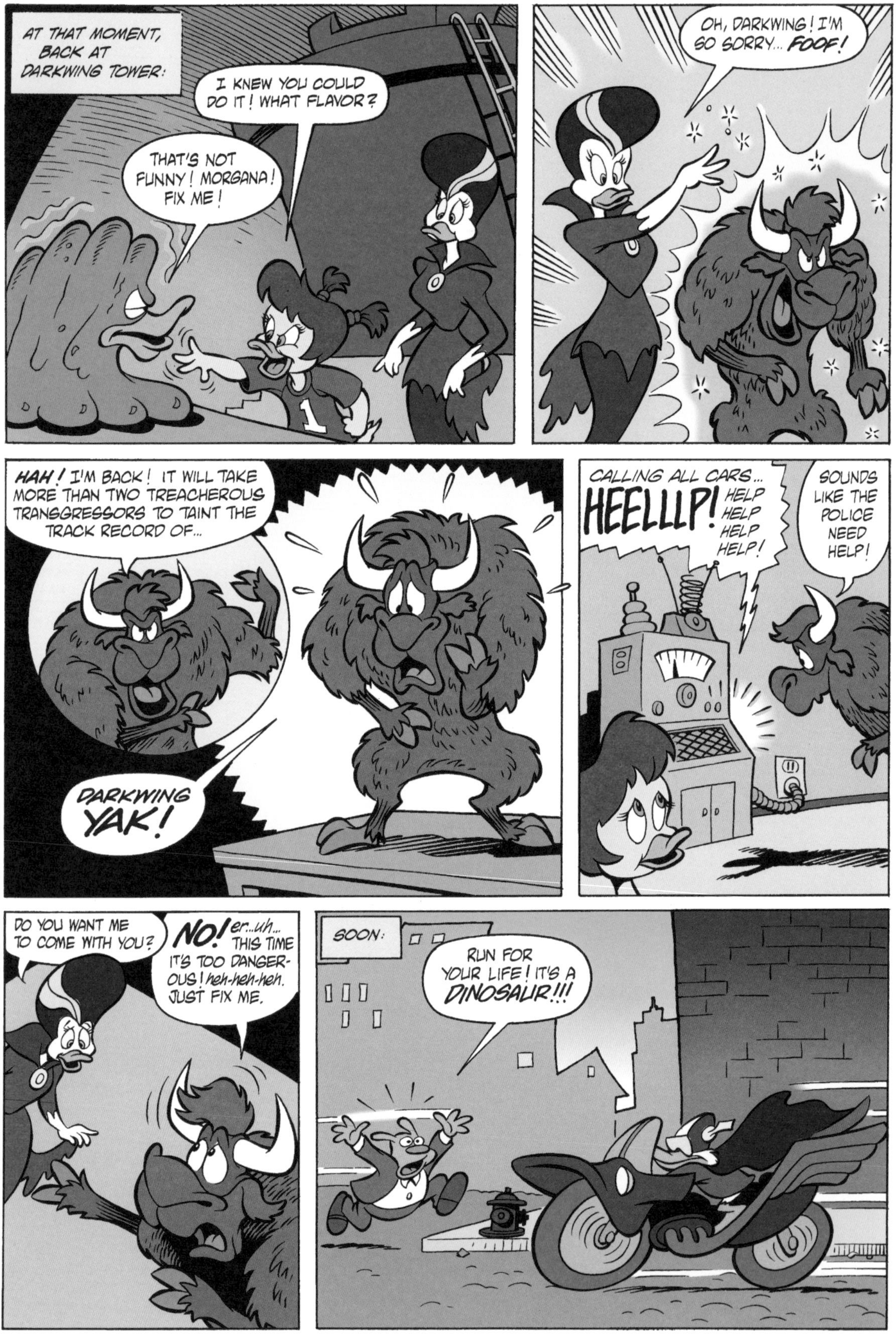
AT THAT MOMENT, BACK AT DARKWING TOWER:
I KNEW YOU COULD DO IT! WHAT FLAVOR?
THAT'S NOT FUNNY! MORGANA! FIX ME!
OH, DARKWING! I'M SO SORRY... FOOF!
HAH! I'M BACK! IT WILL TAKE MORE THAN TWO TREACHEROUS TRANSGRESSORS TO TAINT THE TRACK RECORD OF...
DARKWING YAK!
CALLING ALL CARS... HEELLLP! HELP HELP HELP HELP!
SOUNDS LIKE THE POLICE NEED HELP!
DO YOU WANT ME TO COME WITH YOU?
NO! er...uh... THIS TIME IT'S TOO DANGEROUS! heh-heh-heh. JUST FIX ME.
SOON:
RUN FOR YOUR LIFE! IT'S A DINOSAUR!!!

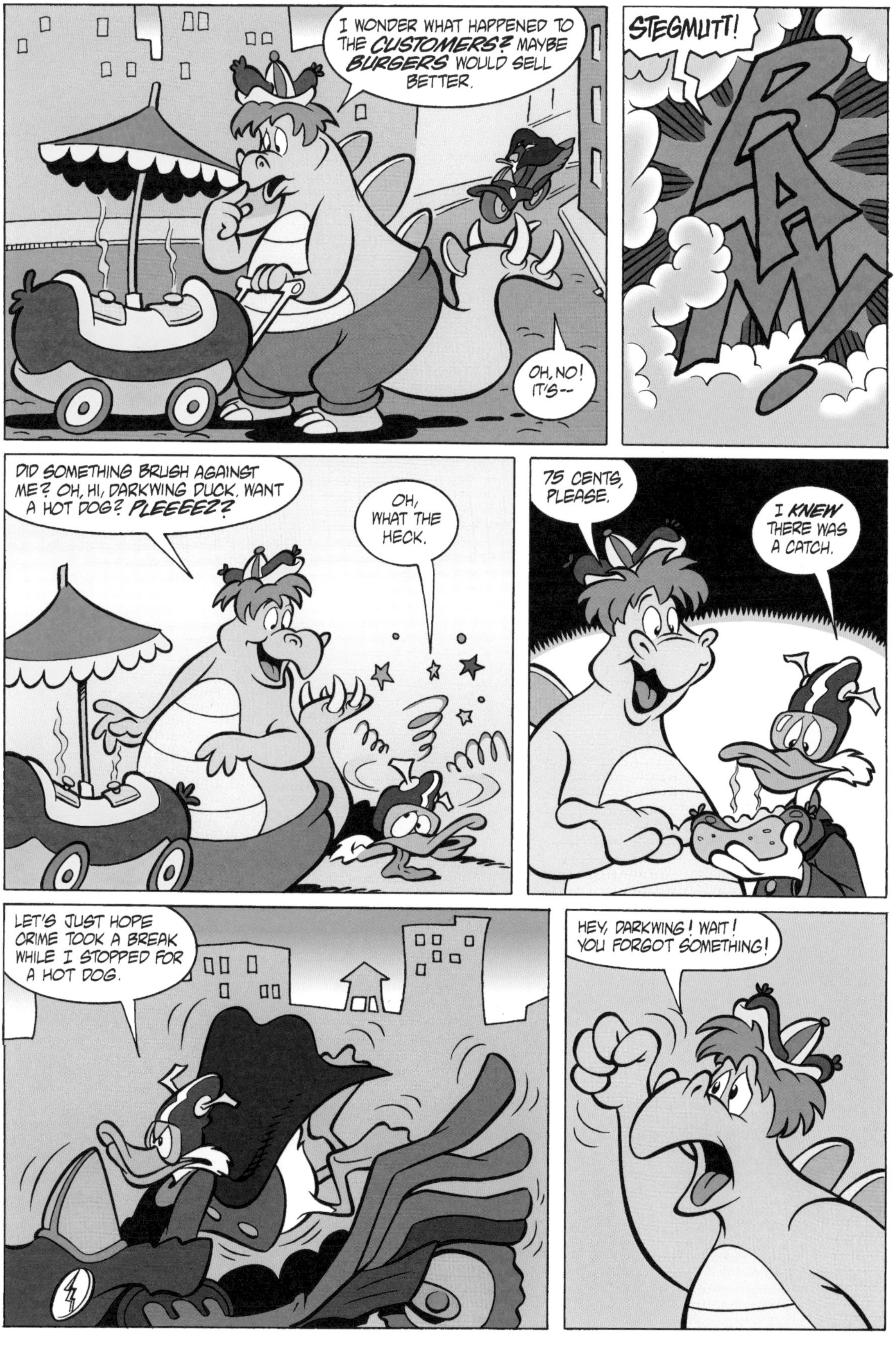
I WONDER WHAT HAPPENED TO THE CUSTOMERS? MAYBE BURGERS WOULD SELL BETTER.
OH, NO! IT'S--
STEGMUTT!
BAM!
DID SOMETHING BRUSH AGAINST ME? OH, HI, DARKWING DUCK. WANT A HOT DOG? PLEEEEZ?
OH, WHAT THE HECK.
75 CENTS, PLEASE.
I KNEW THERE WAS A CATCH.
LET'S JUST HOPE CRIME TOOK A BREAK WHILE I STOPPED FOR A HOT DOG.
HEY, DARKWING! WAIT! YOU FORGOT SOMETHING!

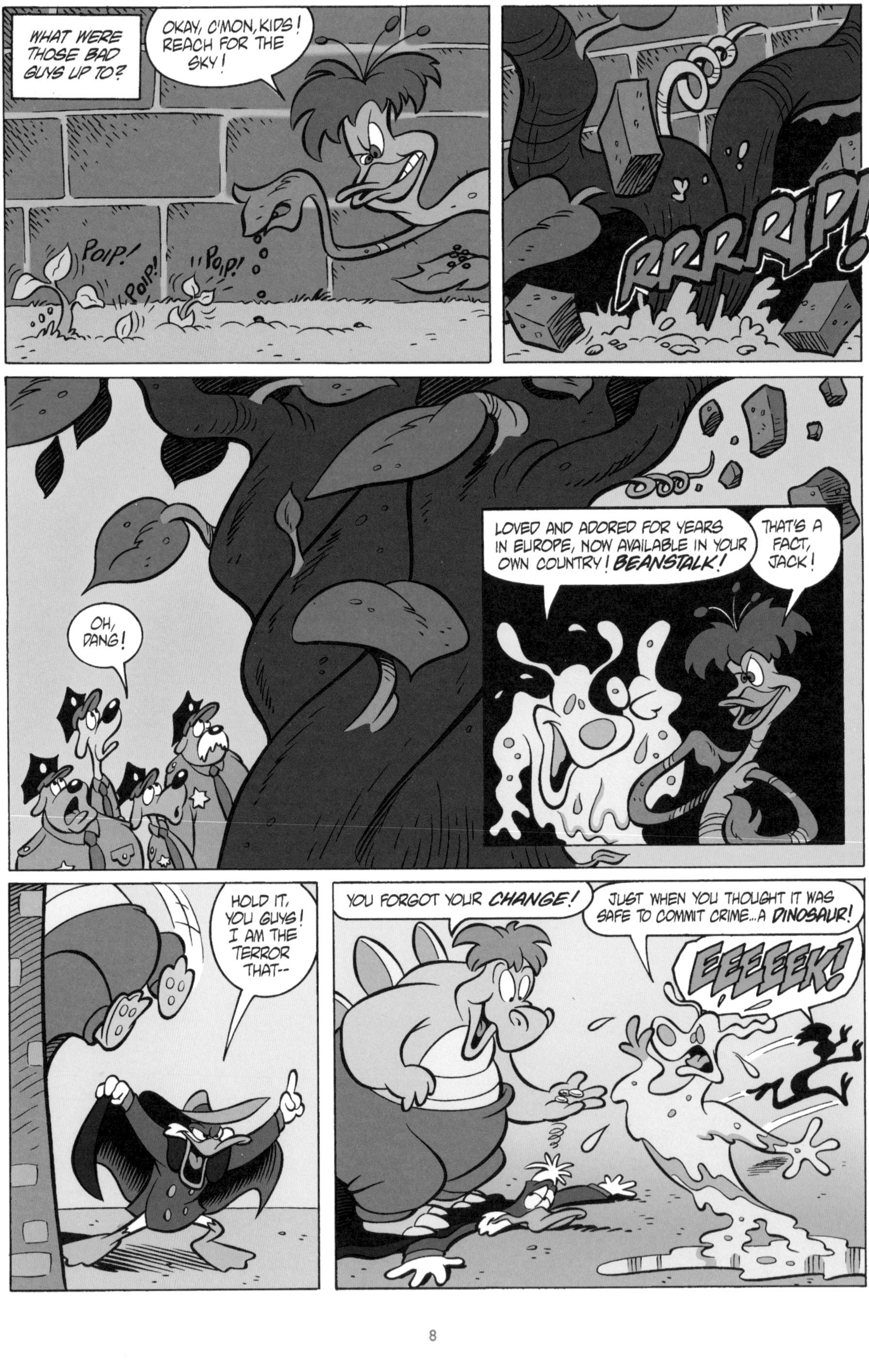
WHAT WERE THOSE BAD GUYS UP TO?
OKAY, C'MON, KIDS! REACH FOR THE SKY!
POIP!
POIP!
POIP!
RRRRIP!
OH, DANG!
LOVED AND ADORED FOR YEARS IN EUROPE, NOW AVAILABLE IN YOUR OWN COUNTRY! BEANSTALK!
THAT'S A FACT, JACK!
HOLD IT, YOU GUYS! I AM THE TERROR THAT--
YOU FORGOT YOUR CHANGE!
JUST WHEN YOU THOUGHT IT WAS SAFE TO COMMIT CRIME...A DINOSAUR!
EEEEEK!

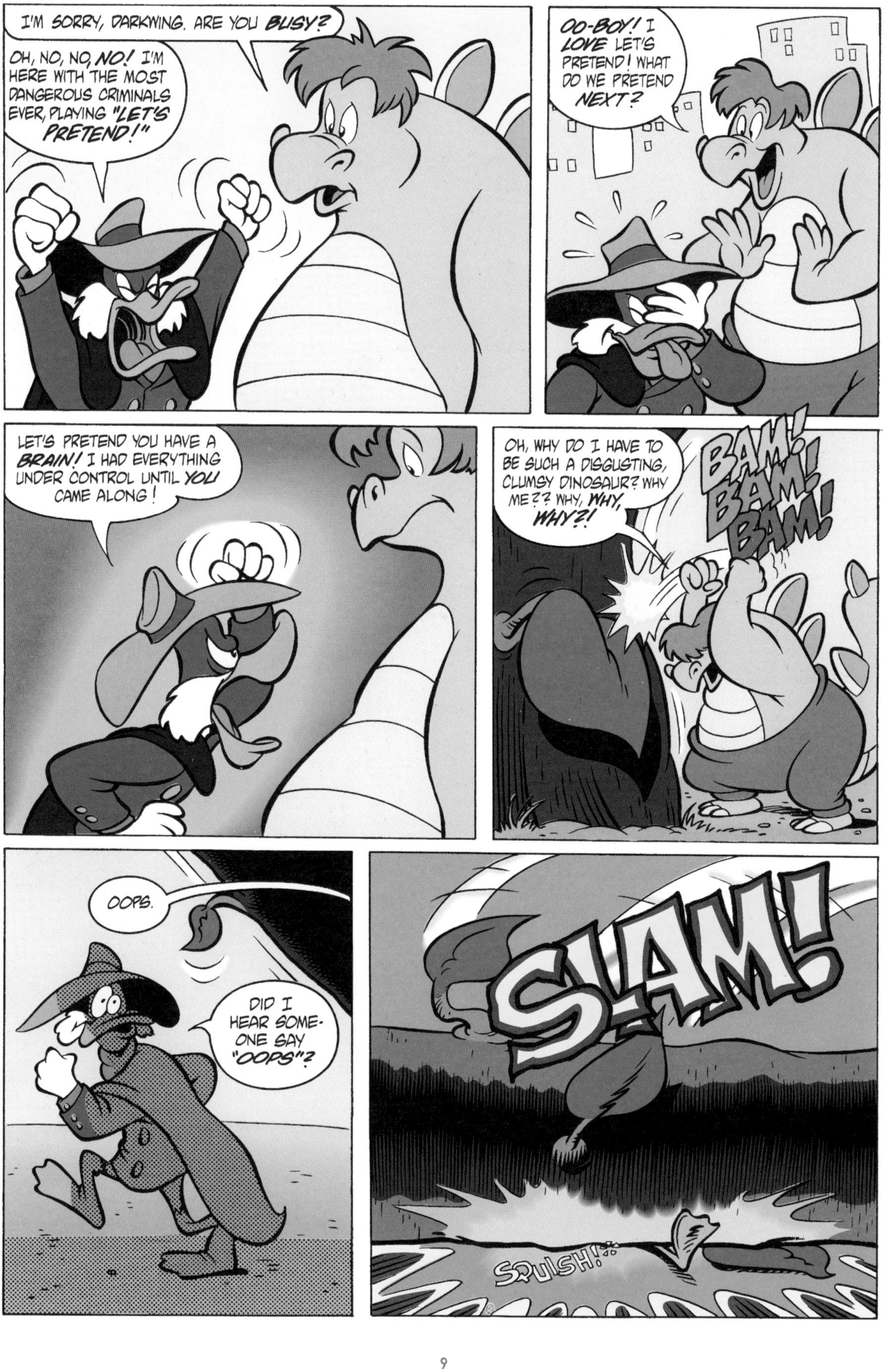
I'M SORRY, DARKWING. ARE YOU BUSY?
OH, NO, NO, NO! I'M HERE WITH THE MOST DANGEROUS CRIMINALS EVER, PLAYING "LET'S PRETEND!"
OO-BOY! I LOVE LET'S PRETEND! WHAT DO WE PRETEND NEXT?
LET'S PRETEND YOU HAVE A BRAIN! I HAD EVERYTHING UNDER CONTROL UNTIL YOU CAME ALONG!
OH, WHY DO I HAVE TO BE SUCH A DISGUSTING, CLUMSY DINOSAUR? WHY ME?? WHY, WHY, WHY?!
BAM! BAM! BAM!
OOPS.
DID I HEAR SOME-ONE SAY "OOPS"?
SLAM!
SQUISH!

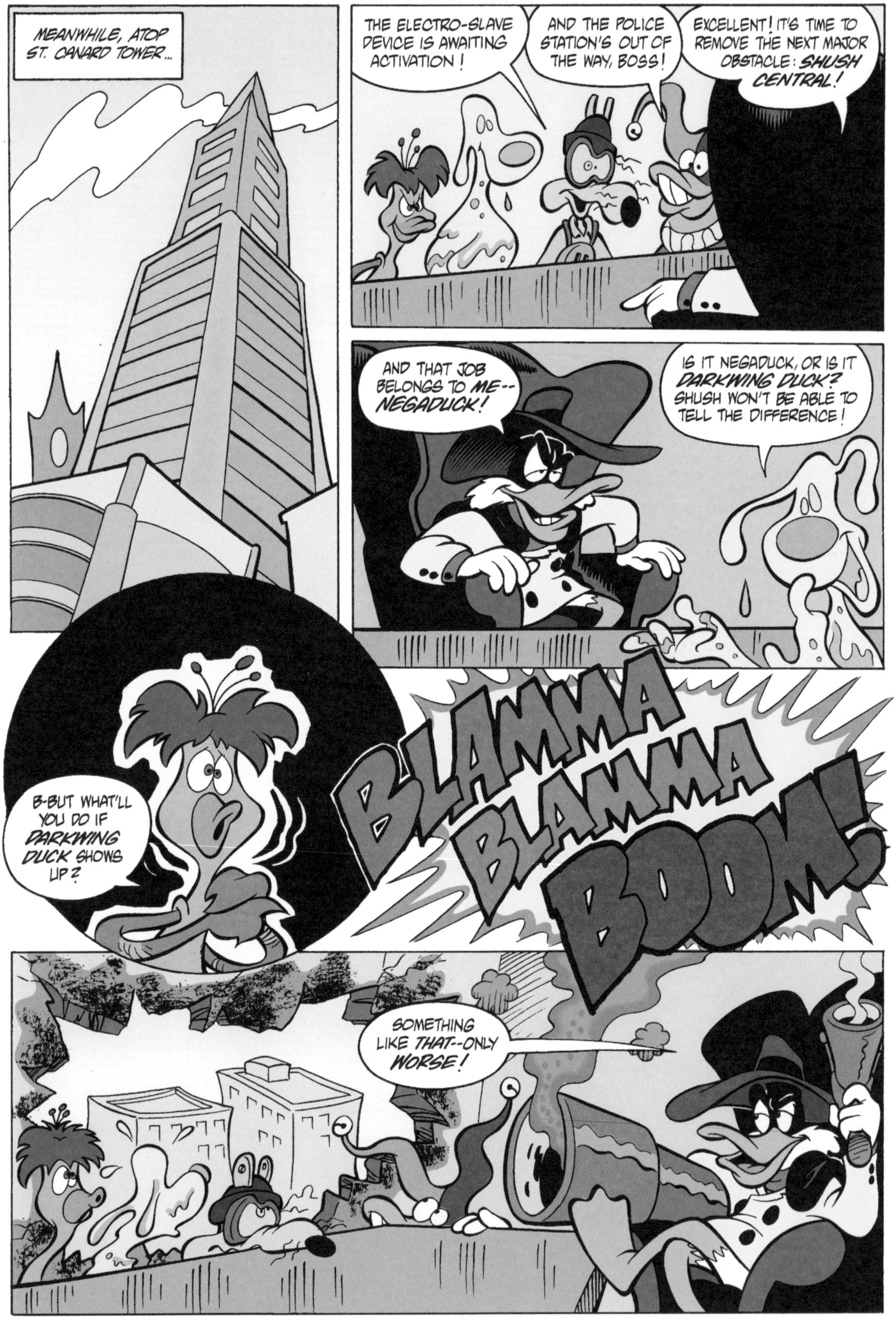

MEANWHILE, ATOP ST. CANARD TOWER...
THE ELECTRO-SLAVE DEVICE IS AWAITING ACTIVATION!
AND THE POLICE STATION'S OUT OF THE WAY, BOSS!
EXCELLENT! IT'S TIME TO REMOVE THE NEXT MAJOR OBSTACLE: SHUSH CENTRAL!
AND THAT JOB BELONGS TO ME-- NEGADUCK!
IS IT NEGADUCK, OR IS IT DARKWING DUCK? SHUSH WON'T BE ABLE TO TELL THE DIFFERENCE!
B-BUT WHAT'LL YOU DO IF DARKWING DUCK SHOWS UP?
BLAMMA BLAMMA BOOM!
SOMETHING LIKE THAT--ONLY WORSE!

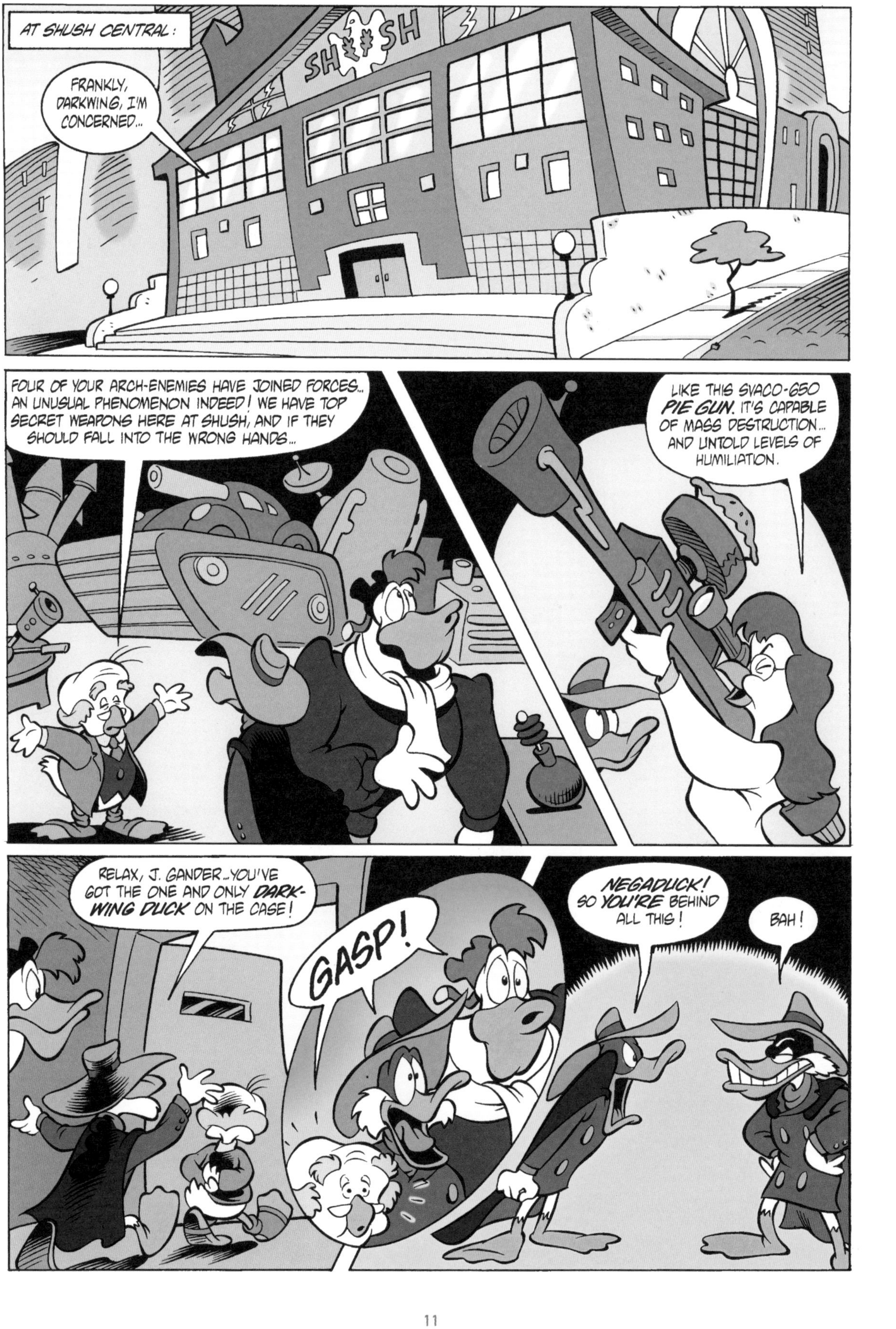
AT SHUSH CENTRAL:
SHUSH
FRANKLY, DARKWING, I'M CONCERNED...
FOUR OF YOUR ARCH-ENEMIES HAVE JOINED FORCES... AN UNUSUAL PHENOMENON INDEED! WE HAVE TOP SECRET WEAPONS HERE AT SHUSH, AND IF THEY SHOULD FALL INTO THE WRONG HANDS...
LIKE THIS SVACO-650 PIE GUN. IT'S CAPABLE OF MASS DESTRUCTION... AND UNTOLD LEVELS OF HUMILIATION.
RELAX, J. GANDER...YOU'VE GOT THE ONE AND ONLY DARKWING DUCK ON THE CASE!
GASP!
NEGADUCK! SO YOU'RE BEHIND ALL THIS!
BAH!

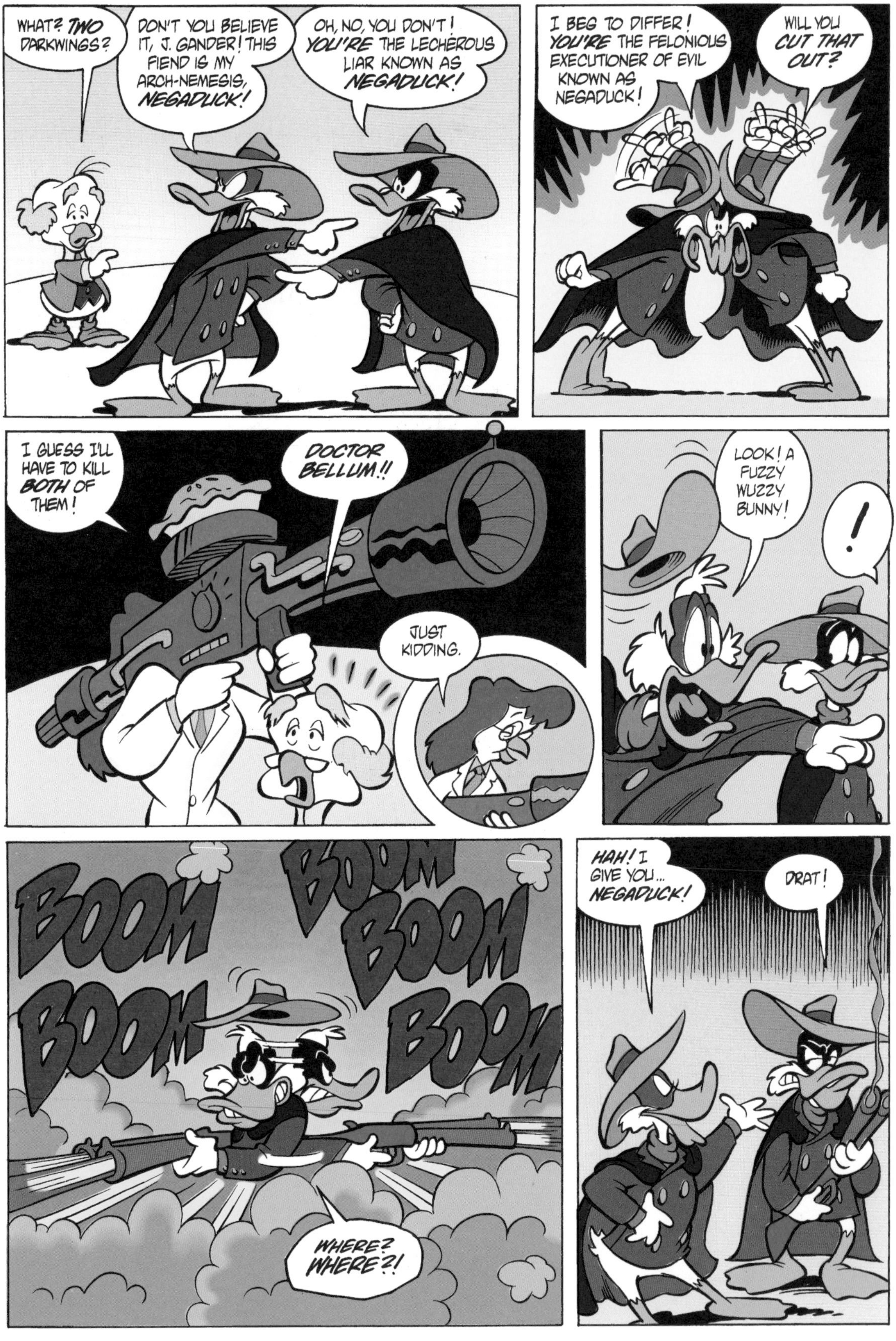
WHAT? TWO DARKWINGS?
DON'T YOU BELIEVE IT, J. GANDER! THIS FIEND IS MY ARCH-NEMESIS, NEGADUCK!
OH, NO, YOU DON'T! YOU'RE THE LECHEROUS LIAR KNOWN AS NEGADUCK!
I BEG TO DIFFER! YOU'RE THE FELONIOUS EXECUTIONER OF EVIL KNOWN AS NEGADUCK!
WILL YOU CUT THAT OUT?
I GUESS I'LL HAVE TO KILL BOTH OF THEM!
DOCTOR BELLUM!!
JUST KIDDING.
LOOK! A FUZZY WUZZY BUNNY!
!
BOOM
BOOM
BOOM
BOOM
BOOM
WHERE? WHERE?!
HAH! I GIVE YOU... NEGADUCK!
DRAT!

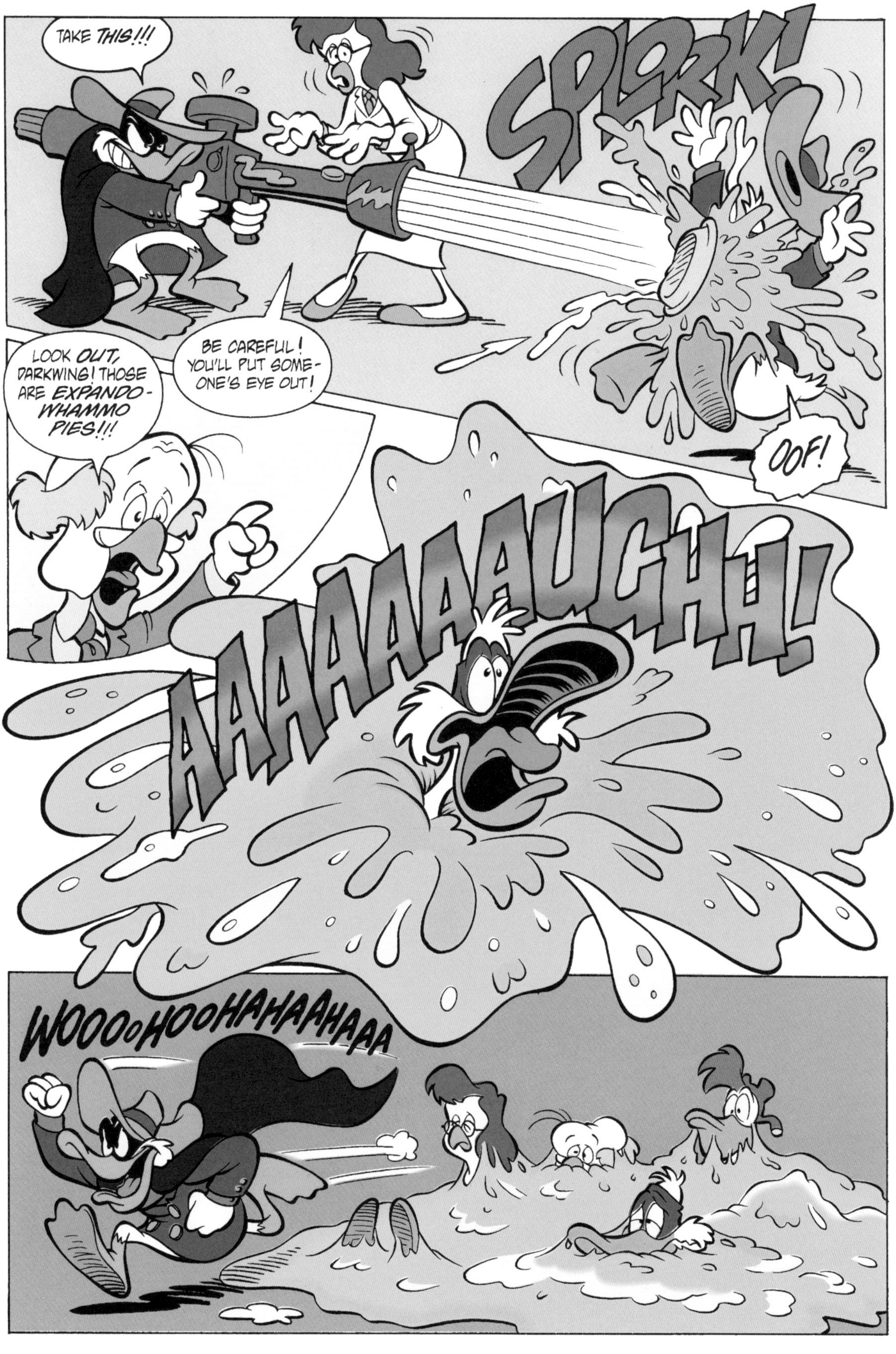
TAKE THIS!!!
SPLORK!
LOOK OUT, DARKWING! THOSE ARE EXPANDO-WHAMMO PIES!!!
BE CAREFUL! YOU'LL PUT SOME-ONE'S EYE OUT!
OOF!
AAAAAAAUGHH!
WOOOoHOOHAHAHAHAAA

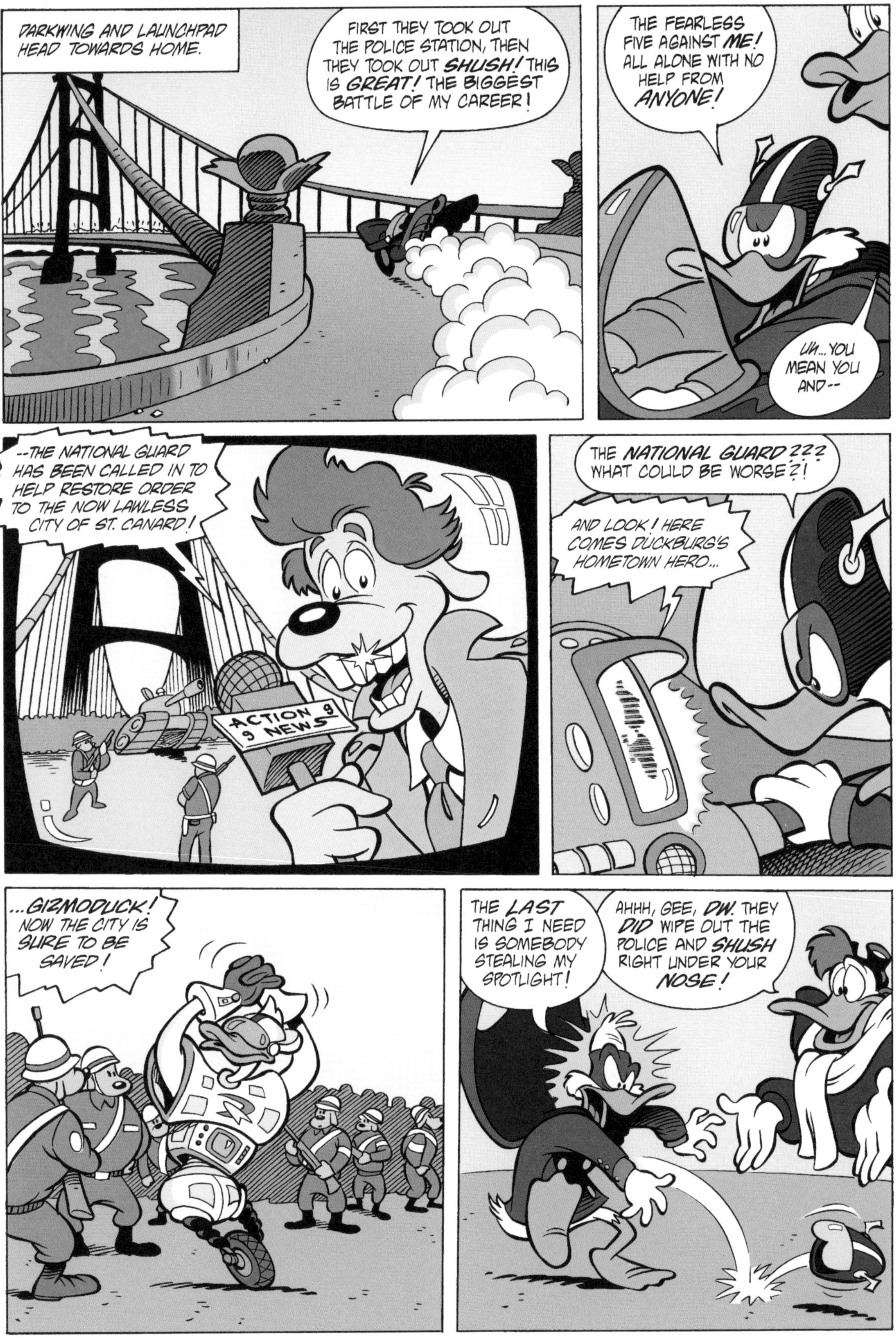
DARKWING AND LAUNCHPAD HEAD TOWARDS HOME.
FIRST THEY TOOK OUT THE POLICE STATION, THEN THEY TOOK OUT SHUSH! THIS IS GREAT! THE BIGGEST BATTLE OF MY CAREER!
THE FEARLESS FIVE AGAINST ME! ALL ALONE WITH NO HELP FROM ANYONE!
UH... YOU MEAN YOU AND--
--THE NATIONAL GUARD HAS BEEN CALLED IN TO HELP RESTORE ORDER TO THE NOW LAWLESS CITY OF ST. CANARD!
ACTION 9 NEWS 9
THE NATIONAL GUARD??? WHAT COULD BE WORSE?!
AND LOOK! HERE COMES DUCKBURG'S HOMETOWN HERO...
...GIZMODUCK! NOW THE CITY IS SURE TO BE SAVED!
THE LAST THING I NEED IS SOMEBODY STEALING MY SPOTLIGHT!
AHHH, GEE, DW. THEY DID WIPE OUT THE POLICE AND SHUSH RIGHT UNDER YOUR NOSE!

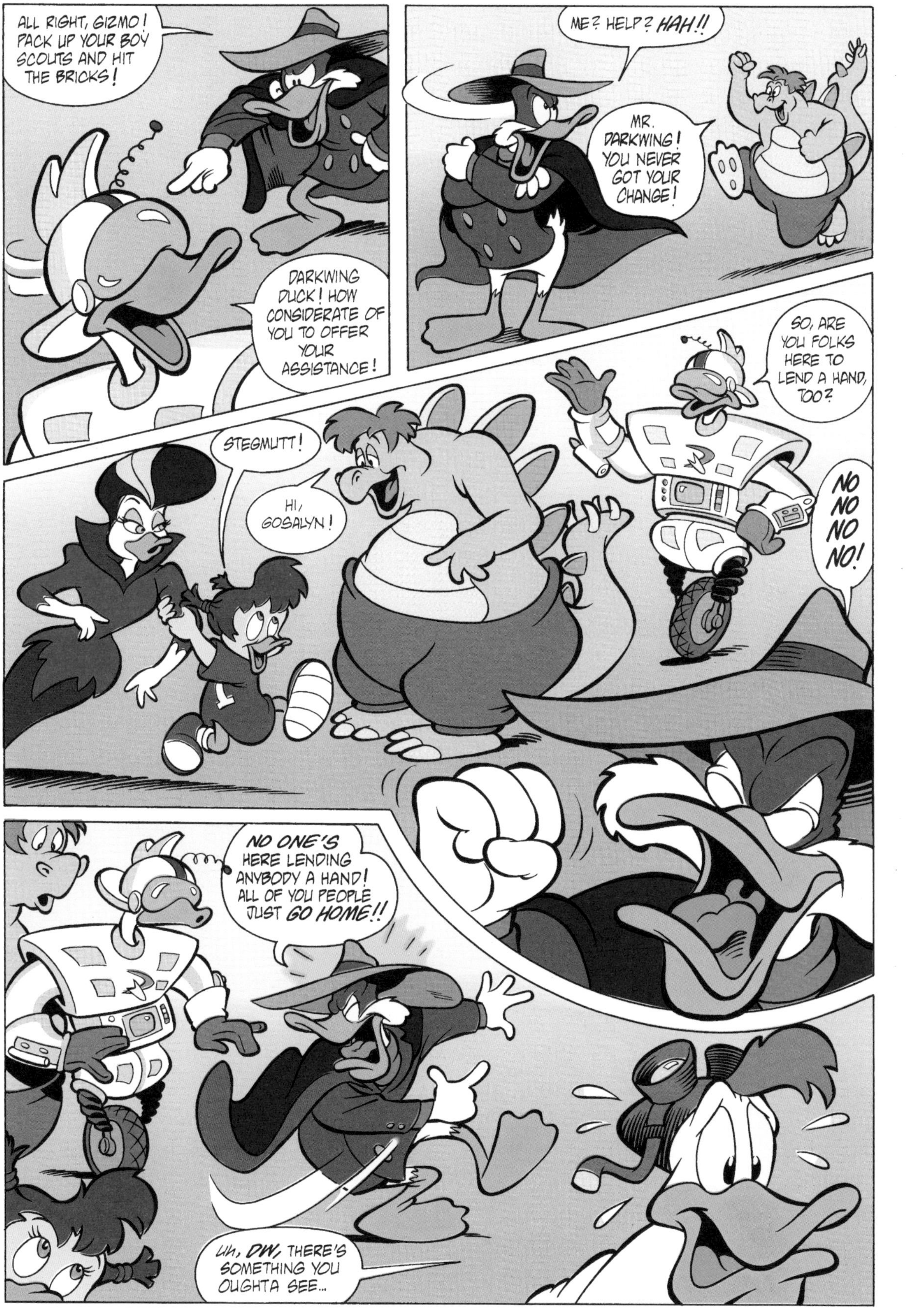
ALL RIGHT, GIZMO! PACK UP YOUR BOY SCOUTS AND HIT THE BRICKS!
DARKWING DUCK! HOW CONSIDERATE OF YOU TO OFFER YOUR ASSISTANCE!
ME? HELP? HAH!!
MR. DARKWING! YOU NEVER GOT YOUR CHANGE!
STEGMUTT!
HI, GOSALYN!
SO, ARE YOU FOLKS HERE TO LEND A HAND, TOO?
NO NO NO NO!
NO ONE'S HERE LENDING ANYBODY A HAND! ALL OF YOU PEOPLE JUST GO HOME!!
UH, DW, THERE'S SOMETHING YOU OUGHTA SEE...

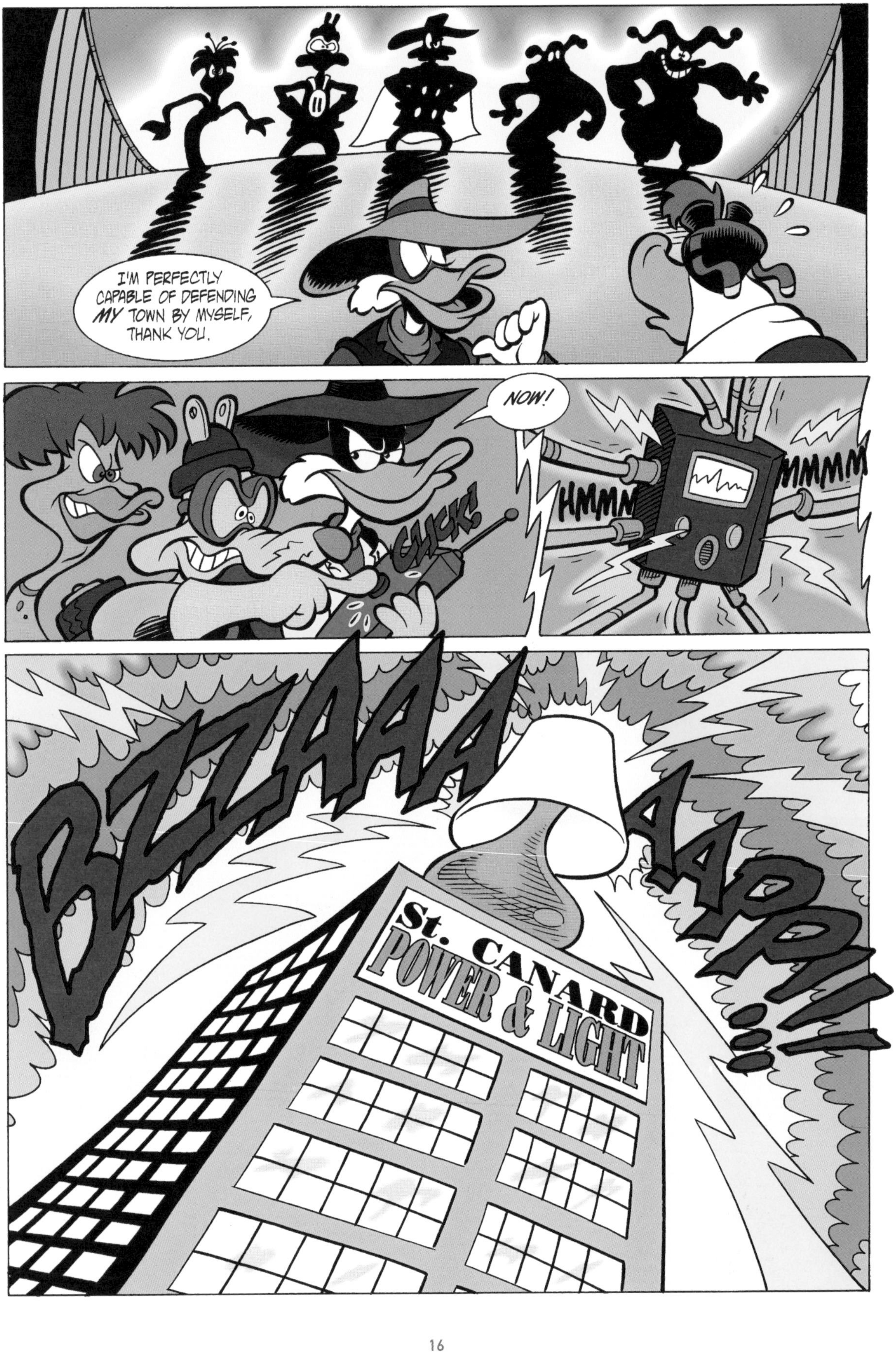
I'M PERFECTLY CAPABLE OF DEFENDING MY TOWN BY MYSELF, THANK YOU.
NOW!
CLICK!
HMMM
MMMM
BZZAAAAAAPP!!!
St. CANARD POWER & LIGHT

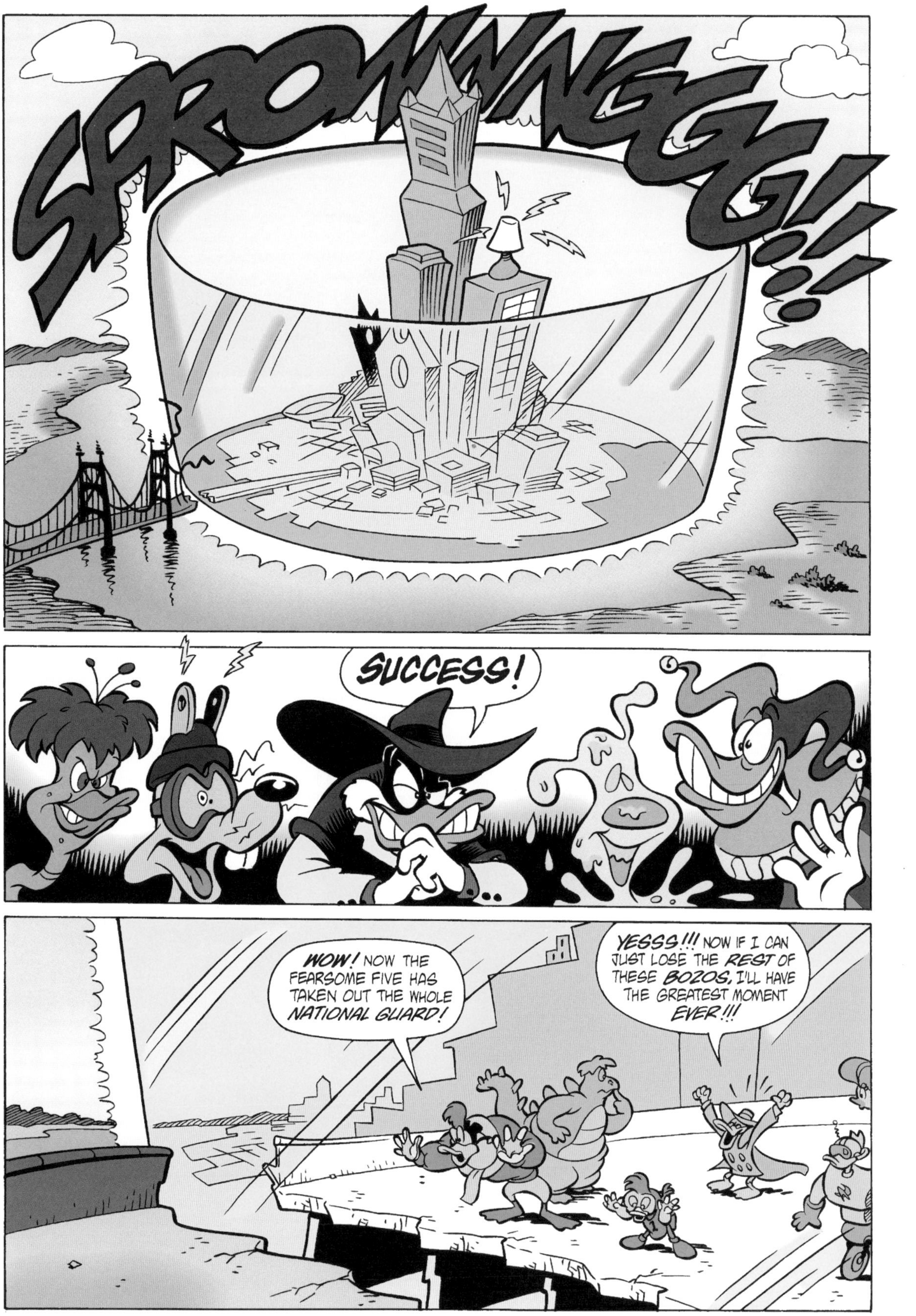
SPROWWNGGG!!!
SUCCESS!
WOW! NOW THE FEARSOME FIVE HAS TAKEN OUT THE WHOLE NATIONAL GUARD!
YESSS!!! NOW IF I CAN JUST LOSE THE REST OF THESE BOZOS, I'LL HAVE THE GREATEST MOMENT EVER!!!

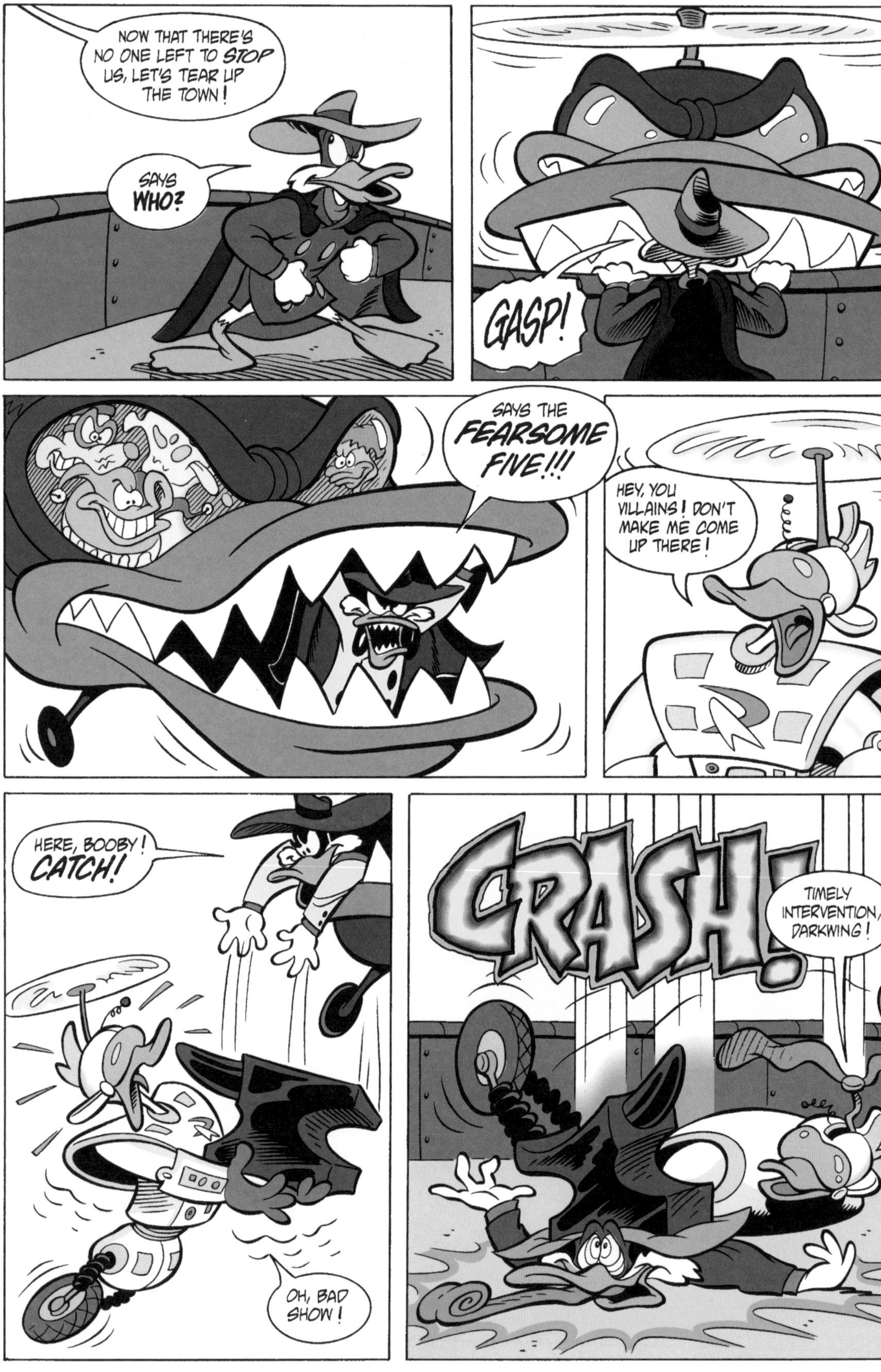

NOW THAT THERE'S NO ONE LEFT TO *STOP* US, LET'S TEAR UP THE TOWN!
SAYS **WHO?**
GASP!
SAYS THE **FEARSOME FIVE!!!**
HEY, YOU VILLAINS! DON'T MAKE ME COME UP THERE!
HERE, BOOBY! **CATCH!**
OH, BAD SHOW!
CRASH!
TIMELY INTERVENTION, DARKWING!

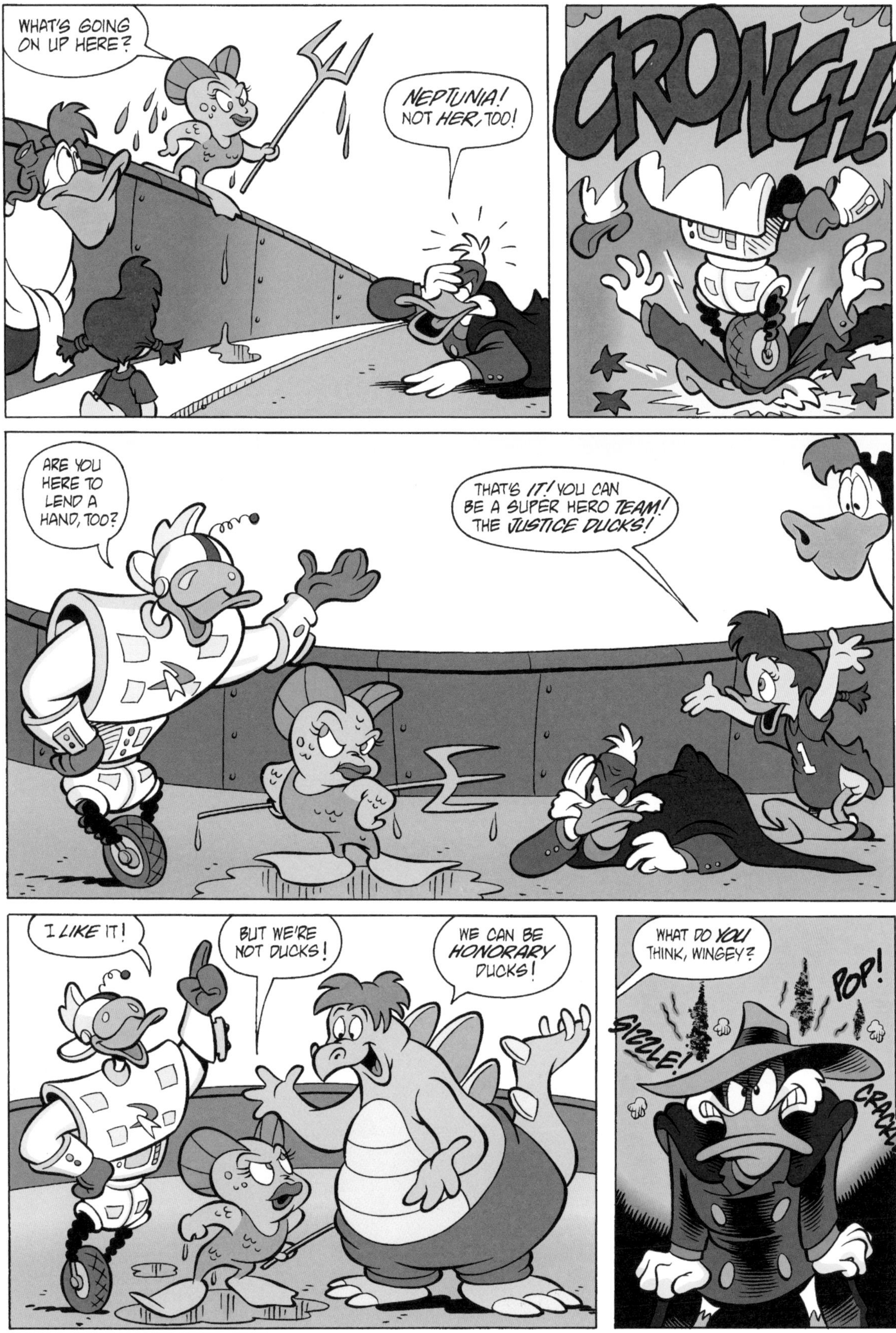
WHAT'S GOING ON UP HERE?
NEPTUNIA! NOT HER, TOO!
CRONCH!
ARE YOU HERE TO LEND A HAND, TOO?
THAT'S IT! YOU CAN BE A SUPER HERO TEAM! THE JUSTICE DUCKS!
I LIKE IT!
BUT WE'RE NOT DUCKS!
WE CAN BE HONORARY DUCKS!
WHAT DO YOU THINK, WINGEY?
SIZZLE!
POP!
CRACKLE!

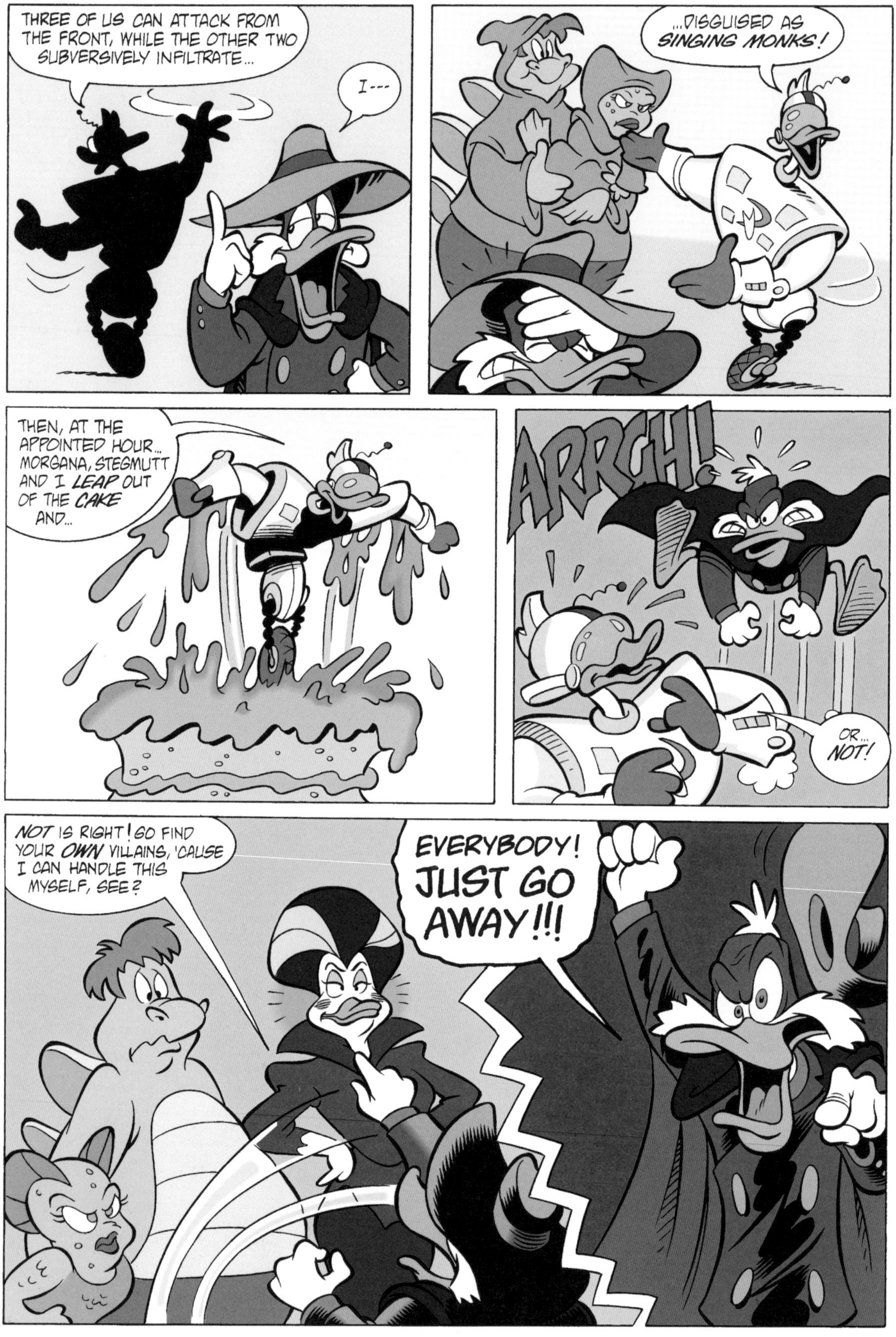
THREE OF US CAN ATTACK FROM THE FRONT, WHILE THE OTHER TWO SUBVERSIVELY INFILTRATE...
I---
...DISGUISED AS SINGING MONKS!
THEN, AT THE APPOINTED HOUR... MORGANA, STEGMUTT AND I LEAP OUT OF THE CAKE AND...
ARRGH!
OR... NOT!
NOT IS RIGHT! GO FIND YOUR OWN VILLAINS, 'CAUSE I CAN HANDLE THIS MYSELF, SEE?
EVERYBODY! JUST GO AWAY!!!

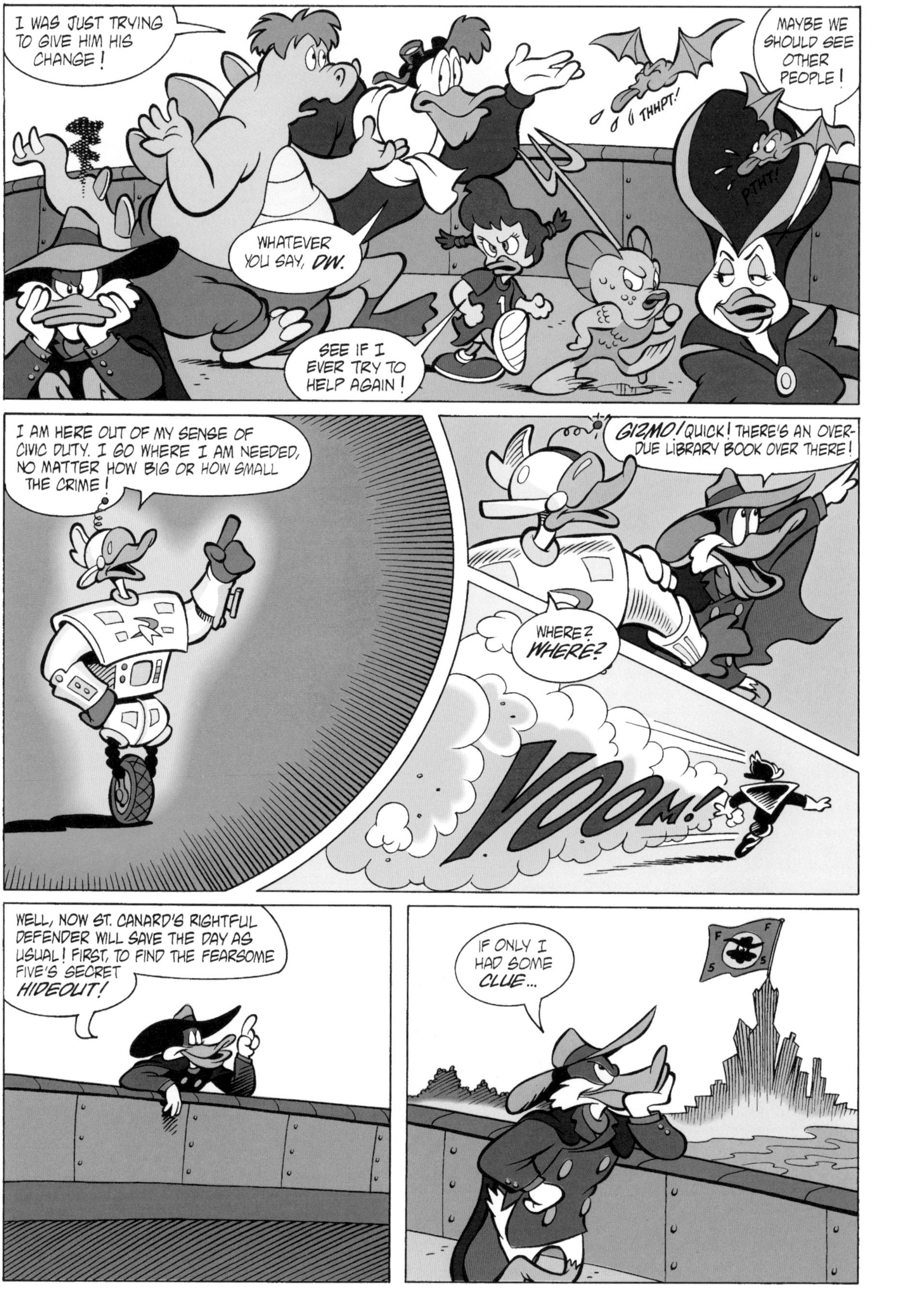
I WAS JUST TRYING TO GIVE HIM HIS CHANGE!
THHPT!
P-THT!
MAYBE WE SHOULD SEE OTHER PEOPLE!
WHATEVER YOU SAY, DW.
SEE IF I EVER TRY TO HELP AGAIN!
I AM HERE OUT OF MY SENSE OF CIVIC DUTY. I GO WHERE I AM NEEDED, NO MATTER HOW BIG OR HOW SMALL THE CRIME!
GIZMO! QUICK! THERE'S AN OVER-DUE LIBRARY BOOK OVER THERE!
WHERE? WHERE?
VOOM!
WELL, NOW ST. CANARD'S RIGHTFUL DEFENDER WILL SAVE THE DAY AS USUAL! FIRST, TO FIND THE FEARSOME FIVE'S SECRET HIDEOUT!
IF ONLY I HAD SOME CLUE...

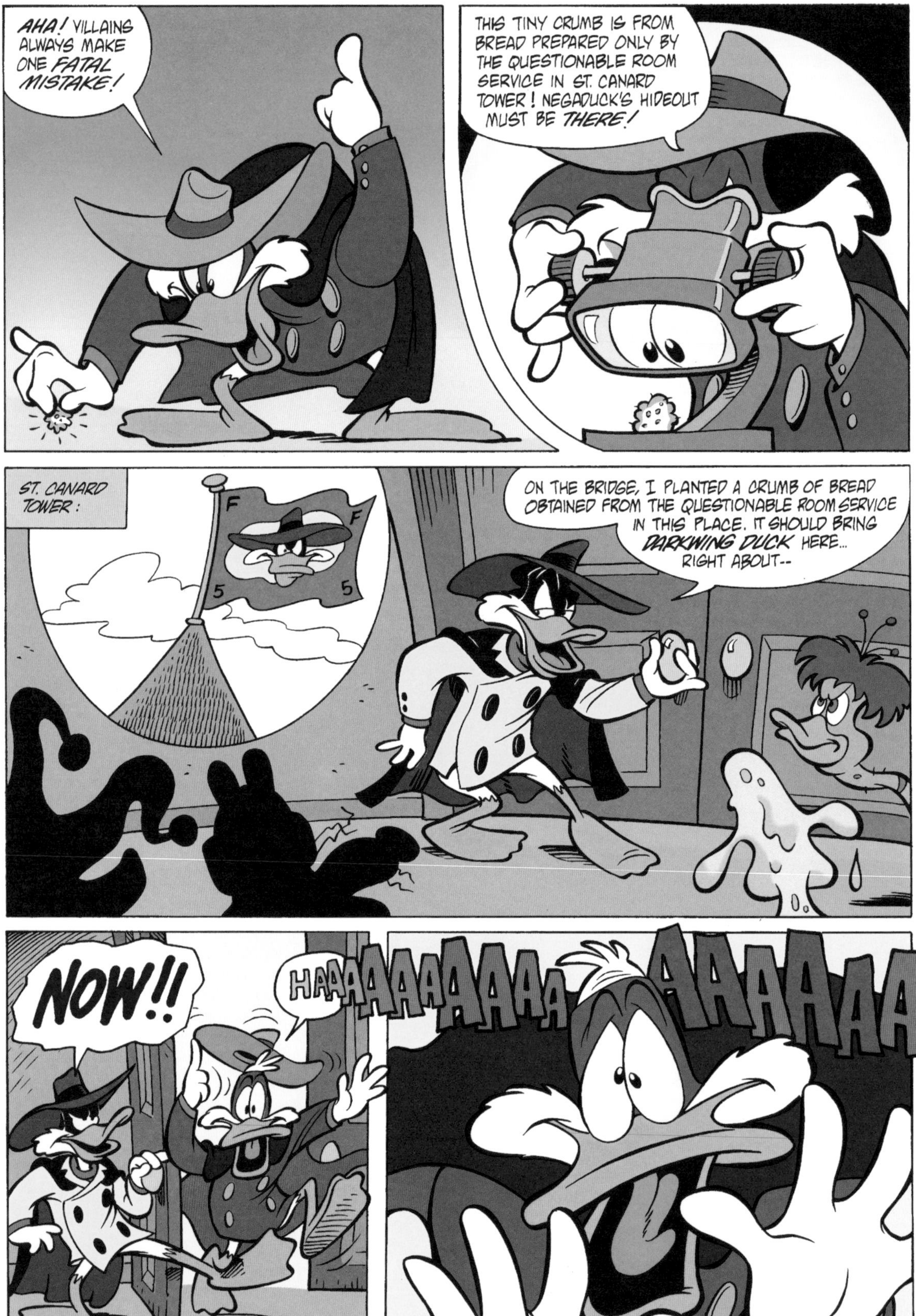
AHA! VILLAINS ALWAYS MAKE ONE FATAL MISTAKE!
THIS TINY CRUMB IS FROM BREAD PREPARED ONLY BY THE QUESTIONABLE ROOM SERVICE IN ST. CANARD TOWER! NEGADUCK'S HIDEOUT MUST BE THERE!
ST. CANARD TOWER:
F F 5 5
ON THE BRIDGE, I PLANTED A CRUMB OF BREAD OBTAINED FROM THE QUESTIONABLE ROOM SERVICE IN THIS PLACE. IT SHOULD BRING DARKWING DUCK HERE... RIGHT ABOUT--
NOW!!
HAAAAAAAAAAAAAAAAAAA

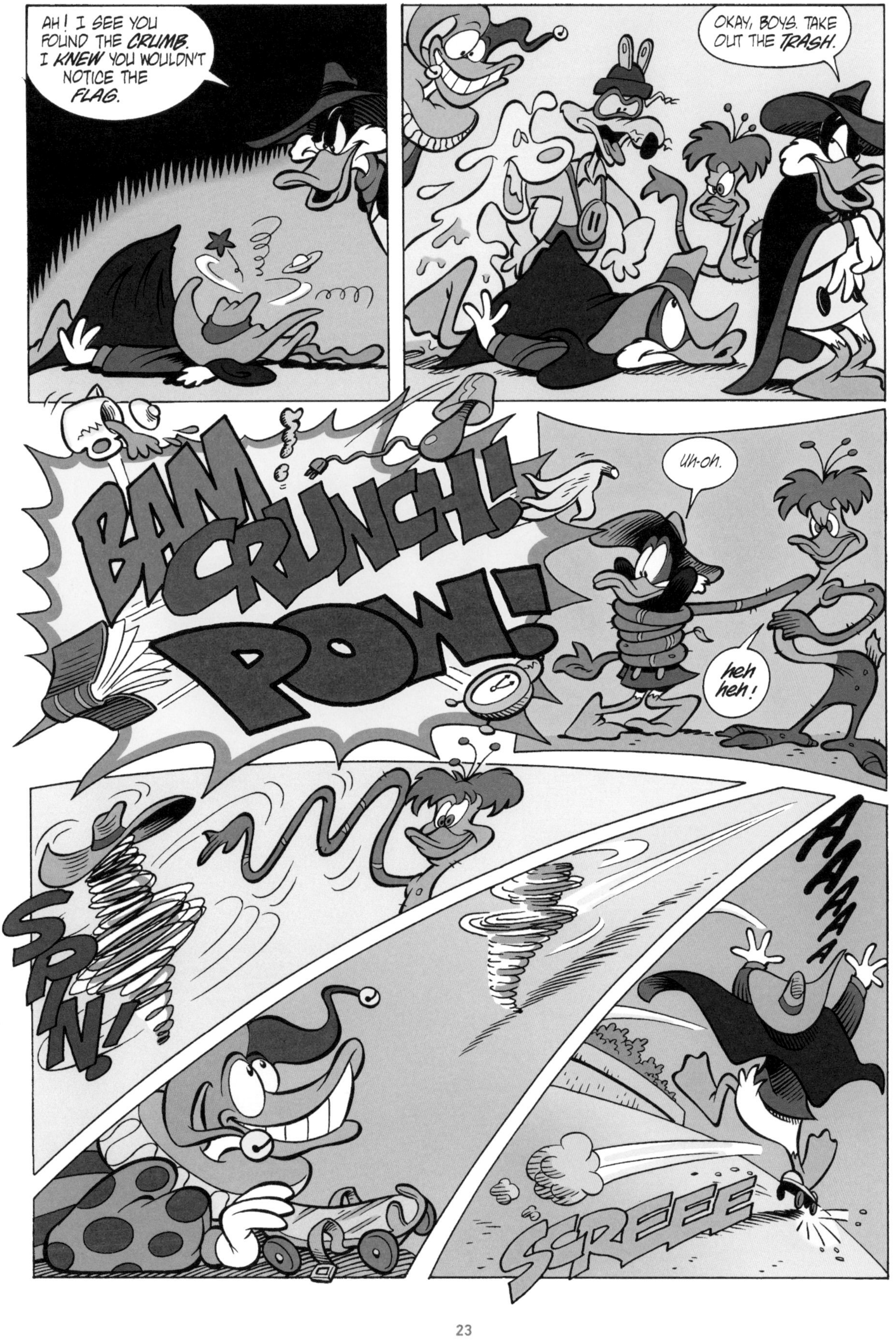
AH! I SEE YOU FOUND THE CRUMB. I KNEW YOU WOULDN'T NOTICE THE FLAG.
OKAY, BOYS. TAKE OUT THE TRASH.
BAM
CRUNCH!
POW!
uh-oh.
heh heh!
SPIN!
AAAAAA
SCREEE

BZZZT!

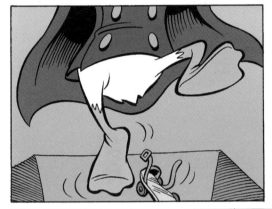

AAAIIEEE

AND THAT'S THE *END* OF *DARKWING DUCK!*

AAAAAAAA

END OF PART ONE!

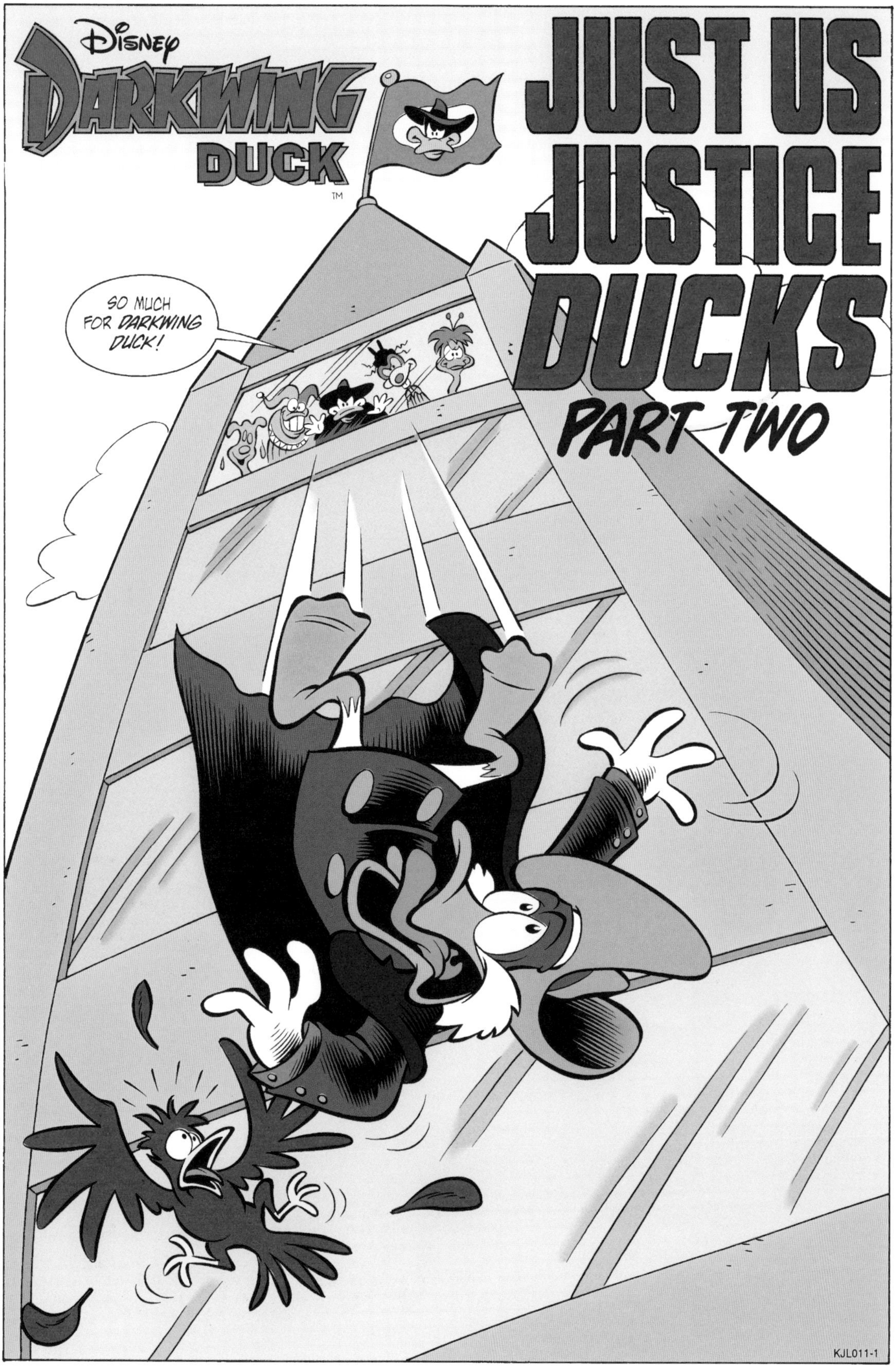
Disney
DARKWING DUCK
JUST US JUSTICE DUCKS
PART TWO
SO MUCH FOR DARKWING DUCK!
KJL011-1

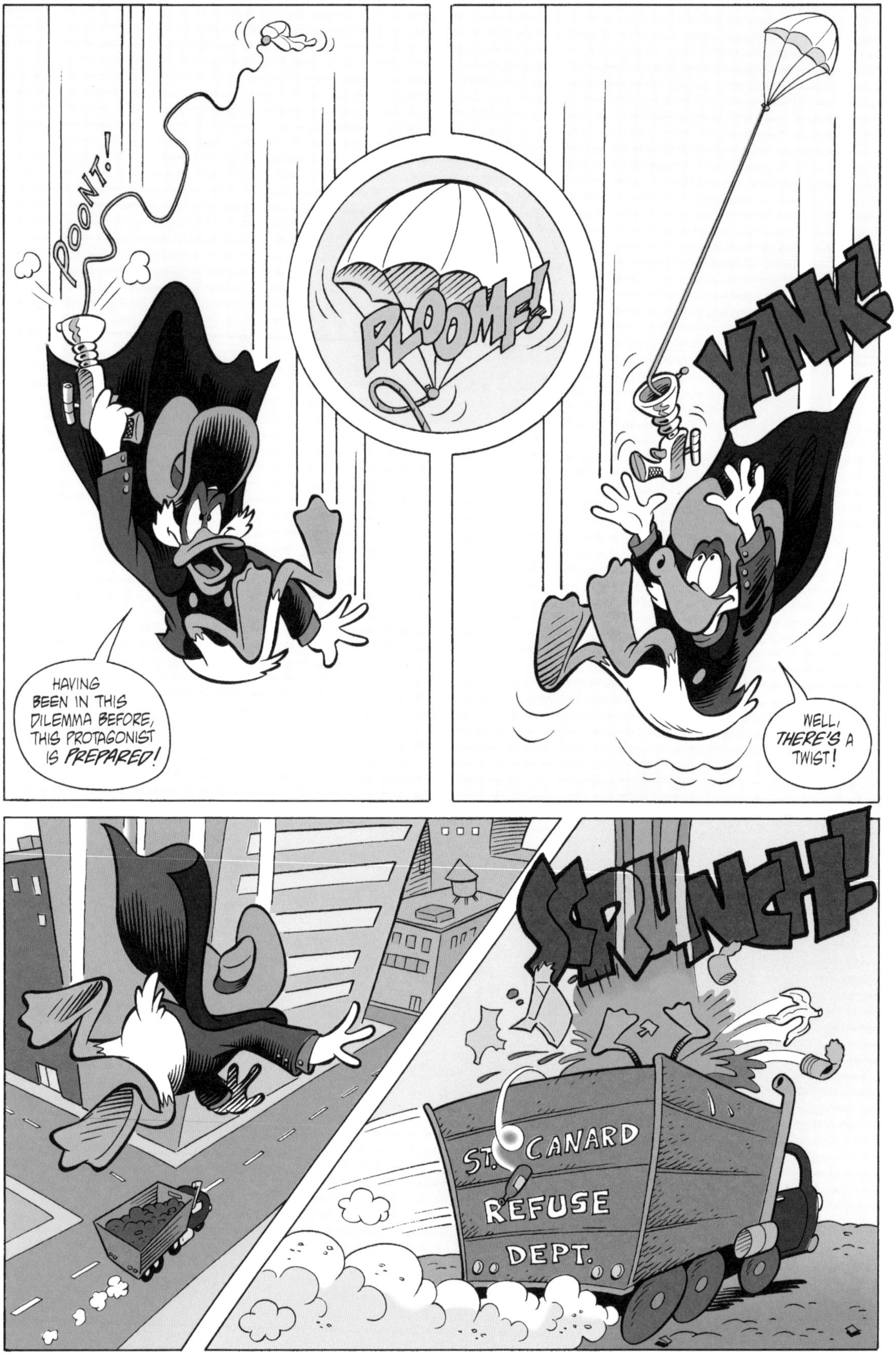

POONT!
PLOOMF!
YANK!
HAVING BEEN IN THIS DILEMMA BEFORE, THIS PROTAGONIST IS *PREPARED*!
WELL, *THERE'S* A TWIST!
SKRUNCH!
ST. CANARD REFUSE DEPT.

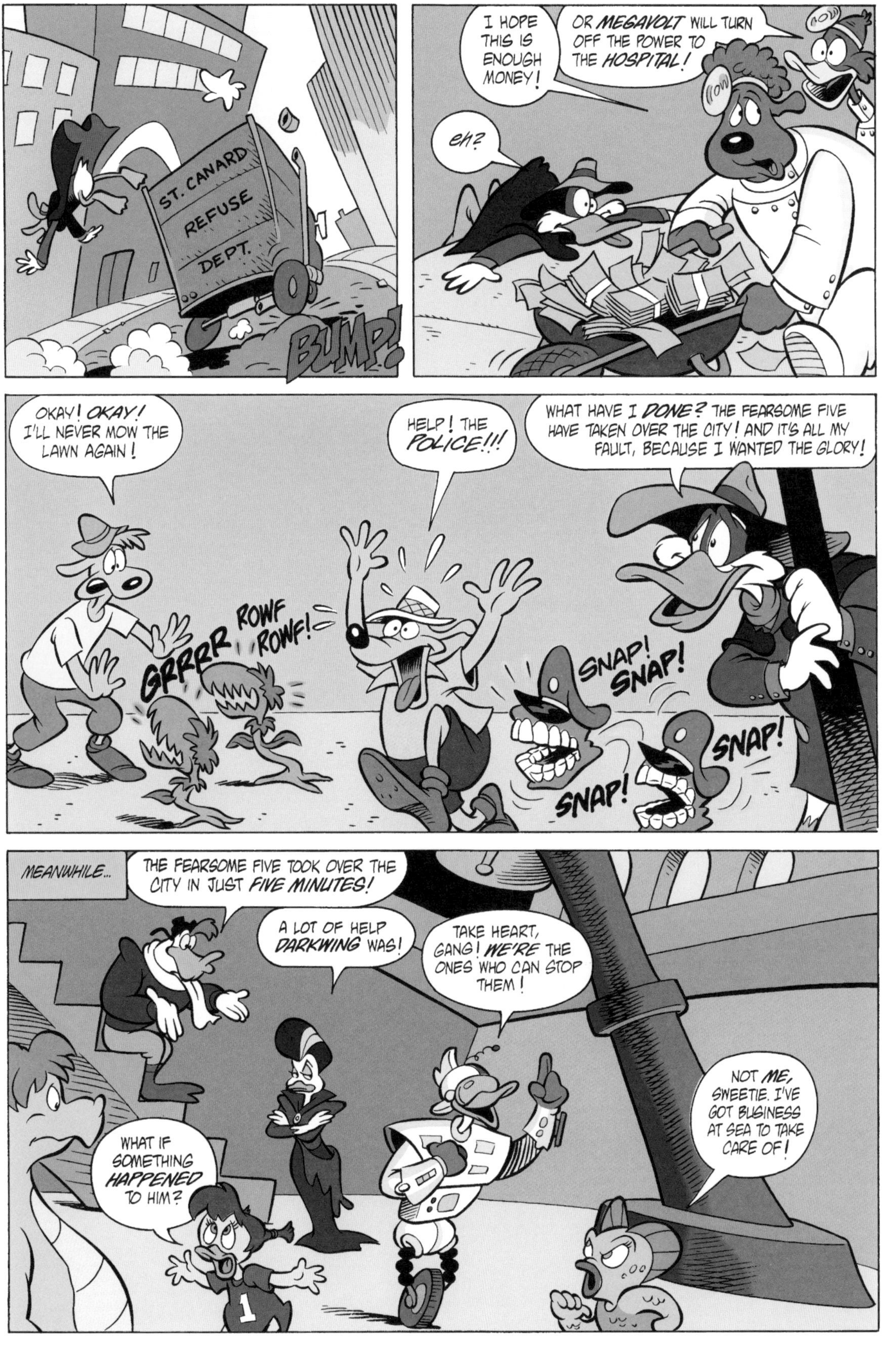
ST. CANARD REFUSE DEPT.
BUMP!
I HOPE THIS IS ENOUGH MONEY!
OR MEGAVOLT WILL TURN OFF THE POWER TO THE HOSPITAL!
eh?
OKAY! OKAY! I'LL NEVER MOW THE LAWN AGAIN!
HELP! THE POLICE!!!
WHAT HAVE I DONE? THE FEARSOME FIVE HAVE TAKEN OVER THE CITY! AND IT'S ALL MY FAULT, BECAUSE I WANTED THE GLORY!
GRRRR
ROWF ROWF!
SNAP! SNAP!
SNAP!
SNAP!
MEANWHILE...
THE FEARSOME FIVE TOOK OVER THE CITY IN JUST FIVE MINUTES!
A LOT OF HELP DARKWING WAS!
TAKE HEART, GANG! WE'RE THE ONES WHO CAN STOP THEM!
NOT ME, SWEETIE. I'VE GOT BUSINESS AT SEA TO TAKE CARE OF!
WHAT IF SOMETHING HAPPENED TO HIM?
1

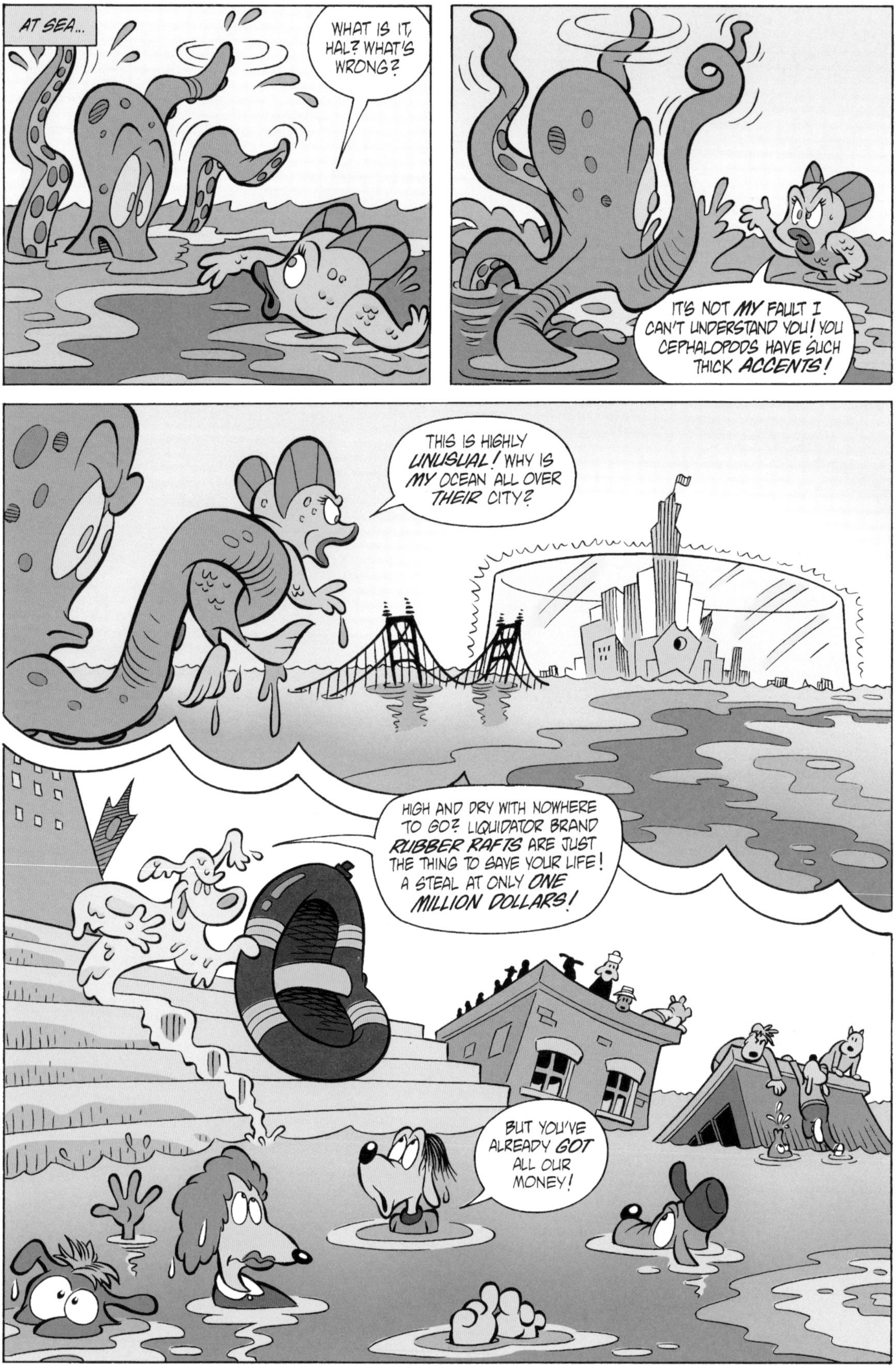
AT SEA...
WHAT IS IT, HAL? WHAT'S WRONG?
IT'S NOT MY FAULT I CAN'T UNDERSTAND YOU! YOU CEPHALOPODS HAVE SUCH THICK ACCENTS!
THIS IS HIGHLY UNUSUAL! WHY IS MY OCEAN ALL OVER THEIR CITY?
HIGH AND DRY WITH NOWHERE TO GO? LIQUIDATOR BRAND RUBBER RAFTS ARE JUST THE THING TO SAVE YOUR LIFE! A STEAL AT ONLY ONE MILLION DOLLARS!
BUT YOU'VE ALREADY GOT ALL OUR MONEY!

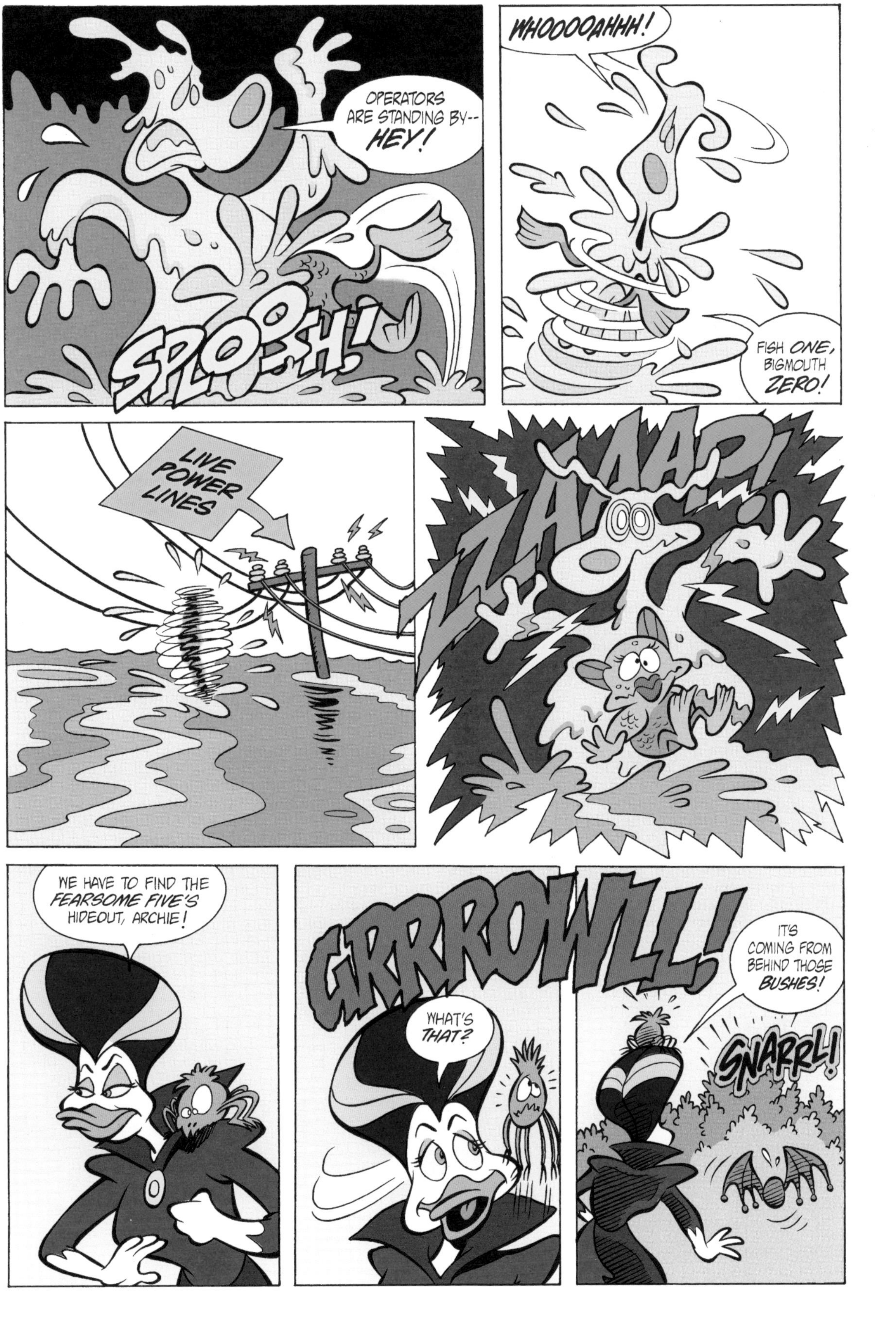
OPERATORS ARE STANDING BY-- HEY!
SPLOOSH!
WHOOOOAHHH!
FISH ONE, BIGMOUTH ZERO!
LIVE POWER LINES
ZZAAAP!
WE HAVE TO FIND THE FEARSOME FIVE'S HIDEOUT, ARCHIE!
GRRROWLL!
WHAT'S THAT?
IT'S COMING FROM BEHIND THOSE BUSHES!
SNARRL!

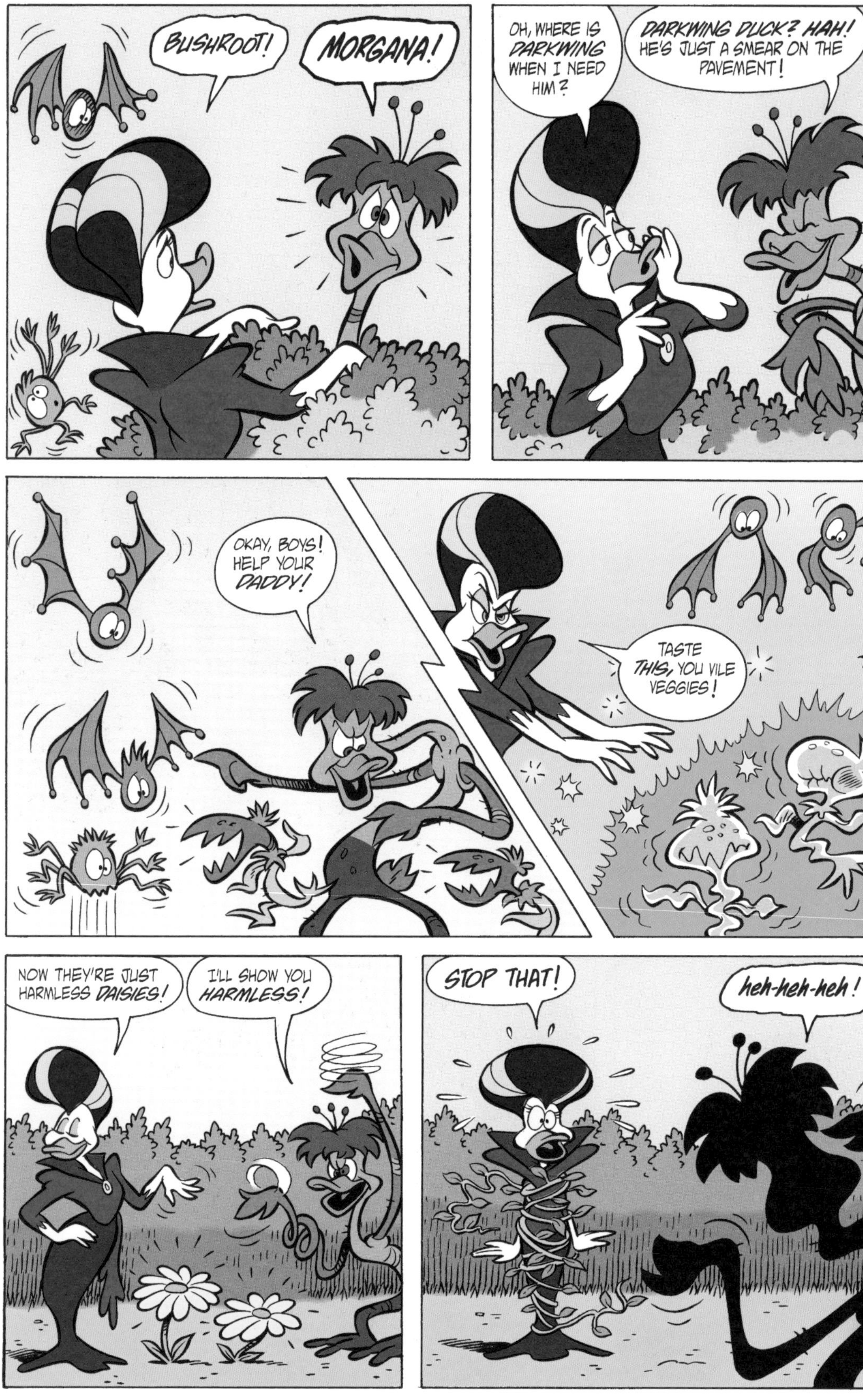
BUSHROOT!
MORGANA!
OH, WHERE IS DARKWING WHEN I NEED HIM?
DARKWING DUCK? HAH! HE'S JUST A SMEAR ON THE PAVEMENT!
OKAY, BOYS! HELP YOUR DADDY!
TASTE THIS, YOU VILE VEGGIES!
NOW THEY'RE JUST HARMLESS DAISIES!
I'LL SHOW YOU HARMLESS!
STOP THAT!
heh-heh-heh!

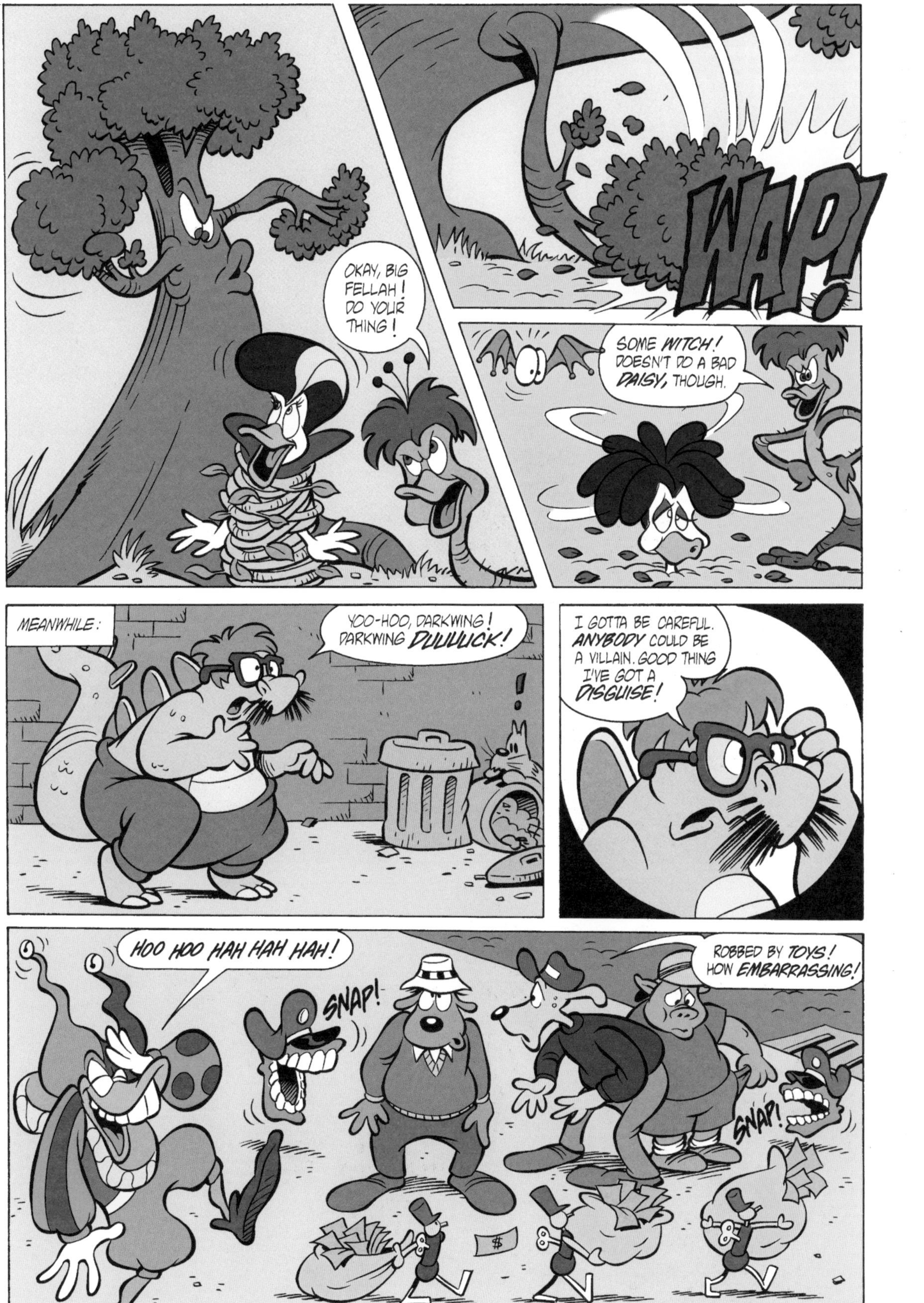
OKAY, BIG FELLAH! DO YOUR THING!
WAP!
SOME WITCH! DOESN'T DO A BAD DAISY, THOUGH.
MEANWHILE:
YOO-HOO, DARKWING! DARKWING DUUUUCK!
!
I GOTTA BE CAREFUL. ANYBODY COULD BE A VILLAIN. GOOD THING I'VE GOT A DISGUISE!
HOO HOO HAH HAH HAH!
SNAP!
ROBBED BY TOYS! HOW EMBARRASSING!
SNAP!

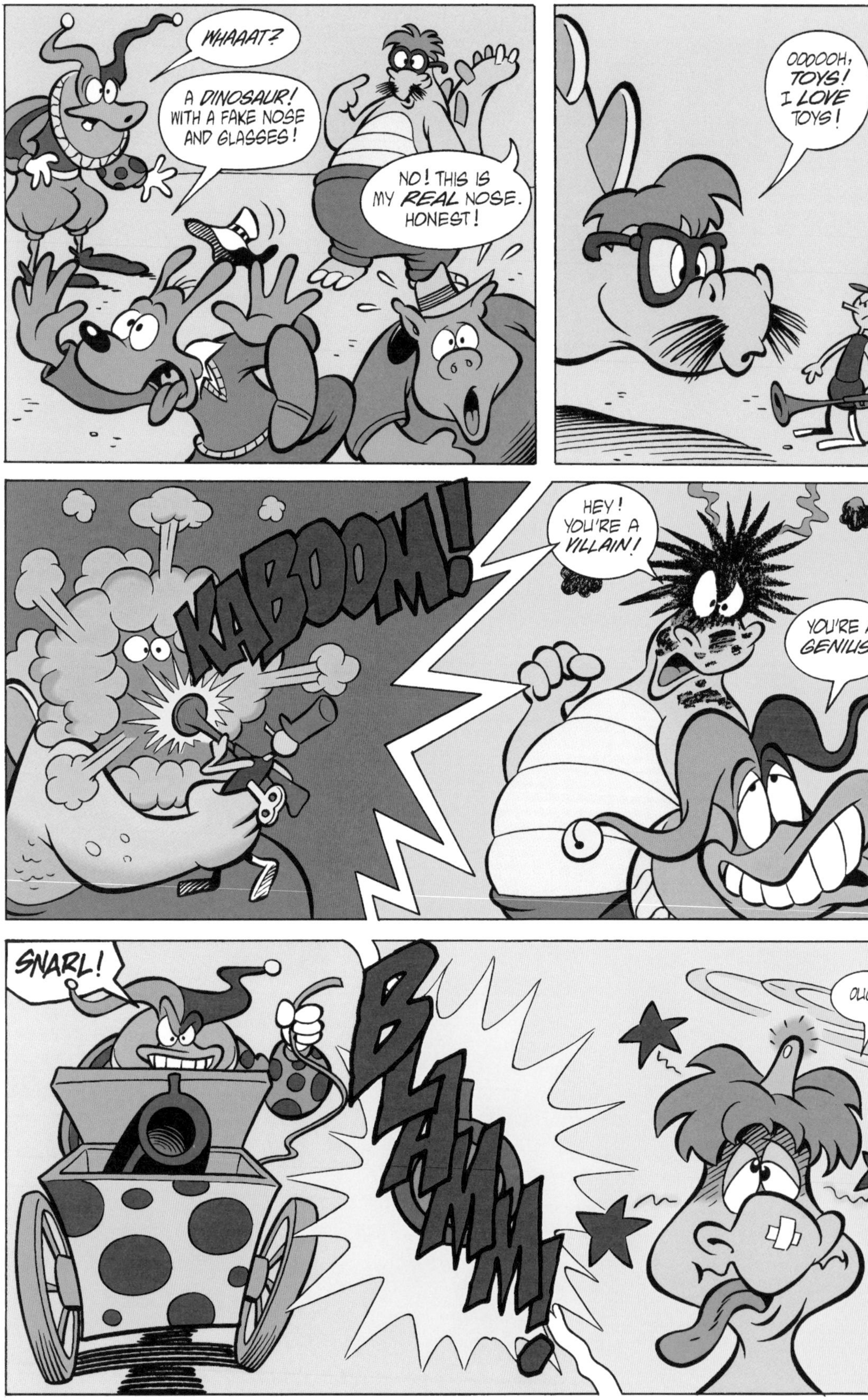
WHAAAT?
A DINOSAUR! WITH A FAKE NOSE AND GLASSES!
NO! THIS IS MY REAL NOSE. HONEST!
OOOOOH, TOYS! I LOVE TOYS!
KABOOM!
HEY! YOU'RE A VILLAIN!
YOU'RE A GENIUS!
SNARL!
BLAMM!
OUCH.

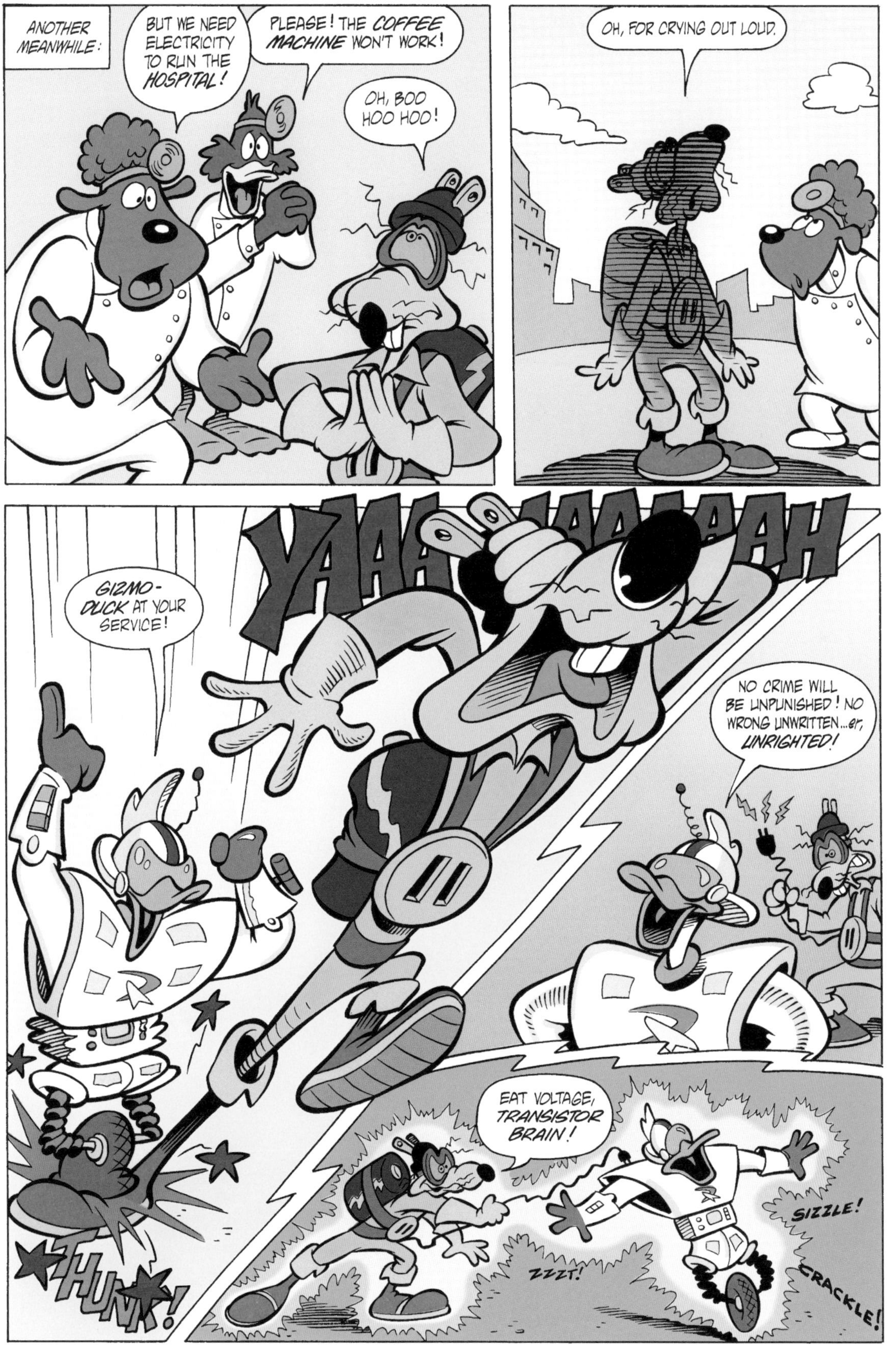

ANOTHER MEANWHILE:
BUT WE NEED ELECTRICITY TO RUN THE HOSPITAL!
PLEASE! THE COFFEE MACHINE WON'T WORK!
OH, BOO HOO HOO!
OH, FOR CRYING OUT LOUD.
YAAAAAAAAAAH
GIZMO-DUCK AT YOUR SERVICE!
NO CRIME WILL BE UNPUNISHED! NO WRONG UNWRITTEN...er, UNRIGHTED!
THUNK!
EAT VOLTAGE, TRANSISTOR BRAIN!
ZZZZT!
SIZZLE!
CRACKLE!

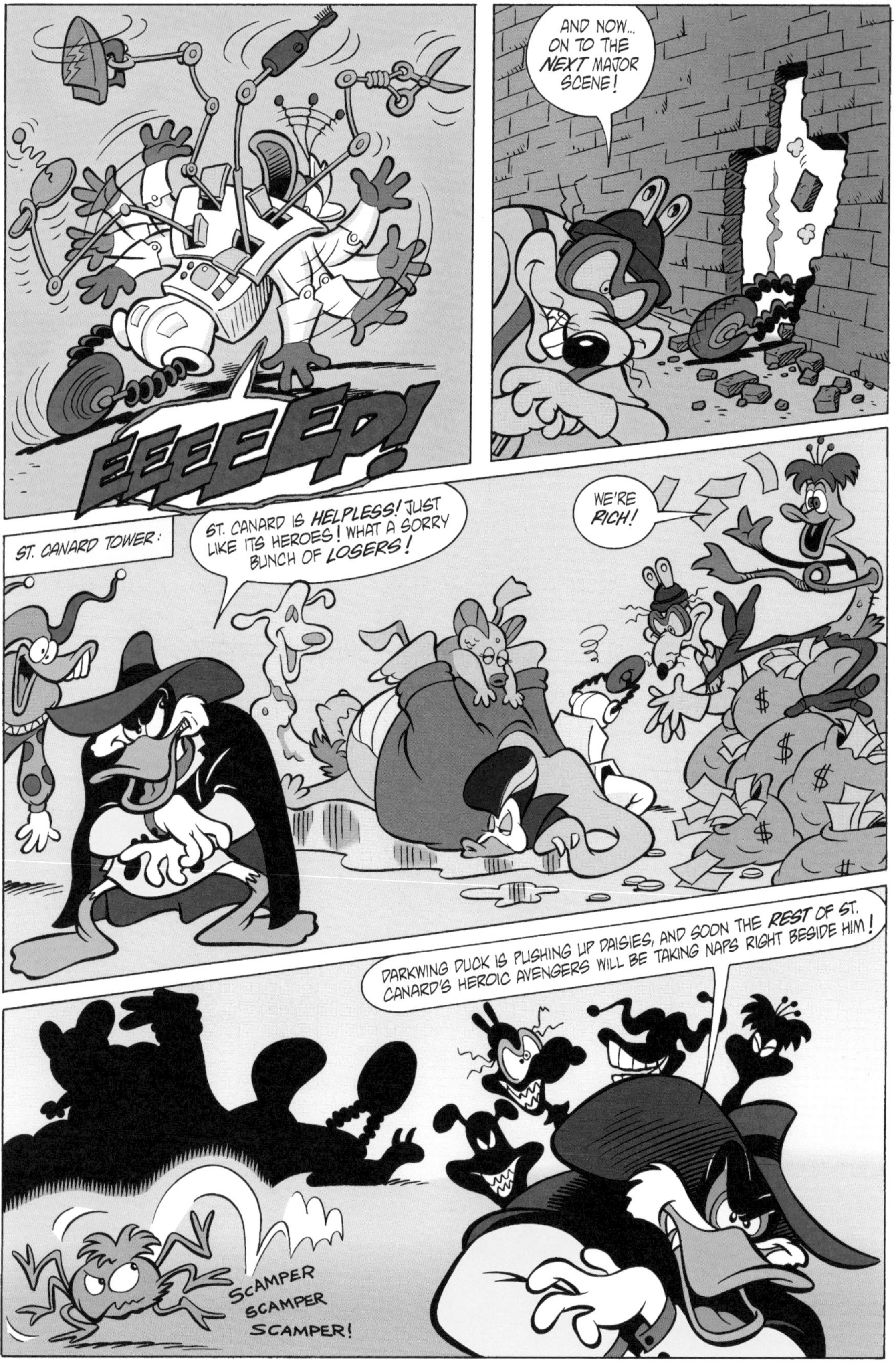
EEEEEP!
AND NOW... ON TO THE NEXT MAJOR SCENE!
ST. CANARD TOWER:
ST. CANARD IS HELPLESS! JUST LIKE ITS HEROES! WHAT A SORRY BUNCH OF LOSERS!
WE'RE RICH!
DARKWING DUCK IS PUSHING UP DAISIES, AND SOON THE REST OF ST. CANARD'S HEROIC AVENGERS WILL BE TAKING NAPS RIGHT BESIDE HIM!
SCAMPER SCAMPER SCAMPER!

BACK AT DARKWING TOWER:

WHERE COULD THEY *BE?*

EW! A *SPIDER!*

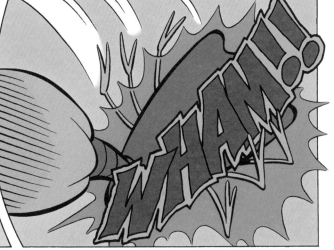

WHAM!!

NO, LAUNCHPAD. IT'S MORGANA'S FRIEND *ARCHIE!*

WHAT *IS* IT, ARCHIE, OL' PAL? WHAT'S HAPPENED?

ECK ECK ZPTHTHT! WAAG! PLGAAH!

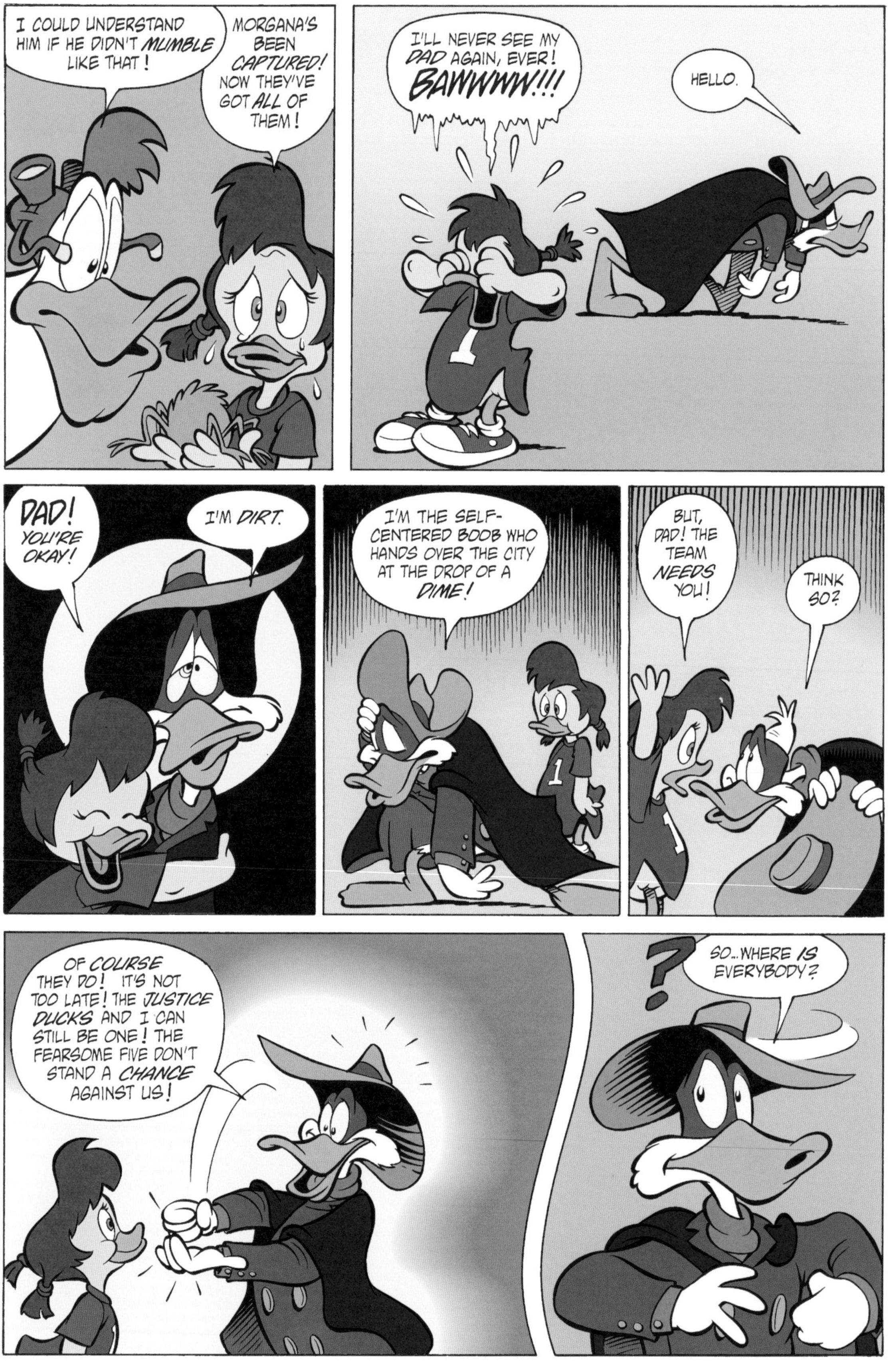

I COULD UNDERSTAND HIM IF HE DIDN'T MUMBLE LIKE THAT!
MORGANA'S BEEN CAPTURED! NOW THEY'VE GOT ALL OF THEM!
I'LL NEVER SEE MY DAD AGAIN, EVER! BAWWWW!!!!
HELLO.
DAD! YOU'RE OKAY!
I'M DIRT.
I'M THE SELF-CENTERED BOOB WHO HANDS OVER THE CITY AT THE DROP OF A DIME!
BUT, DAD! THE TEAM NEEDS YOU!
THINK SO?
OF COURSE THEY DO! IT'S NOT TOO LATE! THE JUSTICE DUCKS AND I CAN STILL BE ONE! THE FEARSOME FIVE DON'T STAND A CHANCE AGAINST US!
?
SO...WHERE IS EVERYBODY?

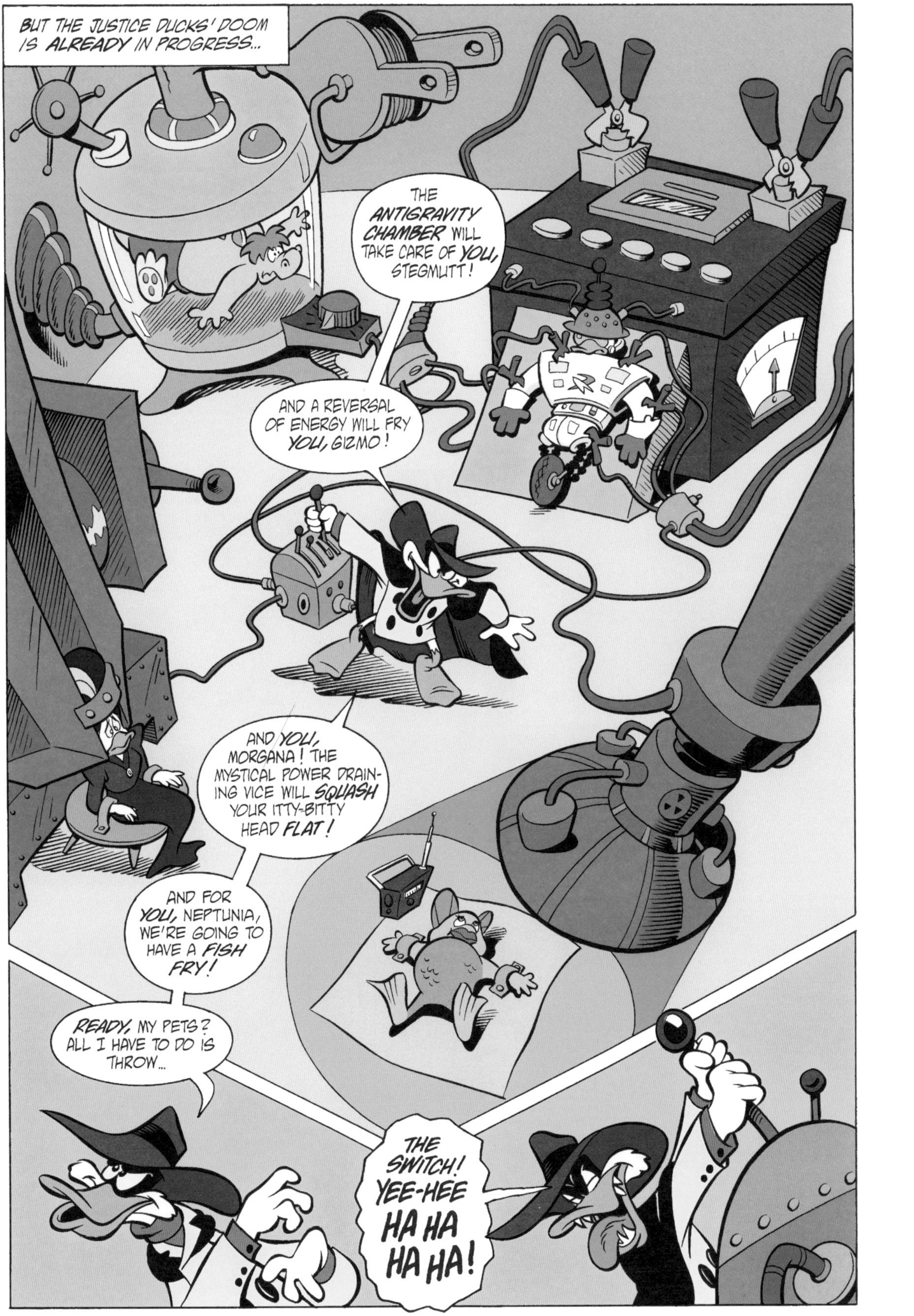
BUT THE JUSTICE DUCKS' DOOM IS ALREADY IN PROGRESS...
THE ANTIGRAVITY CHAMBER WILL TAKE CARE OF YOU, STEGMUTT!
AND A REVERSAL OF ENERGY WILL FRY YOU, GIZMO!
AND YOU, MORGANA! THE MYSTICAL POWER DRAINING VICE WILL SQUASH YOUR ITTY-BITTY HEAD FLAT!
AND FOR YOU, NEPTUNIA, WE'RE GOING TO HAVE A FISH FRY!
READY, MY PETS? ALL I HAVE TO DO IS THROW...
THE SWITCH! YEE-HEE HA HA HA HA!

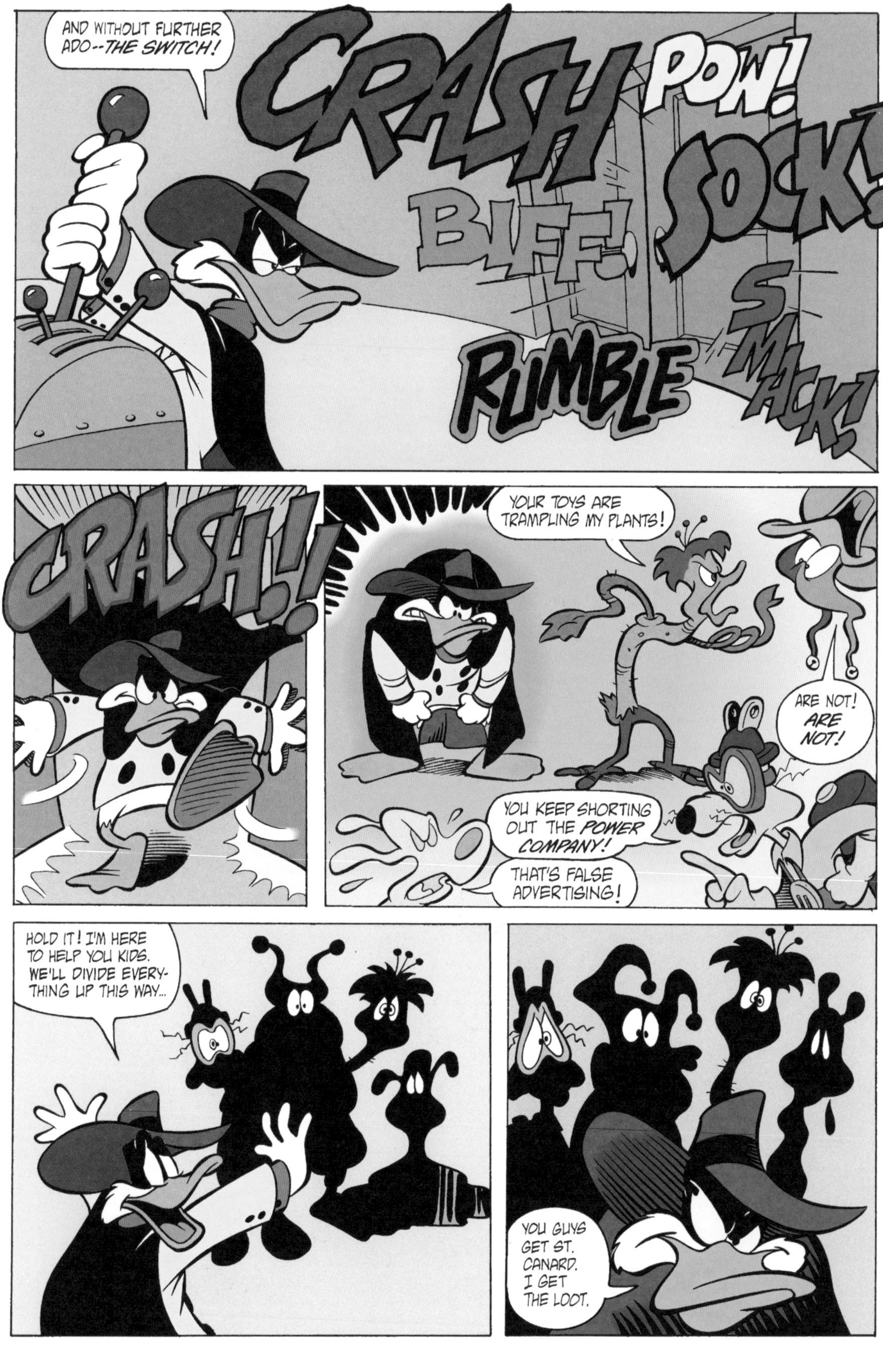
AND WITHOUT FURTHER ADO--THE SWITCH!
CRASH
POW!
SOCK!
BIFF!
SMACK!
RUMBLE
CRASH!!!
YOUR TOYS ARE TRAMPLING MY PLANTS!
ARE NOT! ARE NOT!
YOU KEEP SHORTING OUT THE POWER COMPANY!
THAT'S FALSE ADVERTISING!
HOLD IT! I'M HERE TO HELP YOU KIDS. WE'LL DIVIDE EVERYTHING UP THIS WAY...
YOU GUYS GET ST. CANARD. I GET THE LOOT.

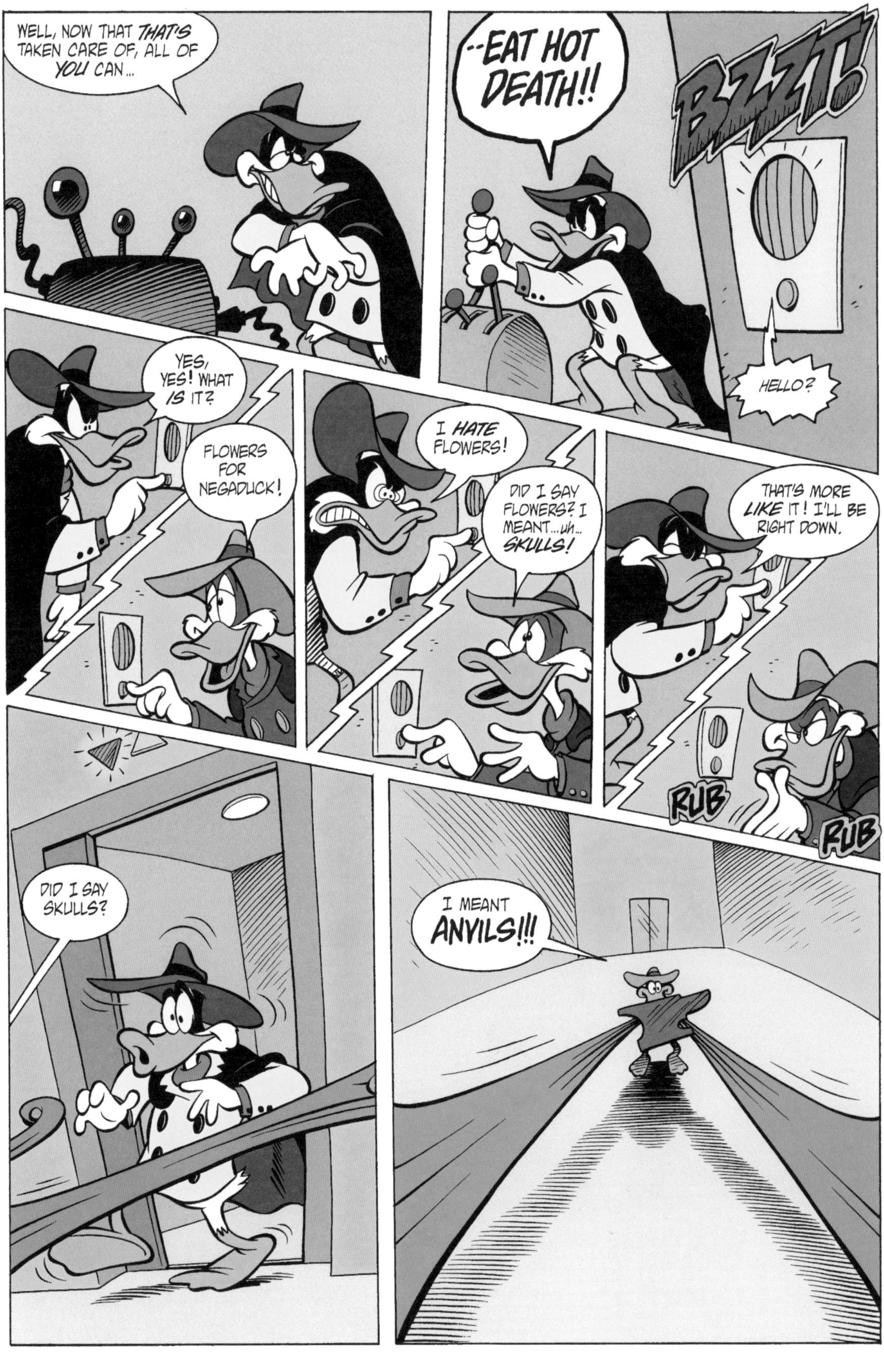
WELL, NOW THAT THAT'S TAKEN CARE OF, ALL OF YOU CAN...
--EAT HOT DEATH!!
BZZT!
HELLO?
YES, YES! WHAT IS IT?
FLOWERS FOR NEGADUCK!
I HATE FLOWERS!
DID I SAY FLOWERS? I MEANT...uh... SKULLS!
THAT'S MORE LIKE IT! I'LL BE RIGHT DOWN.
RUB
RUB
DID I SAY SKULLS?
I MEANT ANVILS!!!

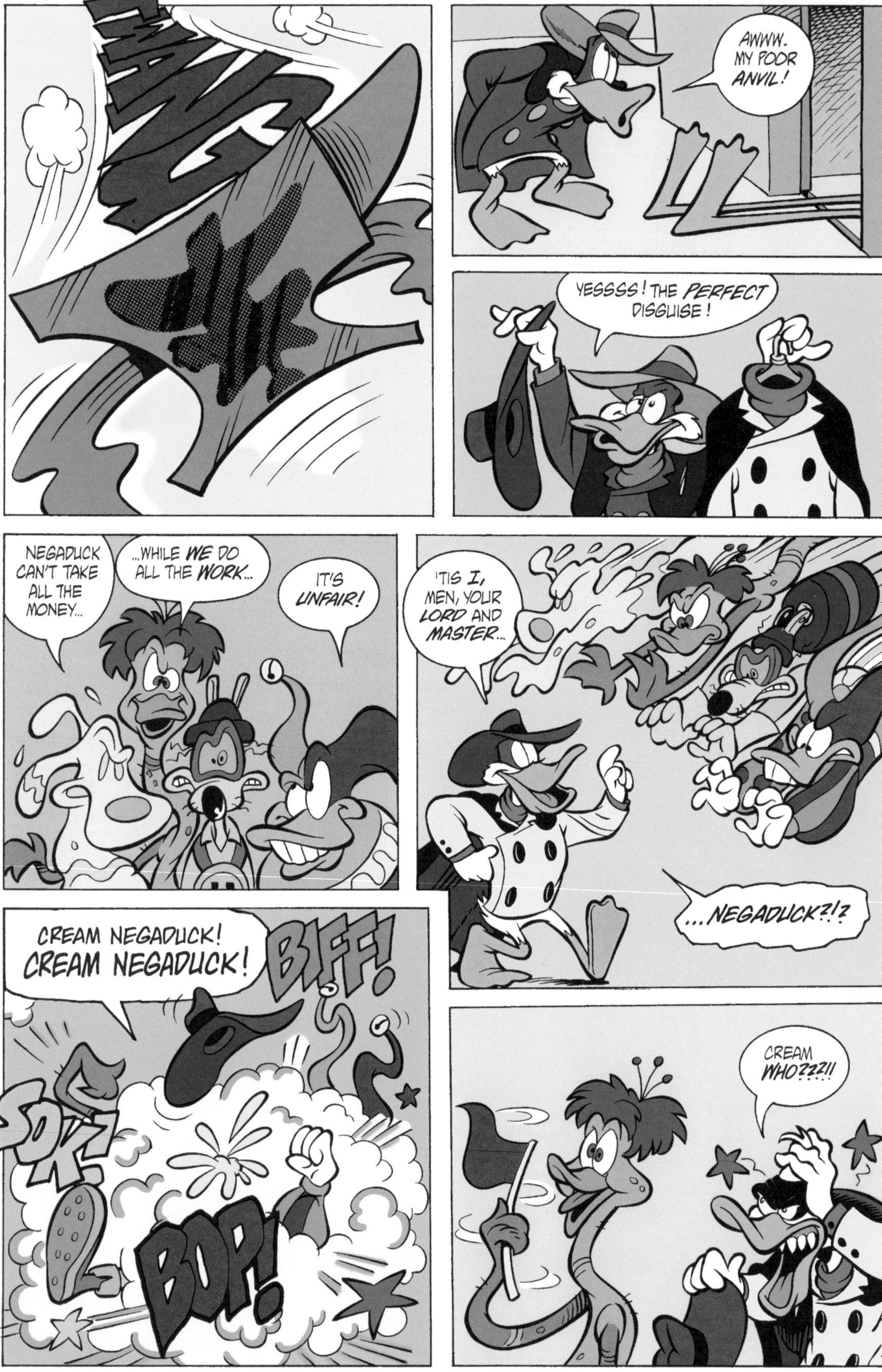

CLANG
AWWW. MY POOR ANVIL!
YESSSS! THE PERFECT DISGUISE!
NEGADUCK CAN'T TAKE ALL THE MONEY...
...WHILE WE DO ALL THE WORK...
IT'S UNFAIR!
'TIS I, MEN, YOUR LORD AND MASTER...
...NEGADUCK?!?
CREAM NEGADUCK! CREAM NEGADUCK!
BIFF!
SOK!
BOP!
CREAM WHO???!!

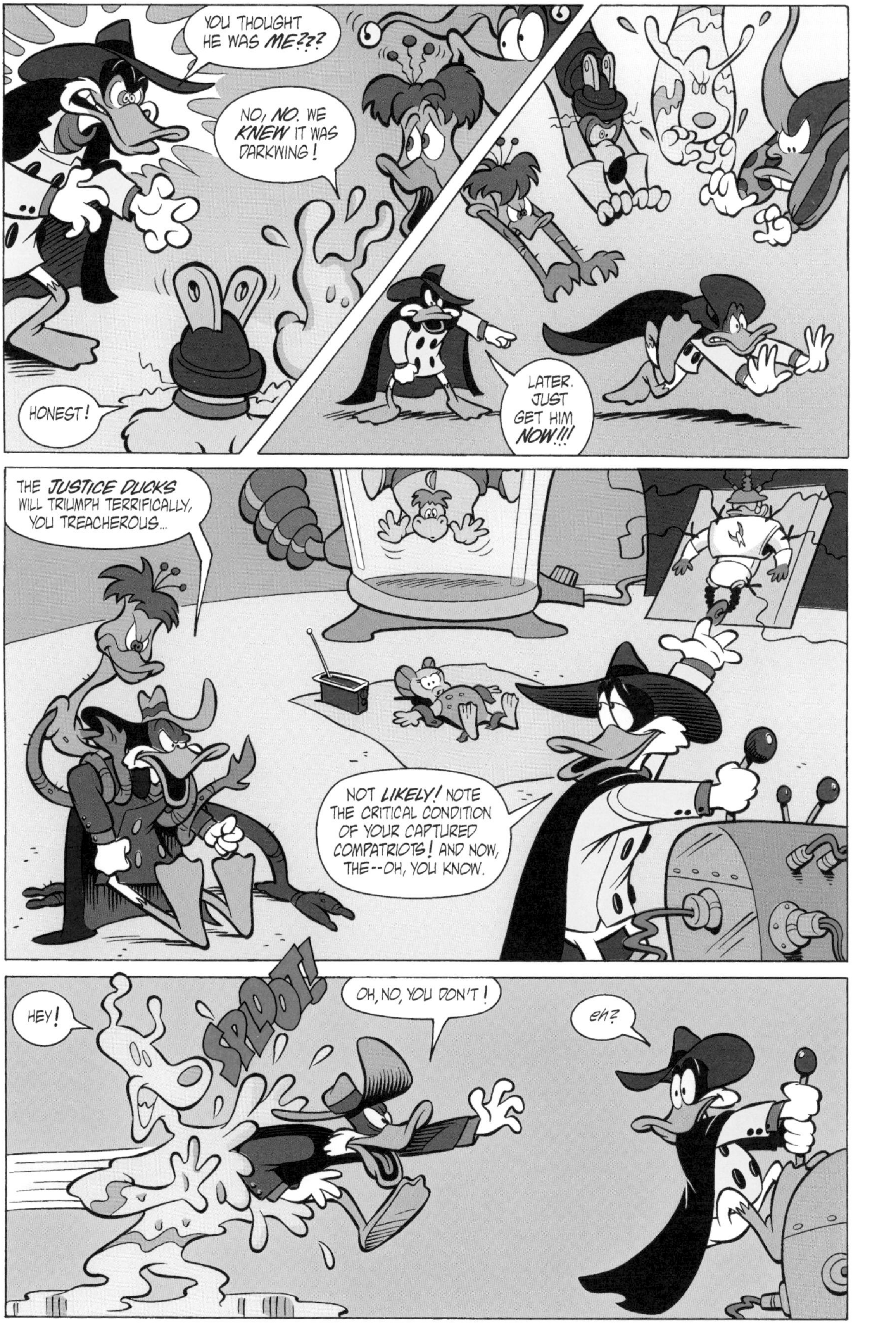
YOU THOUGHT HE WAS ME???
NO, NO. WE KNEW IT WAS DARKWING!
HONEST!
LATER. JUST GET HIM NOW!!!
THE JUSTICE DUCKS WILL TRIUMPH TERRIFICALLY, YOU TREACHEROUS...
NOT LIKELY! NOTE THE CRITICAL CONDITION OF YOUR CAPTURED COMPATRIOTS! AND NOW, THE--OH, YOU KNOW.
HEY!
SPLOOT!
OH, NO, YOU DON'T!
eh?

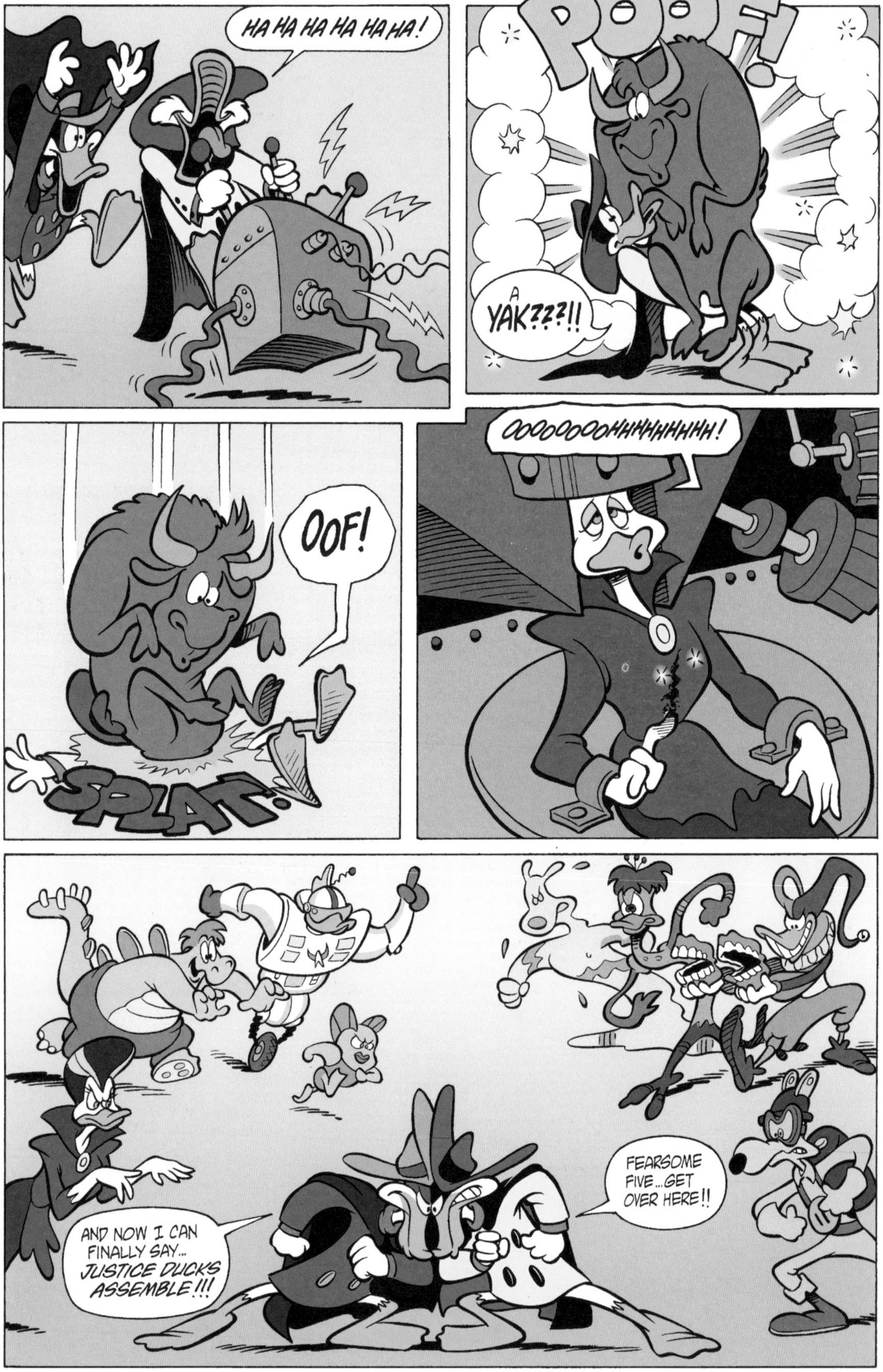
HA HA HA HA HA HA HA!
POOF!
A YAK???!!
OOF!
SPLAT!
OOOOOOOOHHHHHHHH!
FEARSOME FIVE...GET OVER HERE!!
AND NOW I CAN FINALLY SAY... JUSTICE DUCKS ASSEMBLE!!!

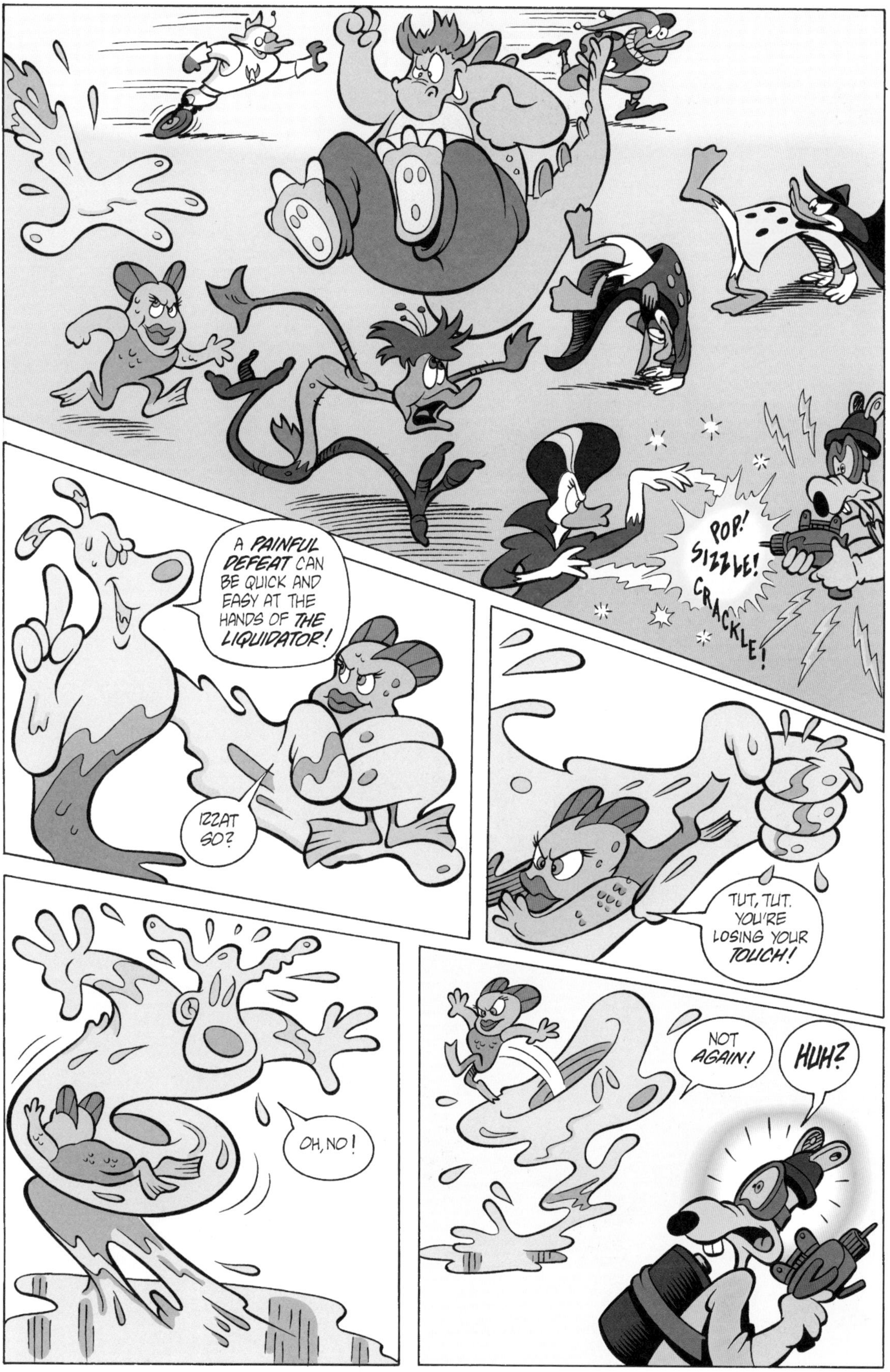
POP! SIZZLE! CRACKLE!
A PAINFUL DEFEAT CAN BE QUICK AND EASY AT THE HANDS OF THE LIQUIDATOR!
IZZAT SO?
TUT, TUT. YOU'RE LOSING YOUR TOUCH!
OH, NO!
NOT AGAIN!
HUH?

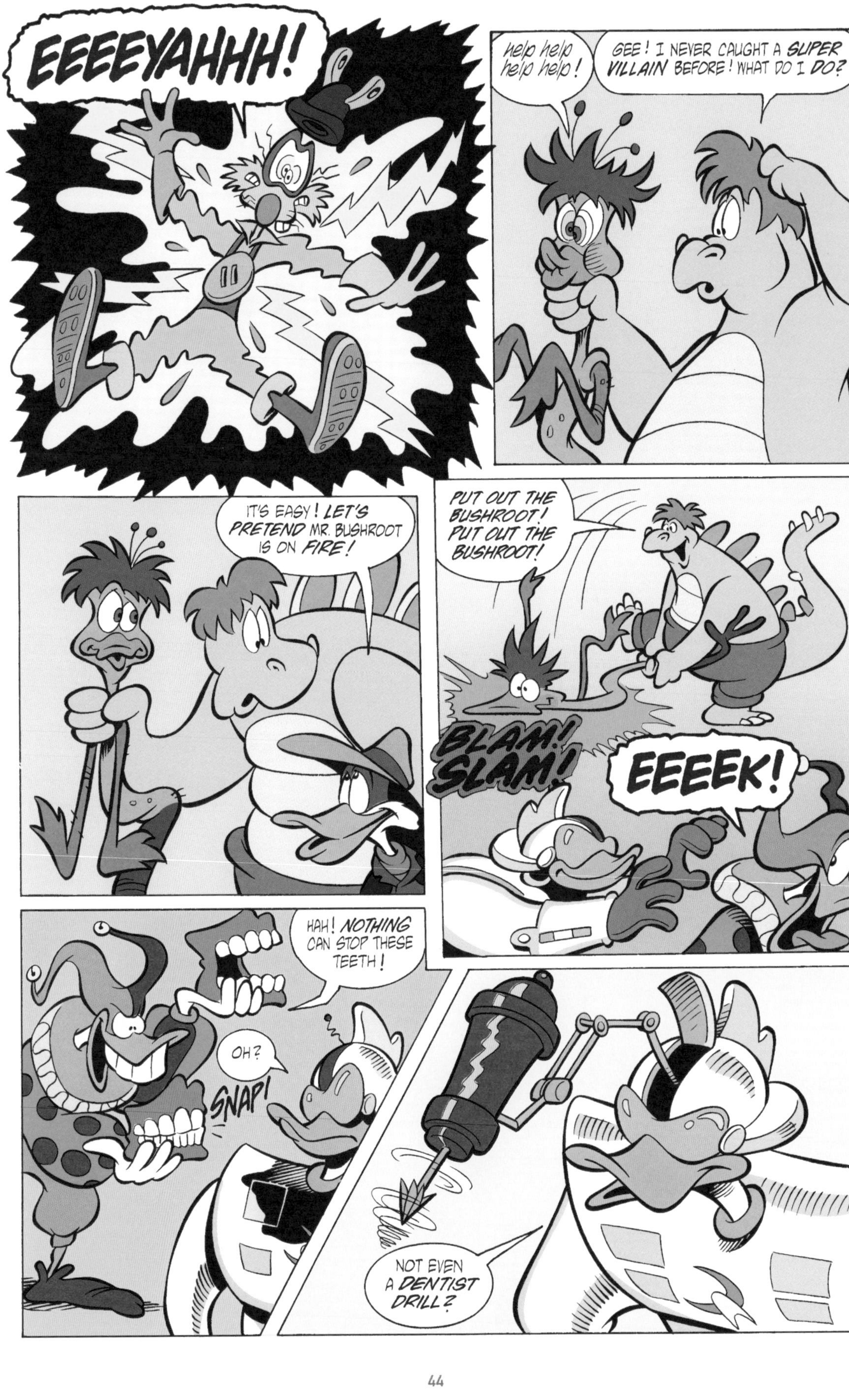
EEEEYAHHH!
help help help help!
GEE! I NEVER CAUGHT A SUPER VILLAIN BEFORE! WHAT DO I DO?
IT'S EASY! LET'S PRETEND MR. BUSHROOT IS ON FIRE!
PUT OUT THE BUSHROOT! PUT OUT THE BUSHROOT!
BLAM! SLAM!
EEEEK!
HAH! NOTHING CAN STOP THESE TEETH!
OH?
SNAP!
NOT EVEN A DENTIST DRILL?

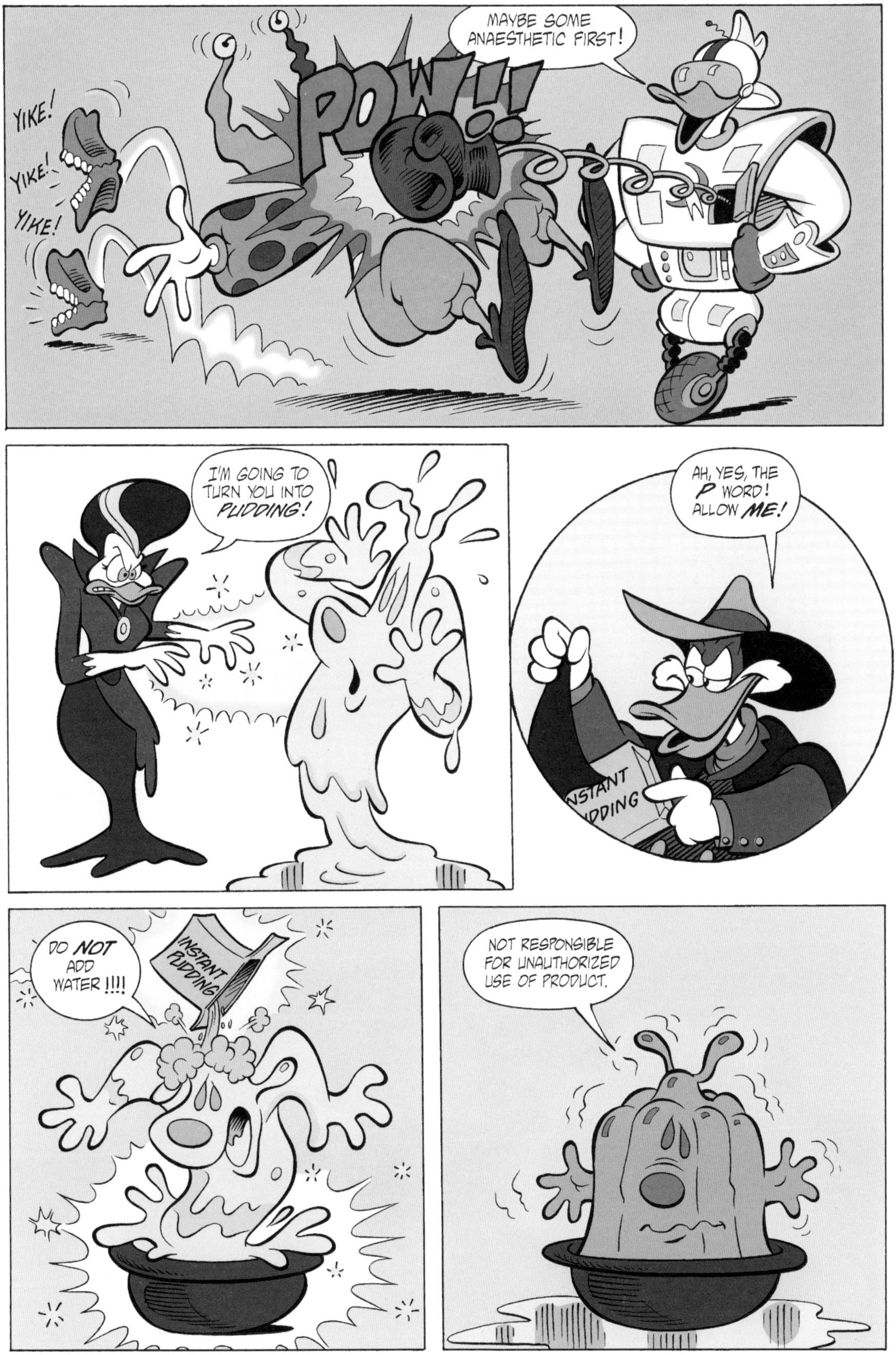
YIKE!
YIKE!
YIKE!
POW!!!
MAYBE SOME ANAESTHETIC FIRST!
I'M GOING TO TURN YOU INTO PUDDING!
AH, YES, THE P WORD! ALLOW ME!
INSTANT PUDDING
DO NOT ADD WATER !!!!
INSTANT PUDDING
NOT RESPONSIBLE FOR UNAUTHORIZED USE OF PRODUCT.

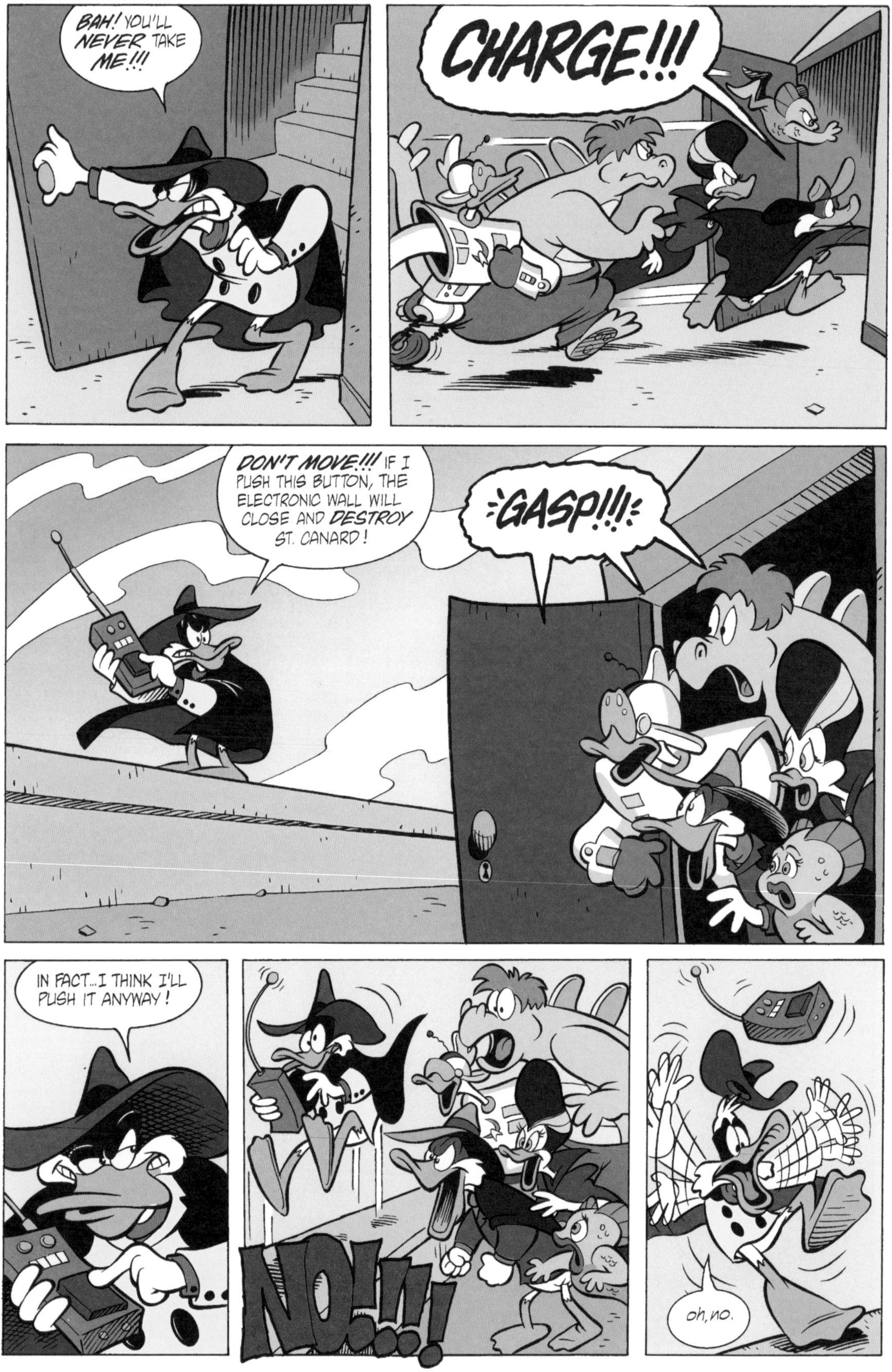
BAH! YOU'LL NEVER TAKE ME!!!
CHARGE!!!
DON'T MOVE!!! IF I PUSH THIS BUTTON, THE ELECTRONIC WALL WILL CLOSE AND DESTROY ST. CANARD!
GASP!!!
IN FACT...I THINK I'LL PUSH IT ANYWAY!
NO!!!!
oh, no.

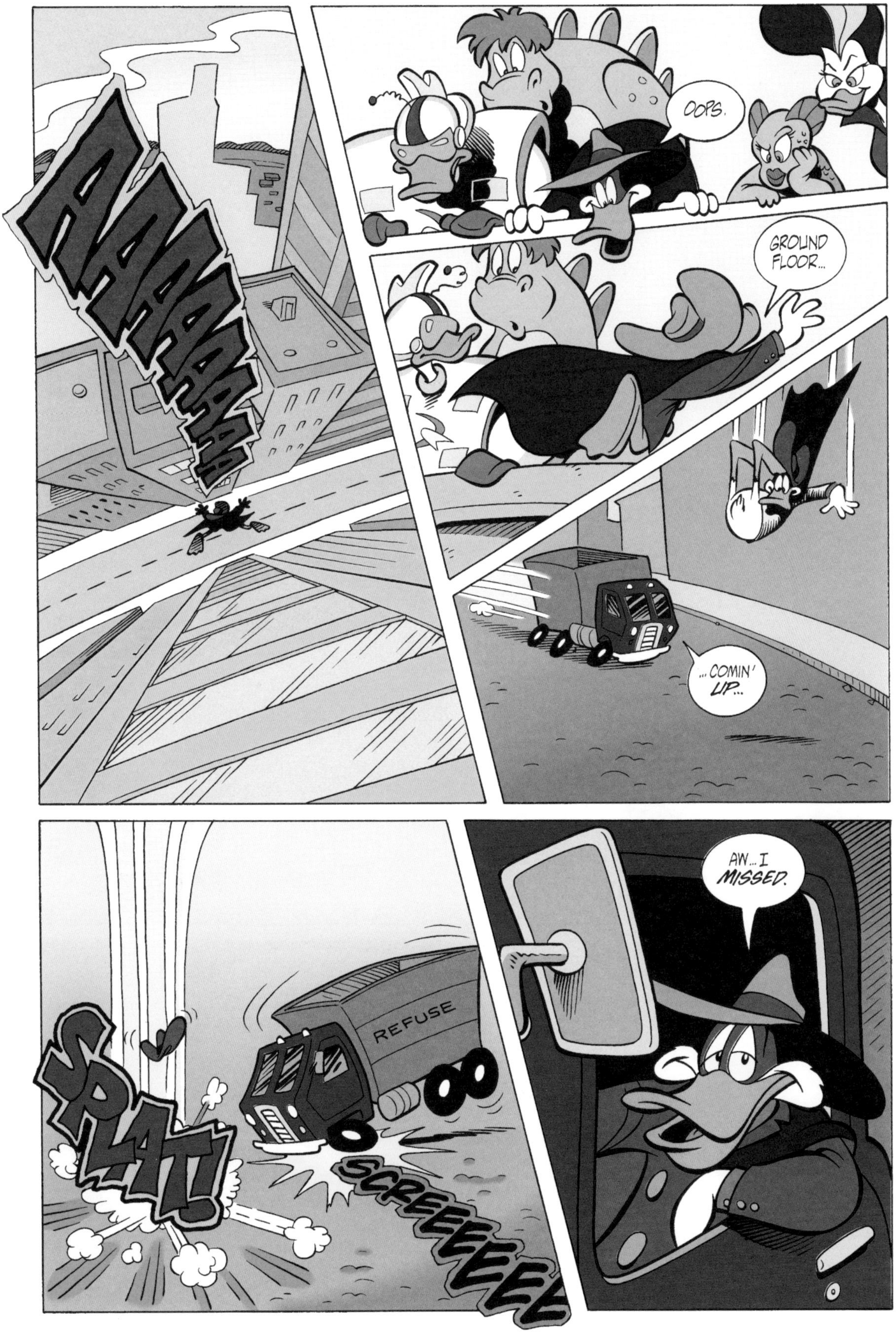
AAAAAAAAAH!
OOPS.
GROUND FLOOR...
...COMIN' UP...
SPLAT!
SCREEEEEEE
REFUSE
AW... I MISSED.

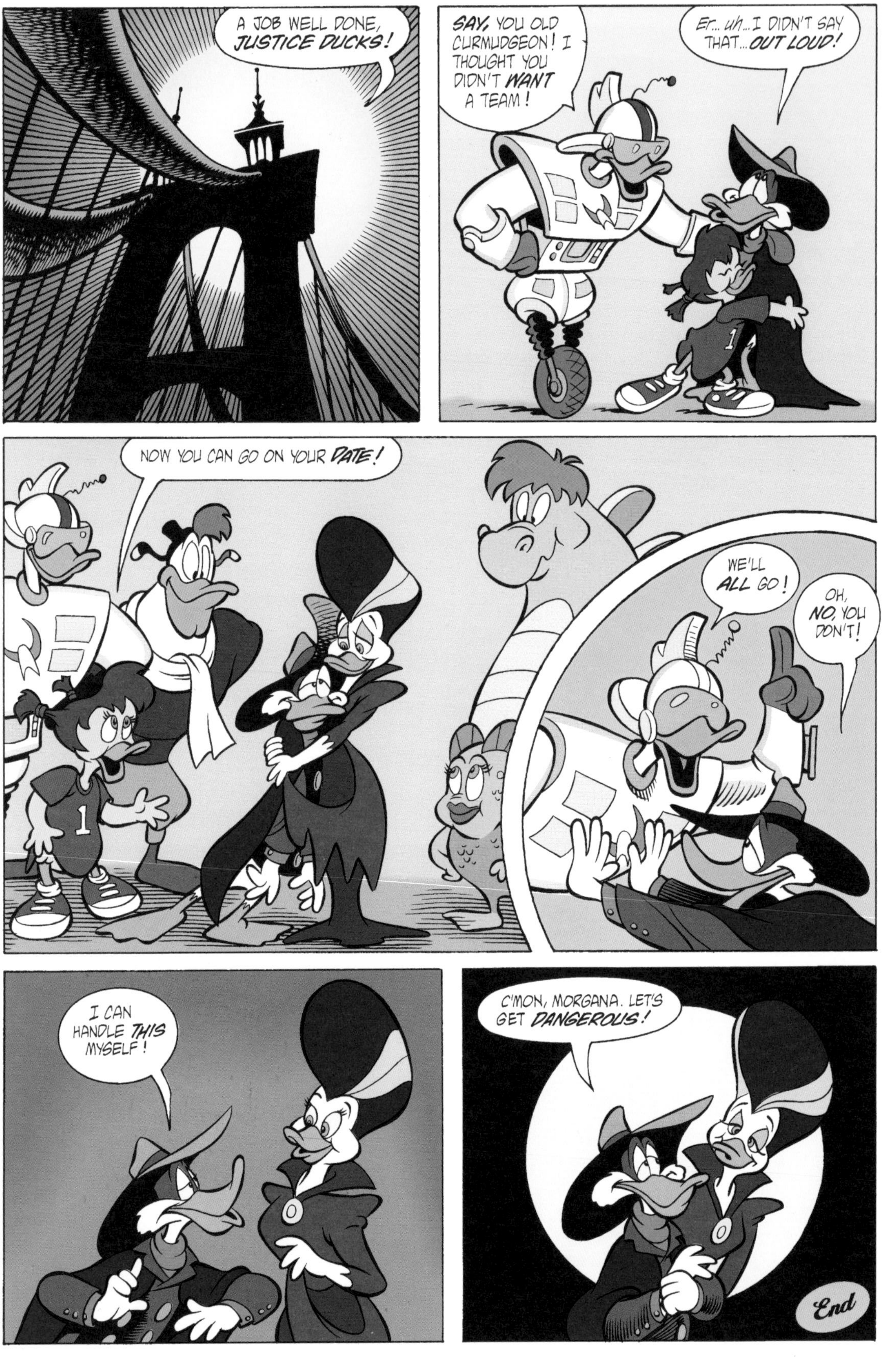
A JOB WELL DONE, JUSTICE DUCKS!
SAY, YOU OLD CURMUDGEON! I THOUGHT YOU DIDN'T WANT A TEAM!
Er... uh... I DIDN'T SAY THAT... OUT LOUD!
NOW YOU CAN GO ON YOUR DATE!
WE'LL ALL GO!
OH, NO, YOU DON'T!
I CAN HANDLE THIS MYSELF!
C'MON, MORGANA. LET'S GET DANGEROUS!
End

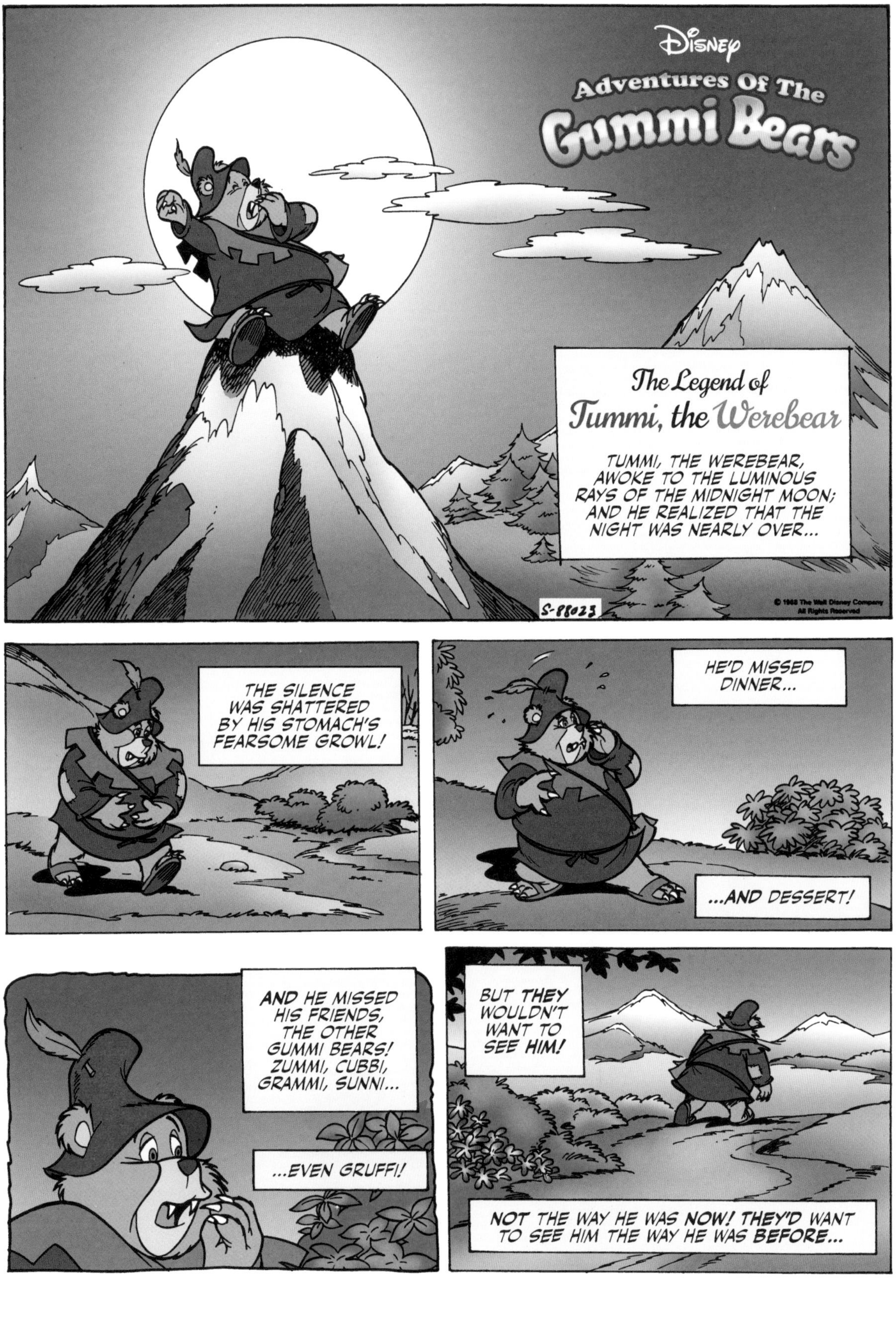
DISNEY
Adventures Of The
Gummi Bears
The Legend of
Tummi, the Werebear
TUMMI, THE WEREBEAR, AWOKE TO THE LUMINOUS RAYS OF THE MIDNIGHT MOON; AND HE REALIZED THAT THE NIGHT WAS NEARLY OVER...
S-88023
© 1988 The Walt Disney Company
All Rights Reserved
THE SILENCE WAS SHATTERED BY HIS STOMACH'S FEARSOME GROWL!
HE'D MISSED DINNER...
...AND DESSERT!
AND HE MISSED HIS FRIENDS, THE OTHER GUMMI BEARS! ZUMMI, CUBBI, GRAMMI, SUNNI...
...EVEN GRUFFI!
BUT THEY WOULDN'T WANT TO SEE HIM!
NOT THE WAY HE WAS NOW! THEY'D WANT TO SEE HIM THE WAY HE WAS BEFORE...

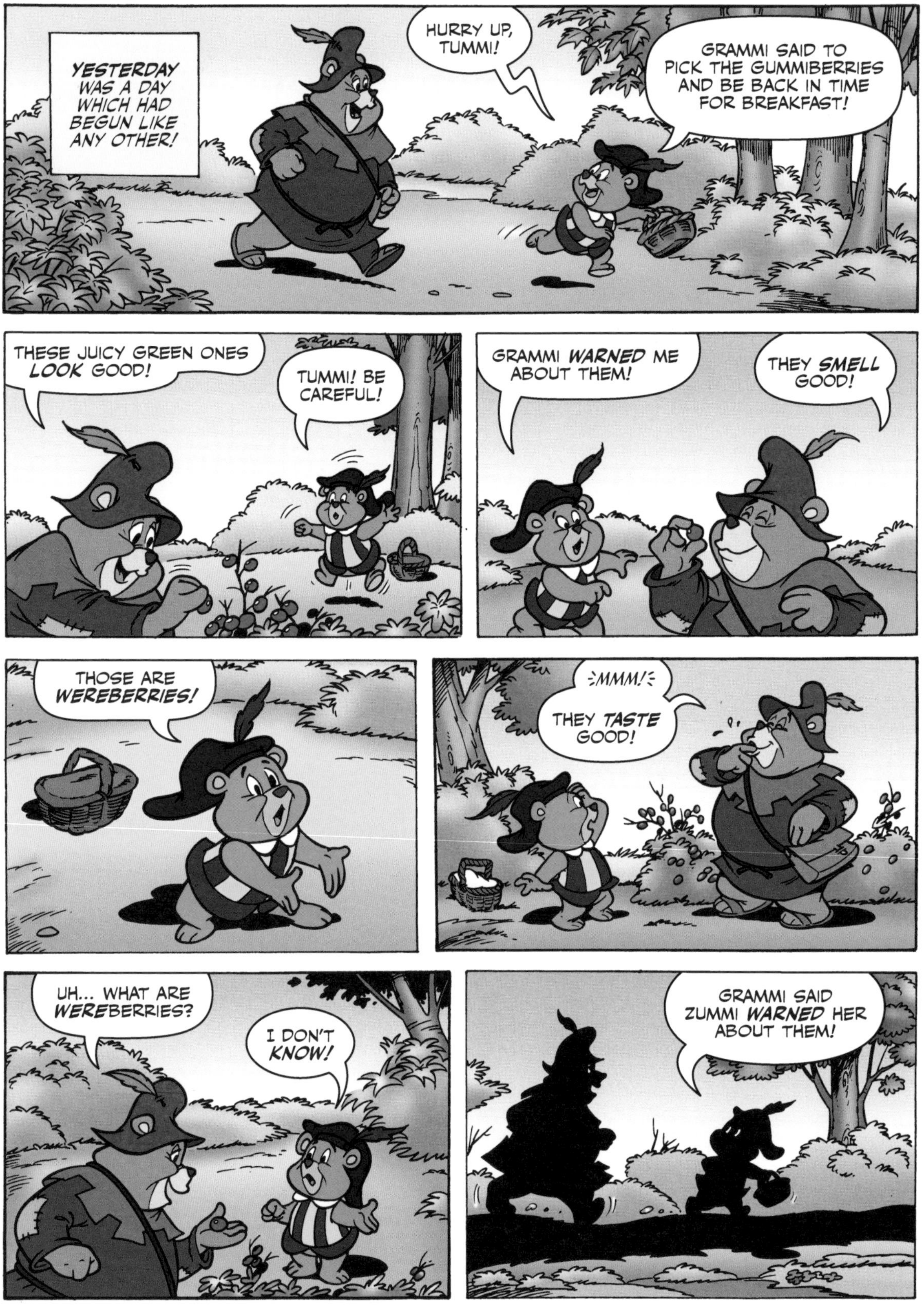
YESTERDAY WAS A DAY WHICH HAD BEGUN LIKE ANY OTHER!
HURRY UP, TUMMI!
GRAMMI SAID TO PICK THE GUMMIBERRIES AND BE BACK IN TIME FOR BREAKFAST!
THESE JUICY GREEN ONES LOOK GOOD!
TUMMI! BE CAREFUL!
GRAMMI WARNED ME ABOUT THEM!
THEY SMELL GOOD!
THOSE ARE WEREBERRIES!
MMM!
THEY TASTE GOOD!
UH... WHAT ARE WEREBERRIES?
I DON'T KNOW!
GRAMMI SAID ZUMMI WARNED HER ABOUT THEM!

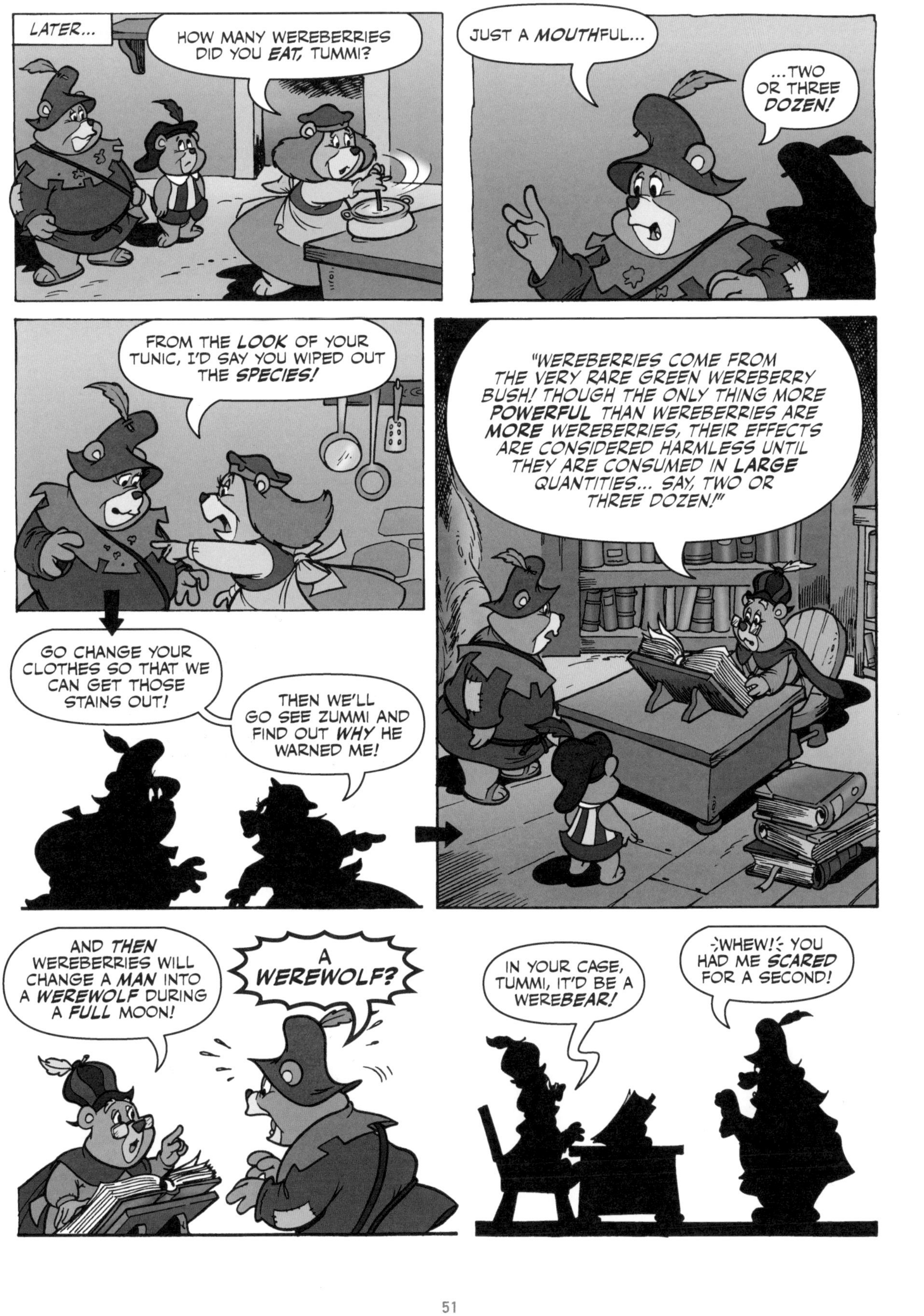
LATER...
HOW MANY WEREBERRIES DID YOU EAT, TUMMI?
JUST A MOUTHFUL...
...TWO OR THREE DOZEN!
FROM THE LOOK OF YOUR TUNIC, I'D SAY YOU WIPED OUT THE SPECIES!
GO CHANGE YOUR CLOTHES SO THAT WE CAN GET THOSE STAINS OUT!
THEN WE'LL GO SEE ZUMMI AND FIND OUT WHY HE WARNED ME!
"WEREBERRIES COME FROM THE VERY RARE GREEN WEREBERRY BUSH! THOUGH THE ONLY THING MORE POWERFUL THAN WEREBERRIES ARE MORE WEREBERRIES, THEIR EFFECTS ARE CONSIDERED HARMLESS UNTIL THEY ARE CONSUMED IN LARGE QUANTITIES... SAY, TWO OR THREE DOZEN!"
AND THEN WEREBERRIES WILL CHANGE A MAN INTO A WEREWOLF DURING A FULL MOON!
A WEREWOLF?
IN YOUR CASE, TUMMI, IT'D BE A WEREBEAR!
WHEW! YOU HAD ME SCARED FOR A SECOND!

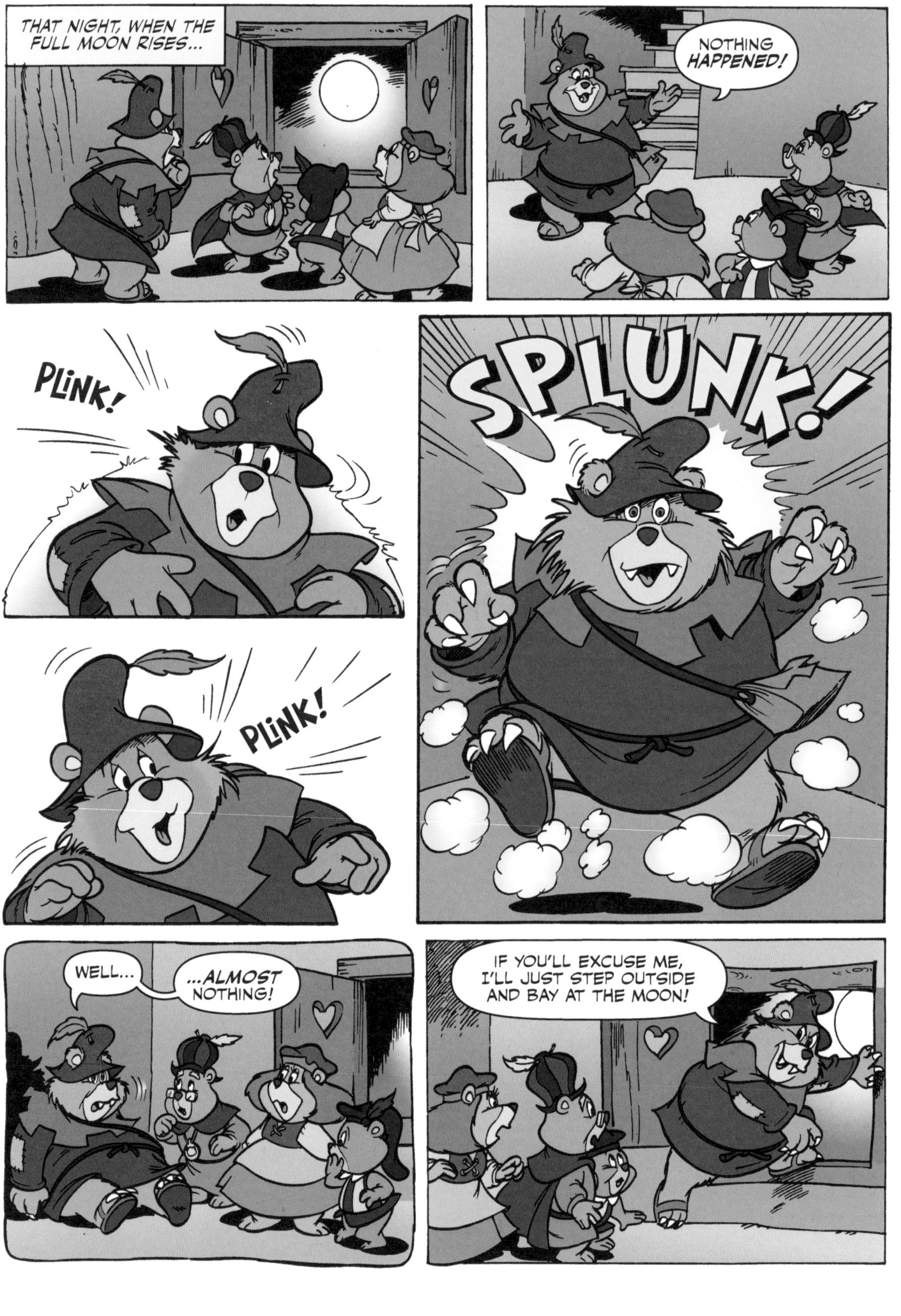
THAT NIGHT, WHEN THE FULL MOON RISES...
NOTHING HAPPENED!
PLINK!
SPLUNK!
PLINK!
WELL...
...ALMOST NOTHING!
IF YOU'LL EXCUSE ME, I'LL JUST STEP OUTSIDE AND BAY AT THE MOON!

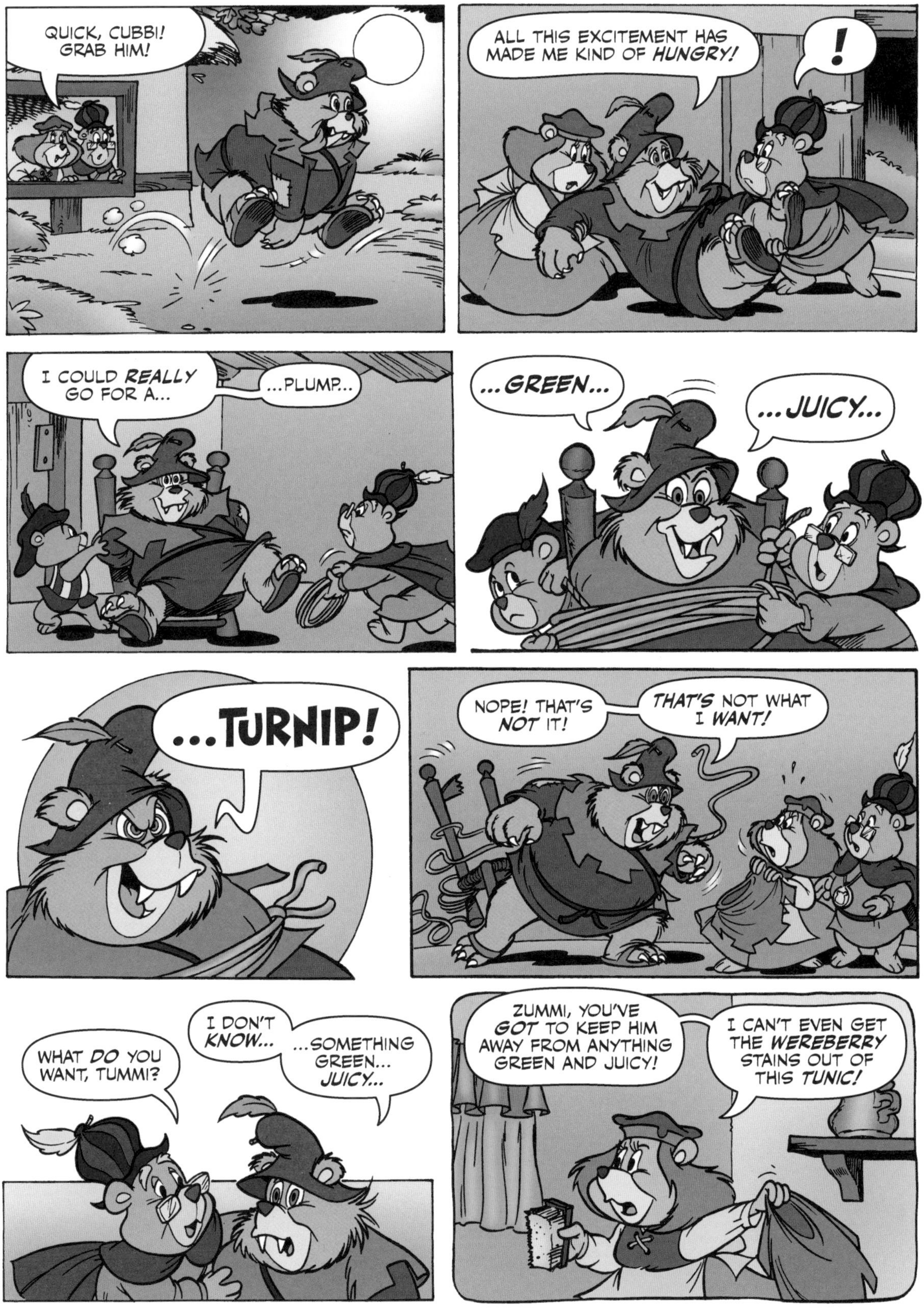
QUICK, CUBBI! GRAB HIM!
ALL THIS EXCITEMENT HAS MADE ME KIND OF HUNGRY!
!
I COULD REALLY GO FOR A...
...PLUMP...
...GREEN...
...JUICY...
...TURNIP!
NOPE! THAT'S NOT IT!
THAT'S NOT WHAT I WANT!
WHAT DO YOU WANT, TUMMI?
I DON'T KNOW...
...SOMETHING GREEN... JUICY...
ZUMMI, YOU'VE GOT TO KEEP HIM AWAY FROM ANYTHING GREEN AND JUICY!
I CAN'T EVEN GET THE WEREBERRY STAINS OUT OF THIS TUNIC!

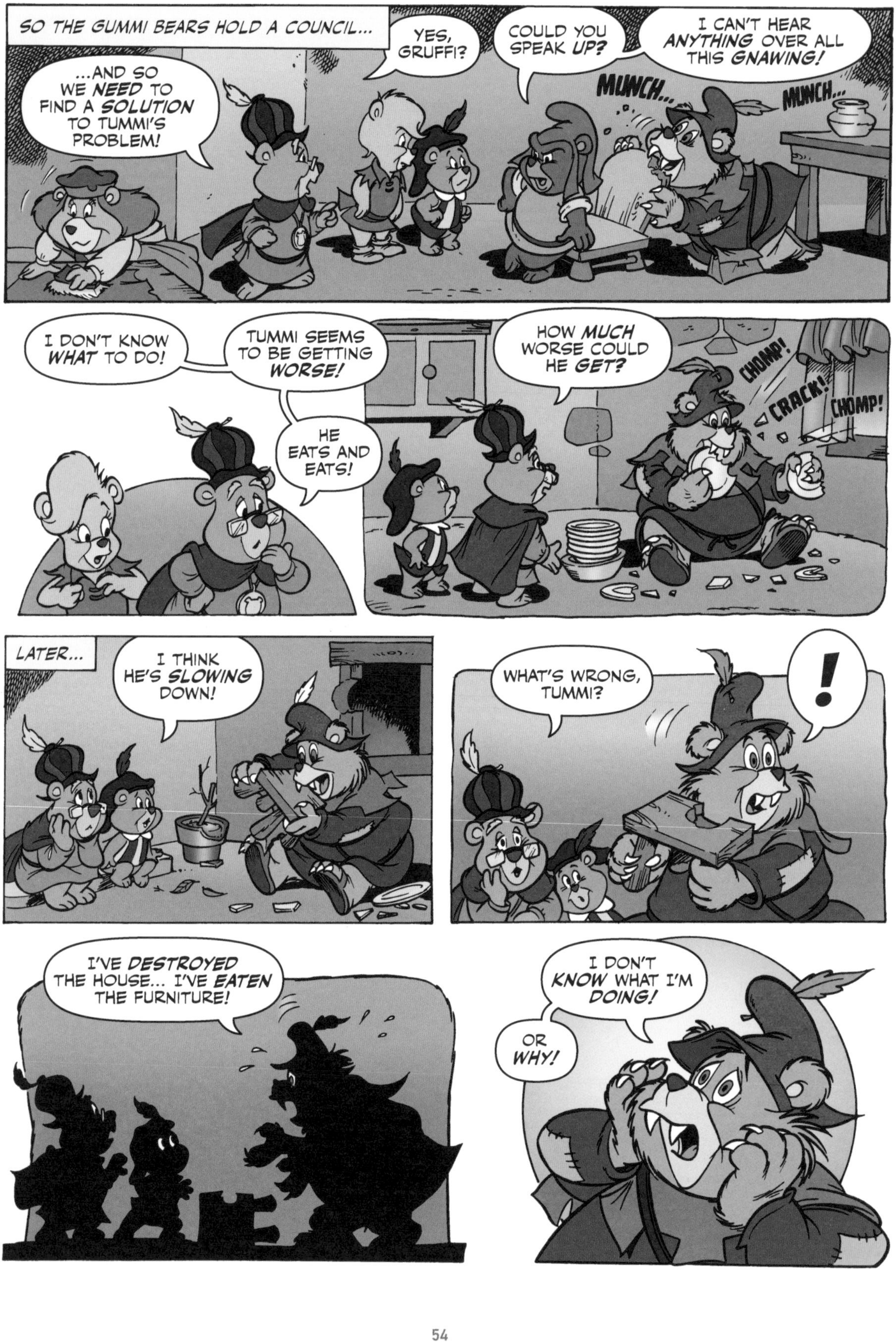

SO THE GUMMI BEARS HOLD A COUNCIL...
...AND SO WE NEED TO FIND A SOLUTION TO TUMMI'S PROBLEM!
YES, GRUFFI?
COULD YOU SPEAK UP?
I CAN'T HEAR ANYTHING OVER ALL THIS GNAWING!
MUNCH...
MUNCH...
I DON'T KNOW WHAT TO DO!
TUMMI SEEMS TO BE GETTING WORSE!
HE EATS AND EATS!
HOW MUCH WORSE COULD HE GET?
CHOMP!
CRACK!
CHOMP!
LATER...
I THINK HE'S SLOWING DOWN!
WHAT'S WRONG, TUMMI?
!
I'VE DESTROYED THE HOUSE... I'VE EATEN THE FURNITURE!
I DON'T KNOW WHAT I'M DOING!
OR WHY!

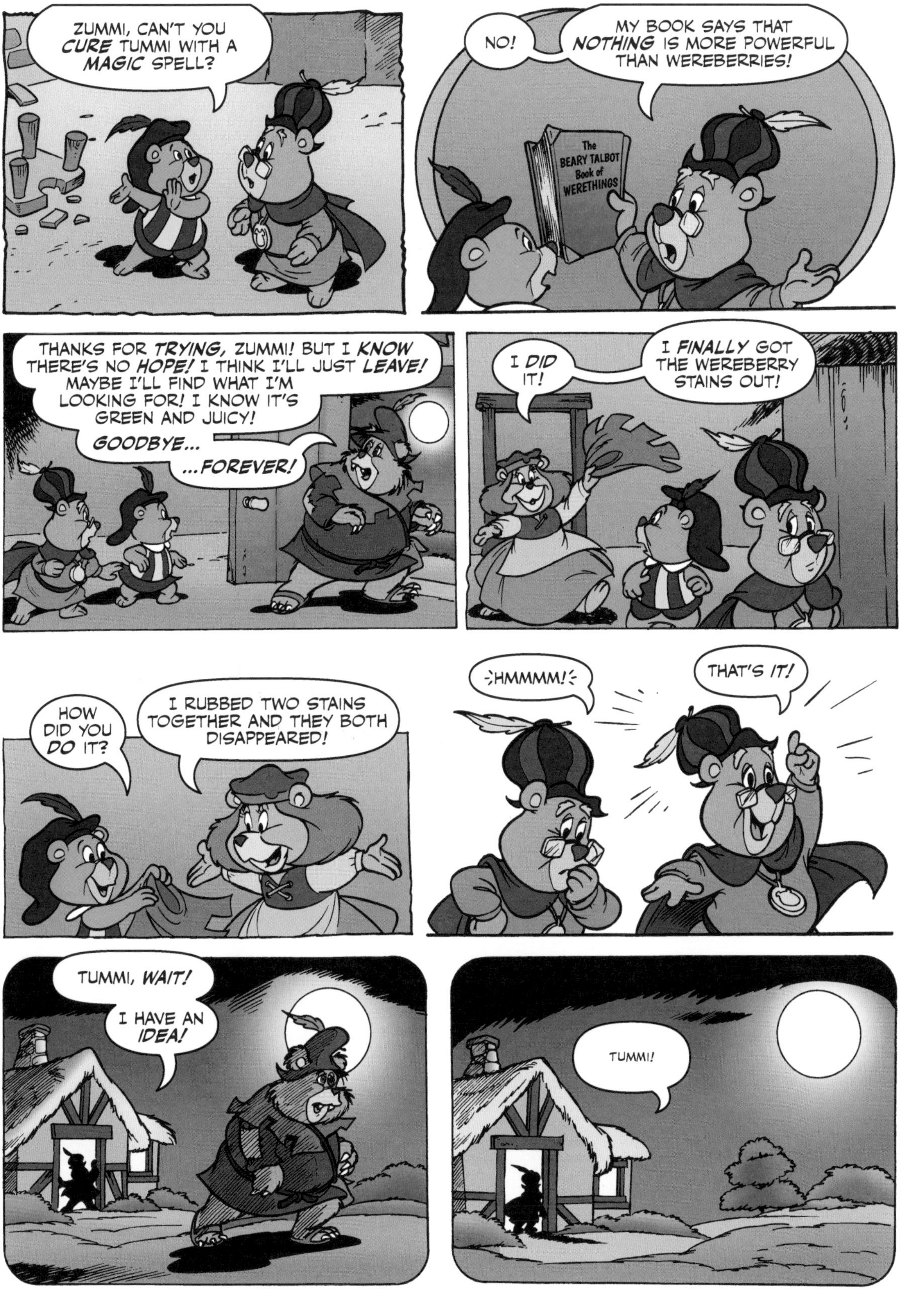
ZUMMI, CAN'T YOU CURE TUMMI WITH A MAGIC SPELL?
NO!
MY BOOK SAYS THAT NOTHING IS MORE POWERFUL THAN WEREBERRIES!
The BEARY TALBOT Book of WERETHINGS
THANKS FOR TRYING, ZUMMI! BUT I KNOW THERE'S NO HOPE! I THINK I'LL JUST LEAVE! MAYBE I'LL FIND WHAT I'M LOOKING FOR! I KNOW IT'S GREEN AND JUICY!
GOODBYE... ...FOREVER!
I DID IT!
I FINALLY GOT THE WEREBERRY STAINS OUT!
HOW DID YOU DO IT?
I RUBBED TWO STAINS TOGETHER AND THEY BOTH DISAPPEARED!
HMMMM!
THAT'S IT!
TUMMI, WAIT!
I HAVE AN IDEA!
TUMMI!

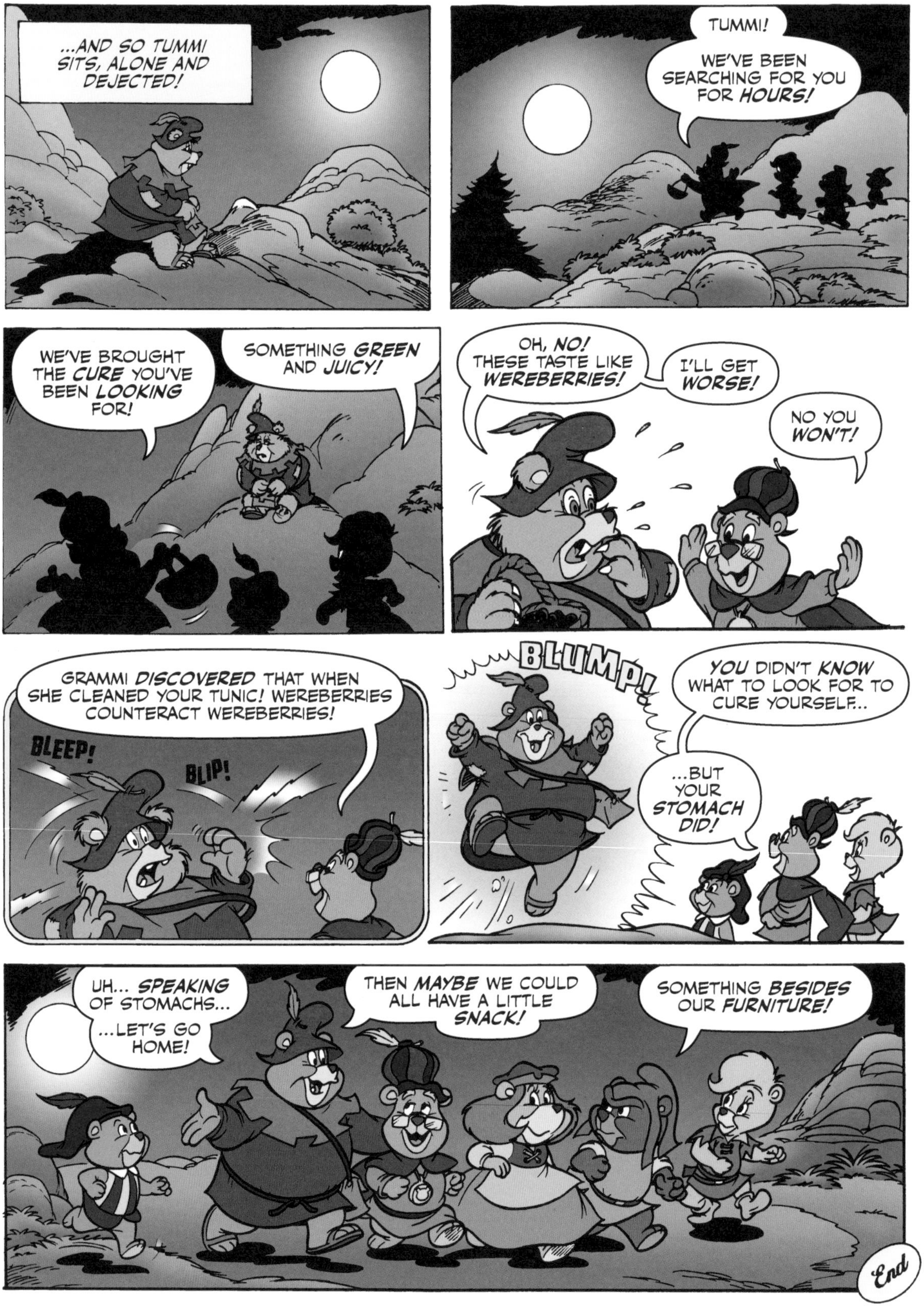
...AND SO TUMMI SITS, ALONE AND DEJECTED!
TUMMI!
WE'VE BEEN SEARCHING FOR YOU FOR HOURS!
WE'VE BROUGHT THE CURE YOU'VE BEEN LOOKING FOR!
SOMETHING GREEN AND JUICY!
OH, NO! THESE TASTE LIKE WEREBERRIES!
I'LL GET WORSE!
NO YOU WON'T!
GRAMMI DISCOVERED THAT WHEN SHE CLEANED YOUR TUNIC! WEREBERRIES COUNTERACT WEREBERRIES!
BLEEP!
BLIP!
BLUMP!
YOU DIDN'T KNOW WHAT TO LOOK FOR TO CURE YOURSELF...
...BUT YOUR STOMACH DID!
UH... SPEAKING OF STOMACHS...
...LET'S GO HOME!
THEN MAYBE WE COULD ALL HAVE A LITTLE SNACK!
SOMETHING BESIDES OUR FURNITURE!
End

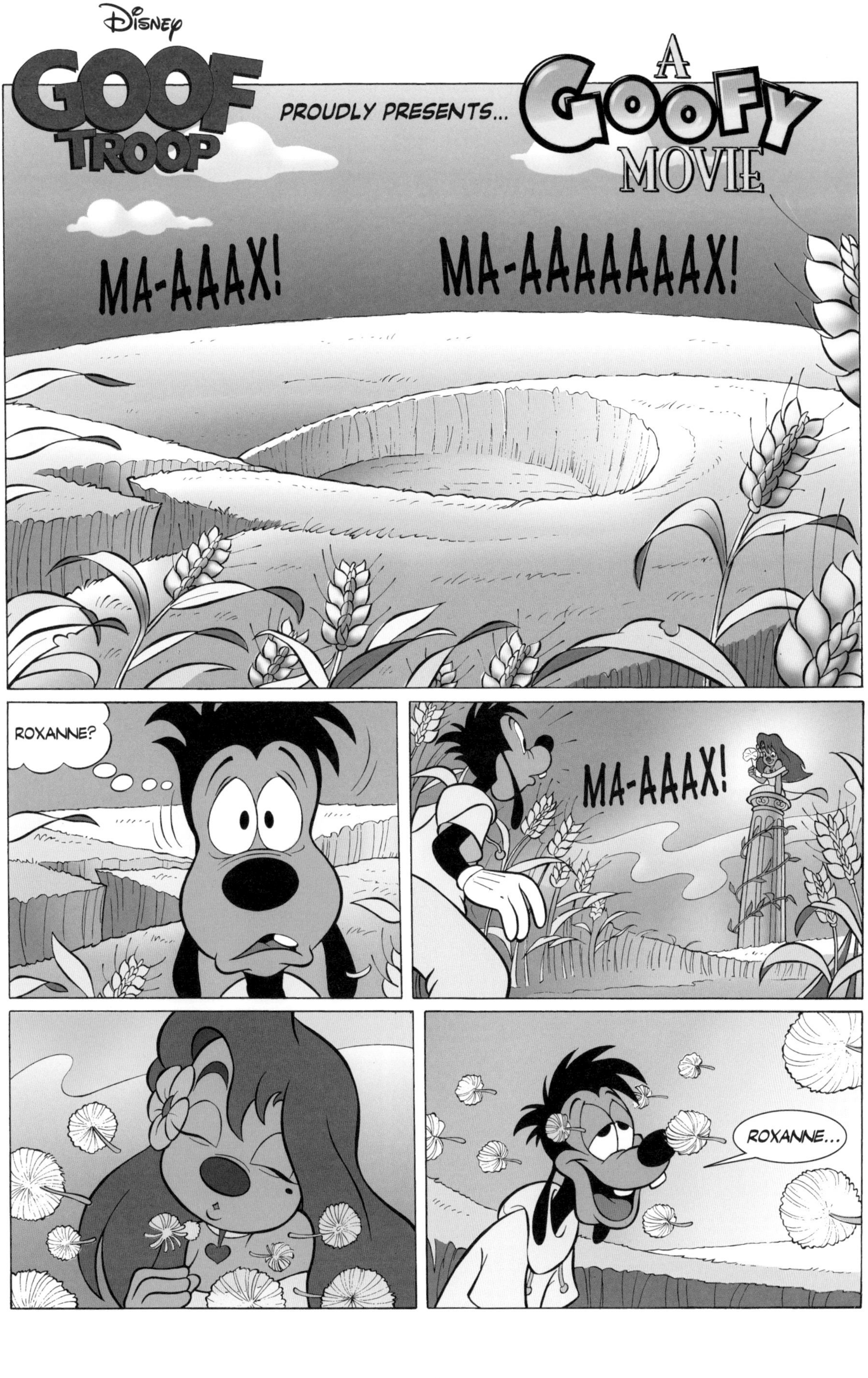
Disney
GOOF TROOP
PROUDLY PRESENTS...
A GOOFY MOVIE
MA-AAAX!
MA-AAAAAAAX!
ROXANNE?
MA-AAAX!
ROXANNE...

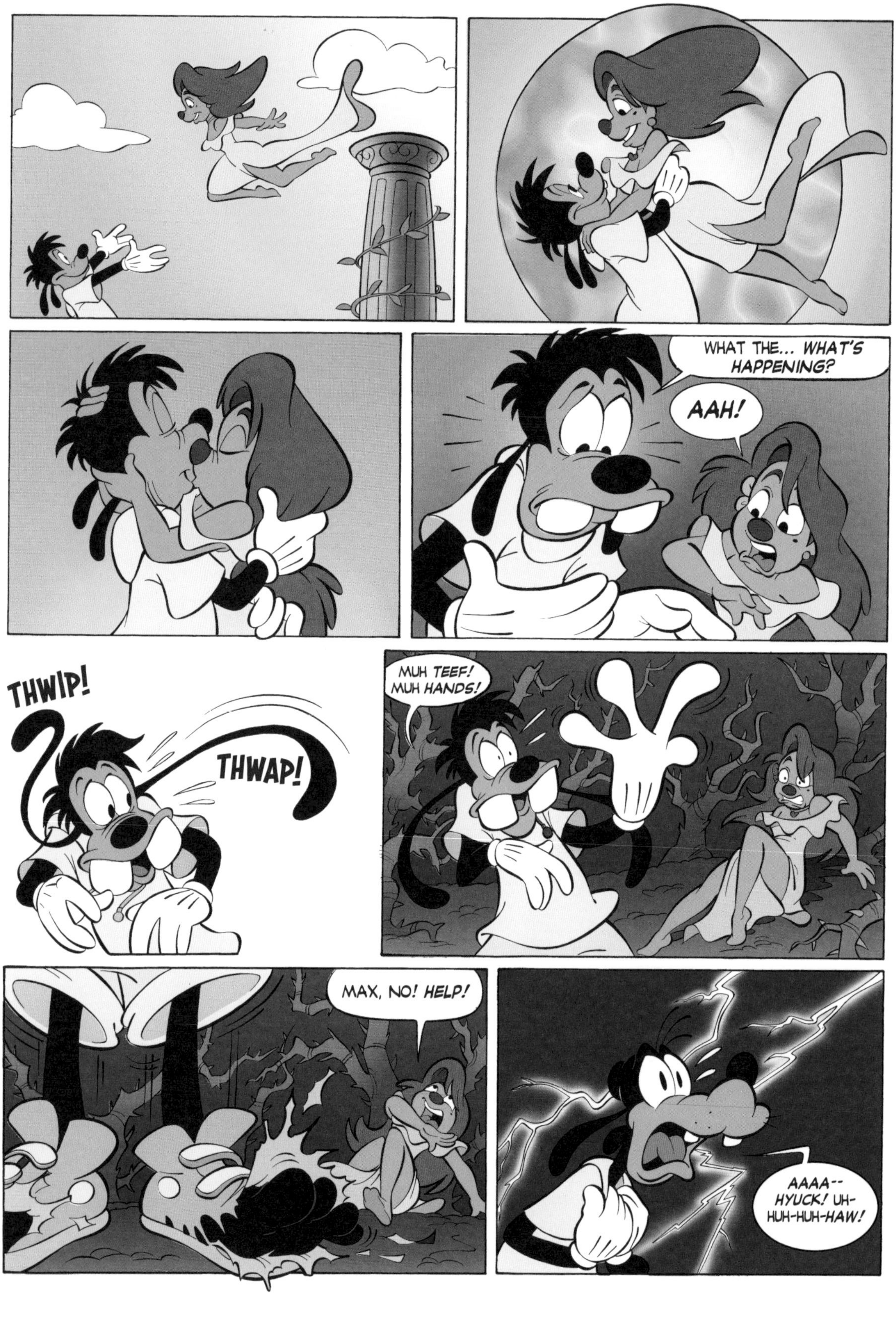
WHAT THE... WHAT'S HAPPENING?
AAH!
THWIP!
THWAP!
MUH TEEF! MUH HANDS!
MAX, NO! HELP!
AAAA-- HYUCK! UH-HUH-HUH-HAW!

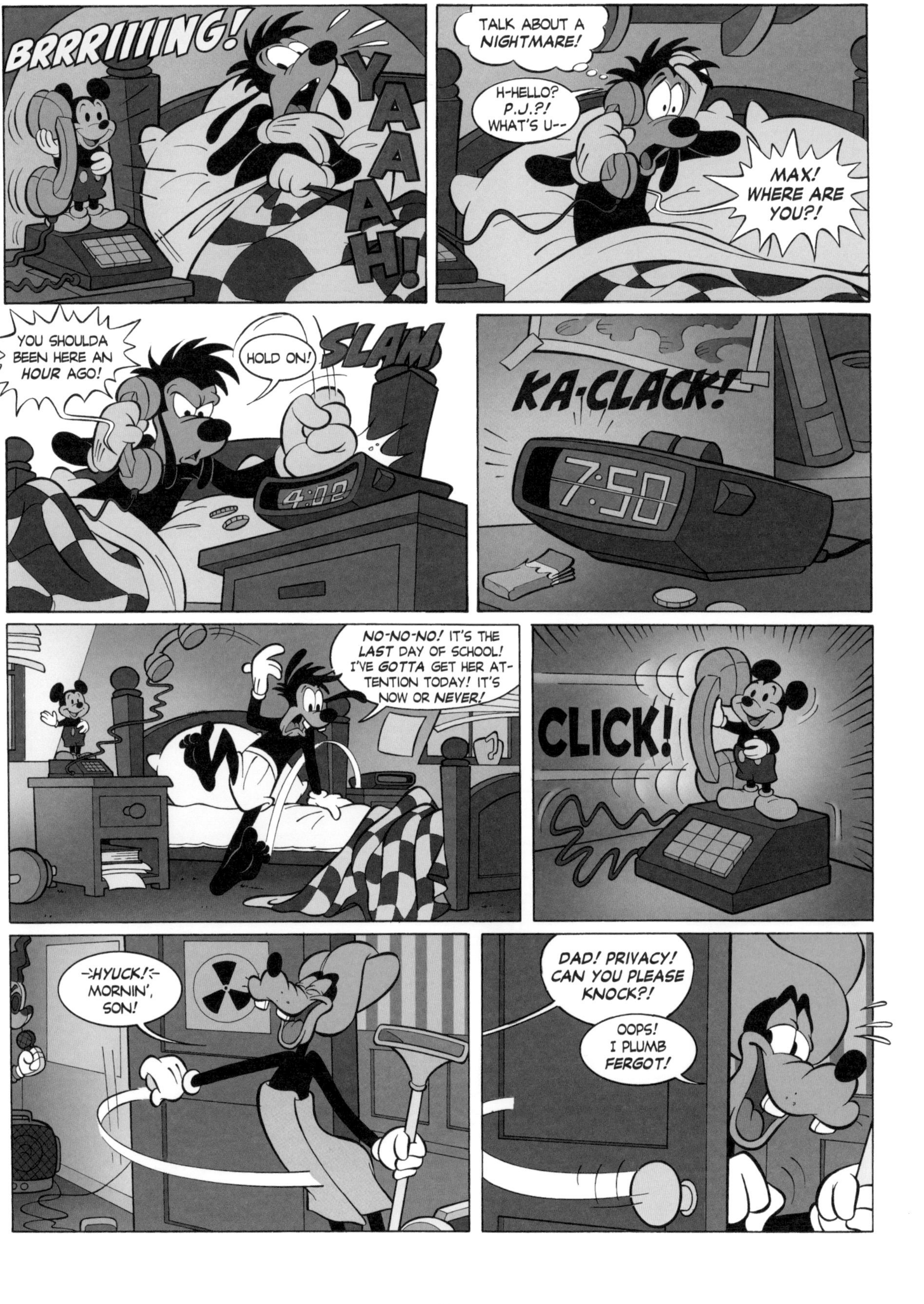
BRRRIIIING!
YAAAAH!
TALK ABOUT A NIGHTMARE!
H-HELLO? P.J.?! WHAT'S U--
MAX! WHERE ARE YOU?!
YOU SHOULDA BEEN HERE AN HOUR AGO!
HOLD ON!
SLAM
4:02
KA-CLACK!
7:50
NO-NO-NO! IT'S THE LAST DAY OF SCHOOL! I'VE GOTTA GET HER ATTENTION TODAY! IT'S NOW OR NEVER!
CLICK!
-HYUCK!- MORNIN', SON!
DAD! PRIVACY! CAN YOU PLEASE KNOCK?!
OOPS! I PLUMB FERGOT!

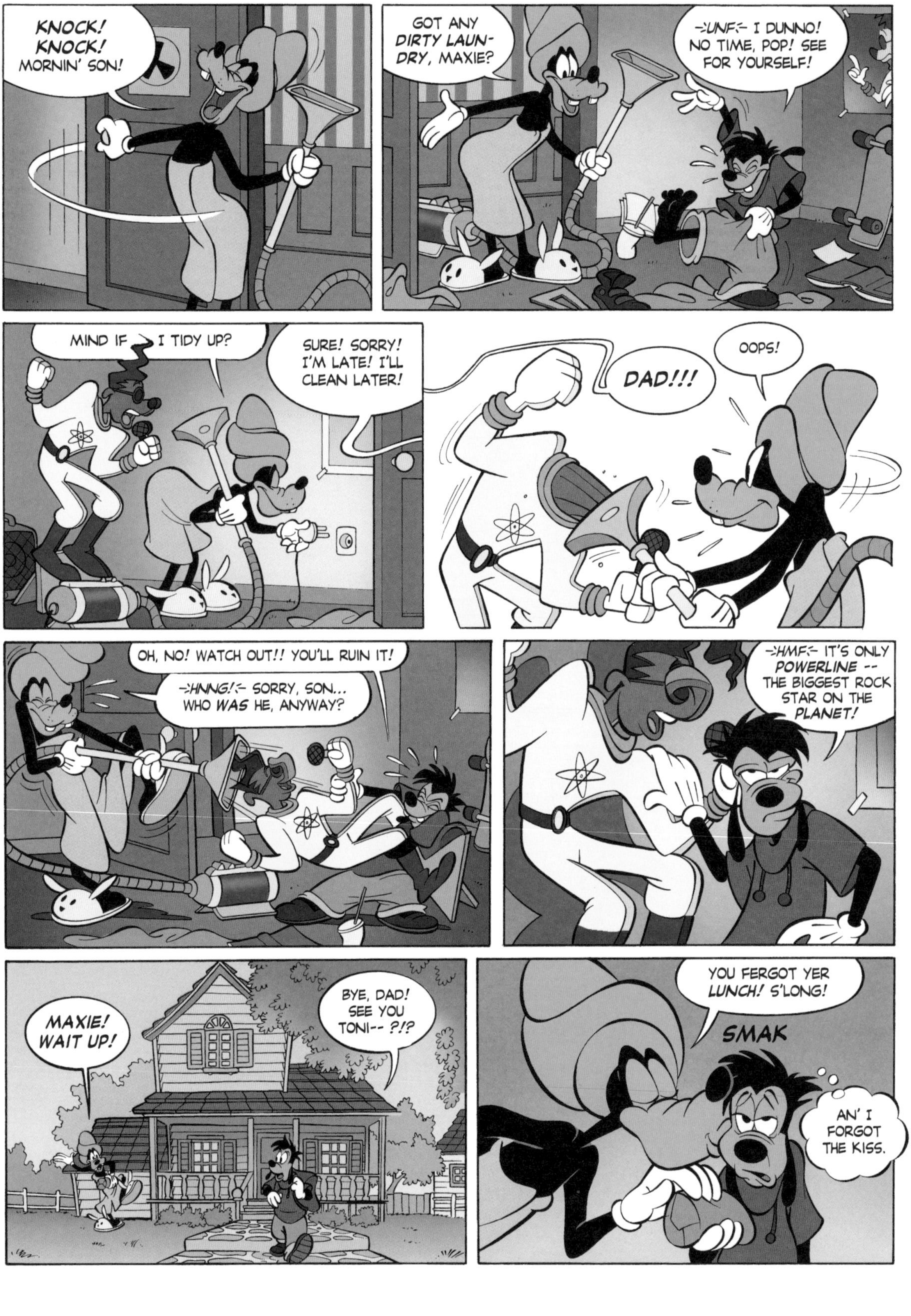
KNOCK! KNOCK! MORNIN' SON!
GOT ANY DIRTY LAUNDRY, MAXIE?
-UNF- I DUNNO! NO TIME, POP! SEE FOR YOURSELF!
MIND IF I TIDY UP?
SURE! SORRY! I'M LATE! I'LL CLEAN LATER!
DAD!!!
OOPS!
OH, NO! WATCH OUT!! YOU'LL RUIN IT!
-HNNG!- SORRY, SON... WHO WAS HE, ANYWAY?
-HMF- IT'S ONLY POWERLINE -- THE BIGGEST ROCK STAR ON THE PLANET!
MAXIE! WAIT UP!
BYE, DAD! SEE YOU TONI-- ?!?
YOU FERGOT YER LUNCH! S'LONG!
SMAK
AN' I FORGOT THE KISS.

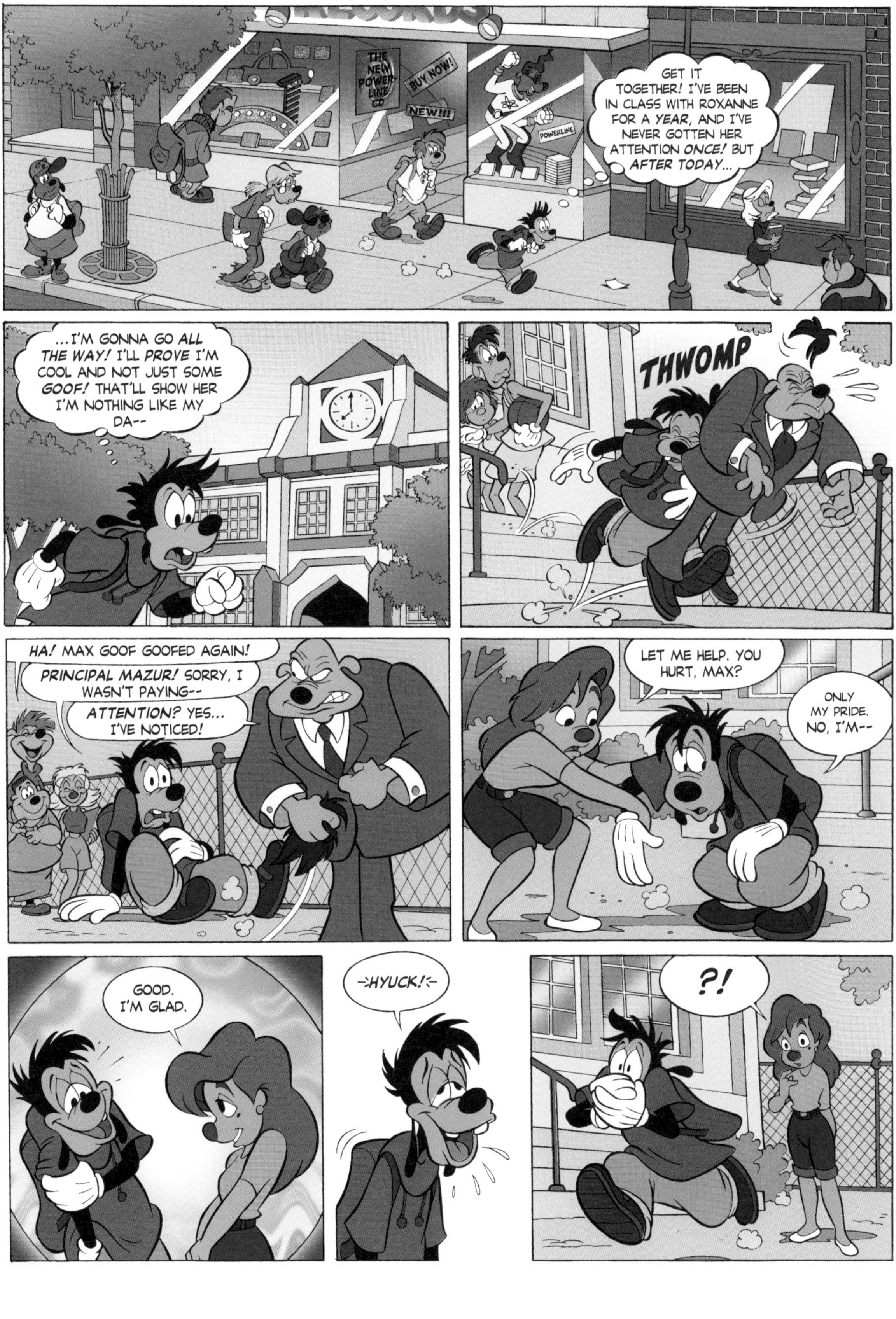
RECORDS
THE NEW POWER-LINE CD
BUY NOW!
NEW!!!
POWERLINE
GET IT TOGETHER! I'VE BEEN IN CLASS WITH ROXANNE FOR A YEAR, AND I'VE NEVER GOTTEN HER ATTENTION ONCE! BUT AFTER TODAY...
...I'M GONNA GO ALL THE WAY! I'LL PROVE I'M COOL AND NOT JUST SOME GOOF! THAT'LL SHOW HER I'M NOTHING LIKE MY DA--
THWOMP
HA! MAX GOOF GOOFED AGAIN!
PRINCIPAL MAZUR! SORRY, I WASN'T PAYING--
ATTENTION? YES... I'VE NOTICED!
LET ME HELP. YOU HURT, MAX?
ONLY MY PRIDE. NO, I'M--
GOOD. I'M GLAD.
HYUCK!
?!

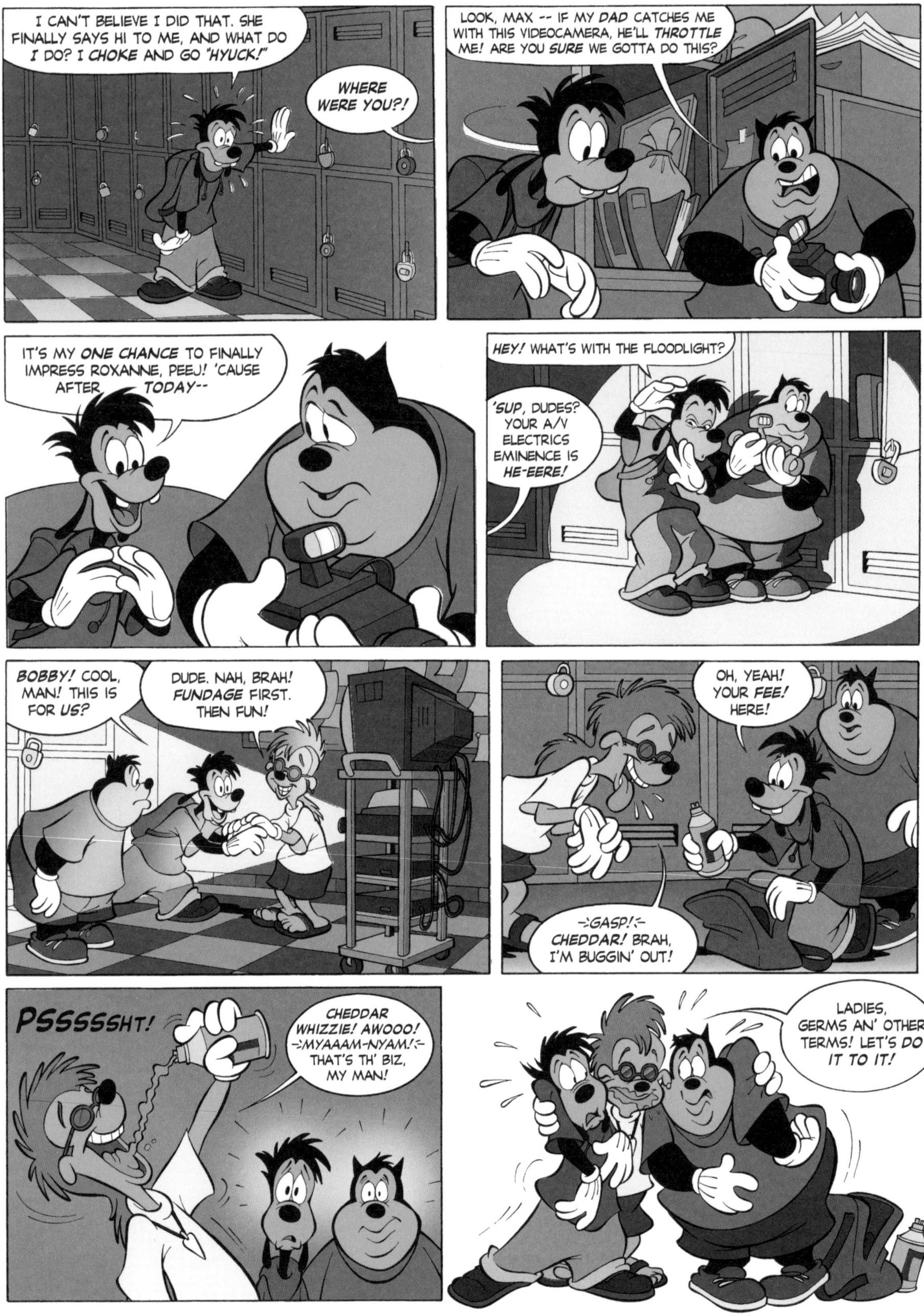

I CAN'T BELIEVE I DID THAT. SHE FINALLY SAYS HI TO ME, AND WHAT DO I DO? I CHOKE AND GO "HYUCK!"
WHERE WERE YOU?!
LOOK, MAX -- IF MY DAD CATCHES ME WITH THIS VIDEOCAMERA, HE'LL THROTTLE ME! ARE YOU SURE WE GOTTA DO THIS?
IT'S MY ONE CHANCE TO FINALLY IMPRESS ROXANNE, PEEJ! 'CAUSE AFTER TODAY--
HEY! WHAT'S WITH THE FLOODLIGHT?
'SUP, DUDES? YOUR A/V ELECTRICS EMINENCE IS HE-EERE!
BOBBY! COOL, MAN! THIS IS FOR US?
DUDE. NAH, BRAH! FUNDAGE FIRST. THEN FUN!
OH, YEAH! YOUR FEE! HERE!
-GASP!- CHEDDAR! BRAH, I'M BUGGIN' OUT!
PSSSSSHT!
CHEDDAR WHIZZIE! AWOOO! -MYAAAM-NYAM!- THAT'S TH' BIZ, MY MAN!
LADIES, GERMS AN' OTHER TERMS! LET'S DO IT TO IT!

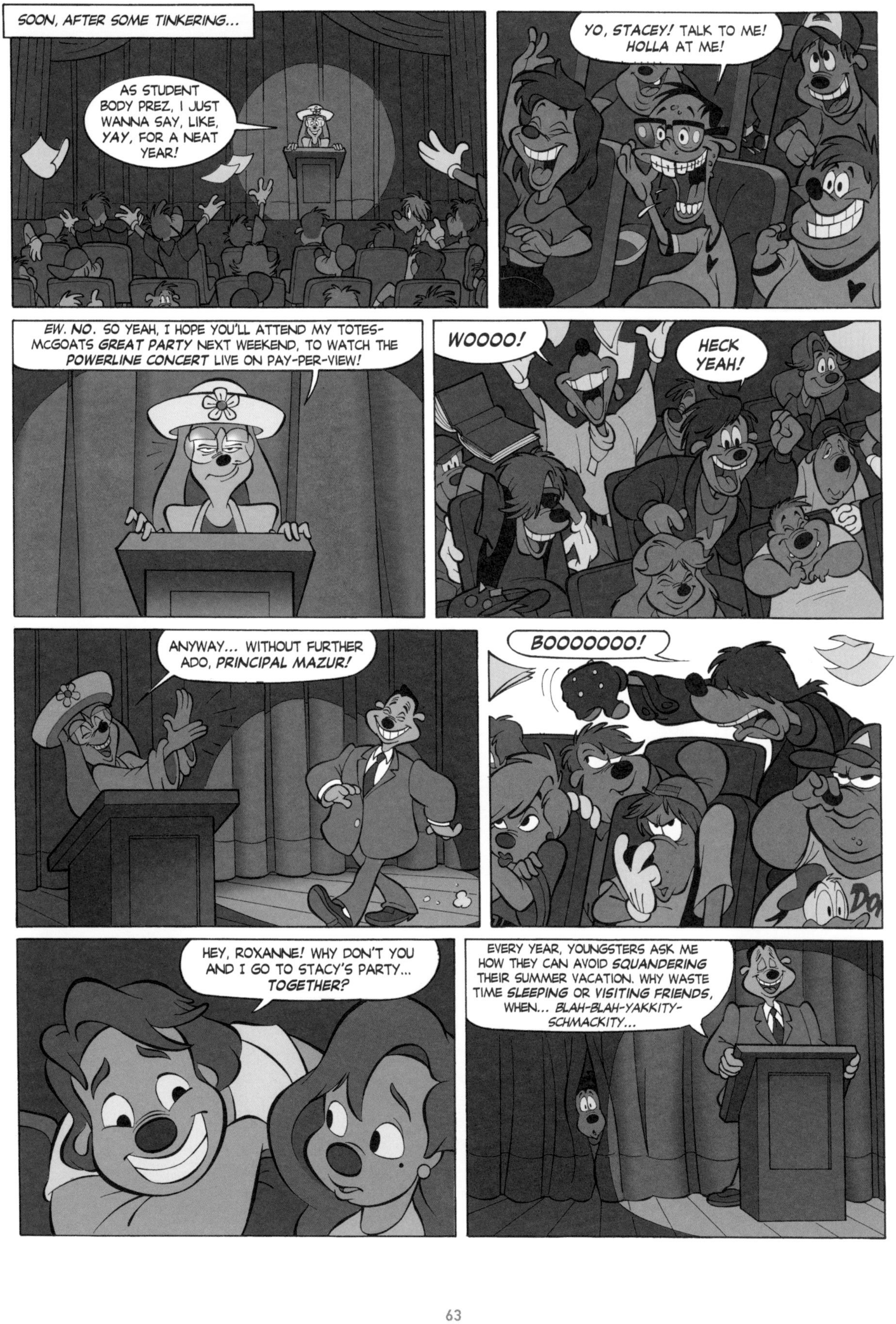
SOON, AFTER SOME TINKERING...
AS STUDENT BODY PREZ, I JUST WANNA SAY, LIKE, YAY, FOR A NEAT YEAR!
YO, STACEY! TALK TO ME! HOLLA AT ME!
EW. NO. SO YEAH, I HOPE YOU'LL ATTEND MY TOTES-McGOATS GREAT PARTY NEXT WEEKEND, TO WATCH THE POWERLINE CONCERT LIVE ON PAY-PER-VIEW!
WOOOO!
HECK YEAH!
ANYWAY... WITHOUT FURTHER ADO, PRINCIPAL MAZUR!
BOOOOOOO!
HEY, ROXANNE! WHY DON'T YOU AND I GO TO STACY'S PARTY... TOGETHER?
EVERY YEAR, YOUNGSTERS ASK ME HOW THEY CAN AVOID SQUANDERING THEIR SUMMER VACATION. WHY WASTE TIME SLEEPING OR VISITING FRIENDS, WHEN... BLAH-BLAH-YAKKITY-SCHMACKITY...

HOW, UH... HOW YA DOING DOWN THERE, BOBBY?

CALM DOWN, BUDDY! NO ATTITUDE! I'M DOIN' IT ALL FER YOU!

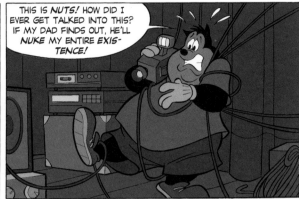

THIS IS *NUTS!* HOW DID I EVER GET TALKED INTO THIS? IF MY DAD FINDS OUT, HE'LL *NUKE* MY ENTIRE *EXISTENCE!*

LESS *STRESS,* PETEY J-R! MAX, IT'S ALL ON *YOU!* WE'RE LIVE IN 3... 2...

...THAT'S WHY I PROPOSE *SCIENCE SLUMBER PARTIES---*

WHAT IN THE WORLD?

HEY!

?!?

AAAAAAH!

STAND OUT ABOVE THE CROWD!

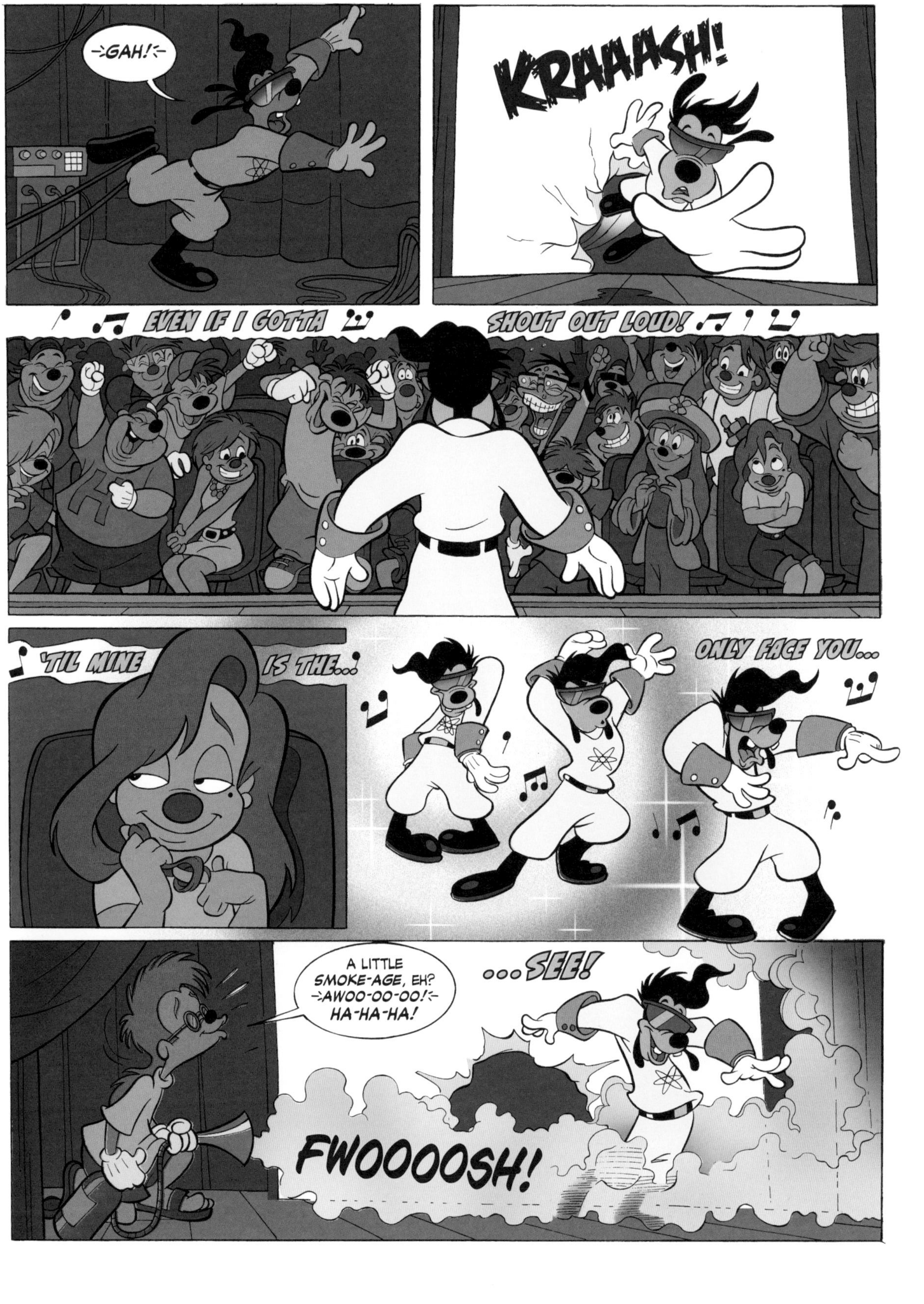

GAH!
KRAAASH!
EVEN IF I GOTTA
SHOUT OUT LOUD!
'TIL MINE
IS THE...
ONLY FACE YOU...
A LITTLE SMOKE-AGE, EH? AWOO-OO-OO! HA-HA-HA!
...SEE!
FWOOOOSH!

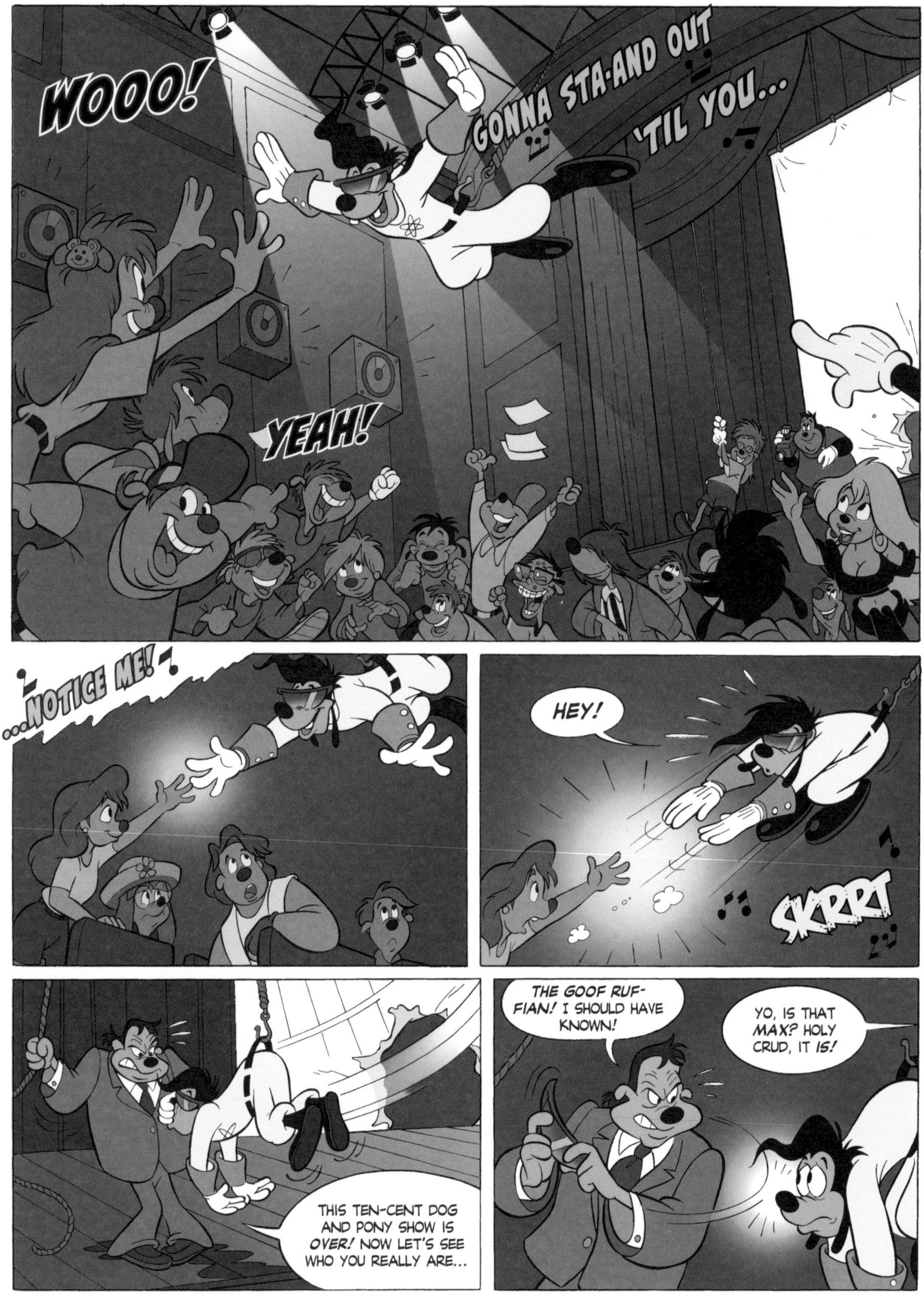
WOOO!
GONNA STA-AND OUT 'TIL YOU...
YEAH!
...NOTICE ME!
HEY!
SKRRT
THIS TEN-CENT DOG AND PONY SHOW IS OVER! NOW LET'S SEE WHO YOU REALLY ARE...
THE GOOF RUFFIAN! I SHOULD HAVE KNOWN!
YO, IS THAT MAX? HOLY CRUD, IT IS!

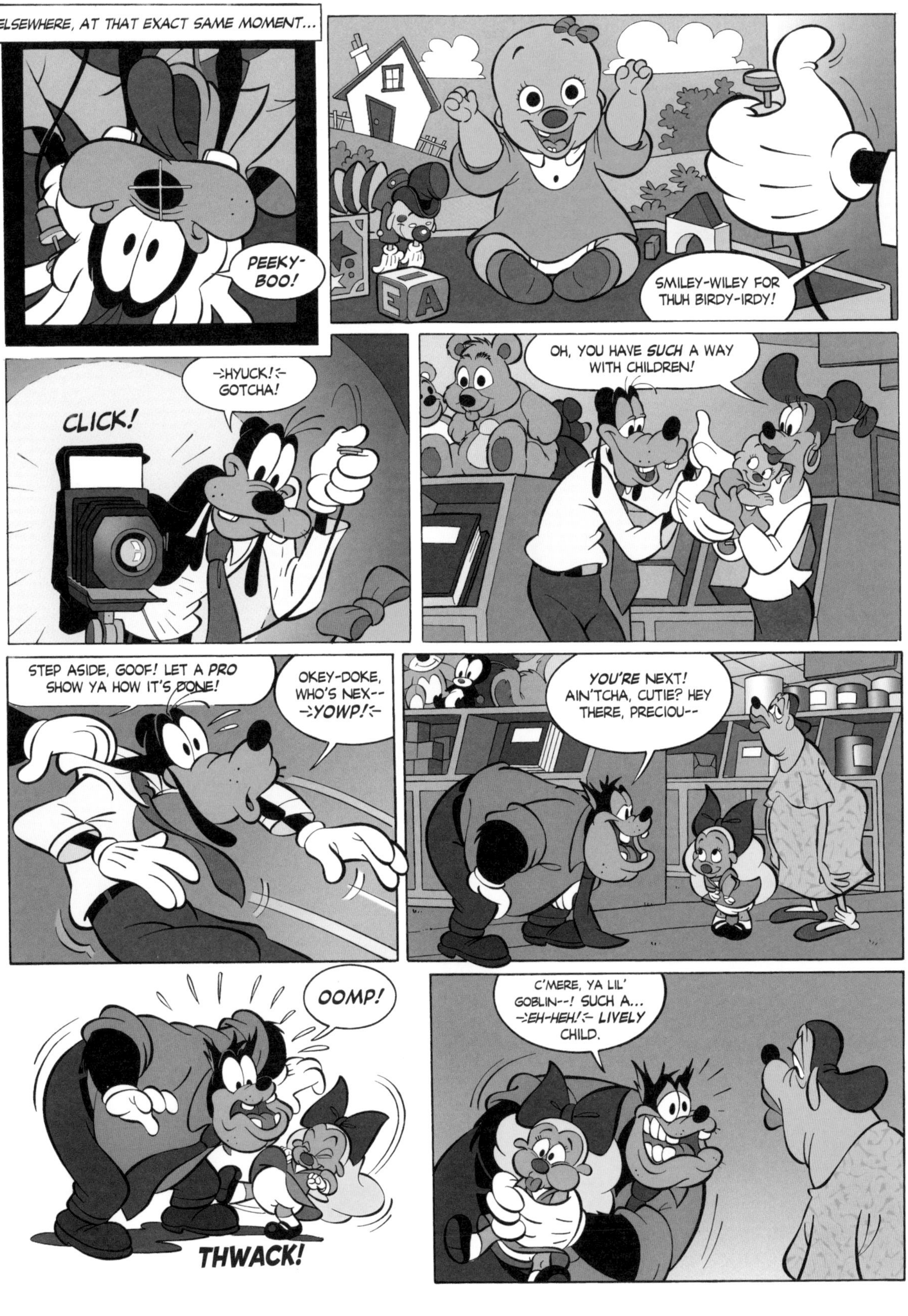
ELSEWHERE, AT THAT EXACT SAME MOMENT...
PEEKY-BOO!
SMILEY-WILEY FOR THUH BIRDY-IRDY!
CLICK!
-HYUCK!- GOTCHA!
OH, YOU HAVE SUCH A WAY WITH CHILDREN!
STEP ASIDE, GOOF! LET A PRO SHOW YA HOW IT'S DONE!
OKEY-DOKE, WHO'S NEX-- -YOWP!-
YOU'RE NEXT! AIN'TCHA, CUTIE? HEY THERE, PRECIOU--
OOMP!
THWACK!
C'MERE, YA LIL' GOBLIN--! SUCH A... -EH-HEH!- LIVELY CHILD.

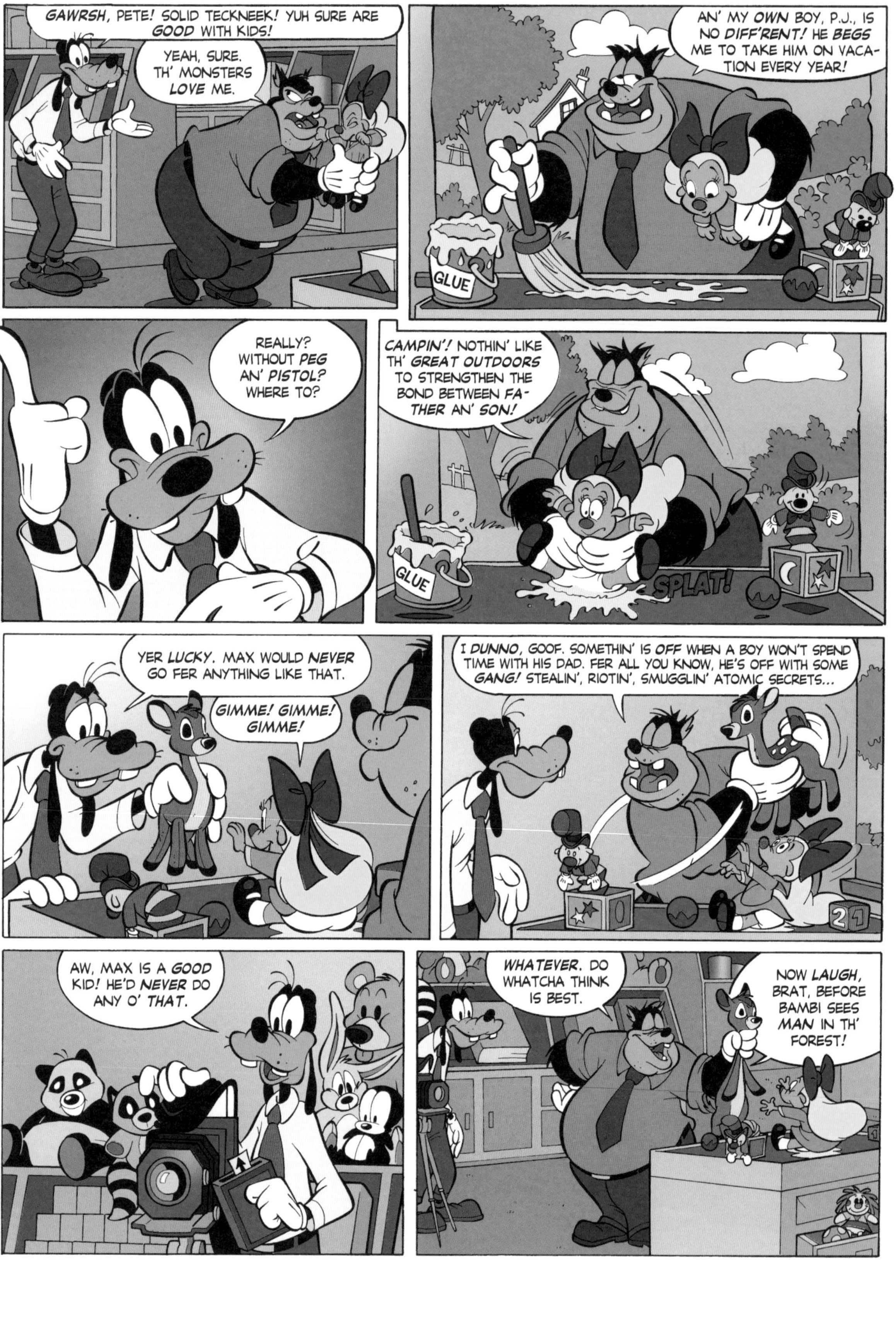
GAWRSH, PETE! SOLID TECKNEEK! YUH SURE ARE GOOD WITH KIDS!
YEAH, SURE. TH' MONSTERS LOVE ME.
AN' MY OWN BOY, P.J., IS NO DIFF'RENT! HE BEGS ME TO TAKE HIM ON VACATION EVERY YEAR!
GLUE
REALLY? WITHOUT PEG AN' PISTOL? WHERE TO?
CAMPIN'! NOTHIN' LIKE TH' GREAT OUTDOORS TO STRENGTHEN THE BOND BETWEEN FATHER AN' SON!
GLUE
SPLAT!
YER LUCKY. MAX WOULD NEVER GO FER ANYTHING LIKE THAT.
GIMME! GIMME! GIMME!
I DUNNO, GOOF. SOMETHIN' IS OFF WHEN A BOY WON'T SPEND TIME WITH HIS DAD. FER ALL YOU KNOW, HE'S OFF WITH SOME GANG! STEALIN', RIOTIN', SMUGGLIN' ATOMIC SECRETS...
AW, MAX IS A GOOD KID! HE'D NEVER DO ANY O' THAT.
WHATEVER. DO WHATCHA THINK IS BEST.
NOW LAUGH, BRAT, BEFORE BAMBI SEES MAN IN TH' FOREST!

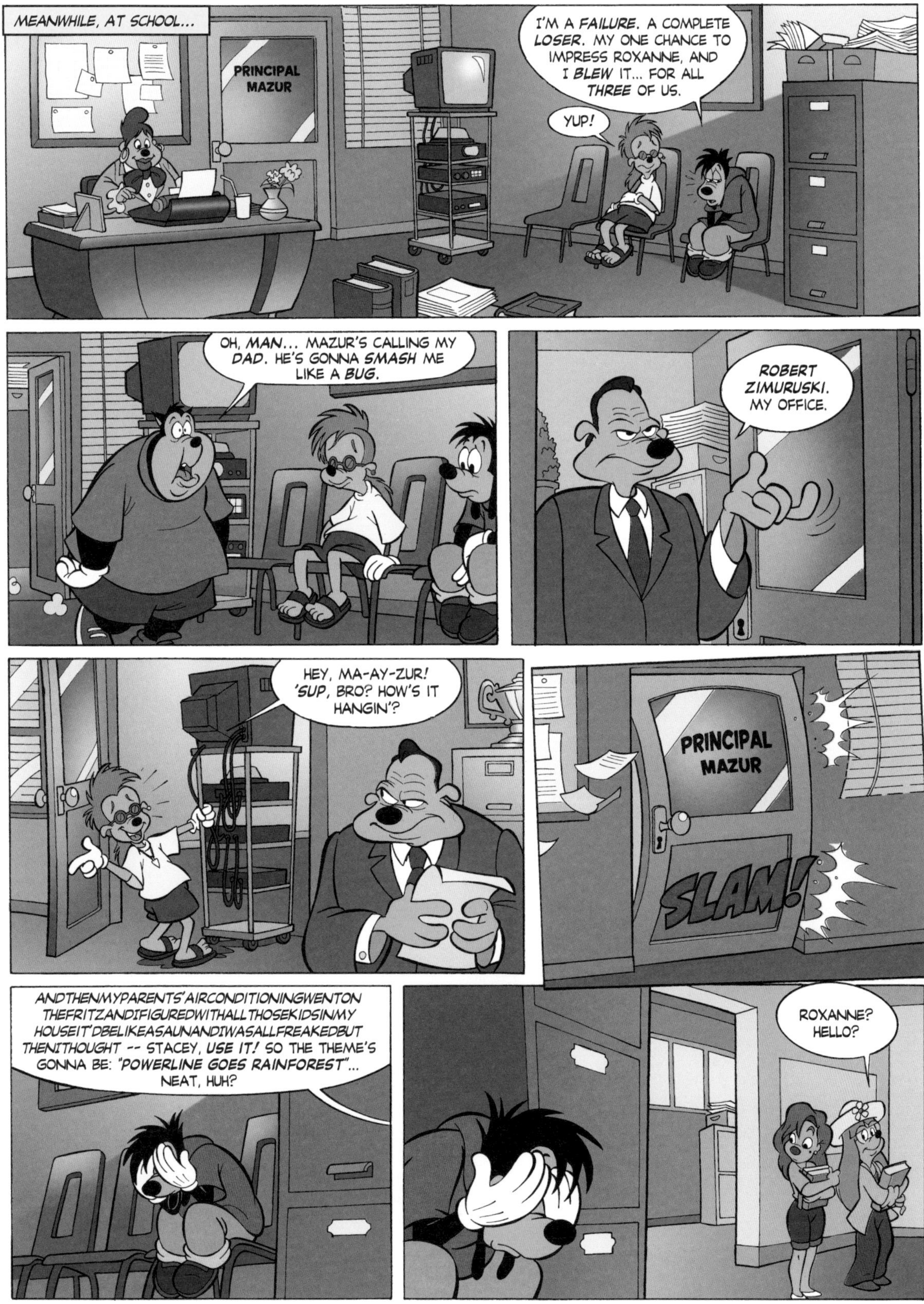

MEANWHILE, AT SCHOOL...
PRINCIPAL MAZUR
I'M A FAILURE. A COMPLETE LOSER. MY ONE CHANCE TO IMPRESS ROXANNE, AND I BLEW IT... FOR ALL THREE OF US.
YUP!
OH, MAN... MAZUR'S CALLING MY DAD. HE'S GONNA SMASH ME LIKE A BUG.
ROBERT ZIMURUSKI. MY OFFICE.
HEY, MA-AY-ZUR! 'SUP, BRO? HOW'S IT HANGIN'?
PRINCIPAL MAZUR
SLAM!
ANDTHENMYPARENTS'AIRCONDITIONINGWENTON THEFRITZANDIFIGUREDWITHALLTHOSEKIDSINMY HOUSEIT'DBELIKEASAUNANDIWASALLFREAKEDBUT THENITHOUGHT -- STACEY, USE IT! SO THE THEME'S GONNA BE: "POWERLINE GOES RAINFOREST"... NEAT, HUH?
ROXANNE? HELLO?

STACEY, NO! I DON'T--

STOP BEING SHY! GO TALK TO HIM!

-GASP!-

OH, GEEZ! ROXANNE! SORRY, I--

NO, IT'S OKAY! I STARTLED YOU!

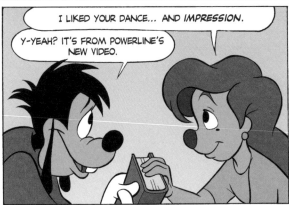

I LIKED YOUR DANCE... AND IMPRESSION.

Y-YEAH? IT'S FROM POWERLINE'S NEW VIDEO.

HE'S A TOTAL GENIUS. FANTASTIC!

YEAH... HE IS. SO, UH, WHILE WE'RE ON THAT... I WAS... SORTA, KINDA WONDERIN' IF YOU'D GO WITH ME TO STACEY'S PARTY ON SATURDAY.

I WAS... SORTA, KINDA THINKIN'... I'D LOVE TO.

COOL! SO, SATURDAY.

YEAH. SATUR- DAY.

70

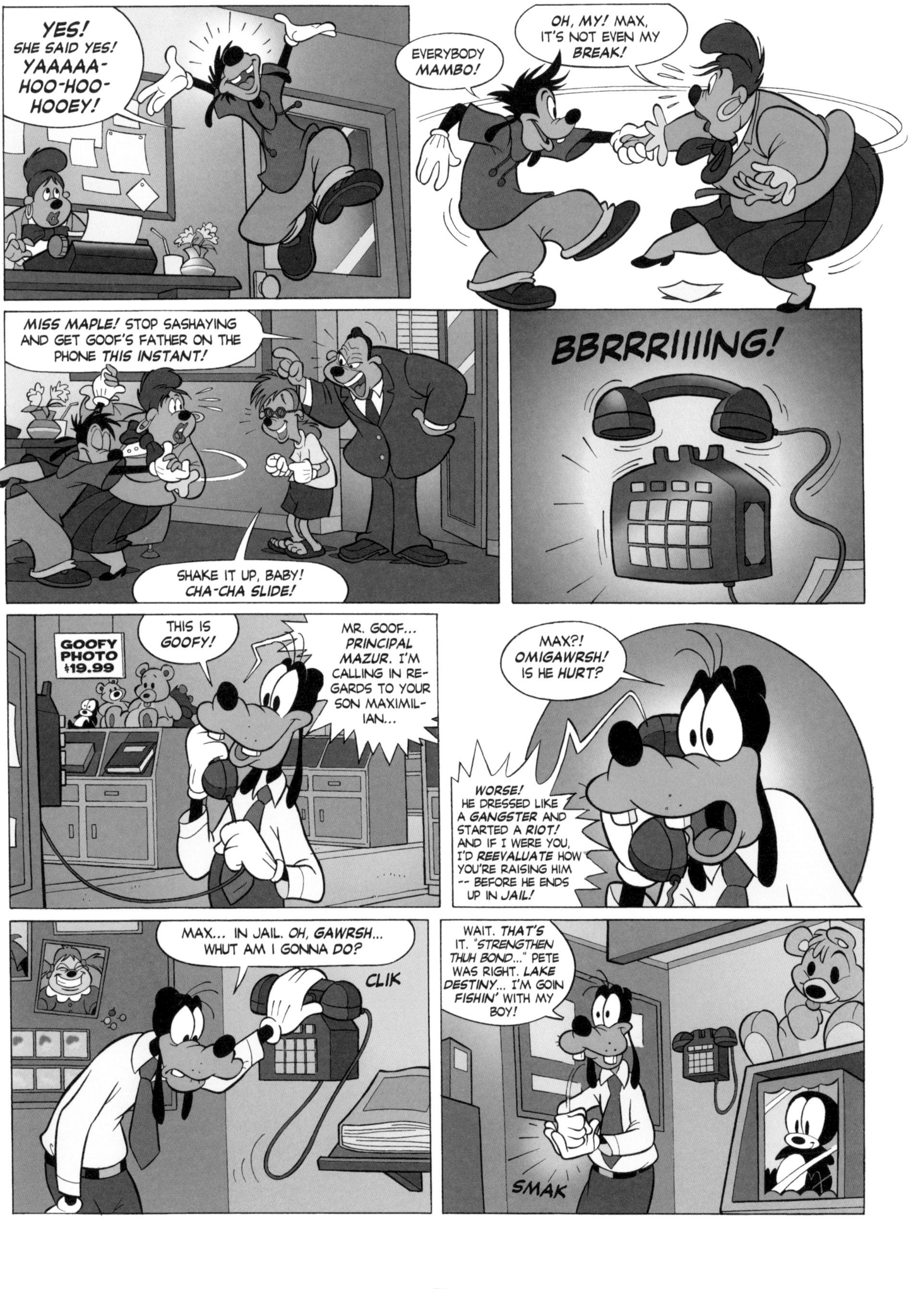
YES! SHE SAID YES! YAAAAA-HOO-HOO-HOOEY!
EVERYBODY MAMBO!
OH, MY! MAX, IT'S NOT EVEN MY BREAK!
MISS MAPLE! STOP SASHAYING AND GET GOOF'S FATHER ON THE PHONE THIS INSTANT!
SHAKE IT UP, BABY! CHA-CHA SLIDE!
BBRRRIIIING!
GOOFY PHOTO $19.99
THIS IS GOOFY!
MR. GOOF... PRINCIPAL MAZUR. I'M CALLING IN REGARDS TO YOUR SON MAXIMILIAN...
MAX?! OMIGAWRSH! IS HE HURT?
WORSE! HE DRESSED LIKE A GANGSTER AND STARTED A RIOT! AND IF I WERE YOU, I'D REEVALUATE HOW YOU'RE RAISING HIM -- BEFORE HE ENDS UP IN JAIL!
MAX... IN JAIL. OH, GAWRSH... WHUT AM I GONNA DO?
CLIK
WAIT. THAT'S IT. "STRENGTHEN THUH BOND..." PETE WAS RIGHT. LAKE DESTINY... I'M GOIN FISHIN' WITH MY BOY!
SMAK

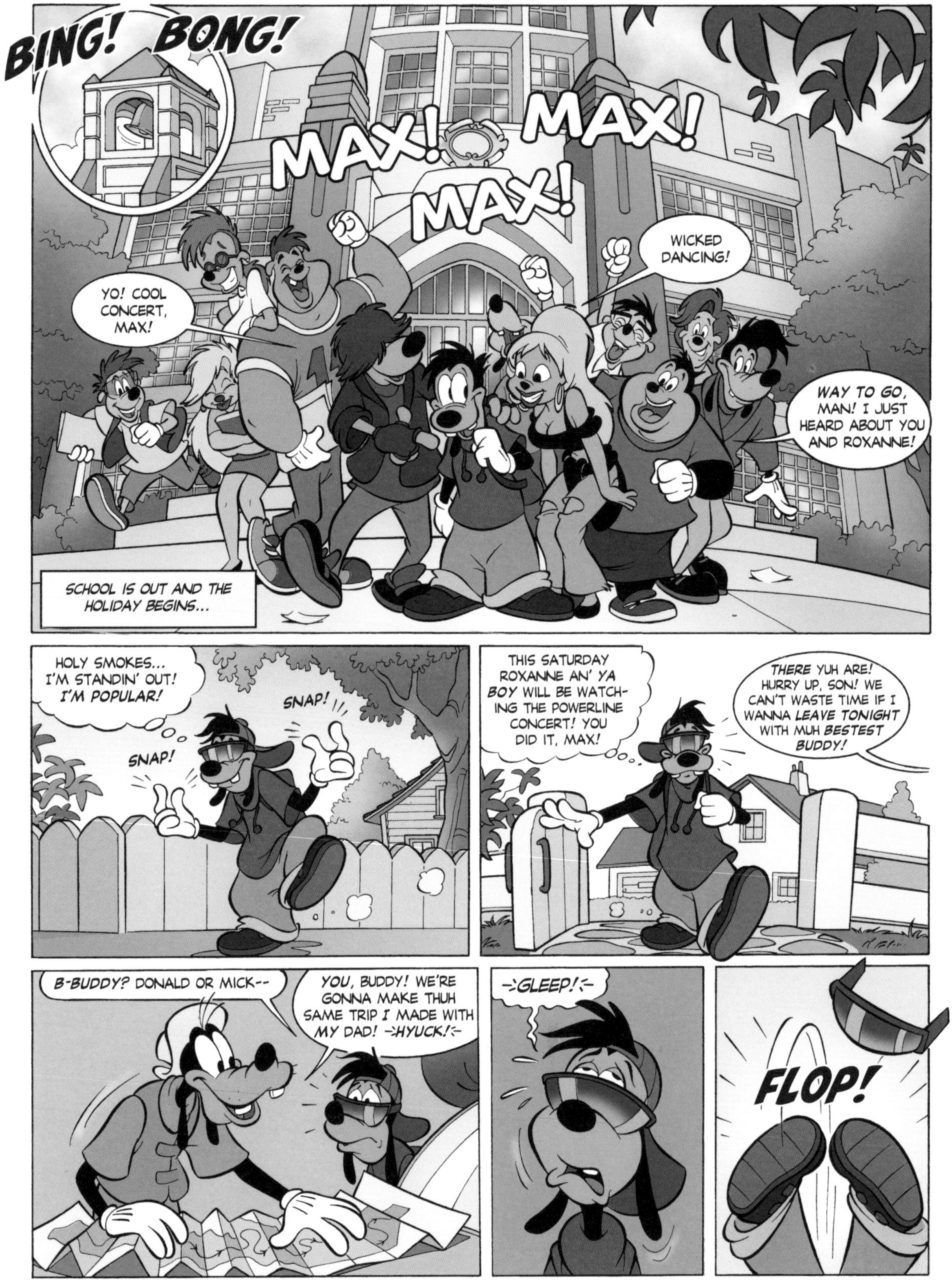
BING! BONG!
MAX! MAX! MAX!
YO! COOL CONCERT, MAX!
WICKED DANCING!
WAY TO GO, MAN! I JUST HEARD ABOUT YOU AND ROXANNE!
SCHOOL IS OUT AND THE HOLIDAY BEGINS...
HOLY SMOKES... I'M STANDIN' OUT! I'M POPULAR!
SNAP!
SNAP!
THIS SATURDAY ROXANNE AN' YA BOY WILL BE WATCHING THE POWERLINE CONCERT! YOU DID IT, MAX!
THERE YUH ARE! HURRY UP, SON! WE CAN'T WASTE TIME IF I WANNA LEAVE TONIGHT WITH MUH BESTEST BUDDY!
B-BUDDY? DONALD OR MICK--
YOU, BUDDY! WE'RE GONNA MAKE THUH SAME TRIP I MADE WITH MY DAD! -HYUCK!-
-GLEEP!-
FLOP!

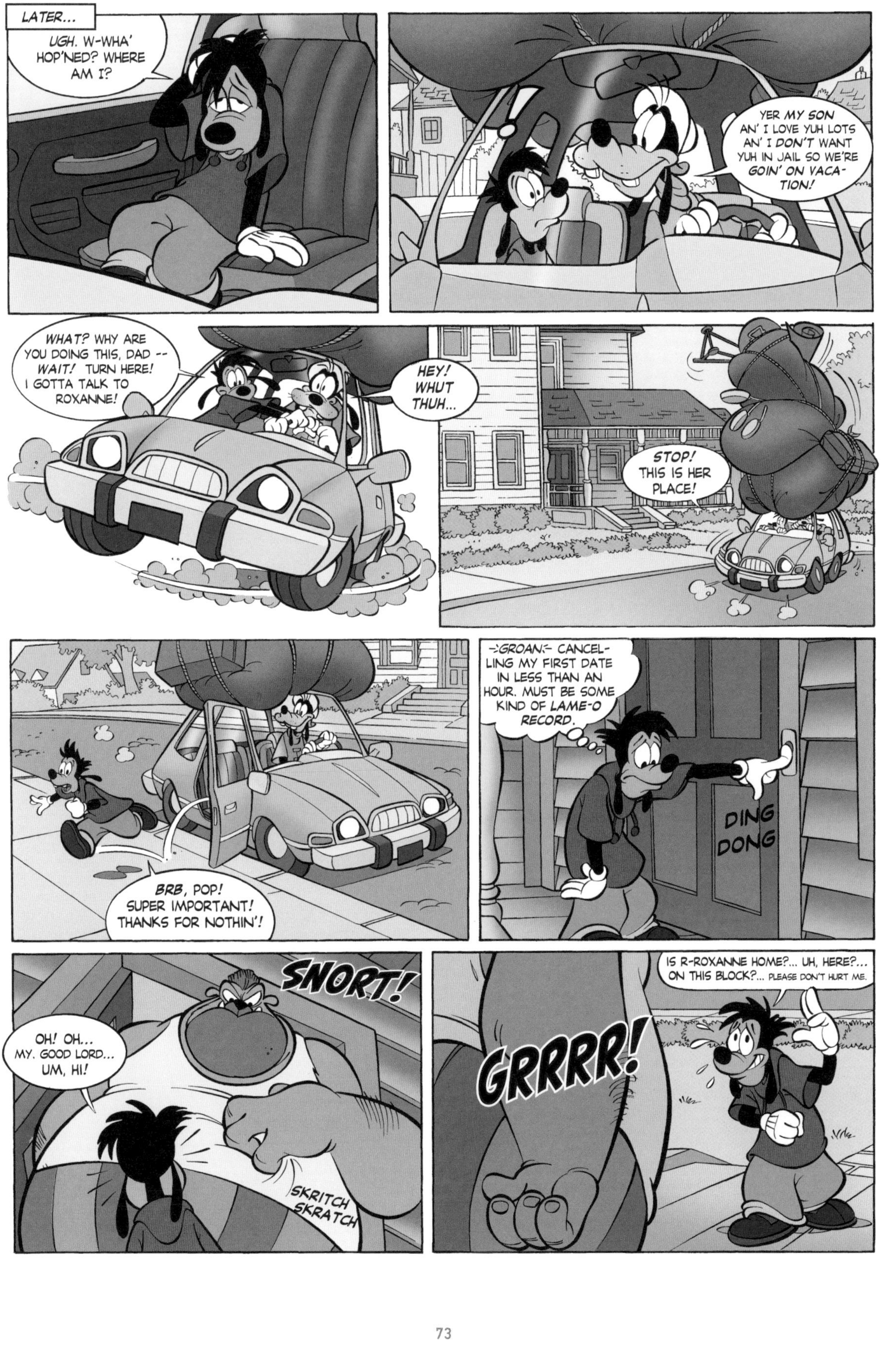
LATER...
UGH. W-WHA' HOP'NED? WHERE AM I?
!
YER MY SON AN' I LOVE YUH LOTS AN' I DON'T WANT YUH IN JAIL SO WE'RE GOIN' ON VACA-TION!
WHAT? WHY ARE YOU DOING THIS, DAD -- WAIT! TURN HERE! I GOTTA TALK TO ROXANNE!
HEY! WHUT THUH...
STOP! THIS IS HER PLACE!
BRB, POP! SUPER IMPORTANT! THANKS FOR NOTHIN'!
-GROAN- CANCEL-LING MY FIRST DATE IN LESS THAN AN HOUR. MUST BE SOME KIND OF LAME-O RECORD.
DING DONG
SNORT!
OH! OH... MY. GOOD LORD... UM, HI!
SKRITCH SKRATCH
IS R-ROXANNE HOME?... UH, HERE?... ON THIS BLOCK?... PLEASE DON'T HURT ME.
GRRRR!

IT'S OKAY, DADDY! MAX IS A FRIEND FROM SCHOOL!

GRUNT?

I PROMISE HE'LL BE FRIENDLIER WHEN YOU PICK ME UP FOR THE PARTY!

SLAM!

WELL... SEE... UM, THAT'S THE PROBLEM, ROXANNE. I CAN'T GO.

OH. THAT'S... OKAY. HOW COME?

SHE'S DISAPPOINTED! MAKE SOMETHING UP!

WELL... I CAN'T GO... 'CAUSE MY DAD'S TAKING ME TO THE POWERLINE CONCERT IN LOS ANGELES!

YOUR DAD'S TAKING YOU CLEAR ACROSS THE COUNTRY FOR A CONCERT?!

UH, YEAH... MY DAD KNEW... KNOWS POWERLINE! THEY PLAYED TOGETHER! MUSIC! IN A BAND!

YOU'RE SERIOUS!

ABSOLUTELY! AND I WAS HOPIN' I COULD WAVE TO YOU WHEN WE'RE ON STAGE... FOR THE FINAL NUMBER! YEAH! EHEH... THAT'S IT!

THAT'S SO SWEET! THEN I'LL SEE YOU ON TV!

SMAK!

S'LONG... I'M IN DEEP SLUDGE.

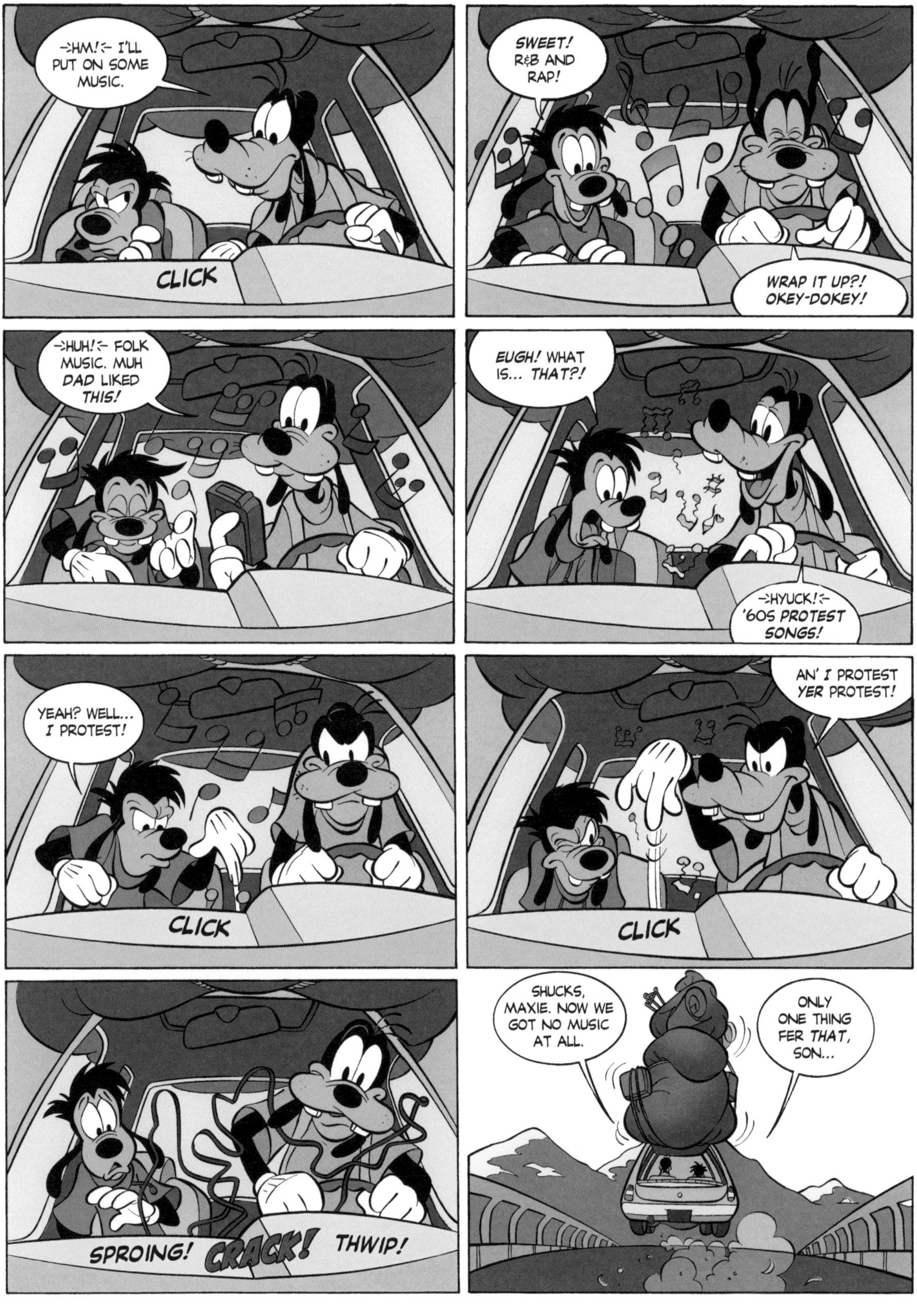

–HM!– I'LL PUT ON SOME MUSIC.
CLICK
SWEET! R&B AND RAP!
WRAP IT UP?! OKEY-DOKEY!
–HUH!– FOLK MUSIC. MUH DAD LIKED THIS!
EUGH! WHAT IS... THAT?!
–HYUCK!– '60S PROTEST SONGS!
YEAH? WELL... I PROTEST!
CLICK
AN' I PROTEST YER PROTEST!
CLICK
SPROING! CRACK! THWIP!
SHUCKS, MAXIE. NOW WE GOT NO MUSIC AT ALL.
ONLY ONE THING FER THAT, SON...

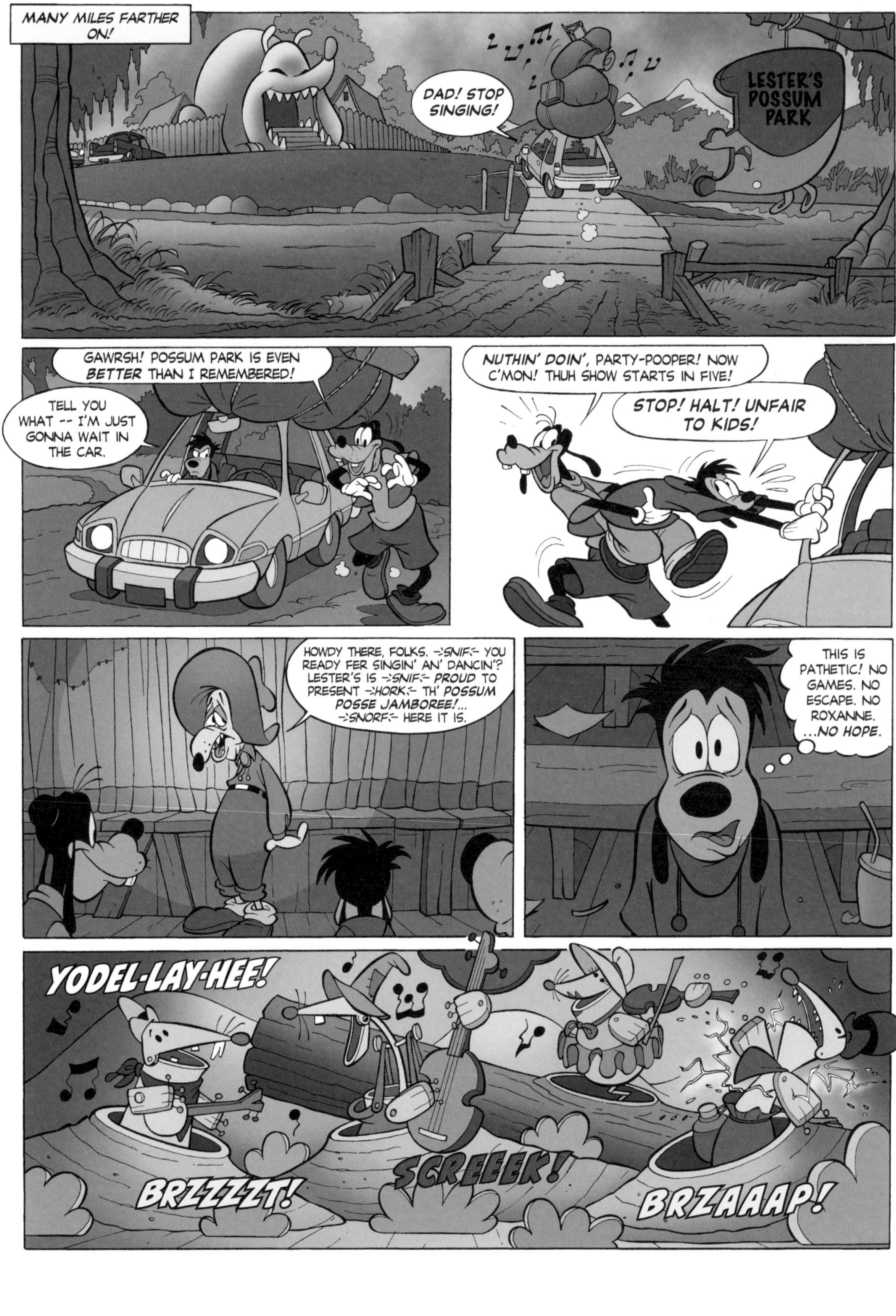
MANY MILES FARTHER ON!
DAD! STOP SINGING!
LESTER'S POSSUM PARK
GAWRSH! POSSUM PARK IS EVEN BETTER THAN I REMEMBERED!
TELL YOU WHAT -- I'M JUST GONNA WAIT IN THE CAR.
NUTHIN' DOIN', PARTY-POOPER! NOW C'MON! THUH SHOW STARTS IN FIVE!
STOP! HALT! UNFAIR TO KIDS!
HOWDY THERE, FOLKS. -SNIF- YOU READY FER SINGIN' AN' DANCIN'? LESTER'S IS -SNIF- PROUD TO PRESENT -HORK- TH' POSSUM POSSE JAMBOREE!... -SNORF- HERE IT IS.
THIS IS PATHETIC! NO GAMES. NO ESCAPE. NO ROXANNE. ...NO HOPE.
YODEL-LAY-HEE!
BRZZZZT!
SCREEEK!
BRZAAAP!

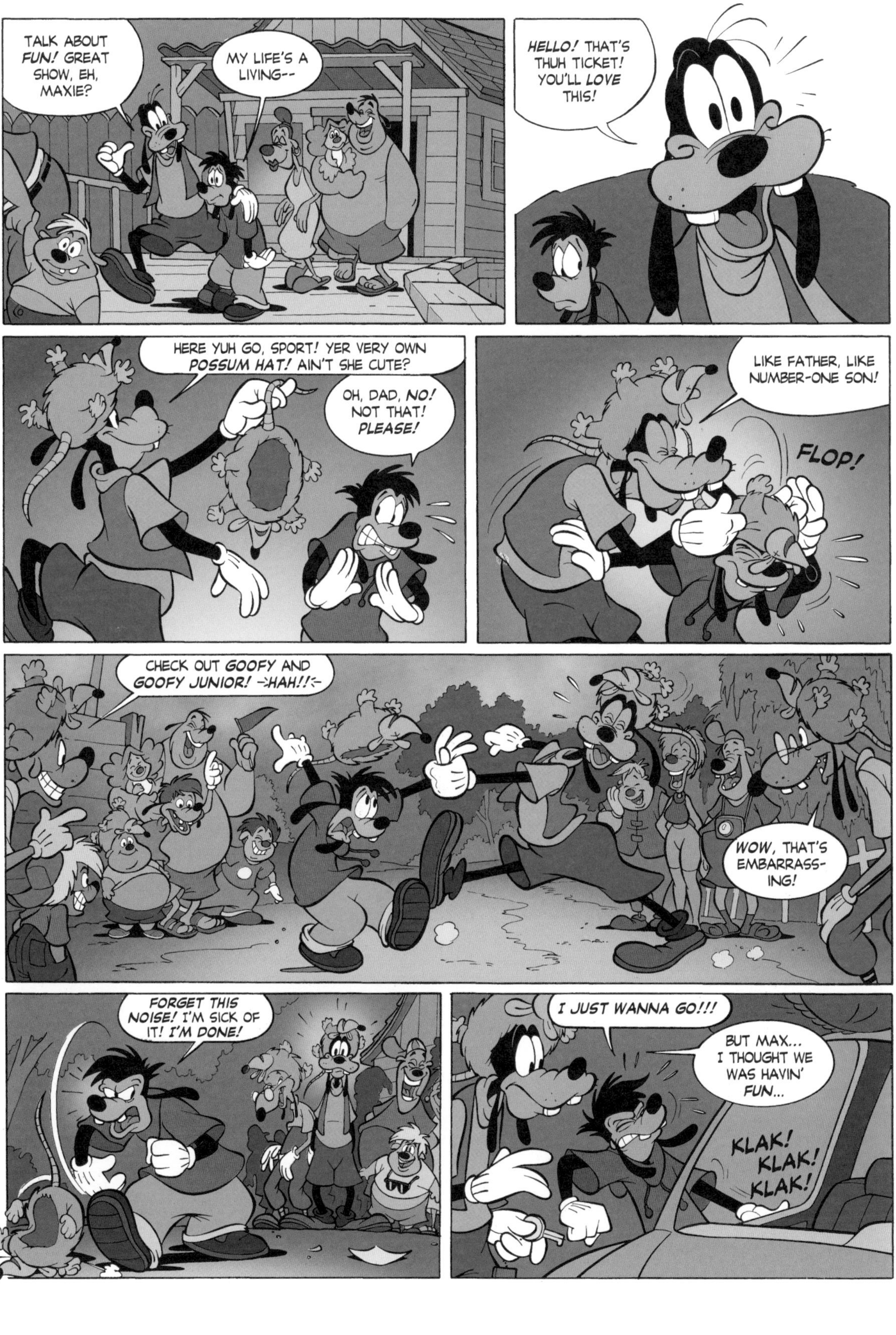
TALK ABOUT FUN! GREAT SHOW, EH, MAXIE?
MY LIFE'S A LIVING--
HELLO! THAT'S THUH TICKET! YOU'LL LOVE THIS!
HERE YUH GO, SPORT! YER VERY OWN POSSUM HAT! AIN'T SHE CUTE?
OH, DAD, NO! NOT THAT! PLEASE!
LIKE FATHER, LIKE NUMBER-ONE SON!
FLOP!
CHECK OUT GOOFY AND GOOFY JUNIOR! -HAH!!-
WOW, THAT'S EMBARRASS-ING!
FORGET THIS NOISE! I'M SICK OF IT! I'M DONE!
I JUST WANNA GO!!!
BUT MAX... I THOUGHT WE WAS HAVIN' FUN...
KLAK! KLAK! KLAK!

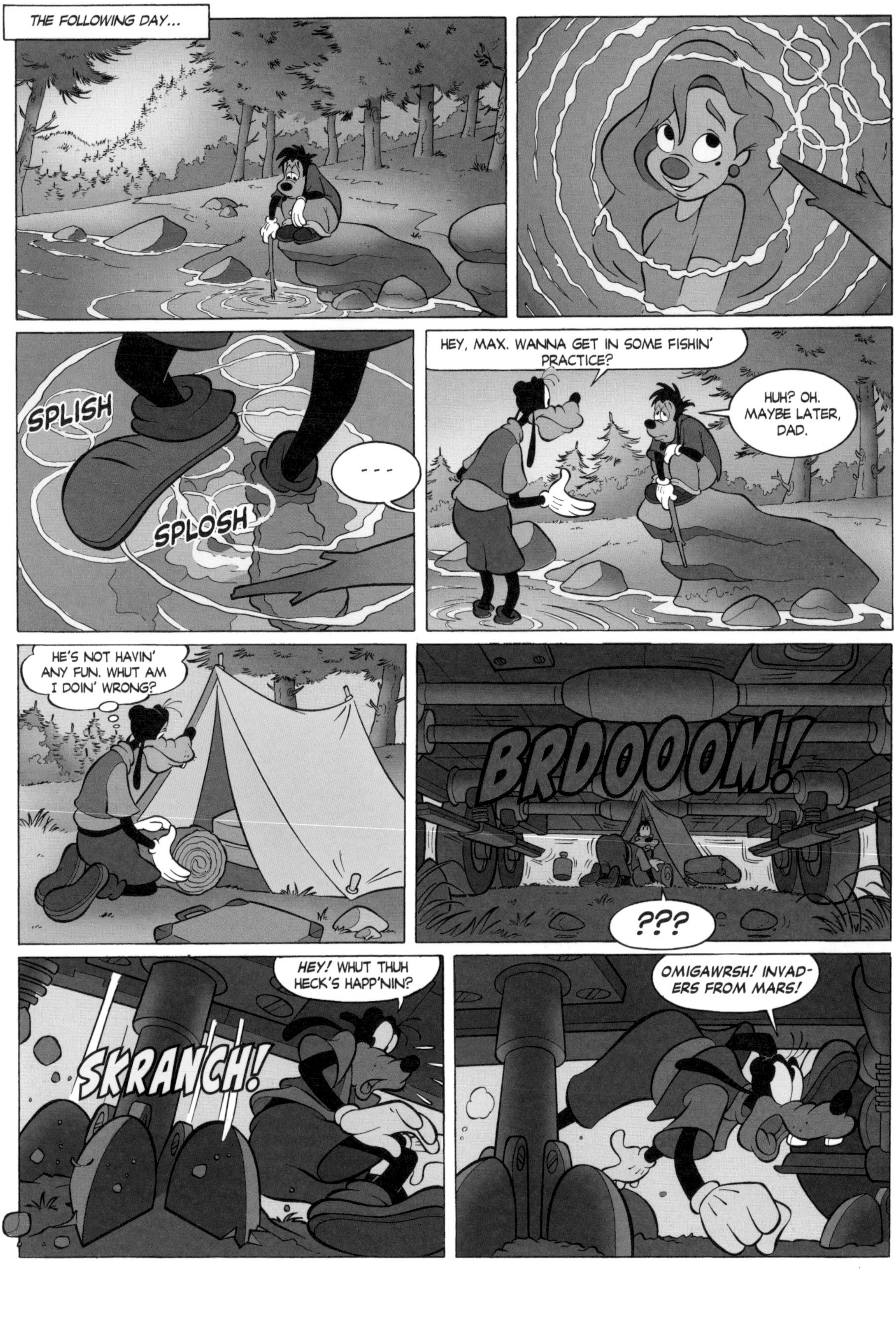

THE FOLLOWING DAY...
SPLISH
SPLOSH
- - -
HEY, MAX. WANNA GET IN SOME FISHIN' PRACTICE?
HUH? OH. MAYBE LATER, DAD.
HE'S NOT HAVIN' ANY FUN. WHUT AM I DOIN' WRONG?
BRDOOOM!
???
HEY! WHUT THUH HECK'S HAPP'NIN?
SKRANCH!
OMIGAWRSH! INVADERS FROM MARS!

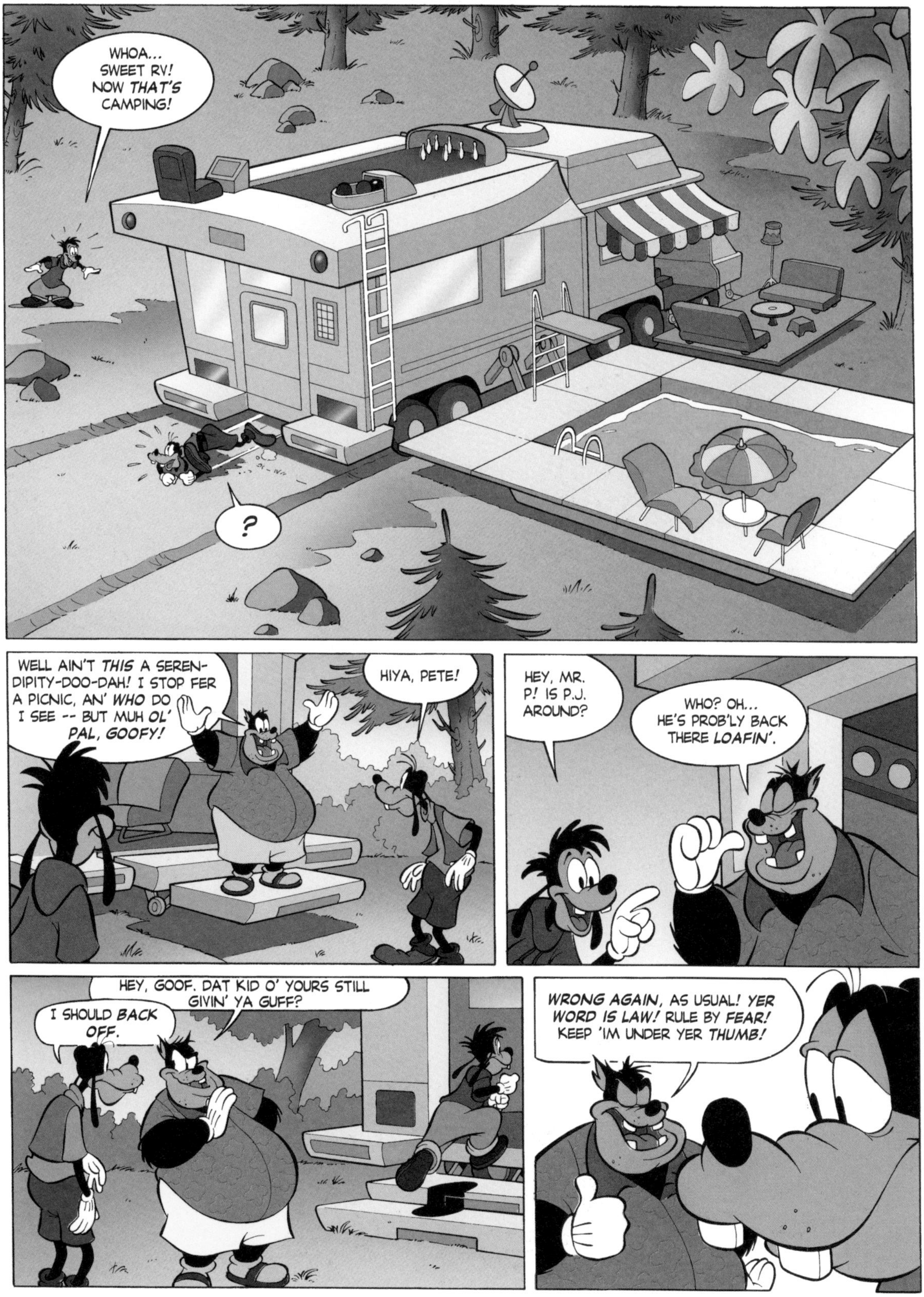
WHOA... SWEET RV! NOW THAT'S CAMPING!
?
WELL AIN'T THIS A SEREN-DIPITY-DOO-DAH! I STOP FER A PICNIC, AN' WHO DO I SEE -- BUT MUH OL' PAL, GOOFY!
HIYA, PETE!
HEY, MR. P! IS P.J. AROUND?
WHO? OH... HE'S PROB'LY BACK THERE LOAFIN'.
HEY, GOOF. DAT KID O' YOURS STILL GIVIN' YA GUFF?
I SHOULD BACK OFF.
WRONG AGAIN, AS USUAL! YER WORD IS LAW! RULE BY FEAR! KEEP 'IM UNDER YER THUMB!

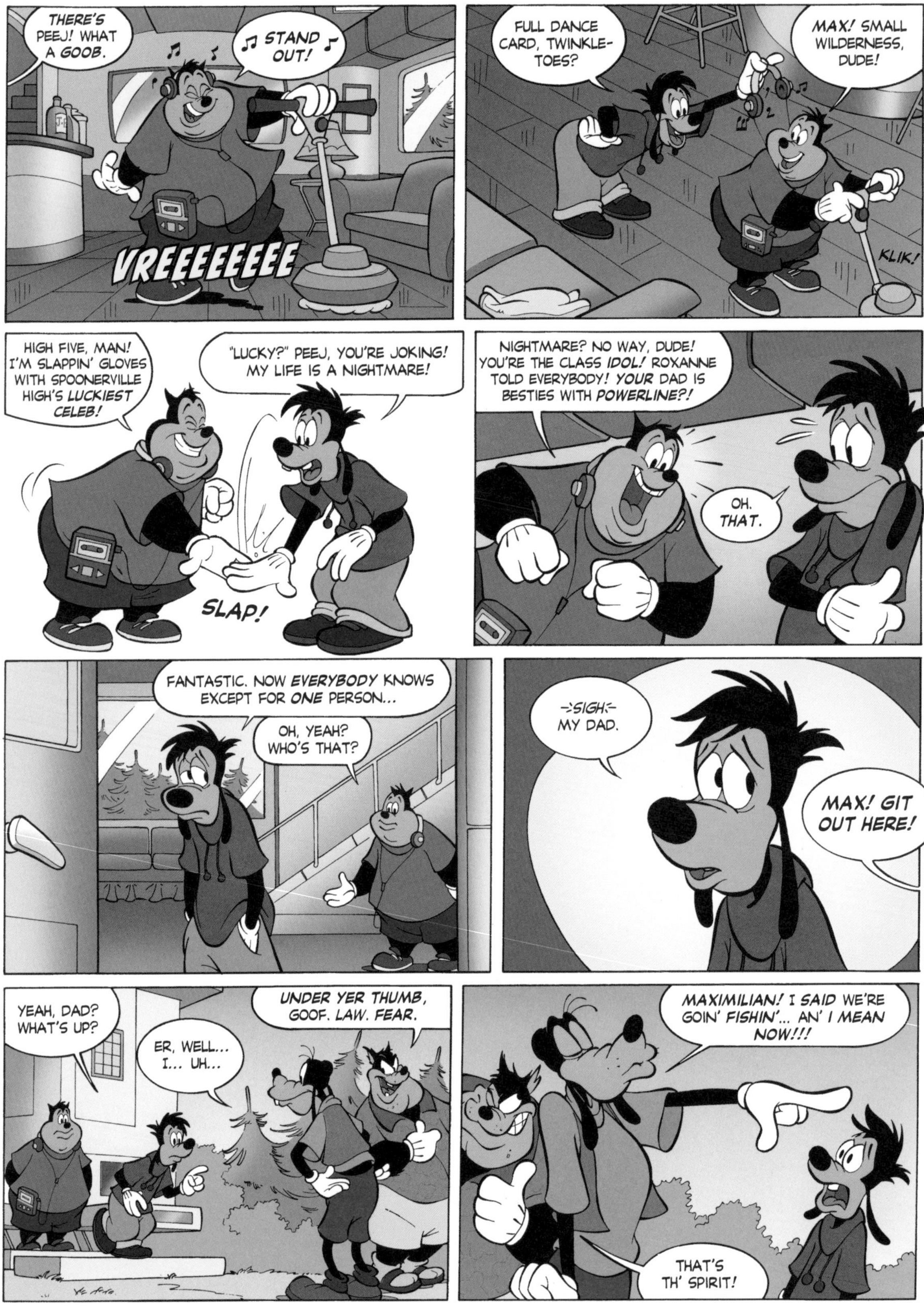

THERE'S PEEJ! WHAT A GOOB.
♫ STAND OUT! ♫
VREEEEEEEE
FULL DANCE CARD, TWINKLE-TOES?
MAX! SMALL WILDERNESS, DUDE!
KLIK!
HIGH FIVE, MAN! I'M SLAPPIN' GLOVES WITH SPOONERVILLE HIGH'S LUCKIEST CELEB!
"LUCKY?" PEEJ, YOU'RE JOKING! MY LIFE IS A NIGHTMARE!
SLAP!
NIGHTMARE? NO WAY, DUDE! YOU'RE THE CLASS IDOL! ROXANNE TOLD EVERYBODY! YOUR DAD IS BESTIES WITH POWERLINE?!
OH. THAT.
FANTASTIC. NOW EVERYBODY KNOWS EXCEPT FOR ONE PERSON...
OH, YEAH? WHO'S THAT?
-SIGH- MY DAD.
MAX! GIT OUT HERE!
YEAH, DAD? WHAT'S UP?
ER, WELL... I... UH...
UNDER YER THUMB, GOOF. LAW. FEAR.
MAXIMILIAN! I SAID WE'RE GOIN' FISHIN'... AN' I MEAN NOW!!!
THAT'S TH' SPIRIT!

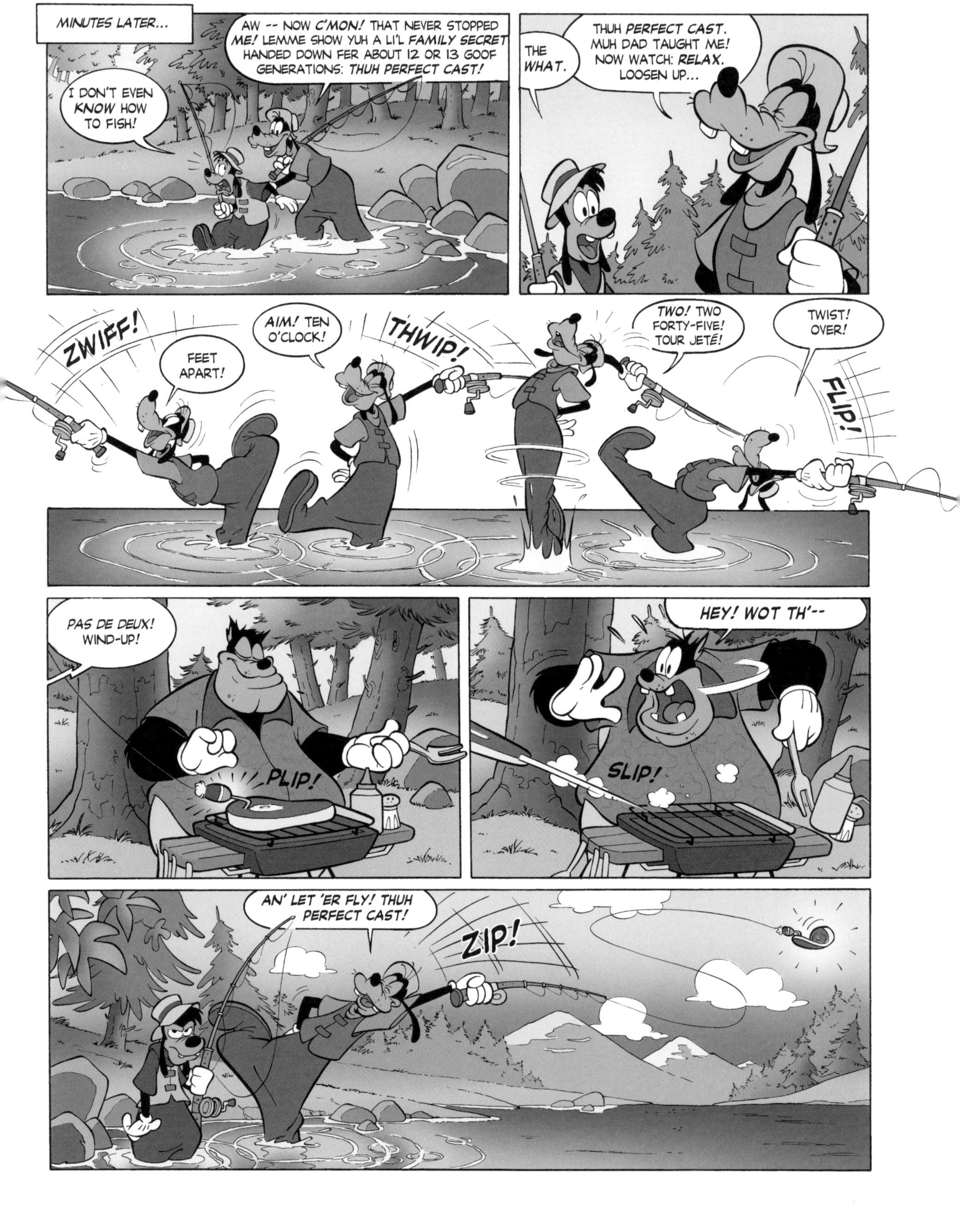

MINUTES LATER...
I DON'T EVEN KNOW HOW TO FISH!
AW -- NOW C'MON! THAT NEVER STOPPED ME! LEMME SHOW YUH A LI'L FAMILY SECRET HANDED DOWN FER ABOUT 12 OR 13 GOOF GENERATIONS: THUH PERFECT CAST!
THE WHAT.
THUH PERFECT CAST. MUH DAD TAUGHT ME! NOW WATCH: RELAX. LOOSEN UP...
ZWIFF!
FEET APART!
AIM! TEN O'CLOCK!
THWIP!
TWO! TWO FORTY-FIVE! TOUR JETÉ!
TWIST! OVER!
FLIP!
PAS DE DEUX! WIND-UP!
PLIP!
HEY! WOT TH'--
SLIP!
AN' LET 'ER FLY! THUH PERFECT CAST!
ZIP!

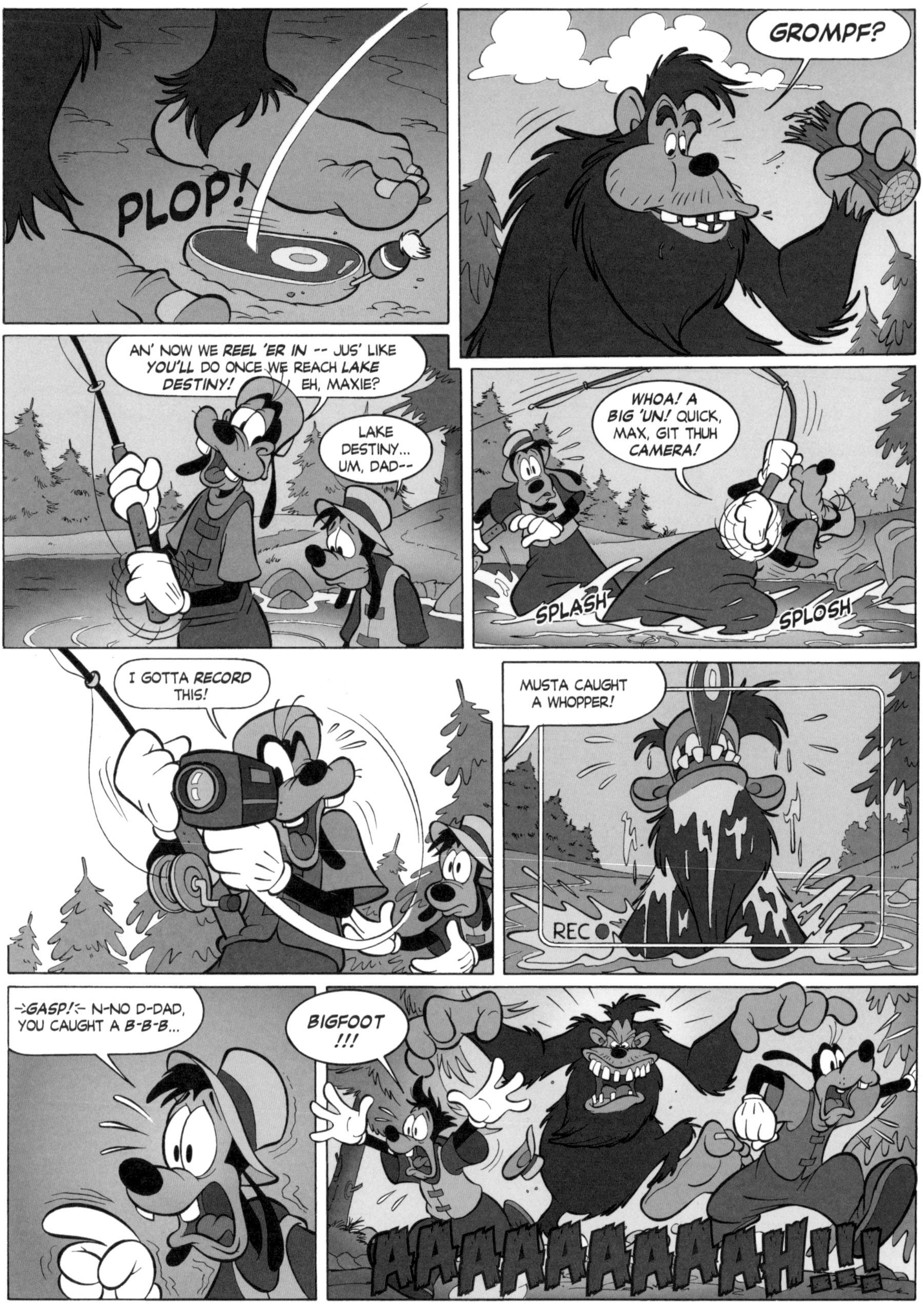
PLOP!
GROMPF?
AN' NOW WE REEL 'ER IN -- JUS' LIKE YOU'LL DO ONCE WE REACH LAKE DESTINY! EH, MAXIE?
LAKE DESTINY... UM, DAD--
WHOA! A BIG 'UN! QUICK, MAX, GIT THUH CAMERA!
SPLASH
SPLOSH
I GOTTA RECORD THIS!
MUSTA CAUGHT A WHOPPER!
REC
-GASP!- N-NO D-DAD, YOU CAUGHT A B-B-B...
BIGFOOT !!!
AAAAAAAAAH!!!

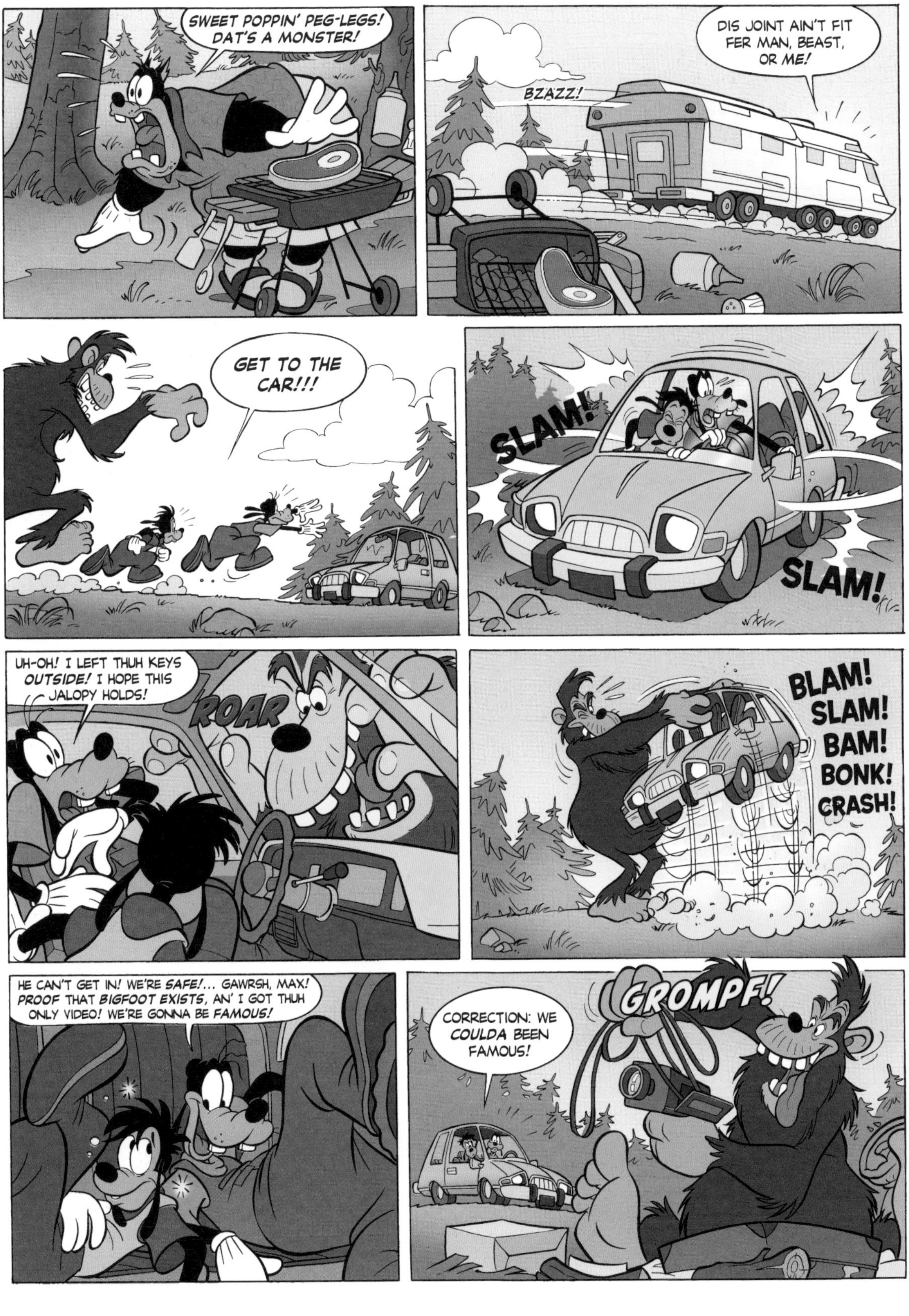
SWEET POPPIN' PEG-LEGS! DAT'S A MONSTER!
DIS JOINT AIN'T FIT FER MAN, BEAST, OR ME!
BZAZZ!
GET TO THE CAR!!!
SLAM!
SLAM!
UH-OH! I LEFT THUH KEYS OUTSIDE! I HOPE THIS JALOPY HOLDS!
ROAR
BLAM! SLAM! BAM! BONK! CRASH!
HE CAN'T GET IN! WE'RE SAFE!... GAWRSH, MAX! PROOF THAT BIGFOOT EXISTS, AN' I GOT THUH ONLY VIDEO! WE'RE GONNA BE FAMOUS!
GROMPF!
CORRECTION: WE COULDA BEEN FAMOUS!

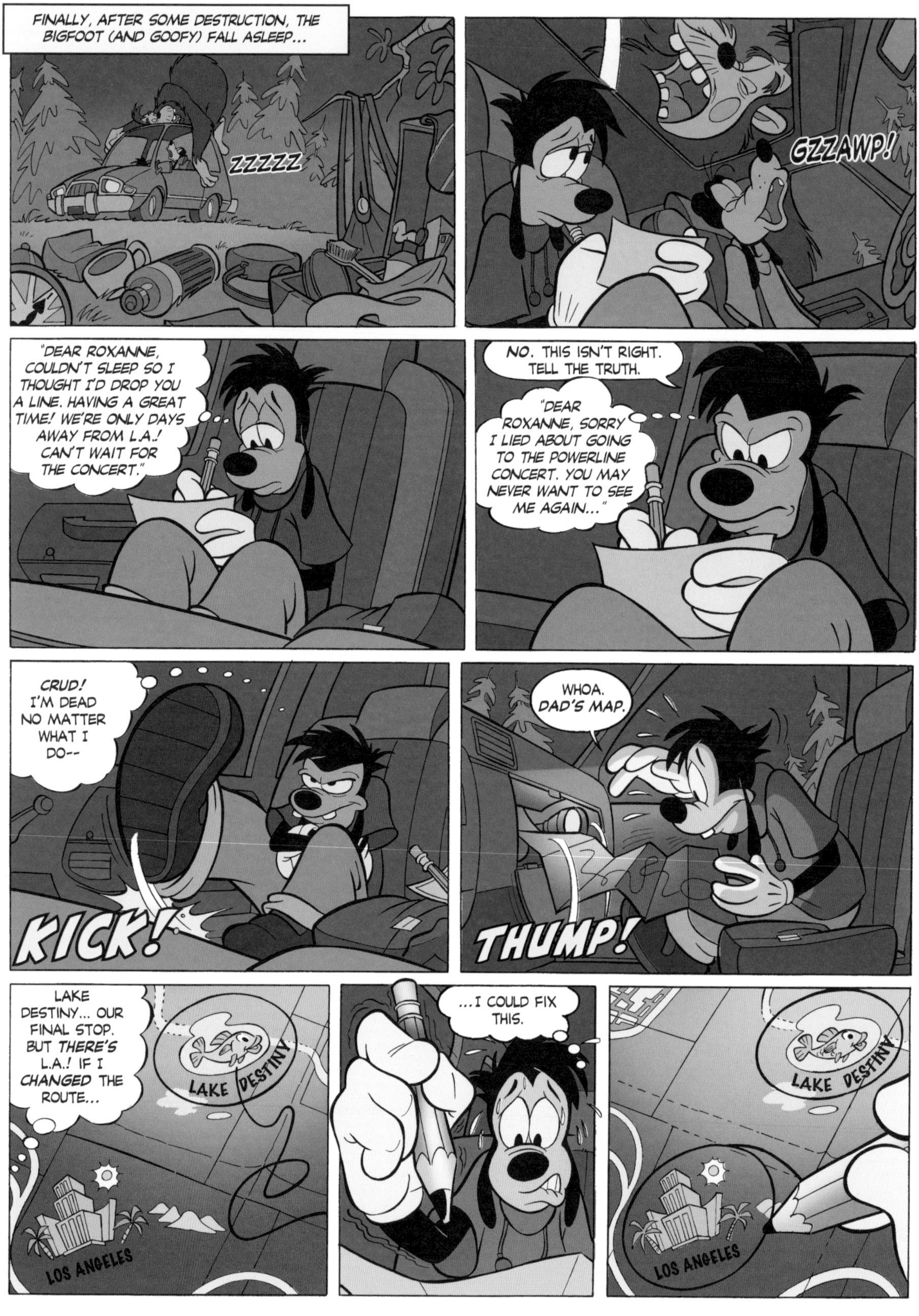

FINALLY, AFTER SOME DESTRUCTION, THE BIGFOOT (AND GOOFY) FALL ASLEEP...
ZZZZZ
GZZAWP!
"DEAR ROXANNE, COULDN'T SLEEP SO I THOUGHT I'D DROP YOU A LINE. HAVING A GREAT TIME! WE'RE ONLY DAYS AWAY FROM L.A.! CAN'T WAIT FOR THE CONCERT."
NO. THIS ISN'T RIGHT. TELL THE TRUTH.
"DEAR ROXANNE, SORRY I LIED ABOUT GOING TO THE POWERLINE CONCERT. YOU MAY NEVER WANT TO SEE ME AGAIN..."
CRUD! I'M DEAD NO MATTER WHAT I DO--
KICK!
WHOA. DAD'S MAP.
THUMP!
LAKE DESTINY... OUR FINAL STOP. BUT THERE'S L.A.! IF I CHANGED THE ROUTE...
LAKE DESTINY
LOS ANGELES
...I COULD FIX THIS.
LAKE DESTINY
LOS ANGELES

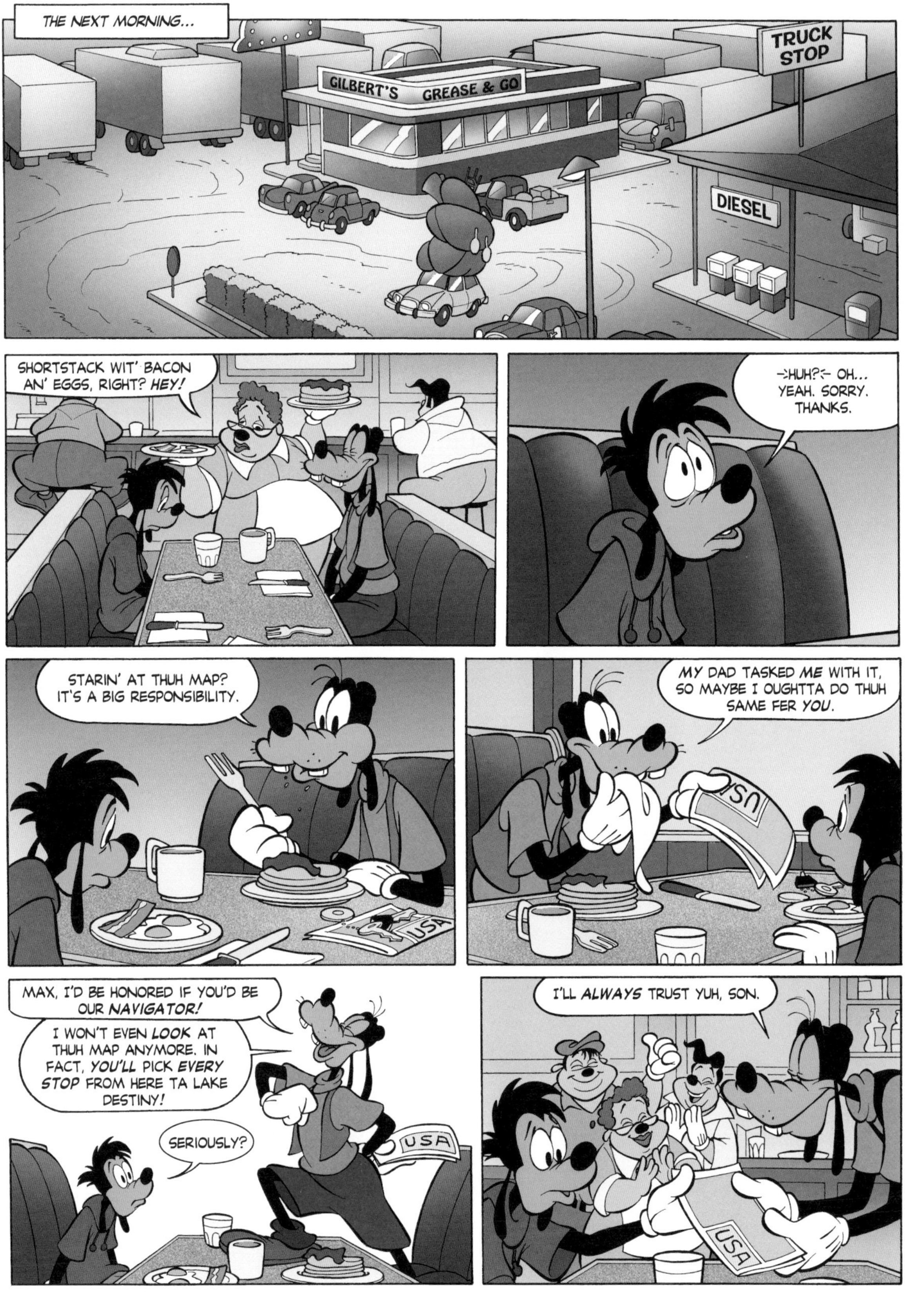
THE NEXT MORNING...
GILBERT'S GREASE & GO
TRUCK STOP
DIESEL
SHORTSTACK WIT' BACON AN' EGGS, RIGHT? HEY!
—HUH?— OH... YEAH. SORRY. THANKS.
STARIN' AT THUH MAP? IT'S A BIG RESPONSIBILITY.
USA
MY DAD TASKED ME WITH IT, SO MAYBE I OUGHTTA DO THUH SAME FER YOU.
MAX, I'D BE HONORED IF YOU'D BE OUR NAVIGATOR!
I WON'T EVEN LOOK AT THUH MAP ANYMORE. IN FACT, YOU'LL PICK EVERY STOP FROM HERE TA LAKE DESTINY!
SERIOUSLY?
I'LL ALWAYS TRUST YUH, SON.

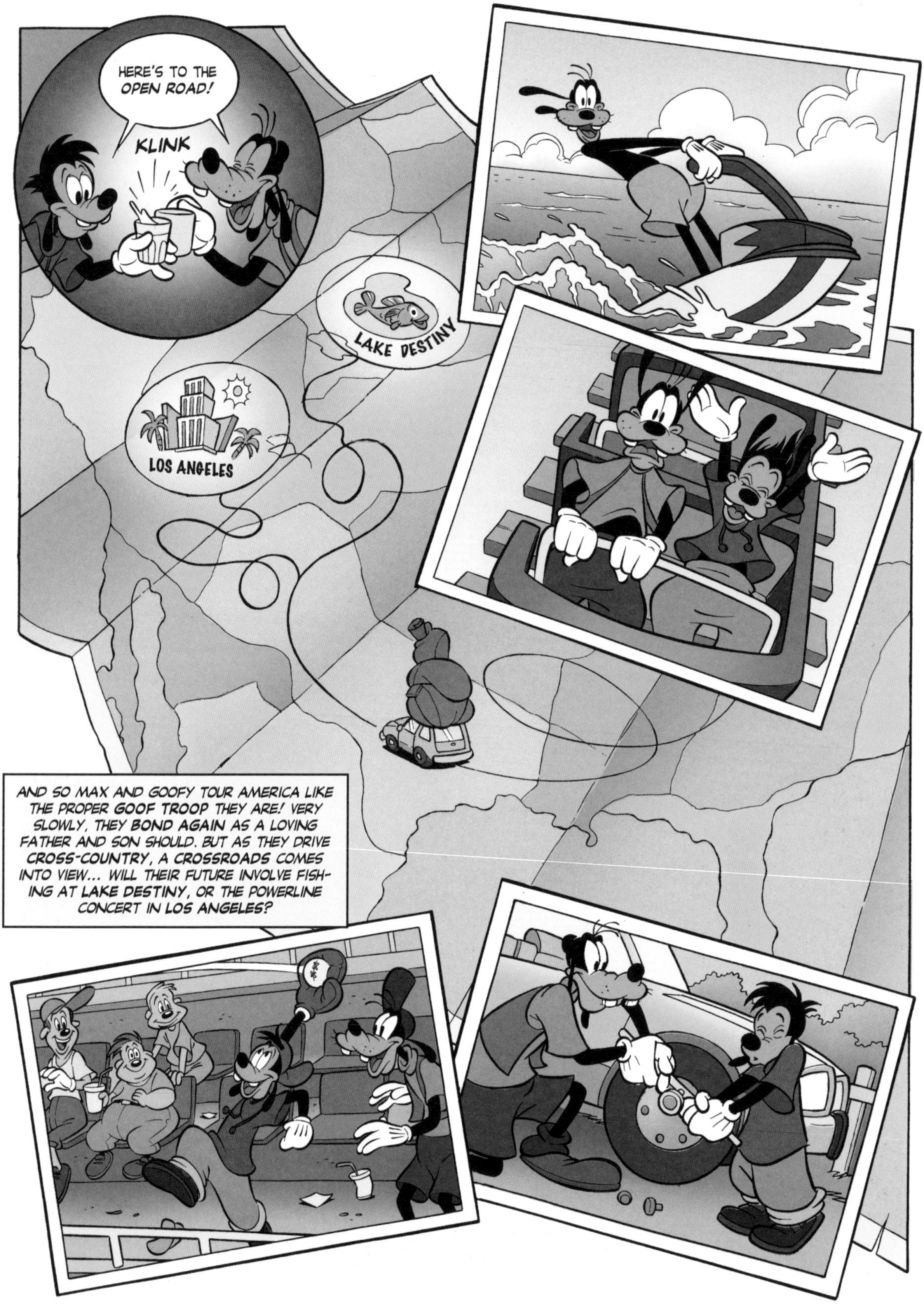

HERE'S TO THE OPEN ROAD!
KLINK
LAKE DESTINY
LOS ANGELES
AND SO MAX AND GOOFY TOUR AMERICA LIKE THE PROPER GOOF TROOP THEY ARE! VERY SLOWLY, THEY BOND AGAIN AS A LOVING FATHER AND SON SHOULD. BUT AS THEY DRIVE CROSS-COUNTRY, A CROSSROADS COMES INTO VIEW... WILL THEIR FUTURE INVOLVE FISHING AT LAKE DESTINY, OR THE POWERLINE CONCERT IN LOS ANGELES?

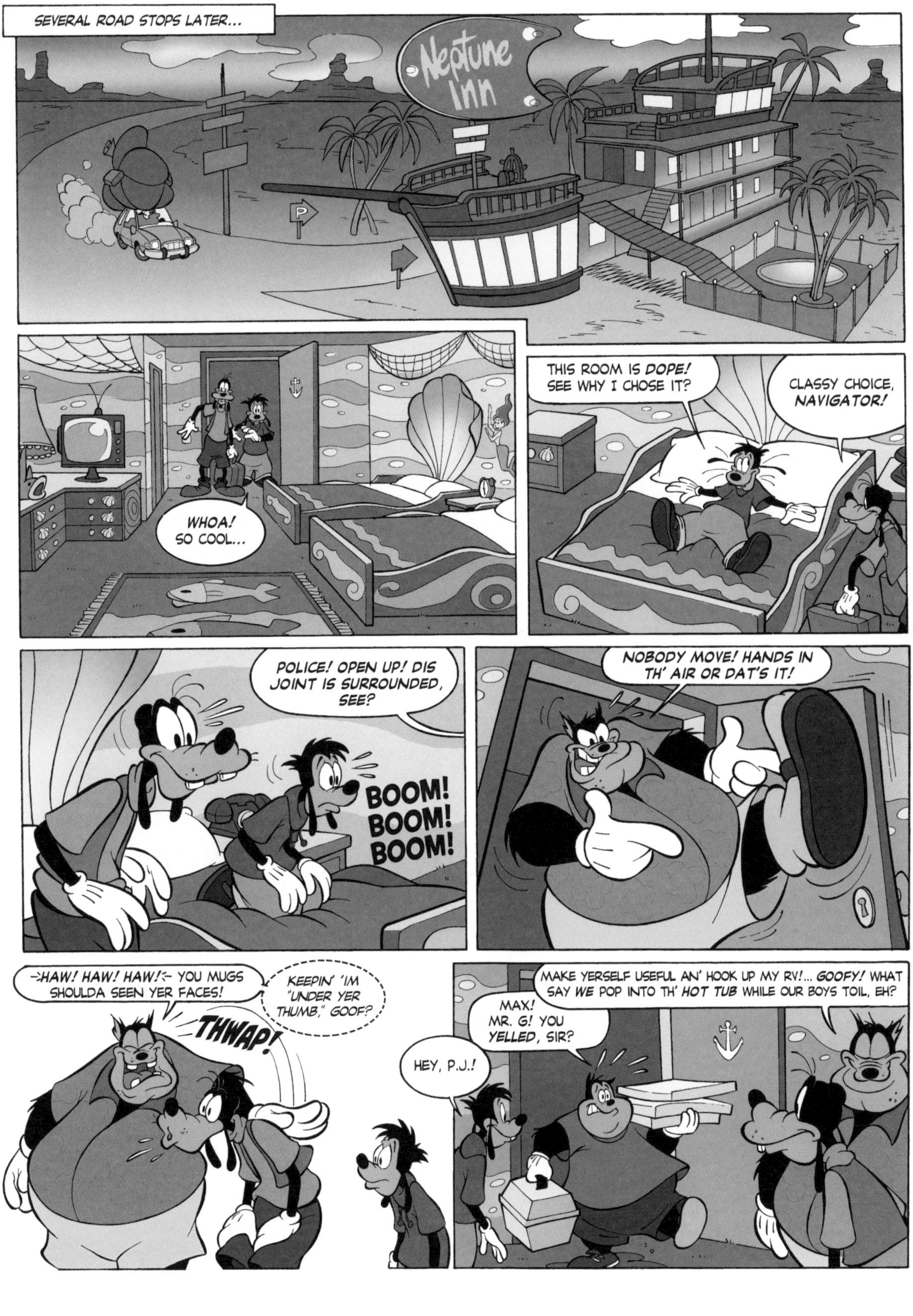
SEVERAL ROAD STOPS LATER...
Neptune Inn
P
WHOA! SO COOL...
THIS ROOM IS DOPE! SEE WHY I CHOSE IT?
CLASSY CHOICE, NAVIGATOR!
POLICE! OPEN UP! DIS JOINT IS SURROUNDED, SEE?
BOOM! BOOM! BOOM!
NOBODY MOVE! HANDS IN TH' AIR OR DAT'S IT!
HAW! HAW! HAW! YOU MUGS SHOULDA SEEN YER FACES!
KEEPIN' 'IM "UNDER YER THUMB," GOOF?
THWAP!
HEY, P.J.!
MAKE YERSELF USEFUL AN' HOOK UP MY RV!... GOOFY! WHAT SAY WE POP INTO TH' HOT TUB WHILE OUR BOYS TOIL, EH?
MAX! MR. G! YOU YELLED, SIR?

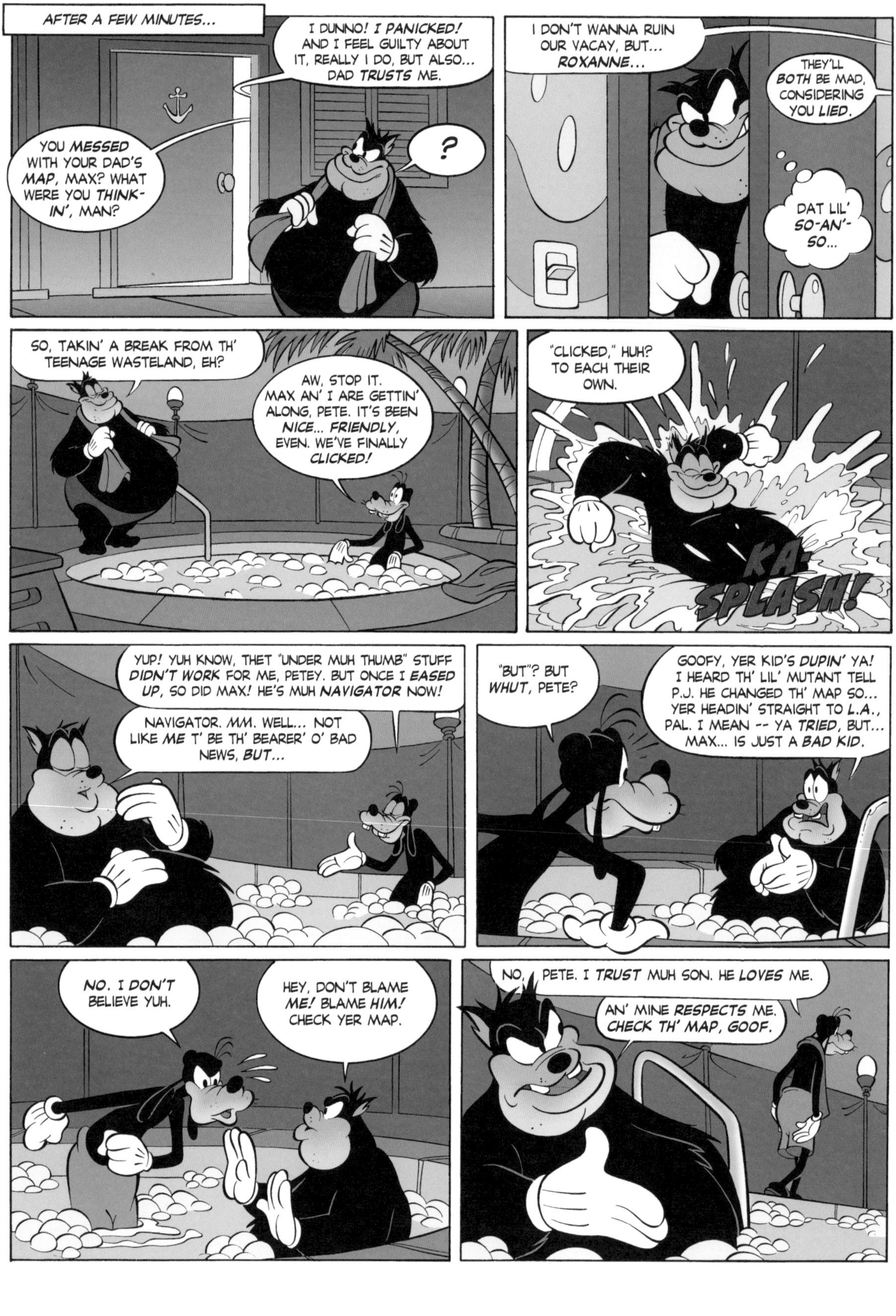
AFTER A FEW MINUTES...
YOU MESSED WITH YOUR DAD'S MAP, MAX? WHAT WERE YOU THINK-IN', MAN?
I DUNNO! I PANICKED! AND I FEEL GUILTY ABOUT IT, REALLY I DO, BUT ALSO... DAD TRUSTS ME.
?
I DON'T WANNA RUIN OUR VACAY, BUT... ROXANNE...
THEY'LL BOTH BE MAD, CONSIDERING YOU LIED.
DAT LIL' SO-AN'-SO...
SO, TAKIN' A BREAK FROM TH' TEENAGE WASTELAND, EH?
AW, STOP IT. MAX AN' I ARE GETTIN' ALONG, PETE. IT'S BEEN NICE... FRIENDLY, EVEN. WE'VE FINALLY CLICKED!
"CLICKED," HUH? TO EACH THEIR OWN.
KA-SPLASH!
YUP! YUH KNOW, THET "UNDER MUH THUMB" STUFF DIDN'T WORK FOR ME, PETEY. BUT ONCE I EASED UP, SO DID MAX! HE'S MUH NAVIGATOR NOW!
NAVIGATOR. MM. WELL... NOT LIKE ME T' BE TH' BEARER' O' BAD NEWS, BUT...
"BUT"? BUT WHUT, PETE?
GOOFY, YER KID'S DUPIN' YA! I HEARD TH' LIL' MUTANT TELL P.J. HE CHANGED TH' MAP SO... YER HEADIN' STRAIGHT TO L.A., PAL. I MEAN -- YA TRIED, BUT... MAX... IS JUST A BAD KID.
NO. I DON'T BELIEVE YUH.
HEY, DON'T BLAME ME! BLAME HIM! CHECK YER MAP.
NO, PETE. I TRUST MUH SON. HE LOVES ME.
AN' MINE RESPECTS ME. CHECK TH' MAP, GOOF.

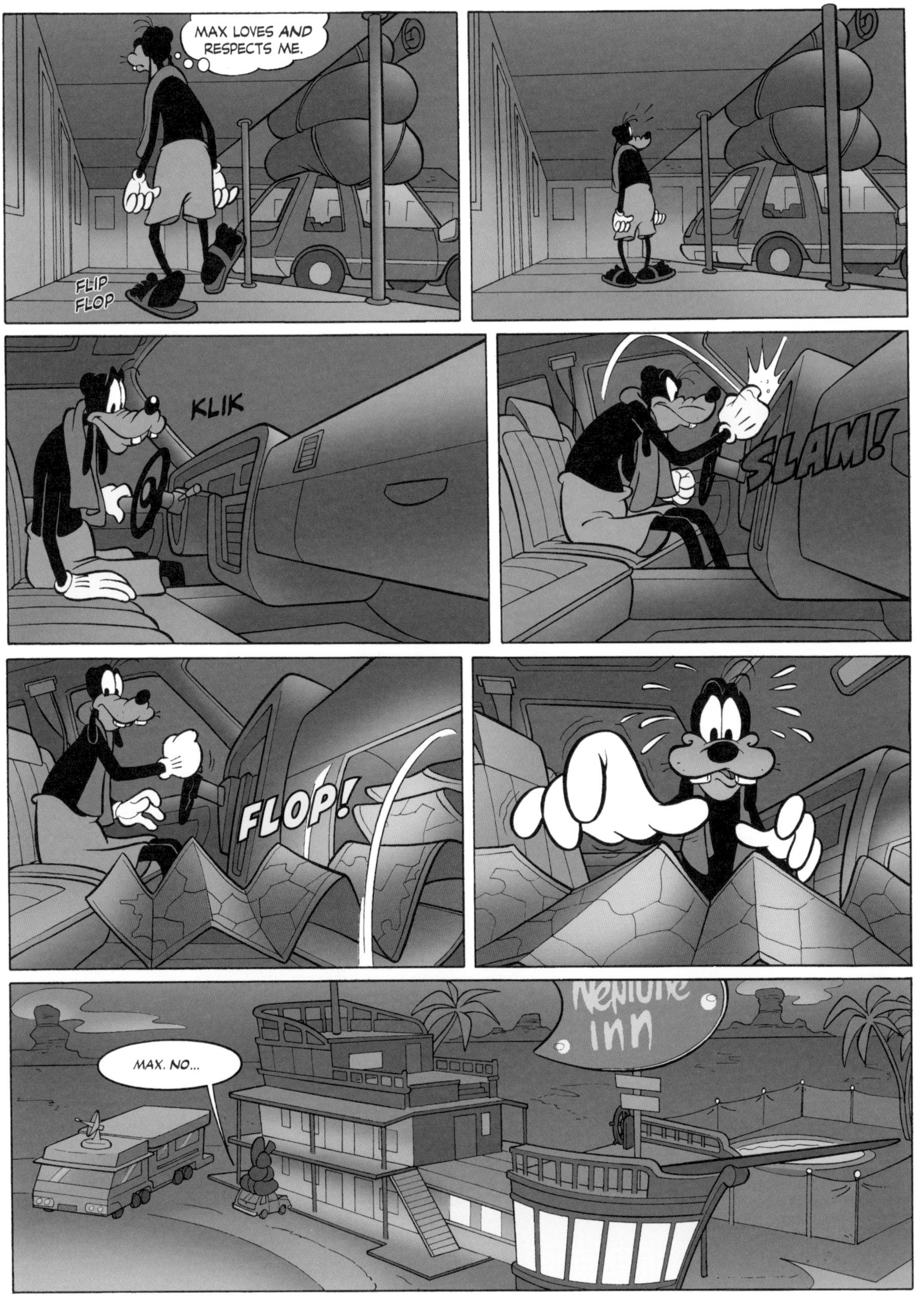
MAX LOVES AND RESPECTS ME.
FLIP FLOP
KLIK
SLAM!
FLOP!
MAX. NO...
inn

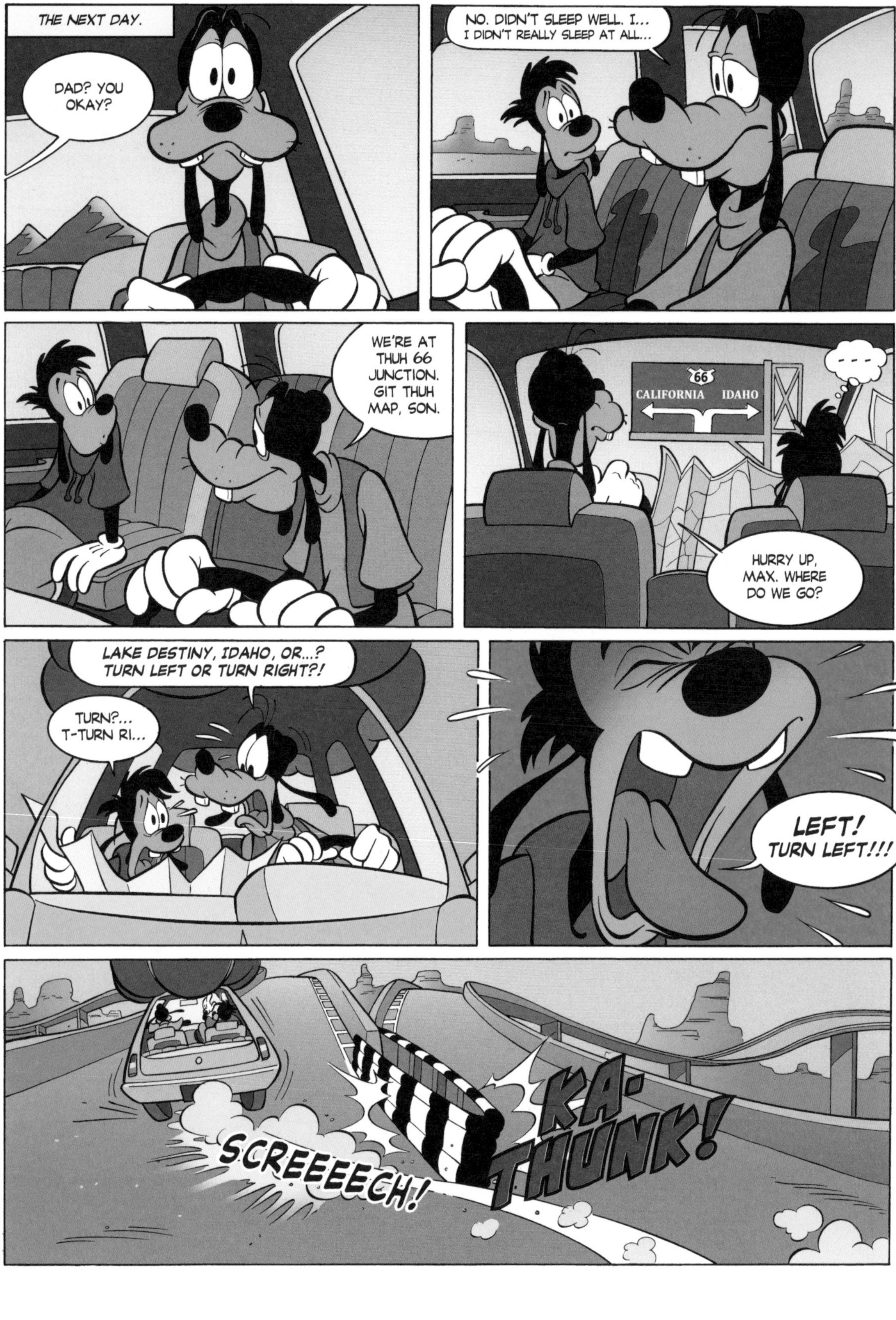
THE NEXT DAY.
DAD? YOU OKAY?
NO. DIDN'T SLEEP WELL. I... I DIDN'T REALLY SLEEP AT ALL...
WE'RE AT THUH 66 JUNCTION. GIT THUH MAP, SON.
66
CALIFORNIA
IDAHO
- - -
HURRY UP, MAX. WHERE DO WE GO?
LAKE DESTINY, IDAHO, OR...? TURN LEFT OR TURN RIGHT?!
TURN?... T-TURN RI...
LEFT! TURN LEFT!!!
KA-THUNK!
SCREEEEECH!

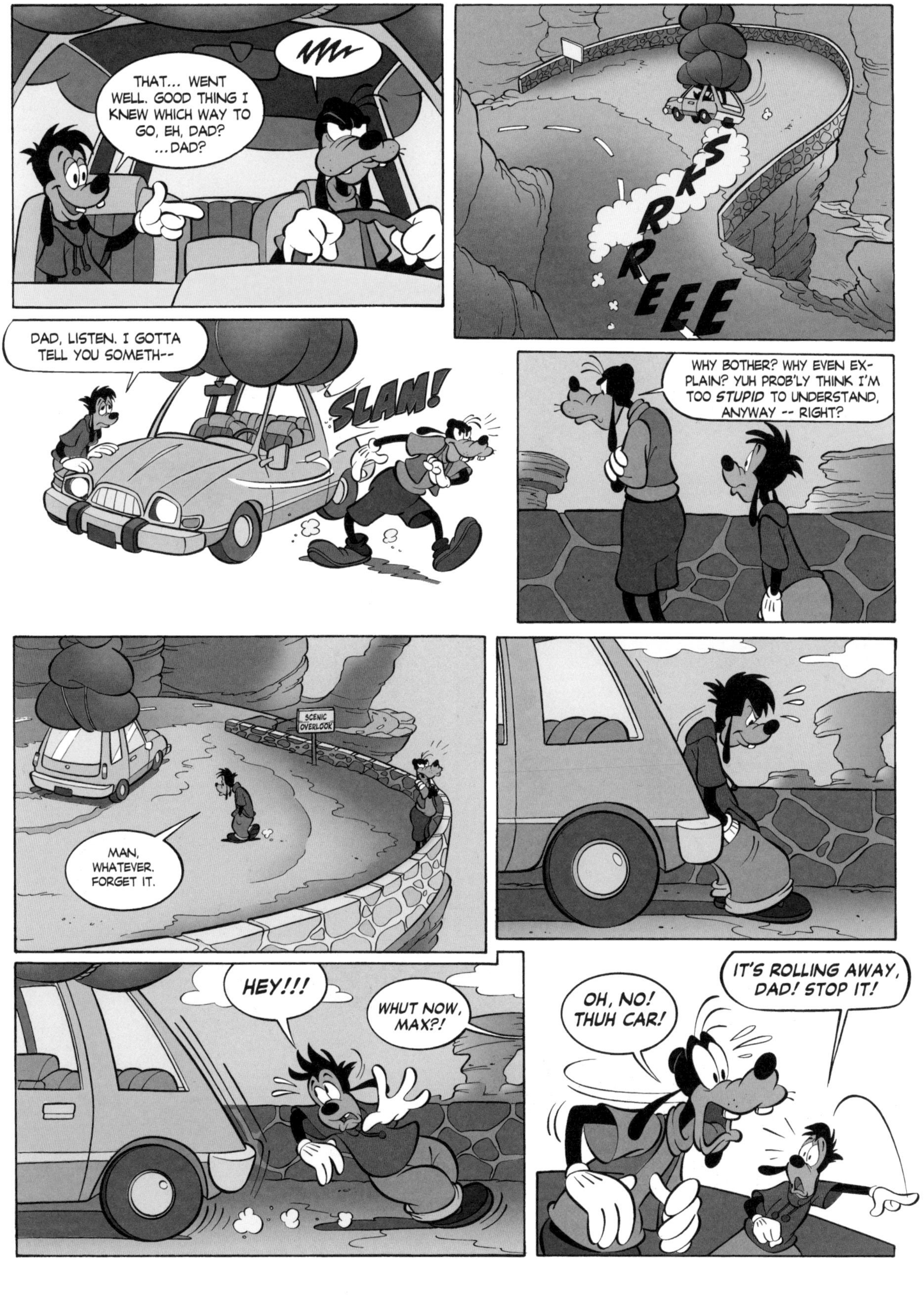
THAT... WENT WELL. GOOD THING I KNEW WHICH WAY TO GO, EH, DAD? ...DAD?
SKRRREEE
DAD, LISTEN. I GOTTA TELL YOU SOMETH--
SLAM!
WHY BOTHER? WHY EVEN EX-PLAIN? YUH PROB'LY THINK I'M TOO *STUPID* TO UNDERSTAND, ANYWAY -- RIGHT?
SCENIC OVERLOOK
MAN, WHATEVER. FORGET IT.
HEY!!!
WHUT NOW, MAX?!
OH, NO! THUH CAR!
IT'S ROLLING AWAY, DAD! STOP IT!

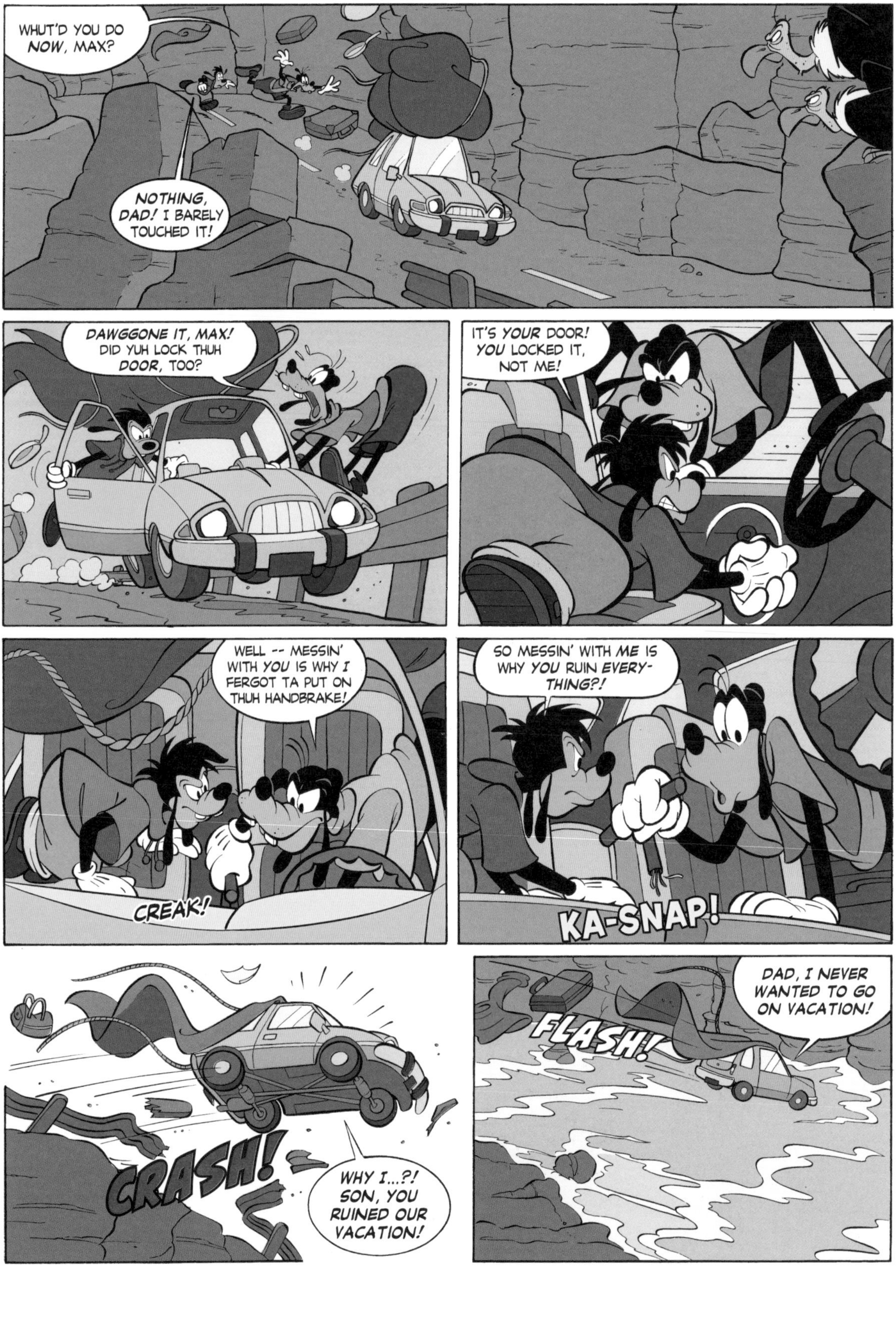
WHUT'D YOU DO NOW, MAX?
NOTHING, DAD! I BARELY TOUCHED IT!
DAWGGONE IT, MAX! DID YUH LOCK THUH DOOR, TOO?
IT'S YOUR DOOR! YOU LOCKED IT, NOT ME!
WELL -- MESSIN' WITH YOU IS WHY I FERGOT TA PUT ON THUH HANDBRAKE!
CREAK!
SO MESSIN' WITH ME IS WHY YOU RUIN EVERY-THING?!
KA-SNAP!
CRASH!
WHY I...?! SON, YOU RUINED OUR VACATION!
FLASH!
DAD, I NEVER WANTED TO GO ON VACATION!

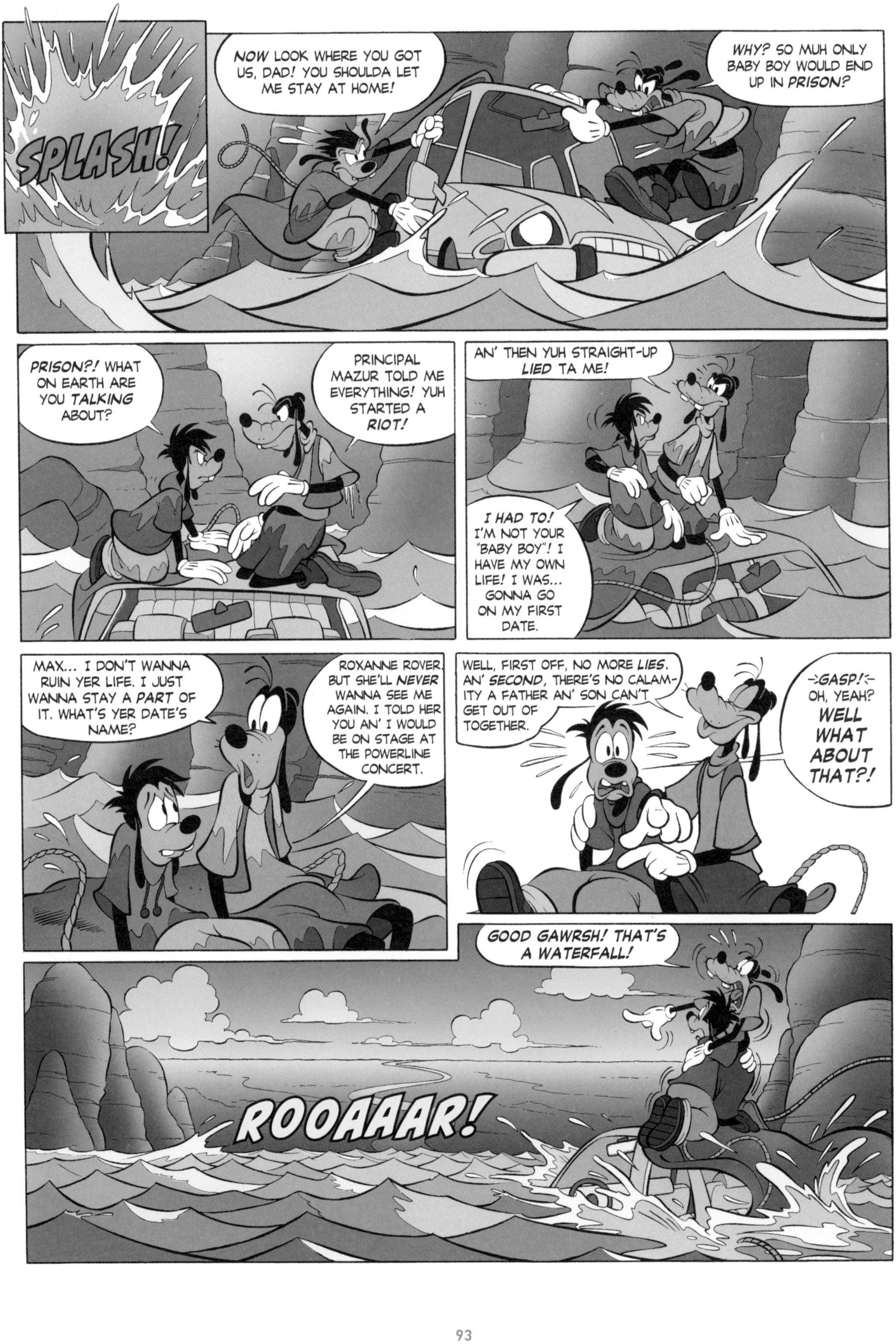
SPLASH!
NOW LOOK WHERE YOU GOT US, DAD! YOU SHOULDA LET ME STAY AT HOME!
WHY? SO MUH ONLY BABY BOY WOULD END UP IN PRISON?
PRISON?! WHAT ON EARTH ARE YOU TALKING ABOUT?
PRINCIPAL MAZUR TOLD ME EVERYTHING! YUH STARTED A RIOT!
AN' THEN YUH STRAIGHT-UP LIED TA ME!
I HAD TO! I'M NOT YOUR "BABY BOY"! I HAVE MY OWN LIFE! I WAS... GONNA GO ON MY FIRST DATE.
MAX... I DON'T WANNA RUIN YER LIFE. I JUST WANNA STAY A PART OF IT. WHAT'S YER DATE'S NAME?
ROXANNE ROVER. BUT SHE'LL NEVER WANNA SEE ME AGAIN. I TOLD HER YOU AN' I WOULD BE ON STAGE AT THE POWERLINE CONCERT.
WELL, FIRST OFF, NO MORE LIES. AN' SECOND, THERE'S NO CALAMITY A FATHER AN' SON CAN'T GET OUT OF TOGETHER.
-GASP!- OH, YEAH? WELL WHAT ABOUT THAT?!
GOOD GAWRSH! THAT'S A WATERFALL!
ROOAAAR!

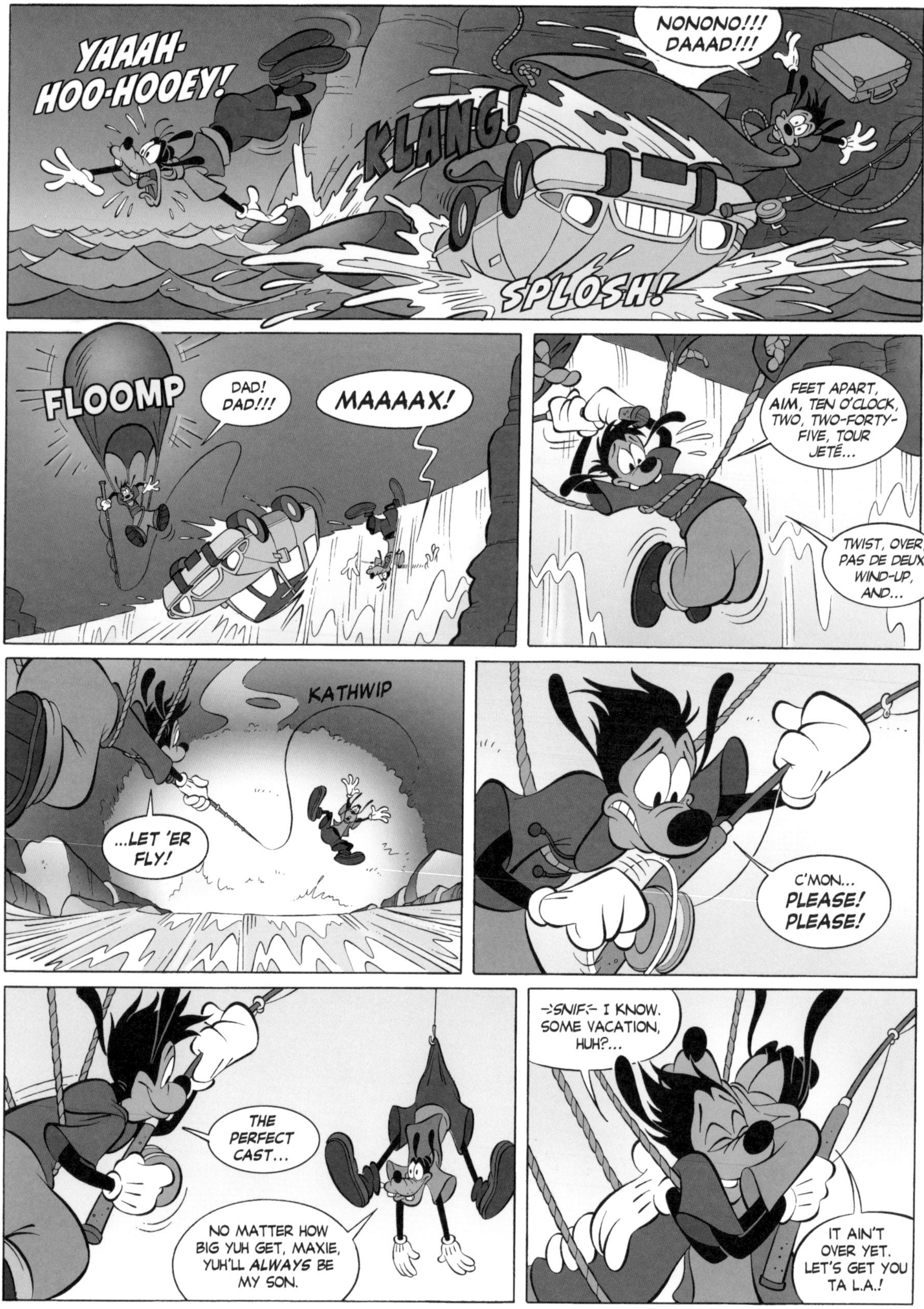
YAAAH-HOO-HOOEY!
NONONO!!! DAAAD!!!
KLANG!
SPLOSH!
FLOOMP
DAD! DAD!!!
MAAAAX!
FEET APART, AIM, TEN O'CLOCK, TWO, TWO-FORTY-FIVE, TOUR JETÉ...
TWIST, OVER, PAS DE DEUX, WIND-UP, AND...
KATHWIP
...LET 'ER FLY!
C'MON... PLEASE! PLEASE!
THE PERFECT CAST...
NO MATTER HOW BIG YUH GET, MAXIE, YUH'LL *ALWAYS* BE MY SON.
-SNIF- I KNOW. SOME VACATION, HUH?...
IT AIN'T OVER YET. LET'S GET YOU TA L.A.!

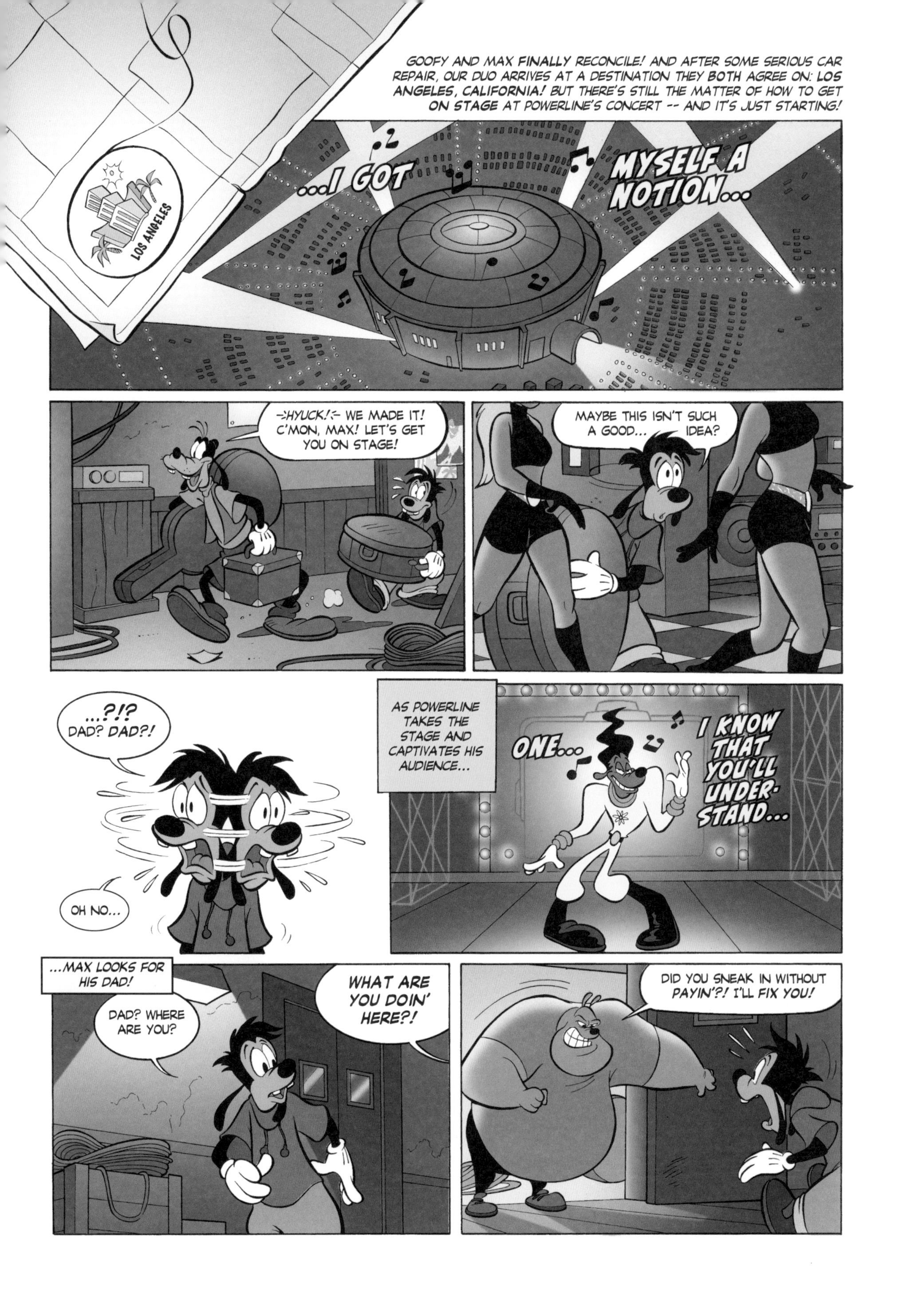
GOOFY AND MAX FINALLY RECONCILE! AND AFTER SOME SERIOUS CAR REPAIR, OUR DUO ARRIVES AT A DESTINATION THEY BOTH AGREE ON: LOS ANGELES, CALIFORNIA! BUT THERE'S STILL THE MATTER OF HOW TO GET ON STAGE AT POWERLINE'S CONCERT -- AND IT'S JUST STARTING!
LOS ANGELES
...I GOT
MYSELF A NOTION...
-HYUCK!- WE MADE IT! C'MON, MAX! LET'S GET YOU ON STAGE!
MAYBE THIS ISN'T SUCH A GOOD... IDEA?
...?!? DAD? DAD?!
OH NO...
AS POWERLINE TAKES THE STAGE AND CAPTIVATES HIS AUDIENCE...
ONE...
I KNOW THAT YOU'LL UNDER-STAND...
...MAX LOOKS FOR HIS DAD!
DAD? WHERE ARE YOU?
WHAT ARE YOU DOIN' HERE?!
DID YOU SNEAK IN WITHOUT PAYIN'?! I'LL FIX YOU!

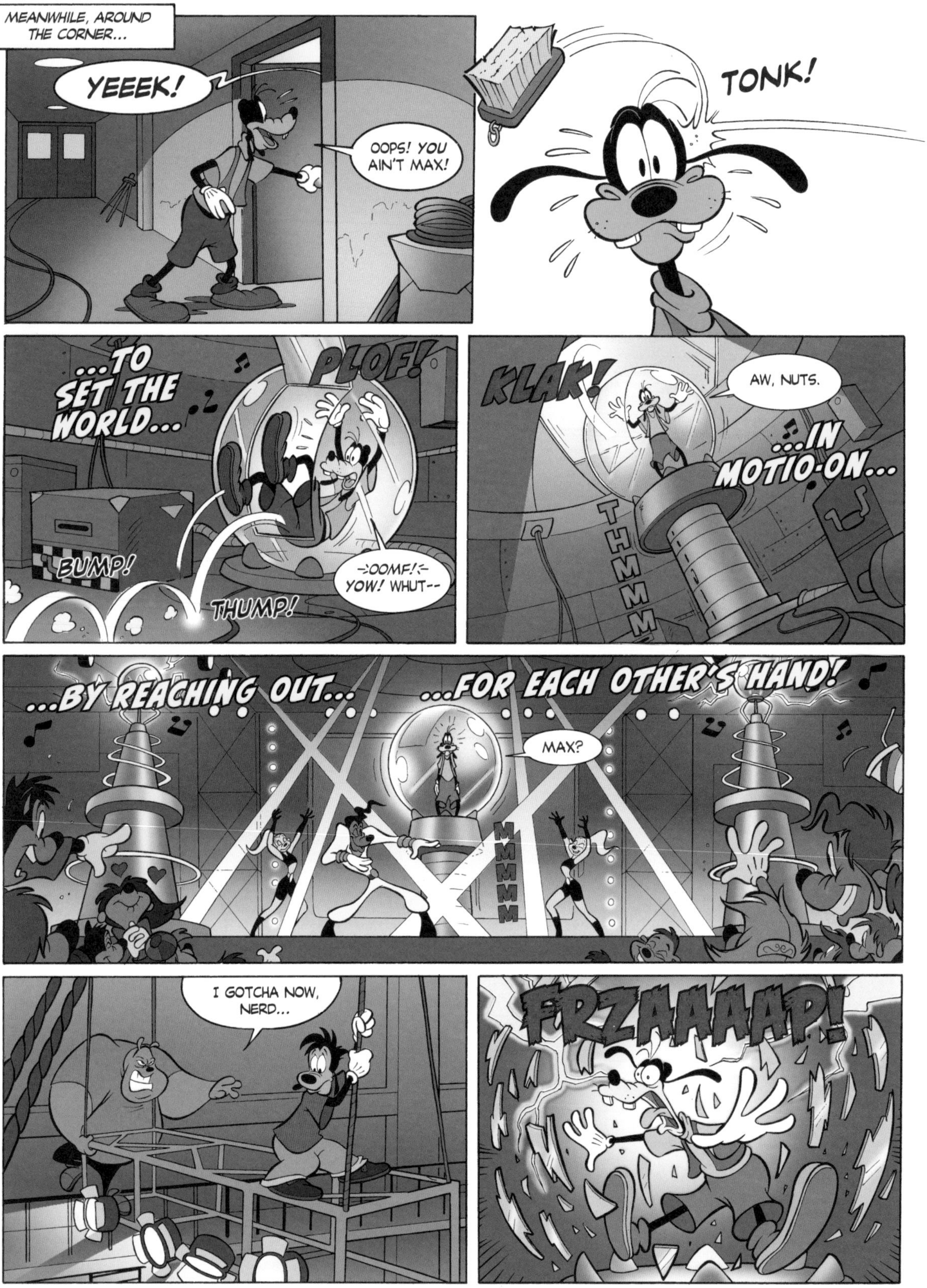
MEANWHILE, AROUND THE CORNER...
YEEEK!
OOPS! YOU AIN'T MAX!
TONK!
...TO SET THE WORLD...
PLOF!
BUMP!
THUMP!
-OOMF!- YOW! WHUT--
KLAK!
AW, NUTS.
...IN MOTIO-ON...
THMMMM
...BY REACHING OUT...
...FOR EACH OTHER'S HAND!
MAX?
MMMM
I GOTCHA NOW, NERD...
FRZAAAAP!

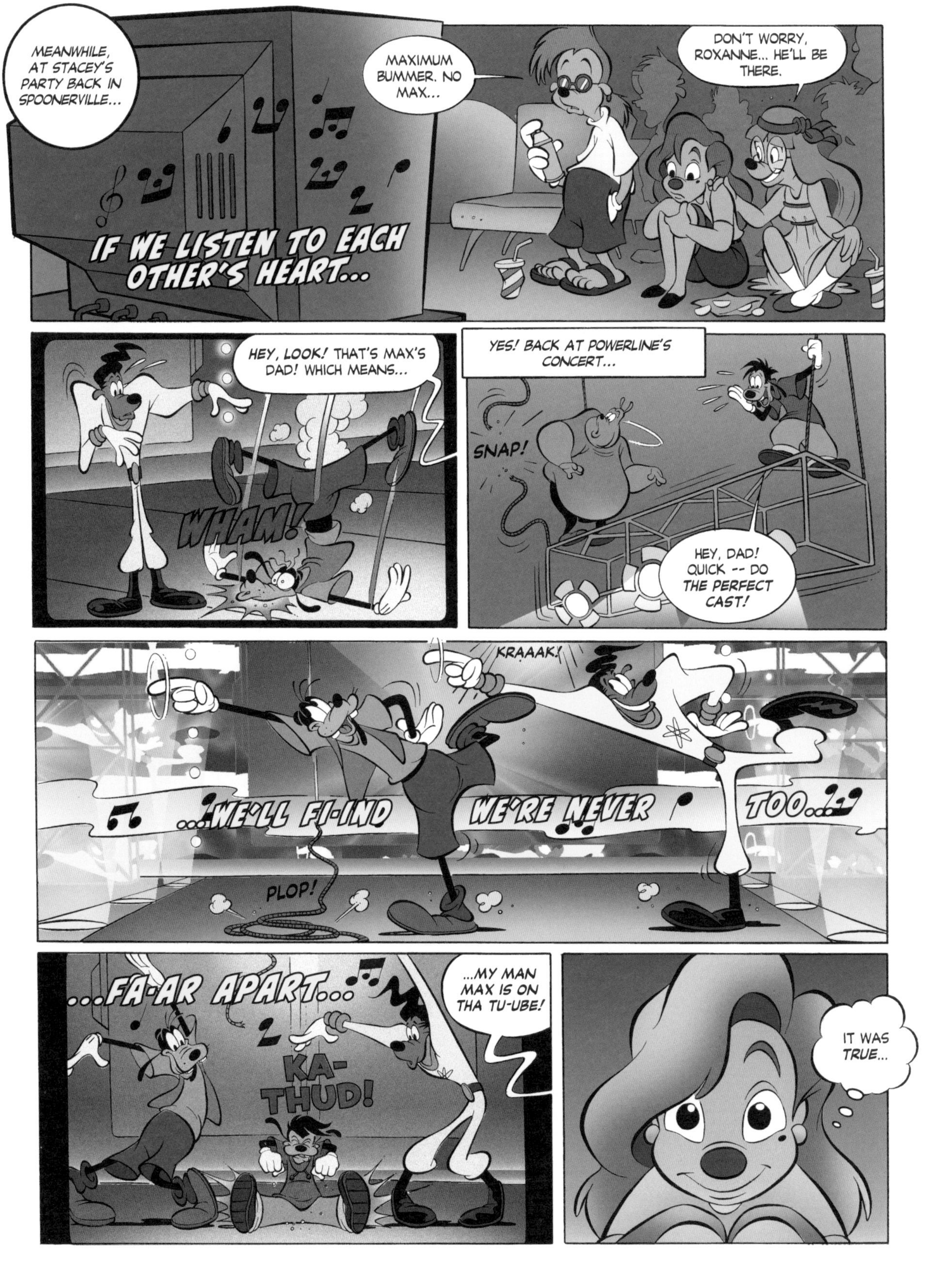
MEANWHILE, AT STACEY'S PARTY BACK IN SPOONERVILLE...
MAXIMUM BUMMER. NO MAX...
DON'T WORRY, ROXANNE... HE'LL BE THERE.
IF WE LISTEN TO EACH OTHER'S HEART...
HEY, LOOK! THAT'S MAX'S DAD! WHICH MEANS...
WHAM!
YES! BACK AT POWERLINE'S CONCERT...
SNAP!
HEY, DAD! QUICK -- DO THE PERFECT CAST!
KRAAAK!
...WE'LL FI-IND WE'RE NEVER TOO...
PLOP!
...FA-AR APART...
...MY MAN MAX IS ON THA TU-UBE!
KA-THUD!
IT WAS TRUE...

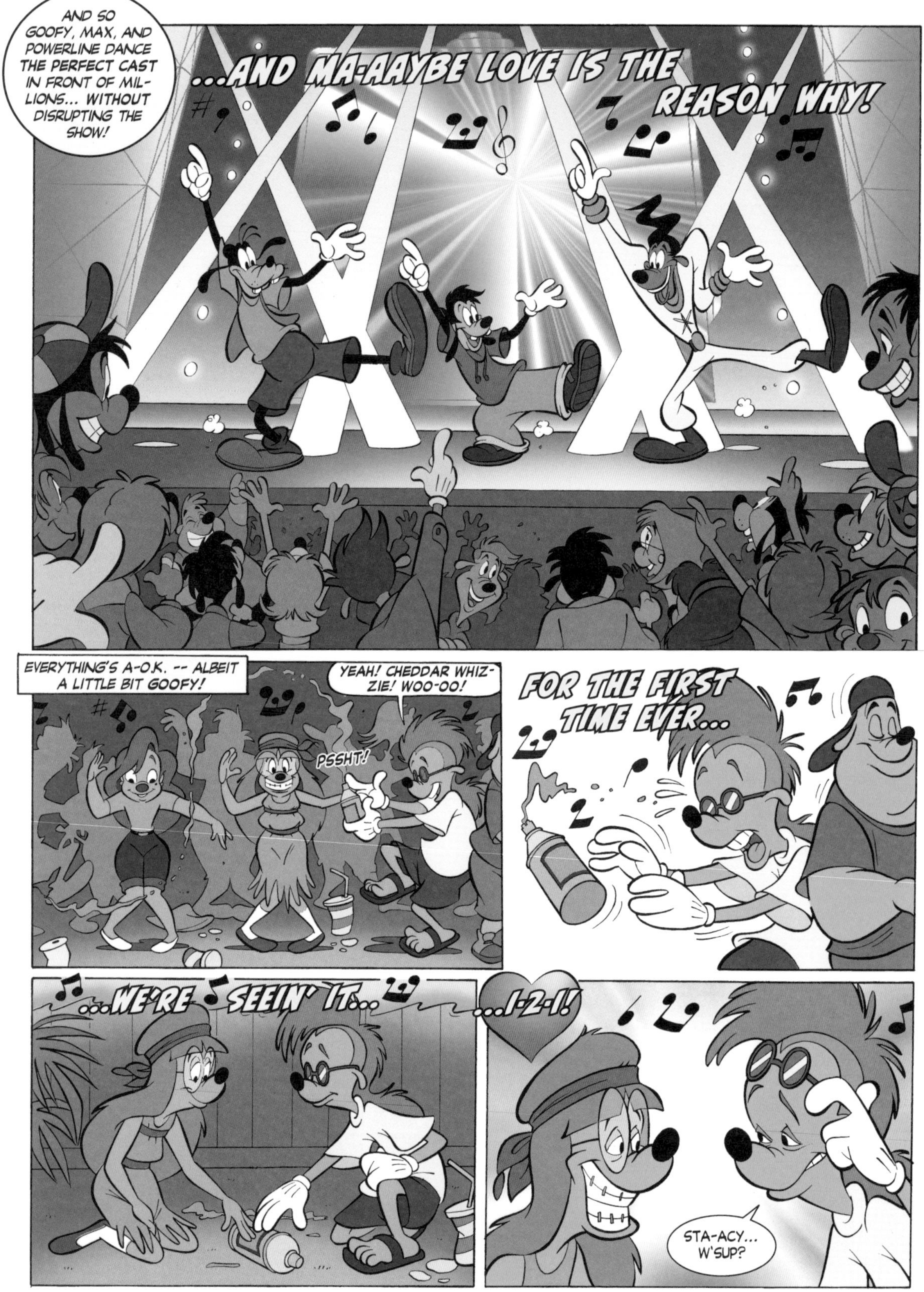

AND SO GOOFY, MAX, AND POWERLINE DANCE THE PERFECT CAST IN FRONT OF MILLIONS... WITHOUT DISRUPTING THE SHOW!
...AND MA-AAYBE LOVE IS THE REASON WHY!
EVERYTHING'S A-O.K. -- ALBEIT A LITTLE BIT GOOFY!
YEAH! CHEDDAR WHIZZIE! WOO-OO!
PSSHT!
FOR THE FIRST TIME EVER...
...WE'RE SEEIN' IT... ...1-2-1!
STA-ACY... W'SUP?

ONE WEEK LATER...

B-R-B, DAD. THANKS FOR THE ADVICE...

OH. HI, ROXANNE.

HEY, MAX! I SAW YOU ON TV. YOU WERE *GREAT!*

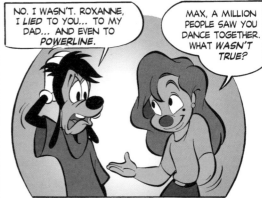

NO. I WASN'T. ROXANNE, I *LIED* TO YOU... TO MY DAD... AND EVEN TO *POWERLINE.*

MAX, A MILLION PEOPLE SAW YOU DANCE TOGETHER. WHAT *WASN'T* TRUE?

WELL... I WASN'T *SUPPOSED* TO BE THERE. BUT I *TOLD* YOU I *WOULD* BE... BECAUSE I *REALLY LIKE* YOU... AND I REALLY WANTED YOU TO LIKE ME. I'M SORRY.

THANKS FOR BEING HONEST...

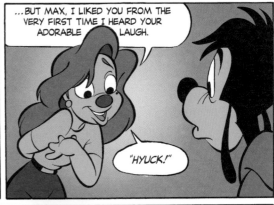

...BUT MAX, I LIKED YOU FROM THE VERY FIRST TIME I HEARD YOUR ADORABLE LAUGH.

"HYUCK!"

OH!

SMEK!

MAX... HEE-HEE...

GAWRSH! ~HYUCK!~

HEY, MAX!

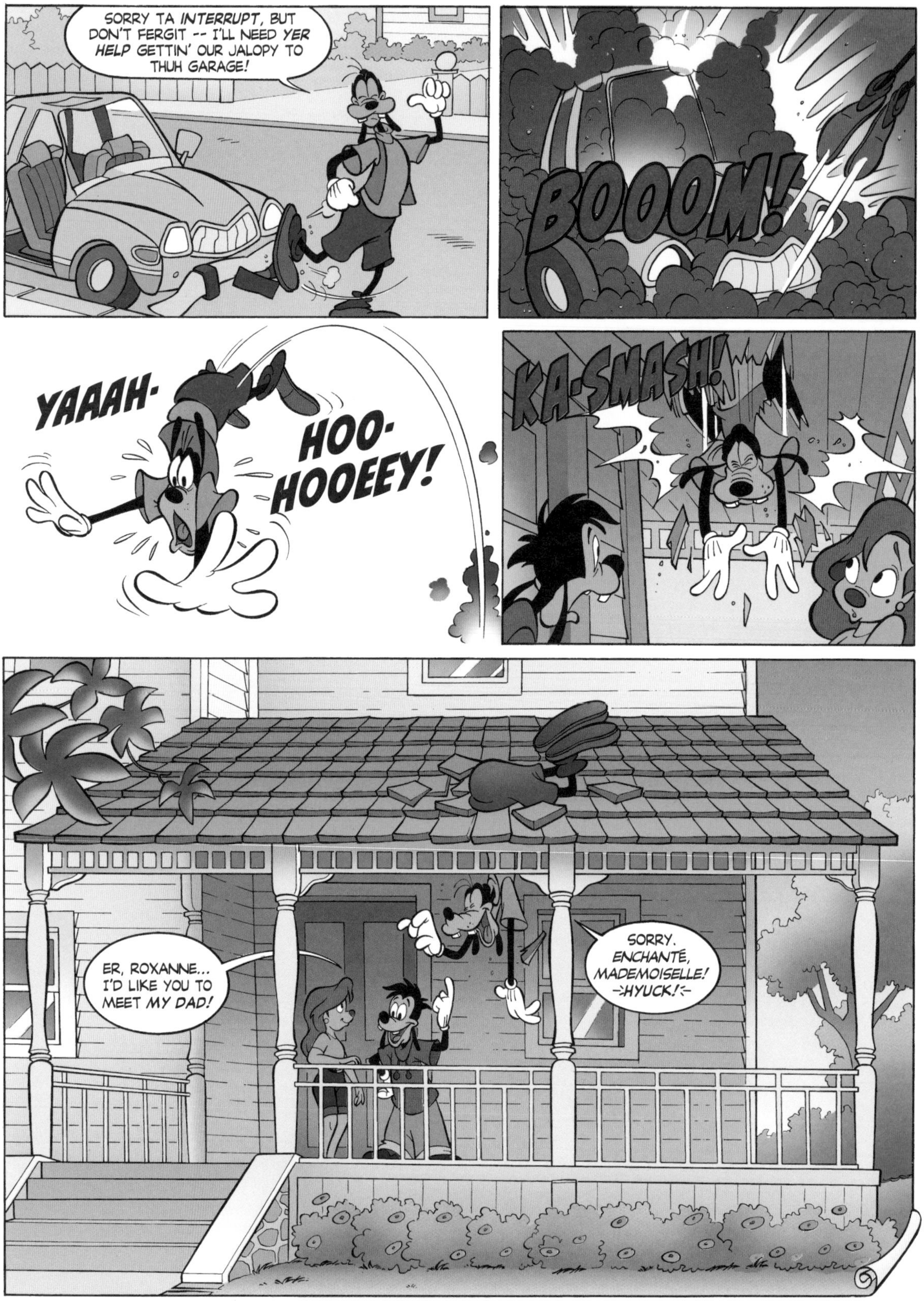
SORRY TA INTERRUPT, BUT DON'T FERGIT -- I'LL NEED YER HELP GETTIN' OUR JALOPY TO THUH GARAGE!
BOOOM!
YAAAH-
HOO-
HOOEEY!
KA-SMASH!
ER, ROXANNE... I'D LIKE YOU TO MEET MY DAD!
SORRY. ENCHANTÉ, MADEMOISELLE! -HYUCK!-

THE START OF SOMETHING GOOFY!

Disney

DuckTales™

A BEAGLE BADTIME STORY

JZ 145-1

SING A SONG OF BEAGLES, PLOTTING THEIR ESCAPE...

TO: THE BEAGLES, STATE PEN FROM: MA

FOUR AND TWENTY BOMBSHELLS, BAKED IN A CAKE...

WHEN THE CAKE EXPLODED, IT MADE A MIGHTY CLAMOR...

WA BOOM!

NOW WASN'T THAT A JOLLY WAY... TO BREAK OUT OF THE SLAMMER?

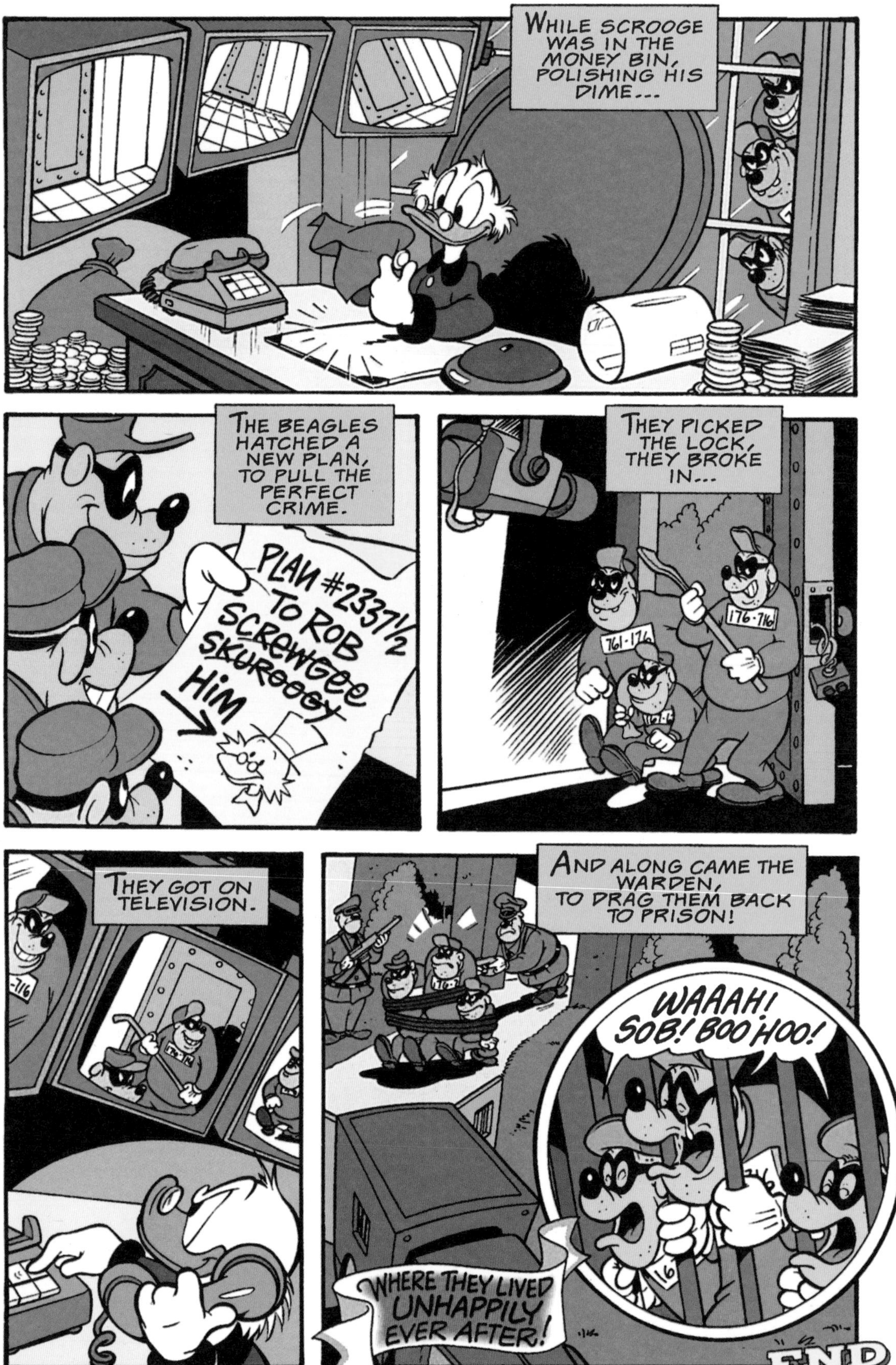
While scrooge was in the money bin, polishing his dime...
The beagles hatched a new plan, to pull the perfect crime.
PLAN #2337½ TO ROB SCREWGEE SKUROOGY HIM
They picked the lock, they broke in...
761-176
176-716
They got on television.
And along came the warden, to drag them back to prison!
WAAAH! SOB! BOO HOO!
WHERE THEY LIVED UNHAPPILY EVER AFTER!
END

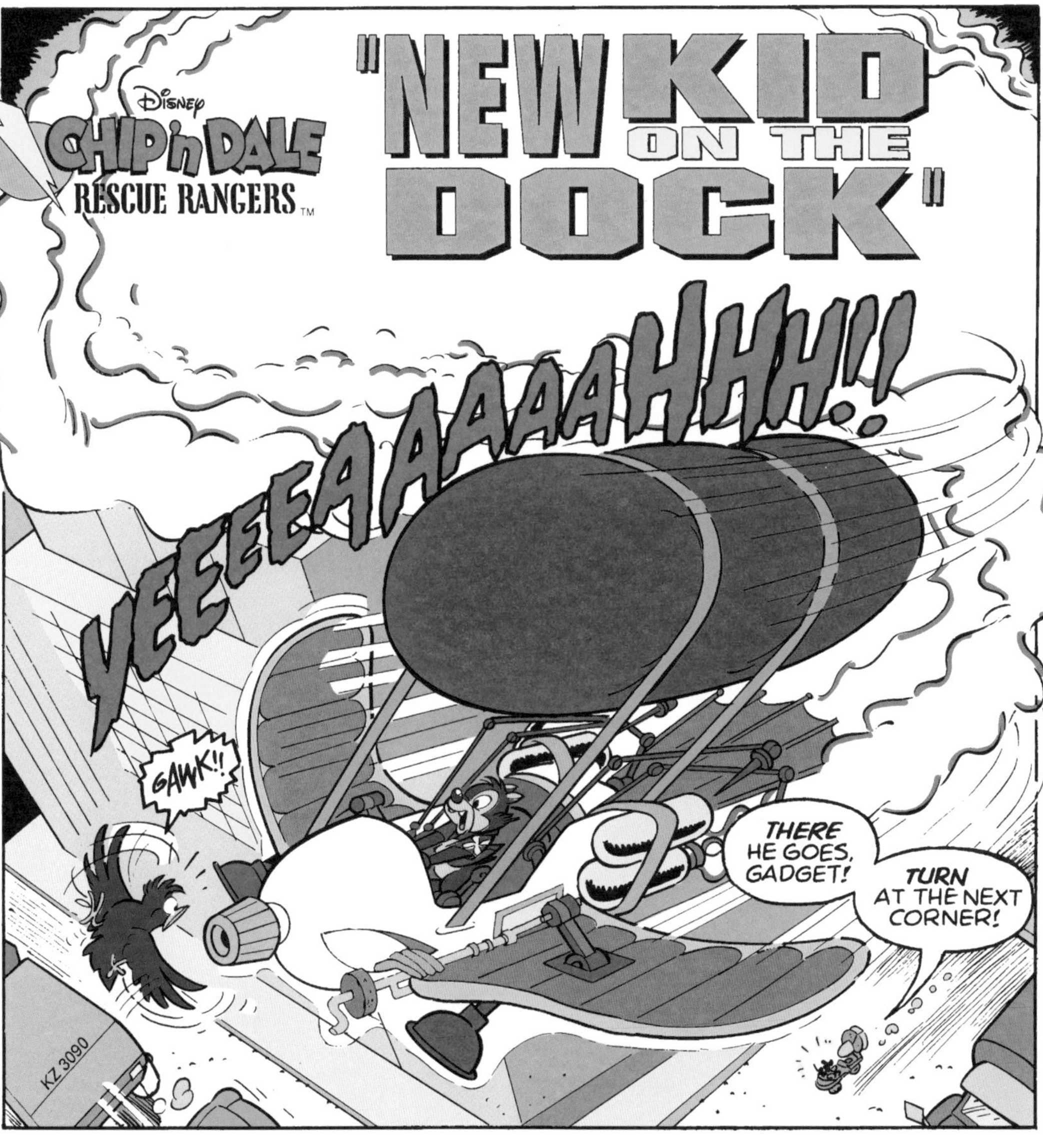
Disney
Chip 'n Dale
RESCUE RANGERS ™
"NEW KID ON THE DOCK"
YEEEEAAAAAHHH!!
GAWK!!
THERE HE GOES, GADGET!
TURN AT THE NEXT CORNER!
KZ 3090

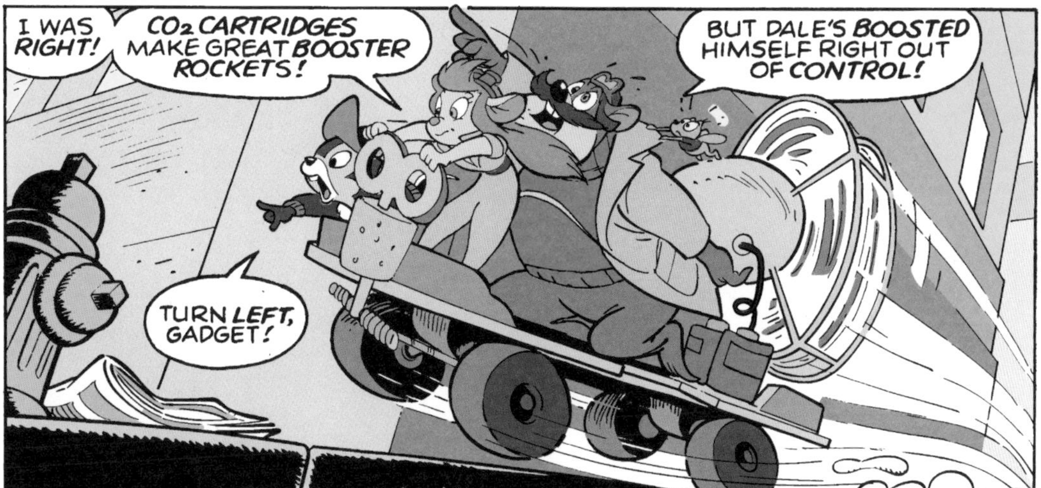
I WAS RIGHT!
CO_2 CARTRIDGES MAKE GREAT BOOSTER ROCKETS!
BUT DALE'S BOOSTED HIMSELF RIGHT OUT OF CONTROL!
TURN LEFT, GADGET!

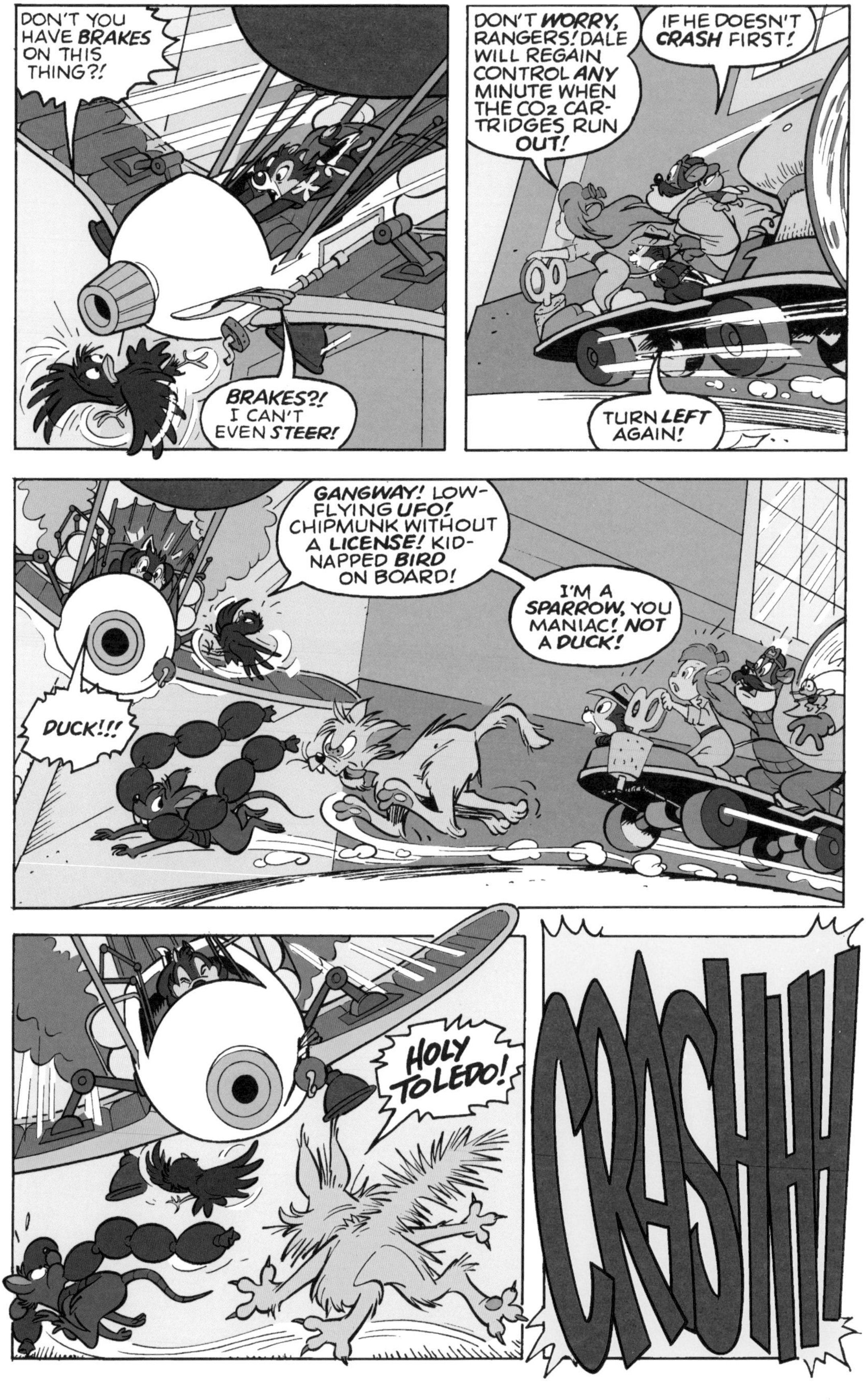
DON'T YOU HAVE BRAKES ON THIS THING?!
BRAKES?! I CAN'T EVEN STEER!
DON'T WORRY, RANGERS! DALE WILL REGAIN CONTROL ANY MINUTE WHEN THE CO2 CAR-TRIDGES RUN OUT!
IF HE DOESN'T CRASH FIRST!
TURN LEFT AGAIN!
GANGWAY! LOW-FLYING UFO! CHIPMUNK WITHOUT A LICENSE! KID-NAPPED BIRD ON BOARD!
I'M A SPARROW, YOU MANIAC! NOT A DUCK!
DUCK!!!
HOLY TOLEDO!
CRASHHH!

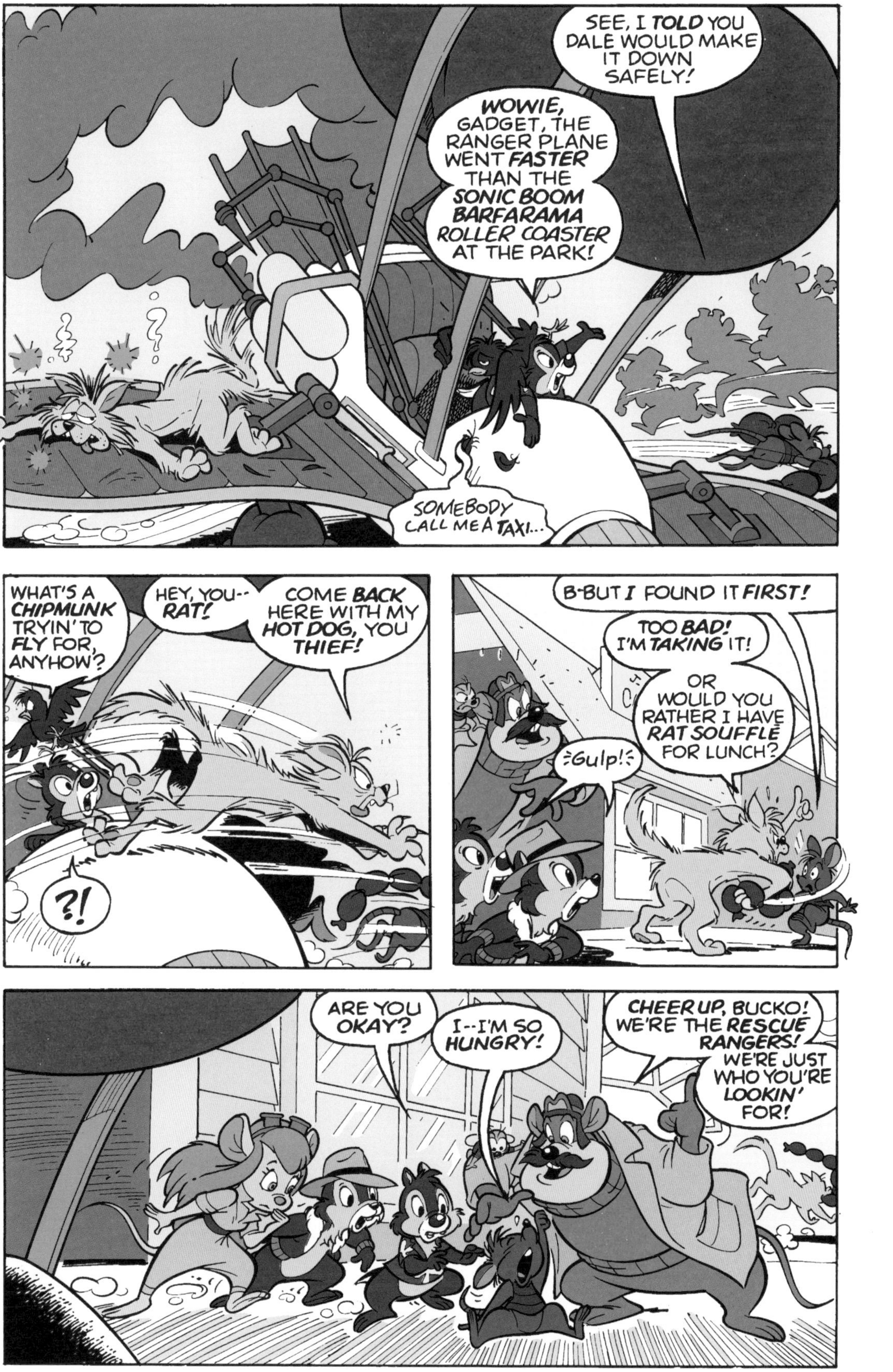
SEE, I TOLD YOU DALE WOULD MAKE IT DOWN SAFELY!
WOWIE, GADGET, THE RANGER PLANE WENT FASTER THAN THE SONIC BOOM BARFARAMA ROLLER COASTER AT THE PARK!
SOMEBODY CALL ME A TAXI...
WHAT'S A CHIPMUNK TRYIN' TO FLY FOR, ANYHOW?
HEY, YOU-- RAT!
COME BACK HERE WITH MY HOT DOG, YOU THIEF!
?!
B-BUT I FOUND IT FIRST!
TOO BAD! I'M TAKING IT!
OR WOULD YOU RATHER I HAVE RAT SOUFFLÉ FOR LUNCH?
Gulp!
ARE YOU OKAY?
I--I'M SO HUNGRY!
CHEER UP, BUCKO! WE'RE THE RESCUE RANGERS!
WE'RE JUST WHO YOU'RE LOOKIN' FOR!

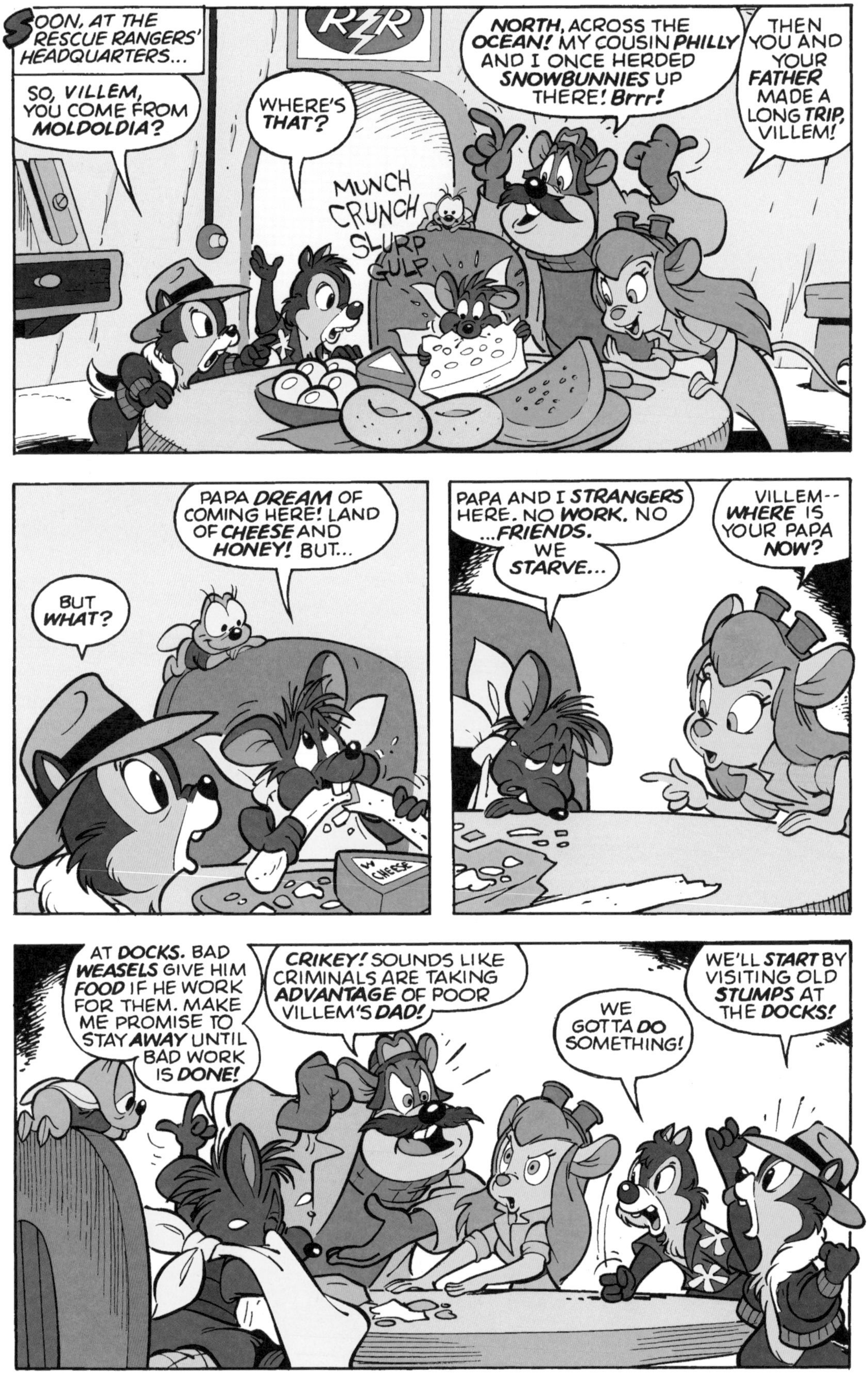
SOON, AT THE RESCUE RANGERS' HEADQUARTERS...
SO, VILLEM, YOU COME FROM MOLDOLDIA?
WHERE'S THAT?
NORTH, ACROSS THE OCEAN! MY COUSIN PHILLY AND I ONCE HERDED SNOWBUNNIES UP THERE! Brrr!
THEN YOU AND YOUR FATHER MADE A LONG TRIP, VILLEM!
MUNCH CRUNCH SLURP GULP
PAPA DREAM OF COMING HERE! LAND OF CHEESE AND HONEY! BUT...
BUT WHAT?
CHEESE
PAPA AND I STRANGERS HERE. NO WORK. NO ...FRIENDS.
WE STARVE...
VILLEM-- WHERE IS YOUR PAPA NOW?
AT DOCKS. BAD WEASELS GIVE HIM FOOD IF HE WORK FOR THEM. MAKE ME PROMISE TO STAY AWAY UNTIL BAD WORK IS DONE!
CRIKEY! SOUNDS LIKE CRIMINALS ARE TAKING ADVANTAGE OF POOR VILLEM'S DAD!
WE GOTTA DO SOMETHING!
WE'LL START BY VISITING OLD STUMPS AT THE DOCKS!

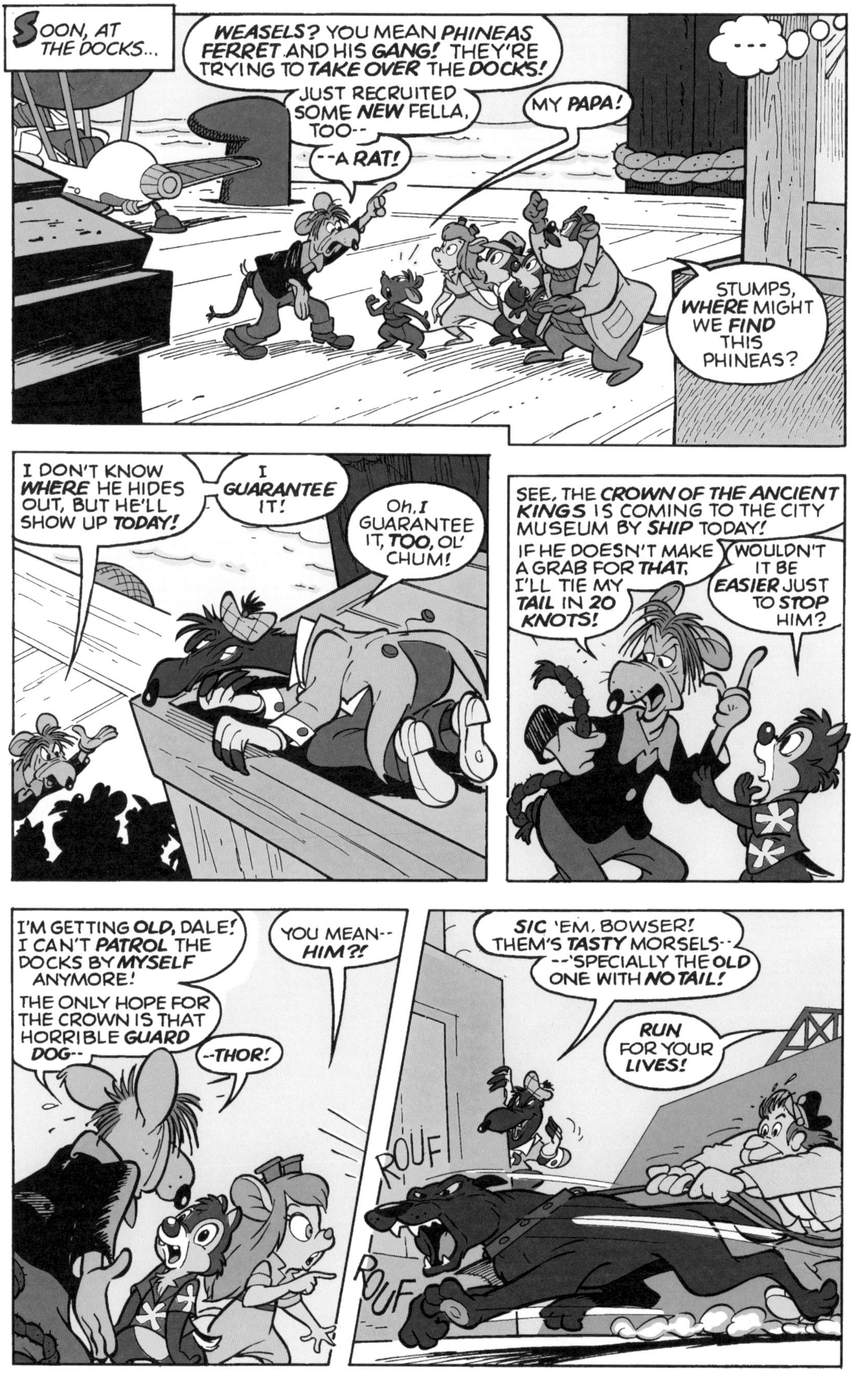
SOON, AT THE DOCKS...
WEASELS? YOU MEAN PHINEAS FERRET AND HIS GANG! THEY'RE TRYING TO TAKE OVER THE DOCKS!
JUST RECRUITED SOME NEW FELLA, TOO--
--A RAT!
MY PAPA!
...
STUMPS, WHERE MIGHT WE FIND THIS PHINEAS?
I DON'T KNOW WHERE HE HIDES OUT, BUT HE'LL SHOW UP TODAY!
I GUARANTEE IT!
Oh, I GUARANTEE IT, TOO, OL' CHUM!
SEE, THE CROWN OF THE ANCIENT KINGS IS COMING TO THE CITY MUSEUM BY SHIP TODAY!
IF HE DOESN'T MAKE A GRAB FOR THAT, I'LL TIE MY TAIL IN 20 KNOTS!
WOULDN'T IT BE EASIER JUST TO STOP HIM?
I'M GETTING OLD, DALE! I CAN'T PATROL THE DOCKS BY MYSELF ANYMORE!
THE ONLY HOPE FOR THE CROWN IS THAT HORRIBLE GUARD DOG--
YOU MEAN-- HIM?!
--THOR!
SIC 'EM, BOWSER! THEM'S TASTY MORSELS--
--'SPECIALLY THE OLD ONE WITH NO TAIL!
RUN FOR YOUR LIVES!
ROUF
ROUF

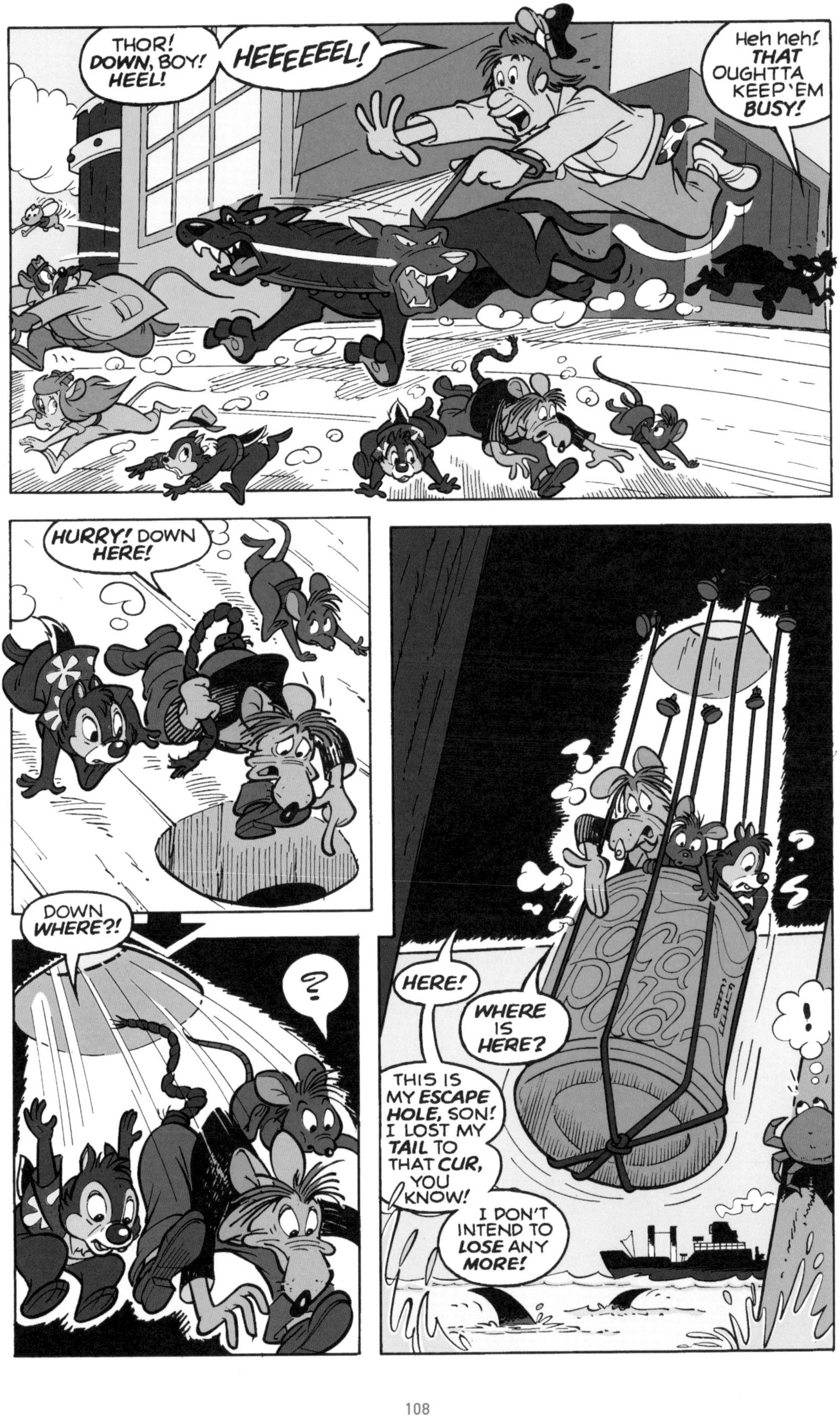
THOR! DOWN, BOY! HEEL!
HEEEEEEL!
Heh heh! THAT OUGHTTA KEEP 'EM BUSY!
HURRY! DOWN HERE!
DOWN WHERE?!
?
HERE!
WHERE IS HERE?
THIS IS MY ESCAPE HOLE, SON! I LOST MY TAIL TO THAT CUR, YOU KNOW!
I DON'T INTEND TO LOSE ANY MORE!
!

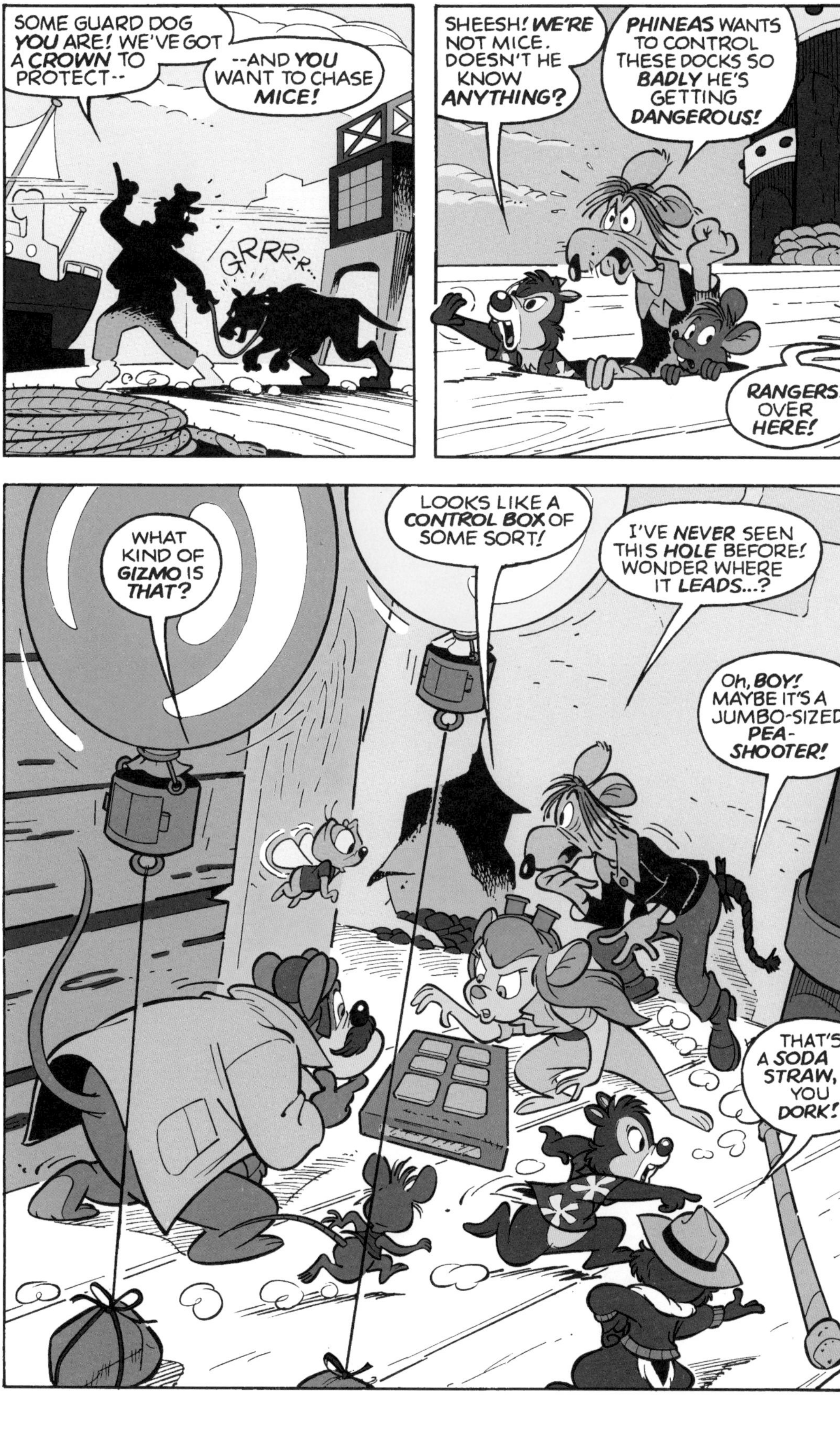

SOME GUARD DOG YOU ARE! WE'VE GOT A CROWN TO PROTECT--
--AND YOU WANT TO CHASE MICE!
GRRRR-R...
SHEESH! WE'RE NOT MICE. DOESN'T HE KNOW ANYTHING?
PHINEAS WANTS TO CONTROL THESE DOCKS SO BADLY HE'S GETTING DANGEROUS!
RANGERS! OVER HERE!
WHAT KIND OF GIZMO IS THAT?
LOOKS LIKE A CONTROL BOX OF SOME SORT!
I'VE NEVER SEEN THIS HOLE BEFORE! WONDER WHERE IT LEADS...?
Oh, BOY! MAYBE IT'S A JUMBO-SIZED PEA-SHOOTER!
THAT'S A SODA STRAW, YOU DORK!

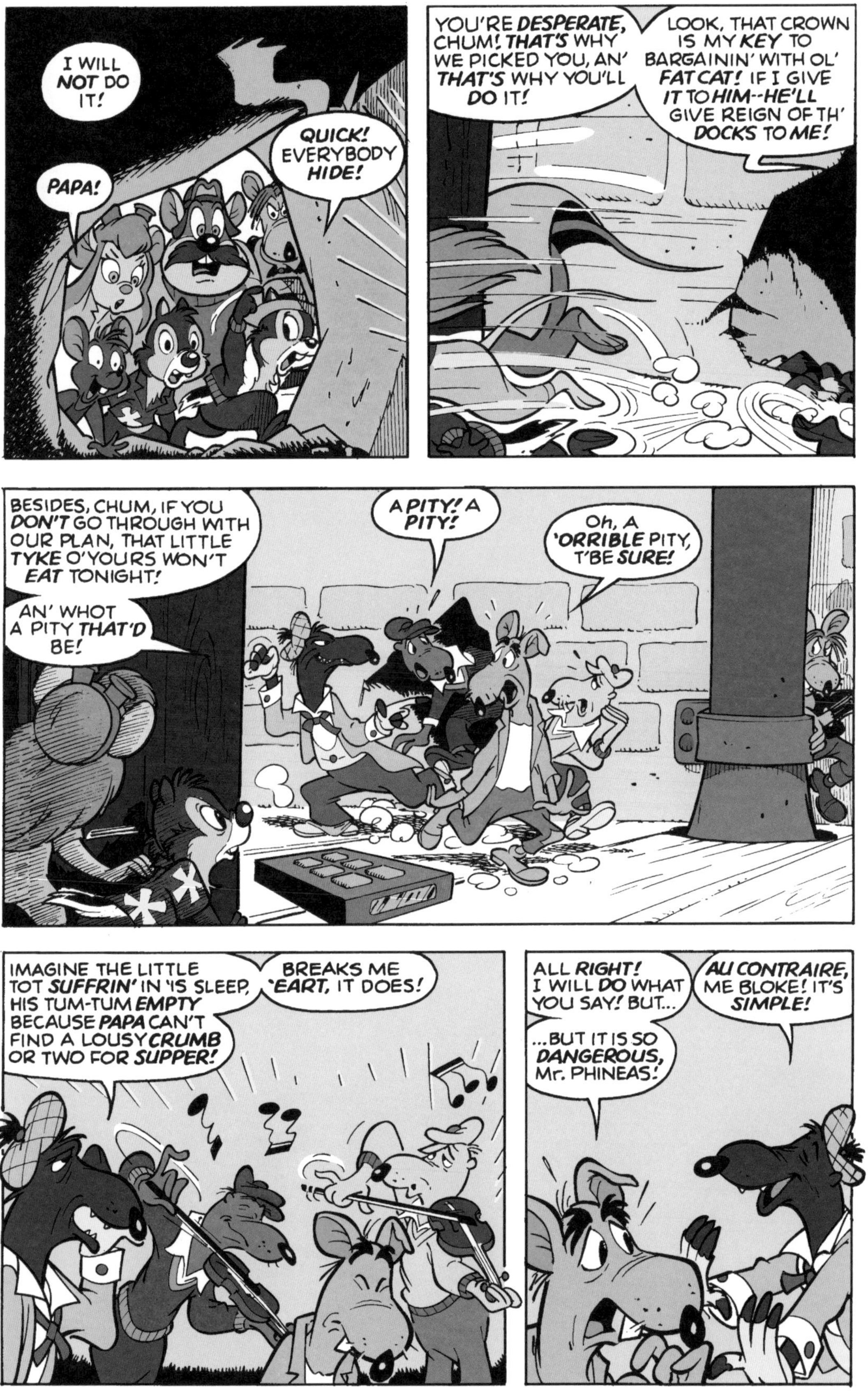
I WILL NOT DO IT!
PAPA!
QUICK! EVERYBODY HIDE!
YOU'RE DESPERATE, CHUM! THAT'S WHY WE PICKED YOU, AN' THAT'S WHY YOU'LL DO IT!
LOOK, THAT CROWN IS MY KEY TO BARGAININ' WITH OL' FAT CAT! IF I GIVE IT TO HIM--HE'LL GIVE REIGN OF TH' DOCKS TO ME!
BESIDES, CHUM, IF YOU DON'T GO THROUGH WITH OUR PLAN, THAT LITTLE TYKE O'YOURS WON'T EAT TONIGHT!
AN' WHOT A PITY THAT'D BE!
A PITY! A PITY!
Oh, A 'ORRIBLE PITY, T'BE SURE!
IMAGINE THE LITTLE TOT SUFFRIN' IN 'IS SLEEP, HIS TUM-TUM EMPTY BECAUSE PAPA CAN'T FIND A LOUSY CRUMB OR TWO FOR SUPPER!
BREAKS ME 'EART, IT DOES!
ALL RIGHT! I WILL DO WHAT YOU SAY! BUT...
...BUT IT IS SO DANGEROUS, Mr. PHINEAS!
AU CONTRAIRE, ME BLOKE! IT'S SIMPLE!

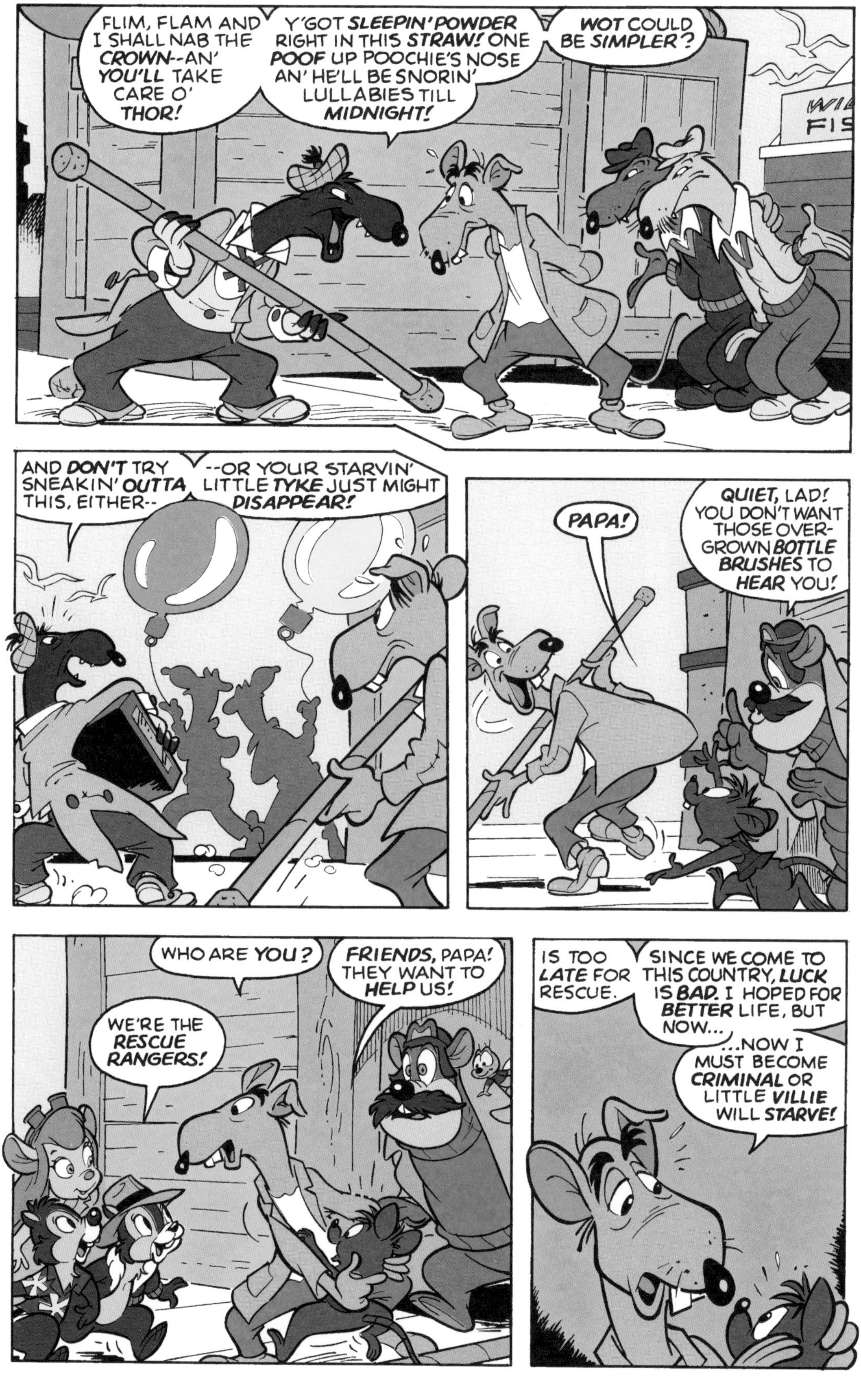
FLIM, FLAM AND I SHALL NAB THE CROWN--AN' YOU'LL TAKE CARE O' THOR!
Y'GOT SLEEPIN' POWDER RIGHT IN THIS STRAW! ONE POOF UP POOCHIE'S NOSE AN' HE'LL BE SNORIN' LULLABIES TILL MIDNIGHT!
WOT COULD BE SIMPLER?
WIL
FIS
AND DON'T TRY SNEAKIN' OUTTA THIS, EITHER--
--OR YOUR STARVIN' LITTLE TYKE JUST MIGHT DISAPPEAR!
PAPA!
QUIET, LAD! YOU DON'T WANT THOSE OVER-GROWN BOTTLE BRUSHES TO HEAR YOU!
WHO ARE YOU?
FRIENDS, PAPA! THEY WANT TO HELP US!
WE'RE THE RESCUE RANGERS!
IS TOO LATE FOR RESCUE.
SINCE WE COME TO THIS COUNTRY, LUCK IS BAD. I HOPED FOR BETTER LIFE, BUT NOW...
...NOW I MUST BECOME CRIMINAL OR LITTLE VILLIE WILL STARVE!

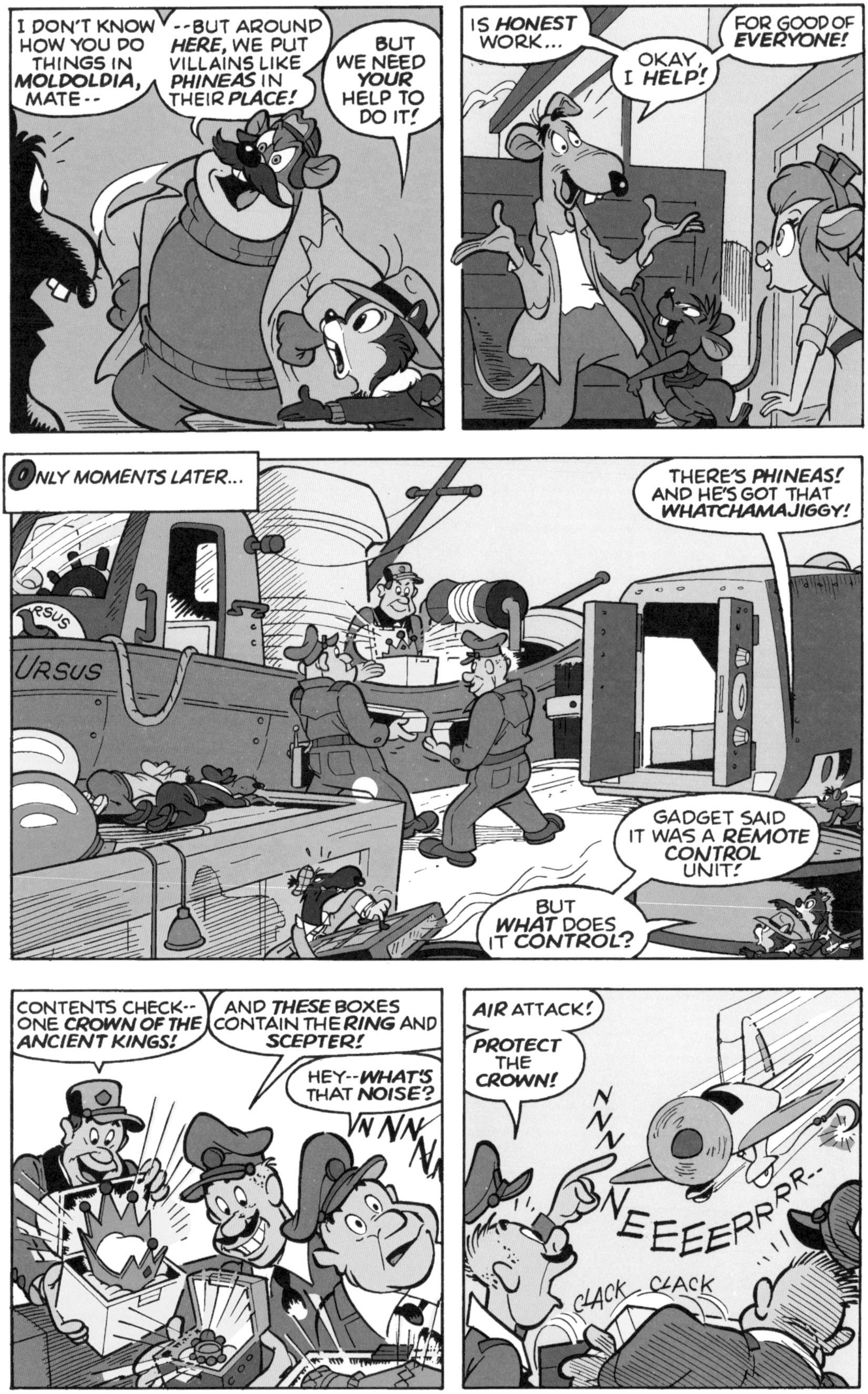
I DON'T KNOW HOW YOU DO THINGS IN MOLDOLDIA, MATE--
--BUT AROUND HERE, WE PUT VILLAINS LIKE PHINEAS IN THEIR PLACE!
BUT WE NEED YOUR HELP TO DO IT!
IS HONEST WORK...
OKAY, I HELP!
FOR GOOD OF EVERYONE!
ONLY MOMENTS LATER...
THERE'S PHINEAS! AND HE'S GOT THAT WHATCHAMAJIGGY!
URSUS
GADGET SAID IT WAS A REMOTE CONTROL UNIT!
BUT WHAT DOES IT CONTROL?
CONTENTS CHECK-- ONE CROWN OF THE ANCIENT KINGS!
AND THESE BOXES CONTAIN THE RING AND SCEPTER!
HEY--WHAT'S THAT NOISE?
NNNNN
AIR ATTACK!
PROTECT THE CROWN!
NNNEEEEERRRRR..
CLACK CLACK

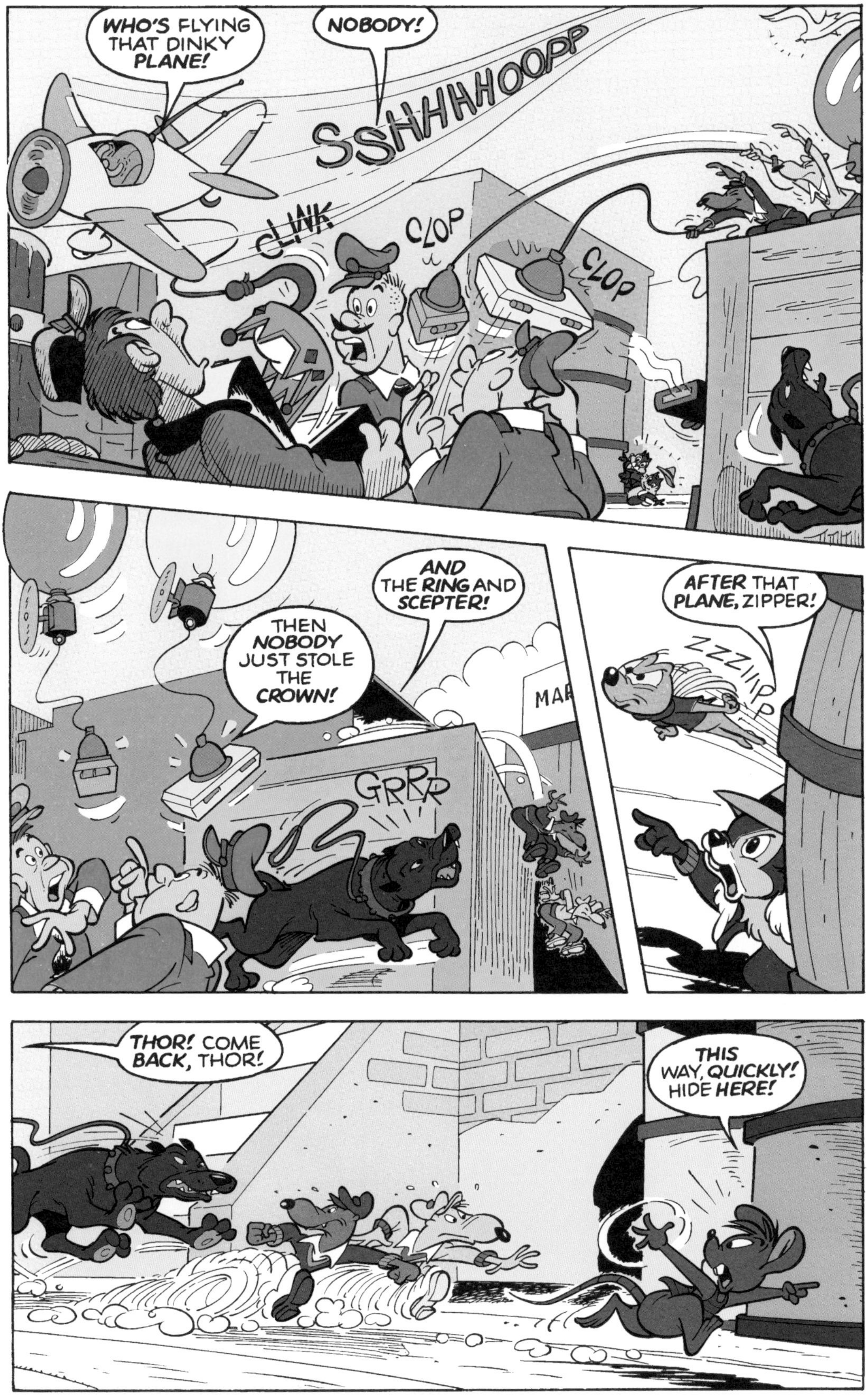
WHO'S FLYING THAT DINKY PLANE!
NOBODY!
SSHHHHOOPP
CLINK
CLOP
CLOP
AND THE RING AND SCEPTER!
THEN NOBODY JUST STOLE THE CROWN!
GRRR
AFTER THAT PLANE, ZIPPER!
ZZZIIIPP
THOR! COME BACK, THOR!
THIS WAY, QUICKLY! HIDE HERE!

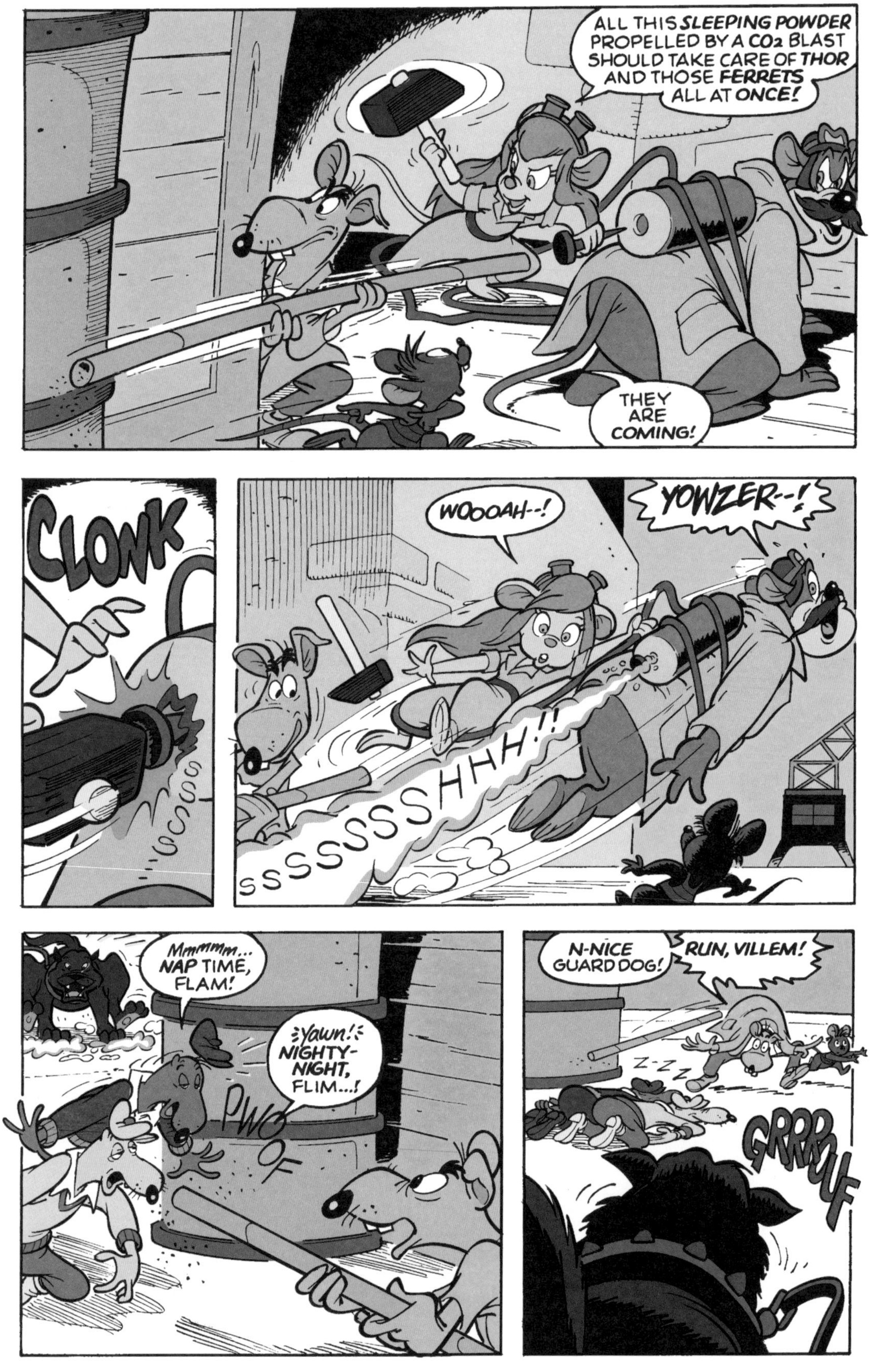
ALL THIS SLEEPING POWDER PROPELLED BY A CO2 BLAST SHOULD TAKE CARE OF THOR AND THOSE FERRETS ALL AT ONCE!
THEY ARE COMING!
CLONK
WOOOAH--!
YOWZER--!
SSSSSSSSHHHH!!
Mmmmm... NAP TIME, FLAM!
Yawn! NIGHTY-NIGHT, FLIM...!
PWOOF
N-NICE GUARD DOG!
RUN, VILLEM!
Z-Z-Z
GRRROUF

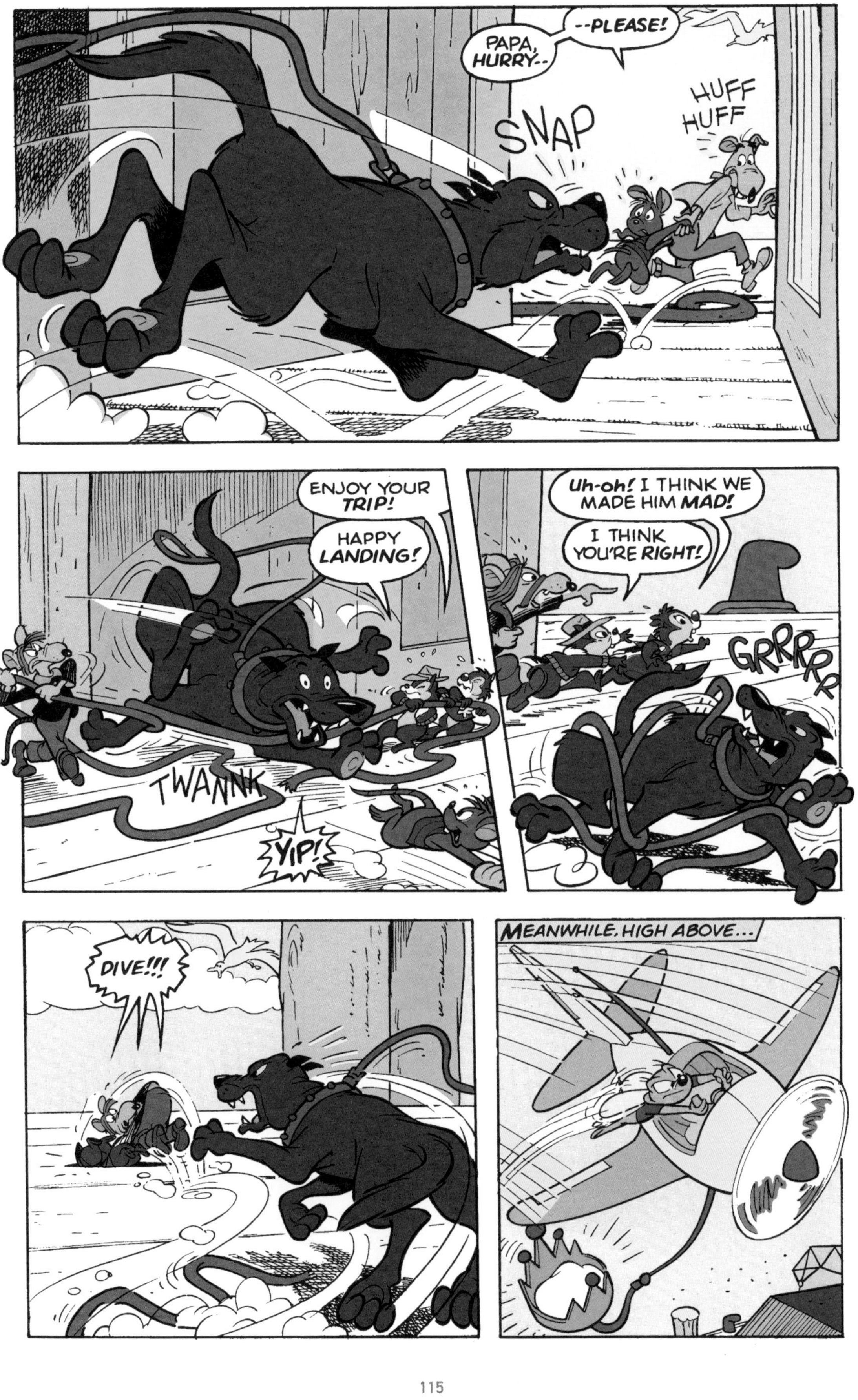
PAPA, HURRY--
--PLEASE!
HUFF HUFF
SNAP
ENJOY YOUR TRIP!
HAPPY LANDING!
TWANNK
YIP!
Uh-oh! I THINK WE MADE HIM MAD!
I THINK YOU'RE RIGHT!
GRRRRR
DIVE!!!
MEANWHILE, HIGH ABOVE...

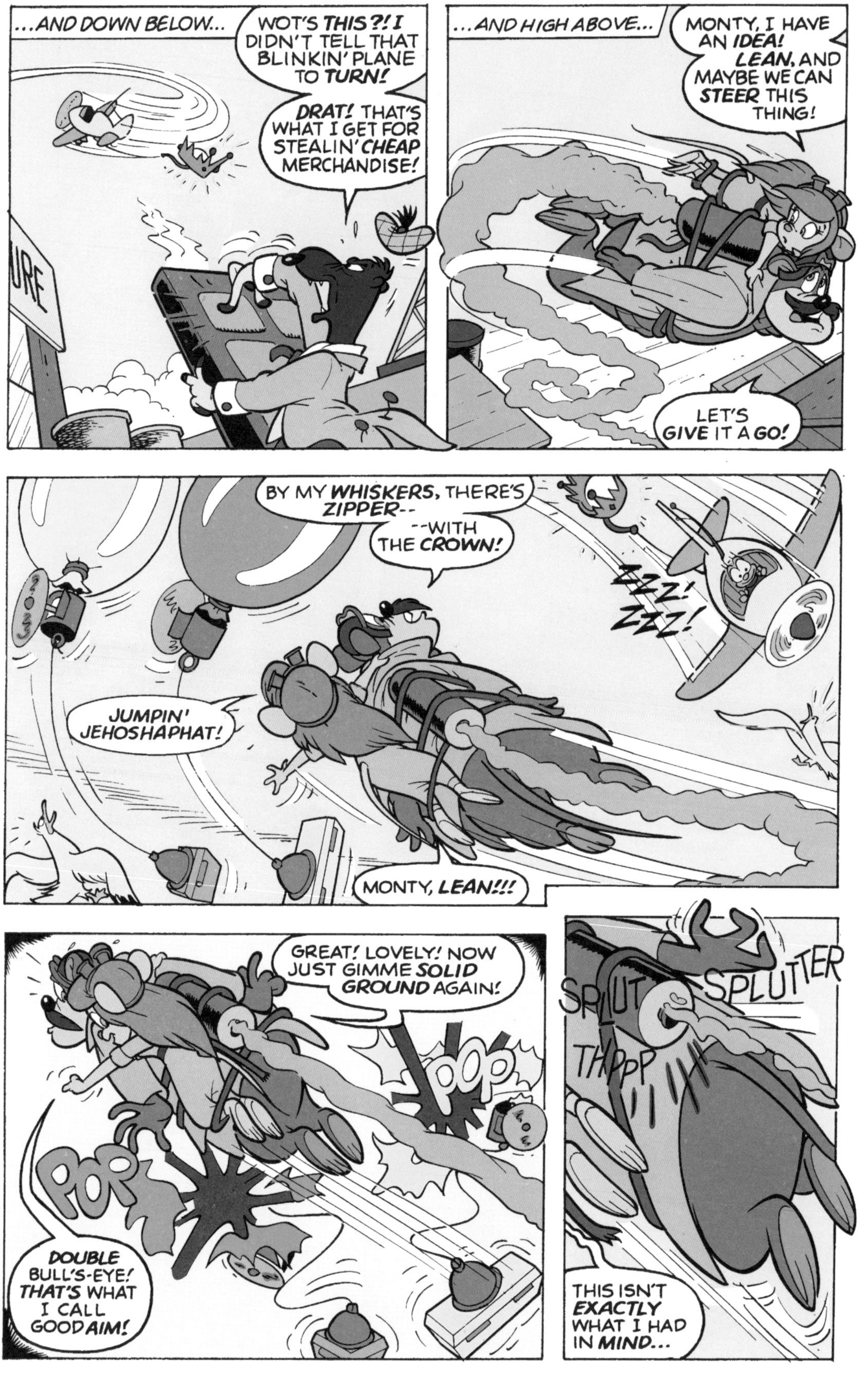

...AND DOWN BELOW...
WOT'S THIS?! I DIDN'T TELL THAT BLINKIN' PLANE TO TURN!
DRAT! THAT'S WHAT I GET FOR STEALIN' CHEAP MERCHANDISE!
...AND HIGH ABOVE...
MONTY, I HAVE AN IDEA! LEAN, AND MAYBE WE CAN STEER THIS THING!
LET'S GIVE IT A GO!
BY MY WHISKERS, THERE'S ZIPPER--
--WITH THE CROWN!
ZZZ! ZZZ!
JUMPIN' JEHOSHAPHAT!
MONTY, LEAN!!!
GREAT! LOVELY! NOW JUST GIMME SOLID GROUND AGAIN!
POP
POP
DOUBLE BULL'S-EYE! THAT'S WHAT I CALL GOOD AIM!
SPLUT
SPLUTTER
THPPP
THIS ISN'T EXACTLY WHAT I HAD IN MIND...

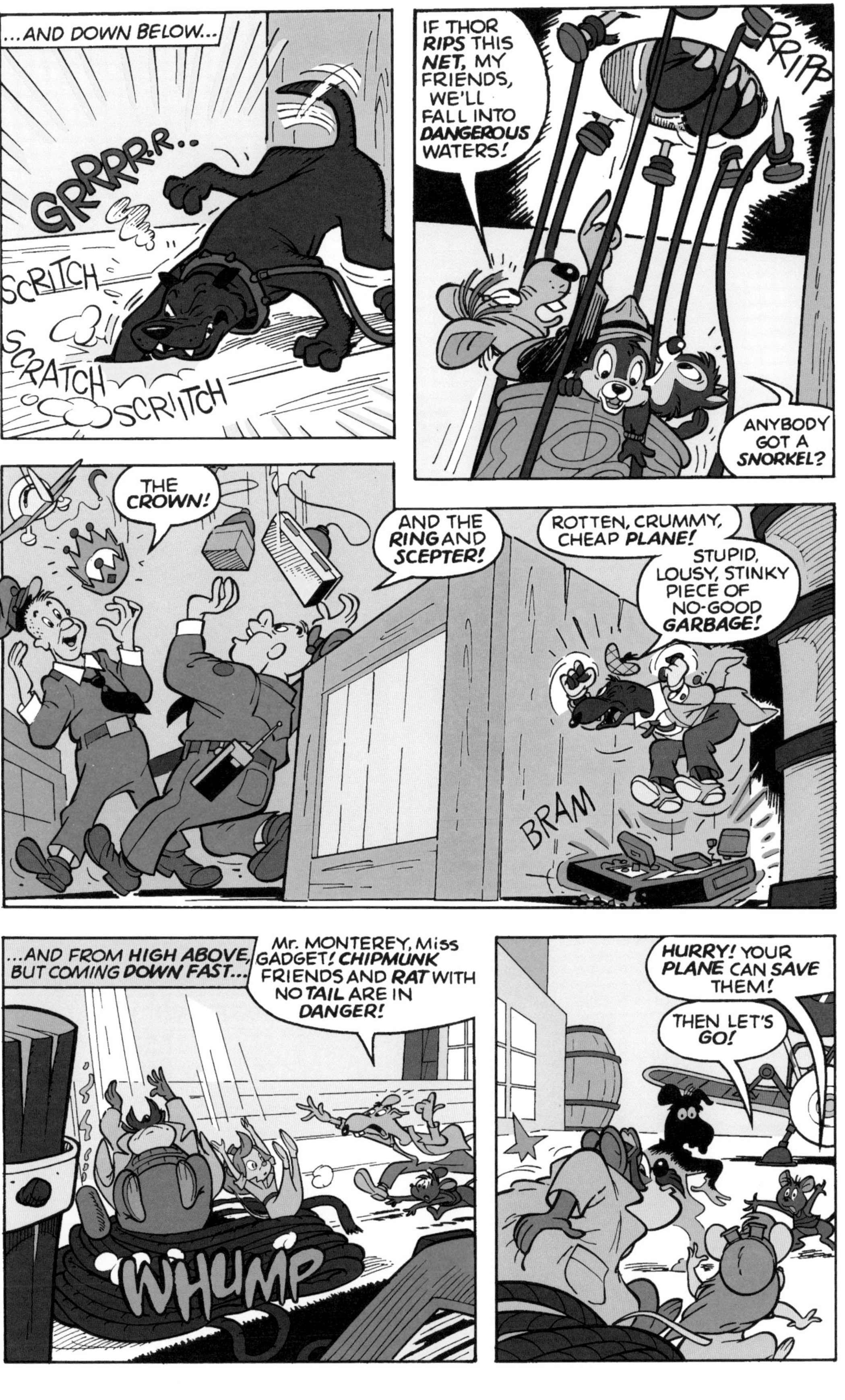
...AND DOWN BELOW...
GRRRR-R..
SCRITCH
SCRATCH
SCRITCH
IF THOR RIPS THIS NET, MY FRIENDS, WE'LL FALL INTO DANGEROUS WATERS!
RRIPP
ANYBODY GOT A SNORKEL?
THE CROWN!
AND THE RING AND SCEPTER!
ROTTEN, CRUMMY, CHEAP PLANE!
STUPID, LOUSY, STINKY PIECE OF NO-GOOD GARBAGE!
BRAM
...AND FROM HIGH ABOVE, BUT COMING DOWN FAST...
Mr. MONTEREY, Miss GADGET! CHIPMUNK FRIENDS AND RAT WITH NO TAIL ARE IN DANGER!
WHUMP
HURRY! YOUR PLANE CAN SAVE THEM!
THEN LET'S GO!

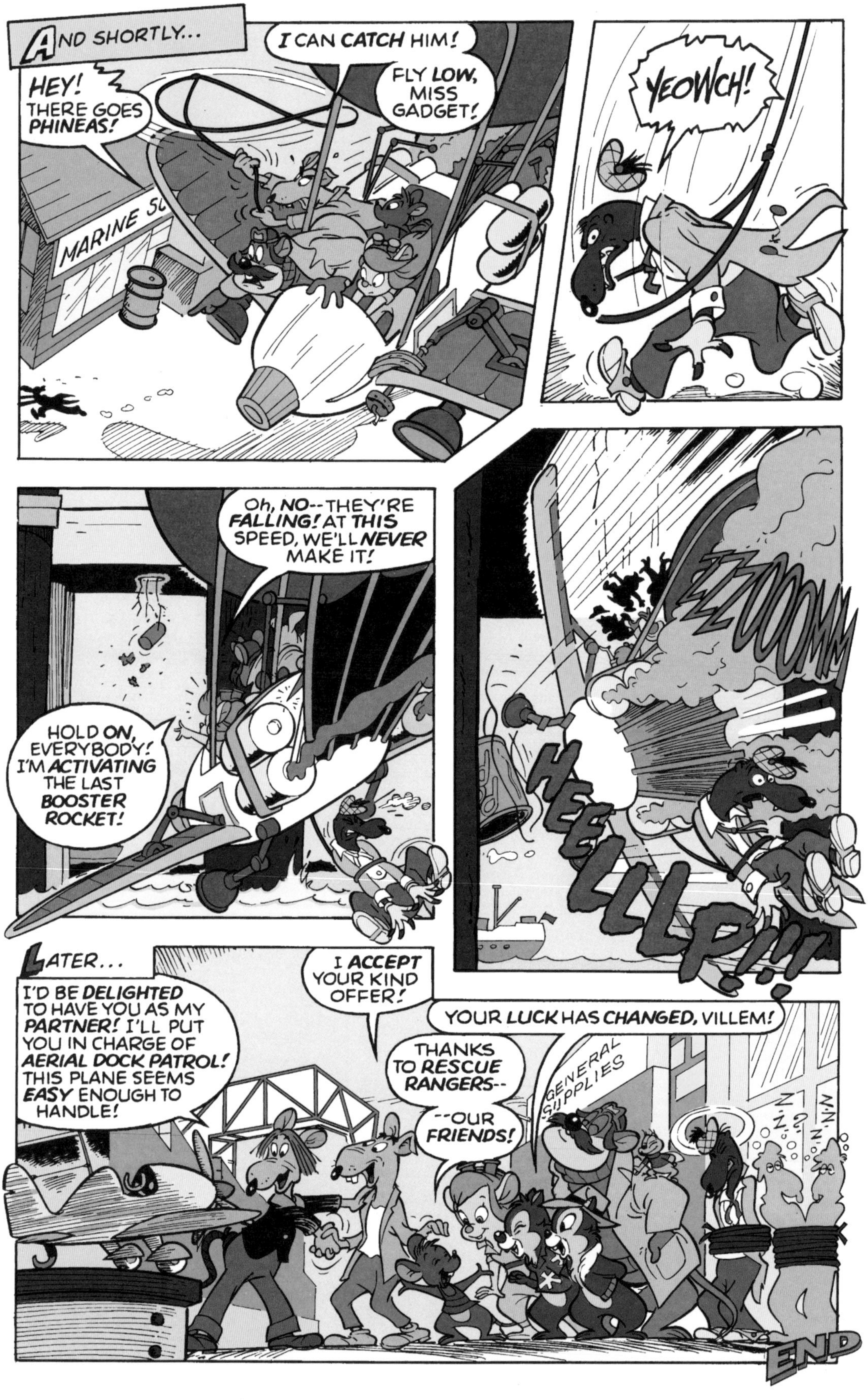
AND SHORTLY...
I CAN CATCH HIM!
HEY! THERE GOES PHINEAS!
FLY LOW, MISS GADGET!
MARINE S
YEOWCH!
Oh, NO--THEY'RE FALLING! AT THIS SPEED, WE'LL NEVER MAKE IT!
HOLD ON, EVERYBODY! I'M ACTIVATING THE LAST BOOSTER ROCKET!
ZZZOOOMM
HEEELLLP!!!
LATER...
I'D BE DELIGHTED TO HAVE YOU AS MY PARTNER! I'LL PUT YOU IN CHARGE OF AERIAL DOCK PATROL! THIS PLANE SEEMS EASY ENOUGH TO HANDLE!
I ACCEPT YOUR KIND OFFER!
YOUR LUCK HAS CHANGED, VILLEM!
THANKS TO RESCUE RANGERS--
--OUR FRIENDS!
GENERAL SUPPLIES
END

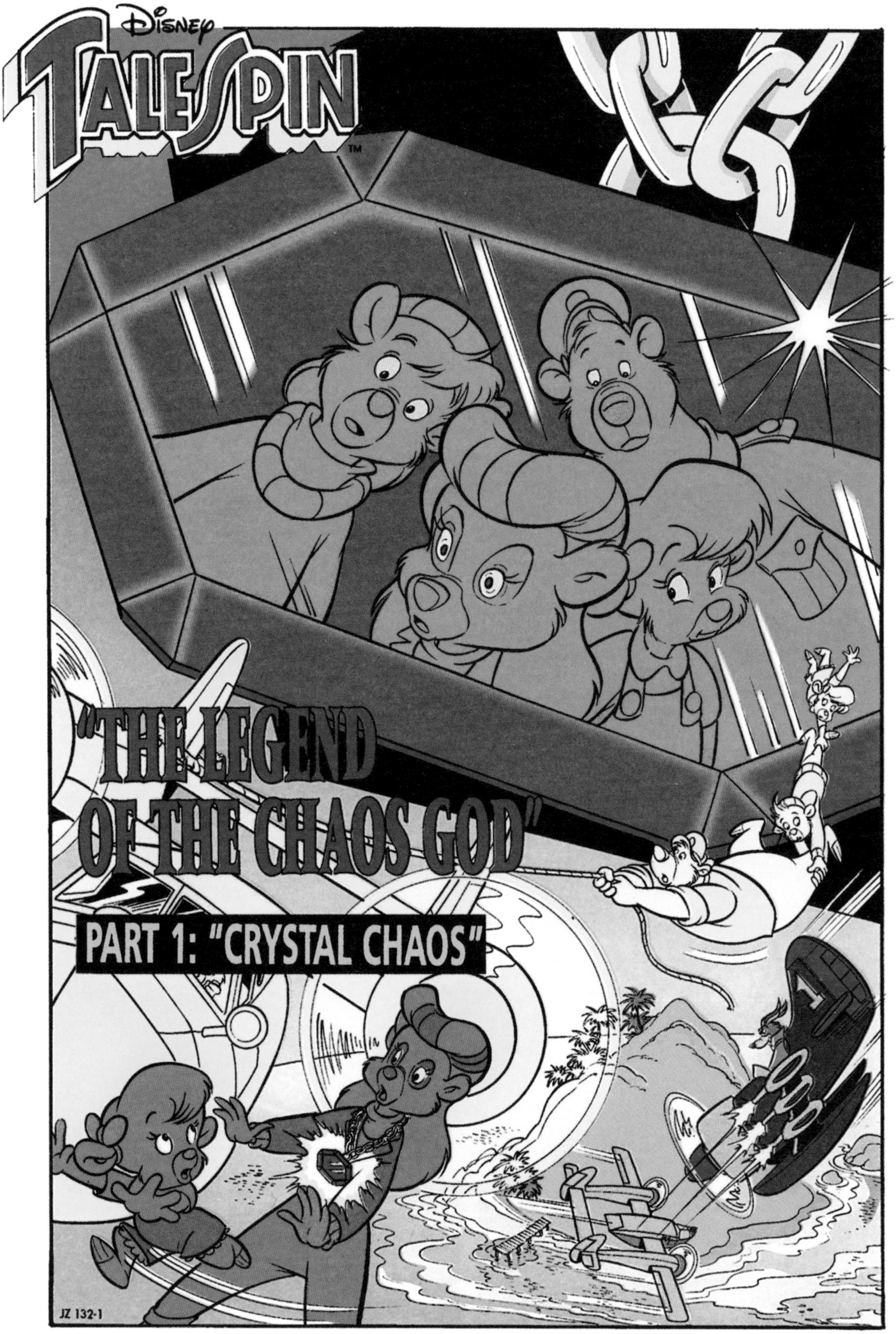
Disney
TaleSpin
"THE LEGEND OF THE CHAOS GOD"
PART 1: "CRYSTAL CHAOS"
JZ 132-1

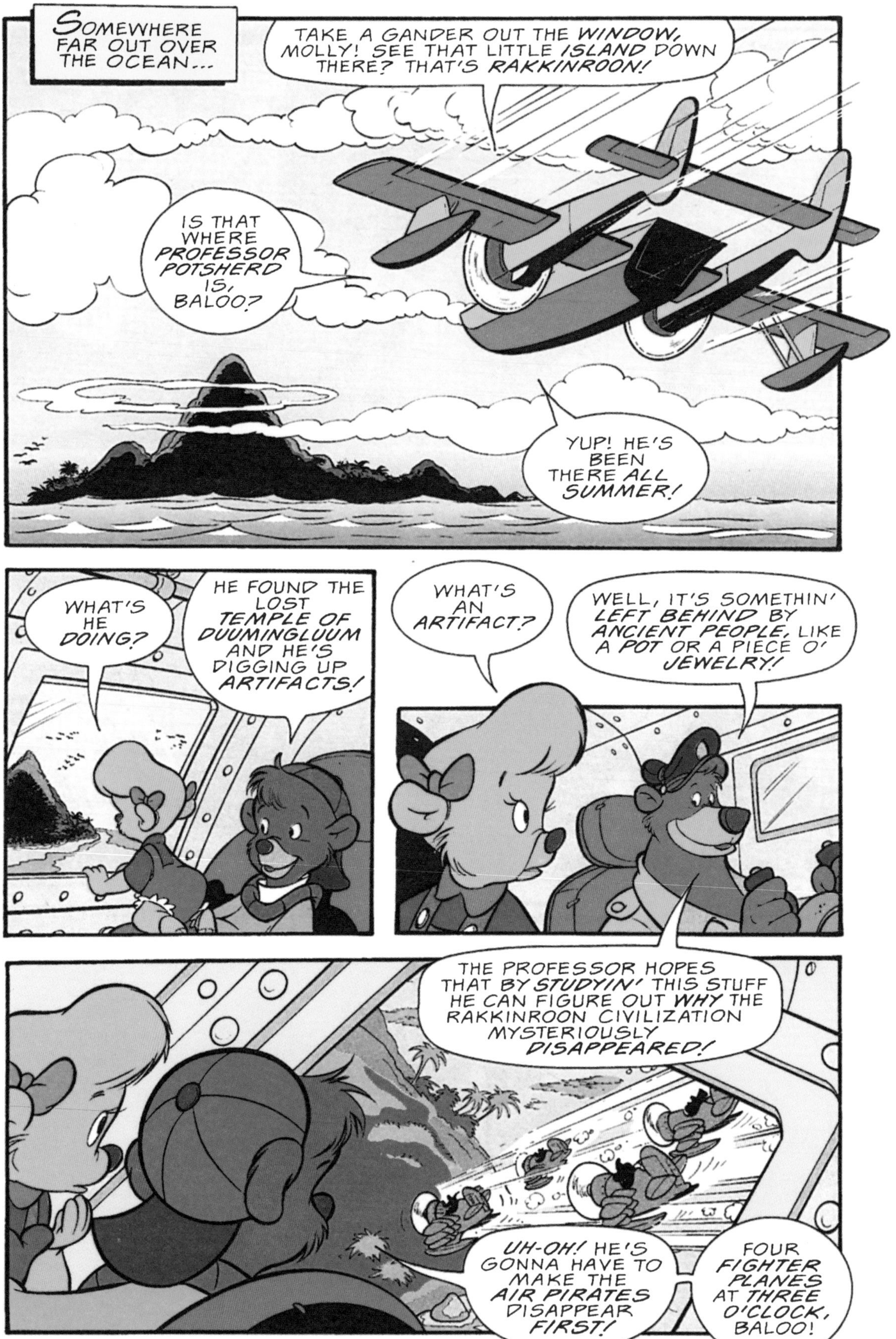
SOMEWHERE FAR OUT OVER THE OCEAN...
TAKE A GANDER OUT THE WINDOW, MOLLY! SEE THAT LITTLE ISLAND DOWN THERE? THAT'S RAKKINROON!
IS THAT WHERE PROFESSOR POTSHERD IS, BALOO?
YUP! HE'S BEEN THERE ALL SUMMER!
WHAT'S HE DOING?
HE FOUND THE LOST TEMPLE OF DUUMINGLUUM AND HE'S DIGGING UP ARTIFACTS!
WHAT'S AN ARTIFACT?
WELL, IT'S SOMETHIN' LEFT BEHIND BY ANCIENT PEOPLE, LIKE A POT OR A PIECE O' JEWELRY!
THE PROFESSOR HOPES THAT BY STUDYIN' THIS STUFF HE CAN FIGURE OUT WHY THE RAKKINROON CIVILIZATION MYSTERIOUSLY DISAPPEARED!
FOUR FIGHTER PLANES AT THREE O'CLOCK, BALOO!
UH-OH! HE'S GONNA HAVE TO MAKE THE AIR PIRATES DISAPPEAR FIRST!

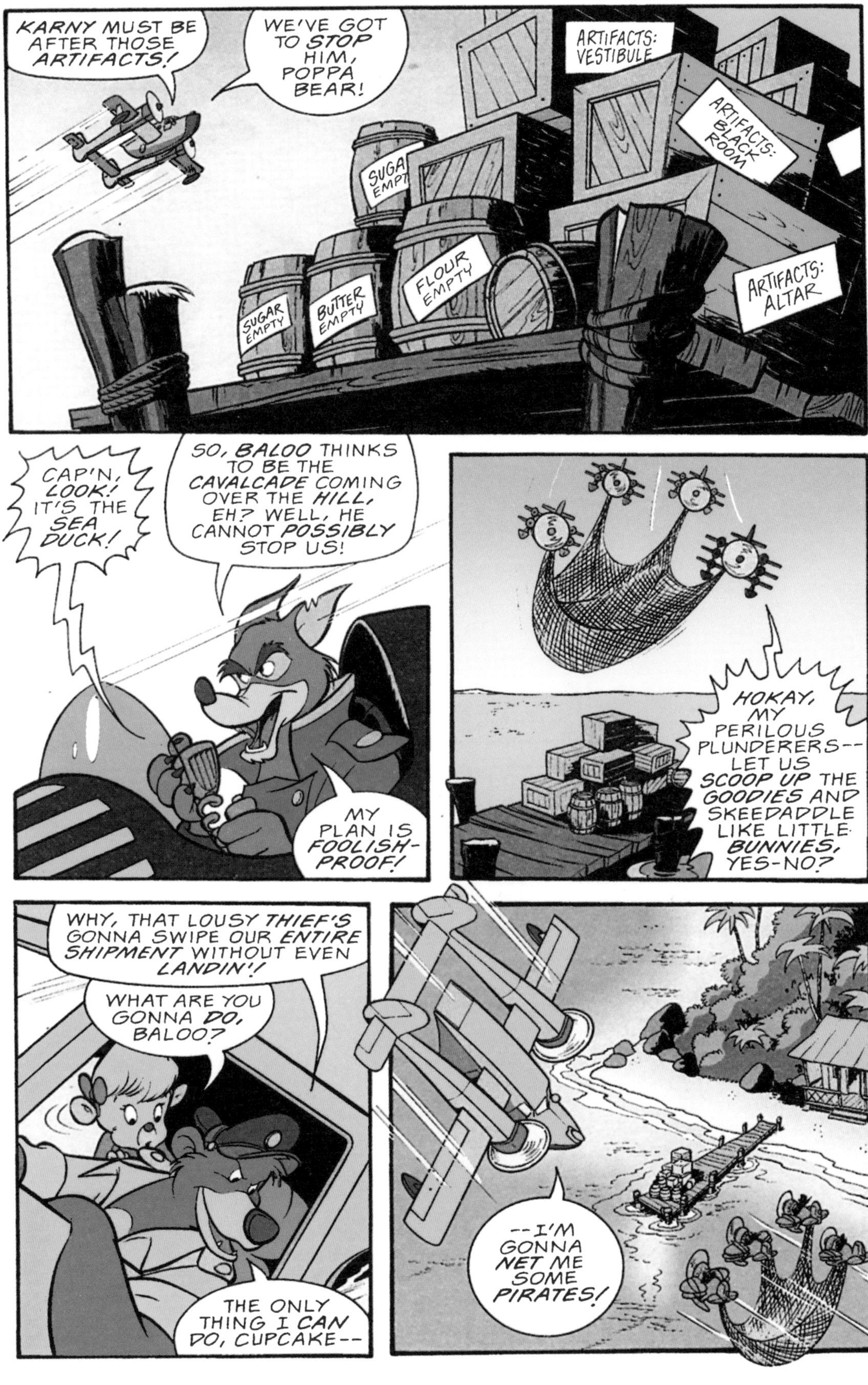
KARNY MUST BE AFTER THOSE ARTIFACTS!
WE'VE GOT TO STOP HIM, POPPA BEAR!
ARTIFACTS: VESTIBULE
ARTIFACTS: BLACK ROOM
SUGAR EMPTY
SUGAR EMPTY
BUTTER EMPTY
FLOUR EMPTY
ARTIFACTS: ALTAR
CAP'N, LOOK! IT'S THE SEA DUCK!
SO, BALOO THINKS TO BE THE CAVALCADE COMING OVER THE HILL, EH? WELL, HE CANNOT POSSIBLY STOP US!
MY PLAN IS FOOLISH-PROOF!
HOKAY, MY PERILOUS PLUNDERERS--LET US SCOOP UP THE GOODIES AND SKEEDADDLE LIKE LITTLE BUNNIES, YES-NO?
WHY, THAT LOUSY THIEF'S GONNA SWIPE OUR ENTIRE SHIPMENT WITHOUT EVEN LANDIN'!
WHAT ARE YOU GONNA DO, BALOO?
THE ONLY THING I CAN DO, CUPCAKE--
--I'M GONNA NET ME SOME PIRATES!

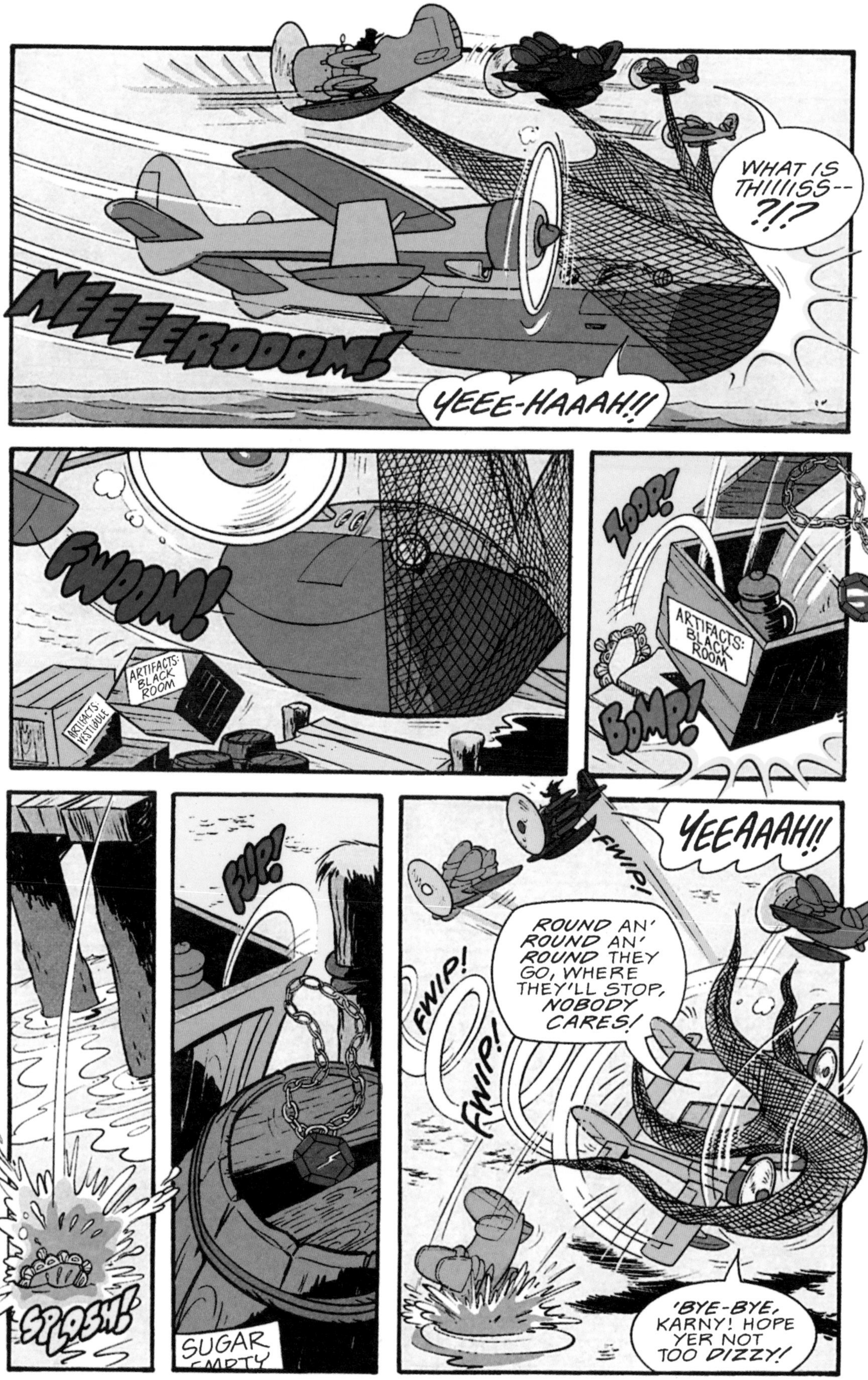
WHAT IS THIIIISS-- ?!?
NEEEEROOOM!
YEEE-HAAAH!!
FWOOM!
ARTIFACTS: BLACK ROOM
ARTIFACTS: VESTIBULE
ZOOP!
ARTIFACTS: BLACK ROOM
BOMP!
FLIP!
SPLOSH!
SUGAR
YEEAAAH!!
FWIP!
ROUND AN' ROUND AN' ROUND THEY GO, WHERE THEY'LL STOP, NOBODY CARES!
FWIP!
FWIP!
'BYE-BYE, KARNY! HOPE YER NOT TOO DIZZY!

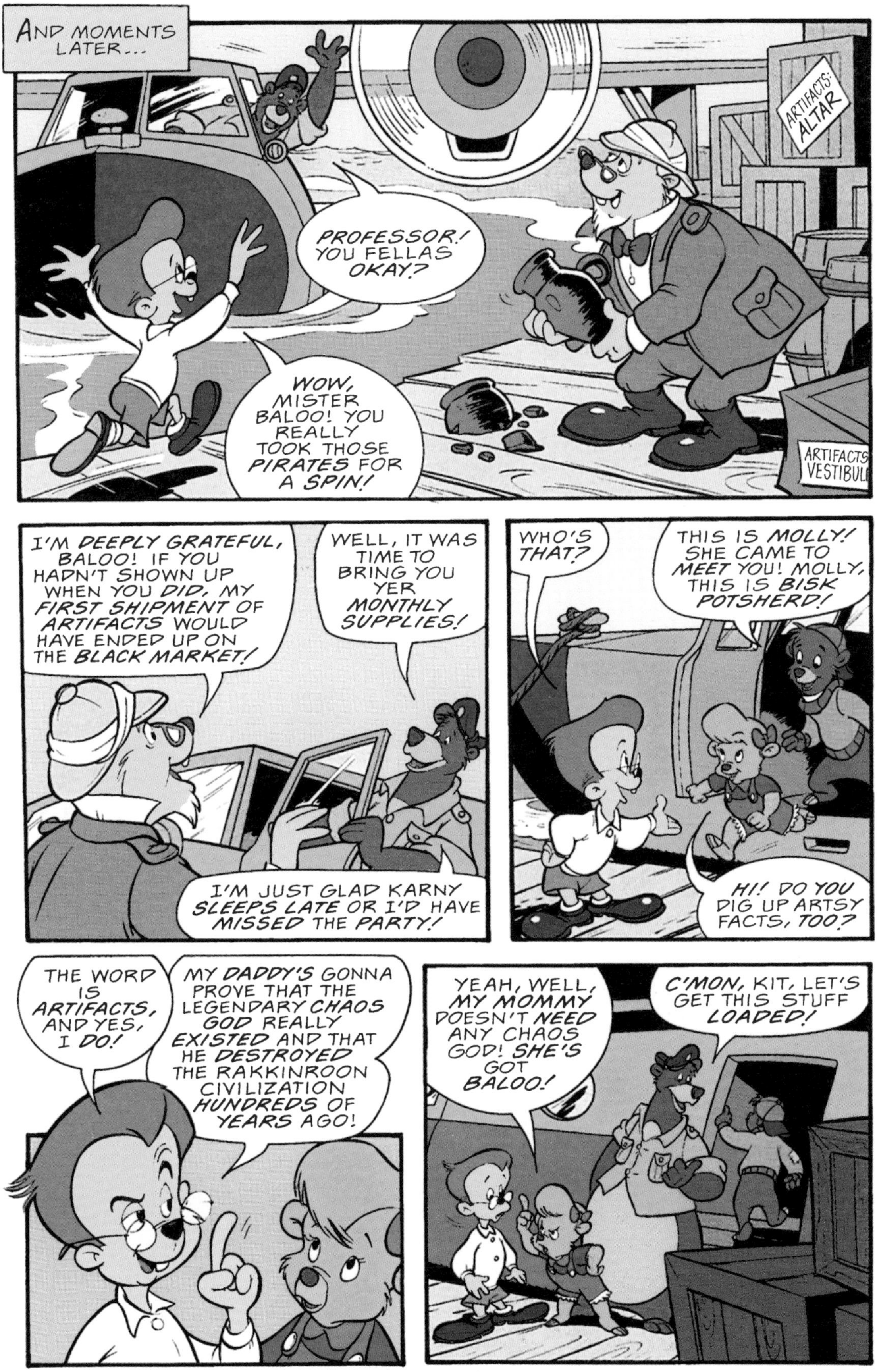

AND MOMENTS LATER...
ARTIFACTS: ALTAR
PROFESSOR! YOU FELLAS OKAY?
WOW, MISTER BALOO! YOU REALLY TOOK THOSE PIRATES FOR A SPIN!
ARTIFACTS VESTIBUL
I'M DEEPLY GRATEFUL, BALOO! IF YOU HADN'T SHOWN UP WHEN YOU DID, MY FIRST SHIPMENT OF ARTIFACTS WOULD HAVE ENDED UP ON THE BLACK MARKET!
WELL, IT WAS TIME TO BRING YOU YER MONTHLY SUPPLIES!
I'M JUST GLAD KARNY SLEEPS LATE OR I'D HAVE MISSED THE PARTY!
WHO'S THAT?
THIS IS MOLLY! SHE CAME TO MEET YOU! MOLLY, THIS IS BISK POTSHERD!
HI! DO YOU DIG UP ARTSY FACTS, TOO?
THE WORD IS ARTIFACTS, AND YES, I DO!
MY DADDY'S GONNA PROVE THAT THE LEGENDARY CHAOS GOD REALLY EXISTED AND THAT HE DESTROYED THE RAKKINROON CIVILIZATION HUNDREDS OF YEARS AGO!
YEAH, WELL, MY MOMMY DOESN'T NEED ANY CHAOS GOD! SHE'S GOT BALOO!
C'MON, KIT, LET'S GET THIS STUFF LOADED!

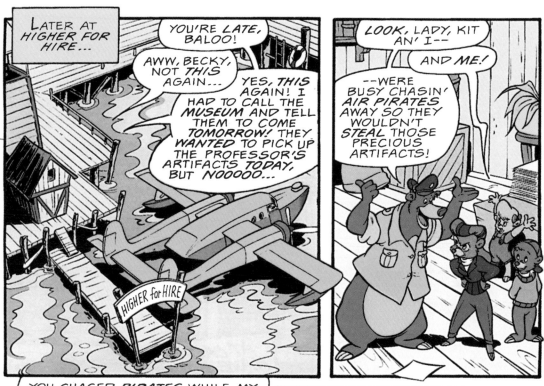

LATER AT *HIGHER FOR HIRE...*

YOU'RE *LATE*, BALOO!

AWW, BECKY, NOT *THIS* AGAIN...

YES, *THIS* AGAIN! I HAD TO CALL THE *MUSEUM* AND TELL THEM TO COME *TOMORROW!* THEY WANTED TO PICK UP THE *PROFESSOR'S* ARTIFACTS *TODAY,* BUT *NOOOOO...*

HIGHER for HIRE

LOOK, LADY, KIT AN' I--

AND *ME!*

--WERE BUSY CHASIN' *AIR PIRATES* AWAY SO THEY WOULDN'T *STEAL* THOSE *PRECIOUS* ARTIFACTS!

YOU CHASED *PIRATES* WHILE MY *DAUGHTER* WAS ON BOARD?!

AW, FER *CRYIN'* OUT LOUD...

MOMMY, *BALOO* SAVED *EVERYTHING* AND *I* DIDN'T GET *HURT!* DON'T BE MAD, *PLEASE?!*

OH, ALL RIGHT...

...IN THE NAME OF *ARCHAEOLOGY* I'LL LET IT *SLIDE.*

YOU KNOW, MOLLY, YOUR MOM'S *LUCKY* TO HAVE YOU *AROUND* ON DAYS LIKE THIS!

SO'S *BALOO!*

OKAY, DISASTER *AVERTED!* NOW EVERYBODY *SHOO!* I'VE GOT *WORK* TO DO!

NO *REST* FOR THE *WICKED,* EH?

NOT WITH *YOU* AROUND!

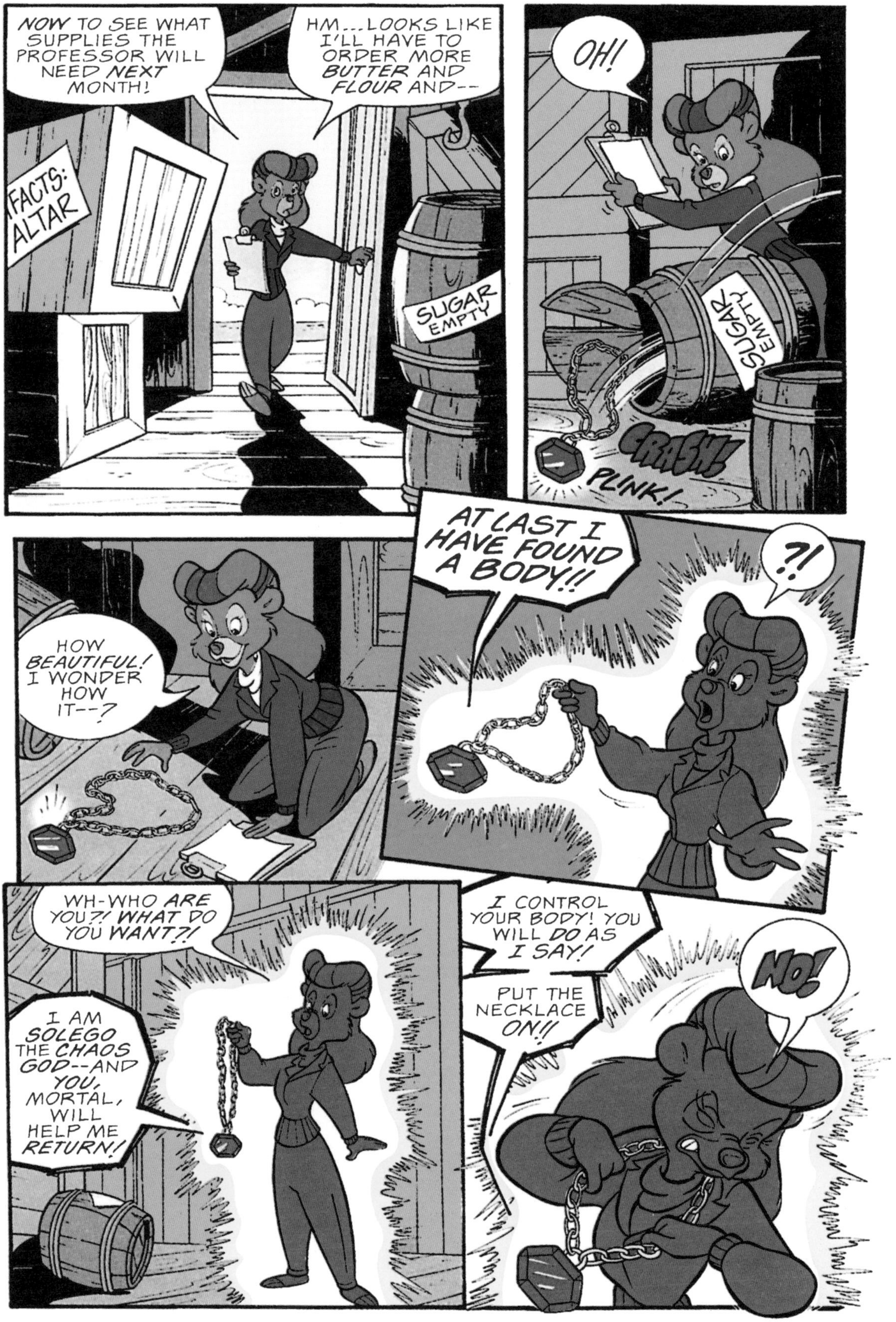
NOW TO SEE WHAT SUPPLIES THE PROFESSOR WILL NEED NEXT MONTH!
HM...LOOKS LIKE I'LL HAVE TO ORDER MORE BUTTER AND FLOUR AND--
FACTS: ALTAR
SUGAR EMPTY
OH!
SUGAR EMPTY
CRASH!
PLINK!
HOW BEAUTIFUL! I WONDER HOW IT--?
AT LAST I HAVE FOUND A BODY!!
?!
WH-WHO ARE YOU?! WHAT DO YOU WANT?!
I AM SOLEGO THE CHAOS GOD--AND YOU, MORTAL, WILL HELP ME RETURN!
I CONTROL YOUR BODY! YOU WILL DO AS I SAY!
PUT THE NECKLACE ON!!
NO!

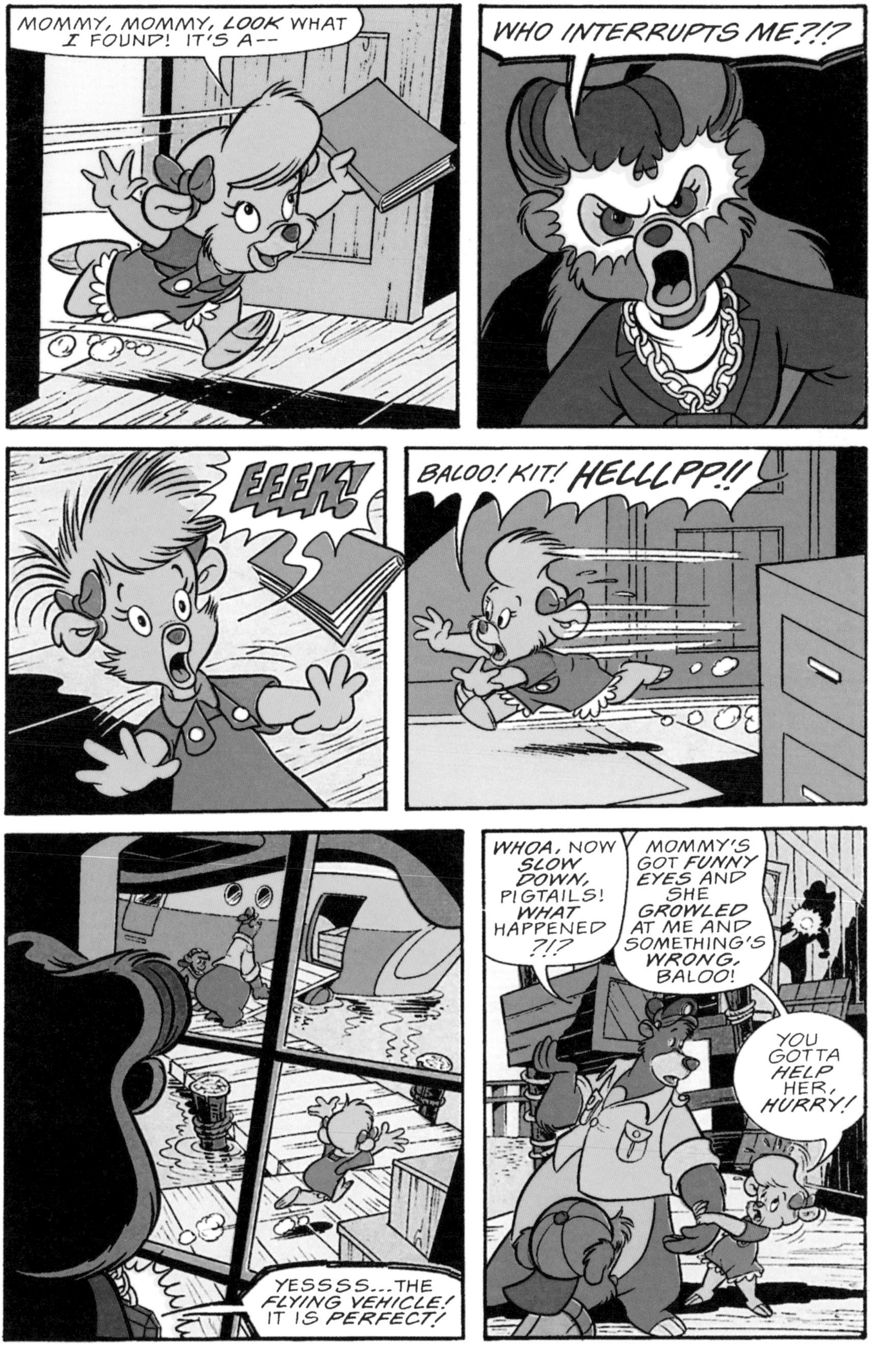
MOMMY, MOMMY, LOOK WHAT I FOUND! IT'S A--
WHO INTERRUPTS ME?!?
EEEK!
BALOO! KIT! HELLLPP!!
YESSSS...THE FLYING VEHICLE! IT IS PERFECT!
WHOA, NOW SLOW DOWN, PIGTAILS! WHAT HAPPENED ?!?
MOMMY'S GOT FUNNY EYES AND SHE GROWLED AT ME AND SOMETHING'S WRONG, BALOO!
YOU GOTTA HELP HER, HURRY!

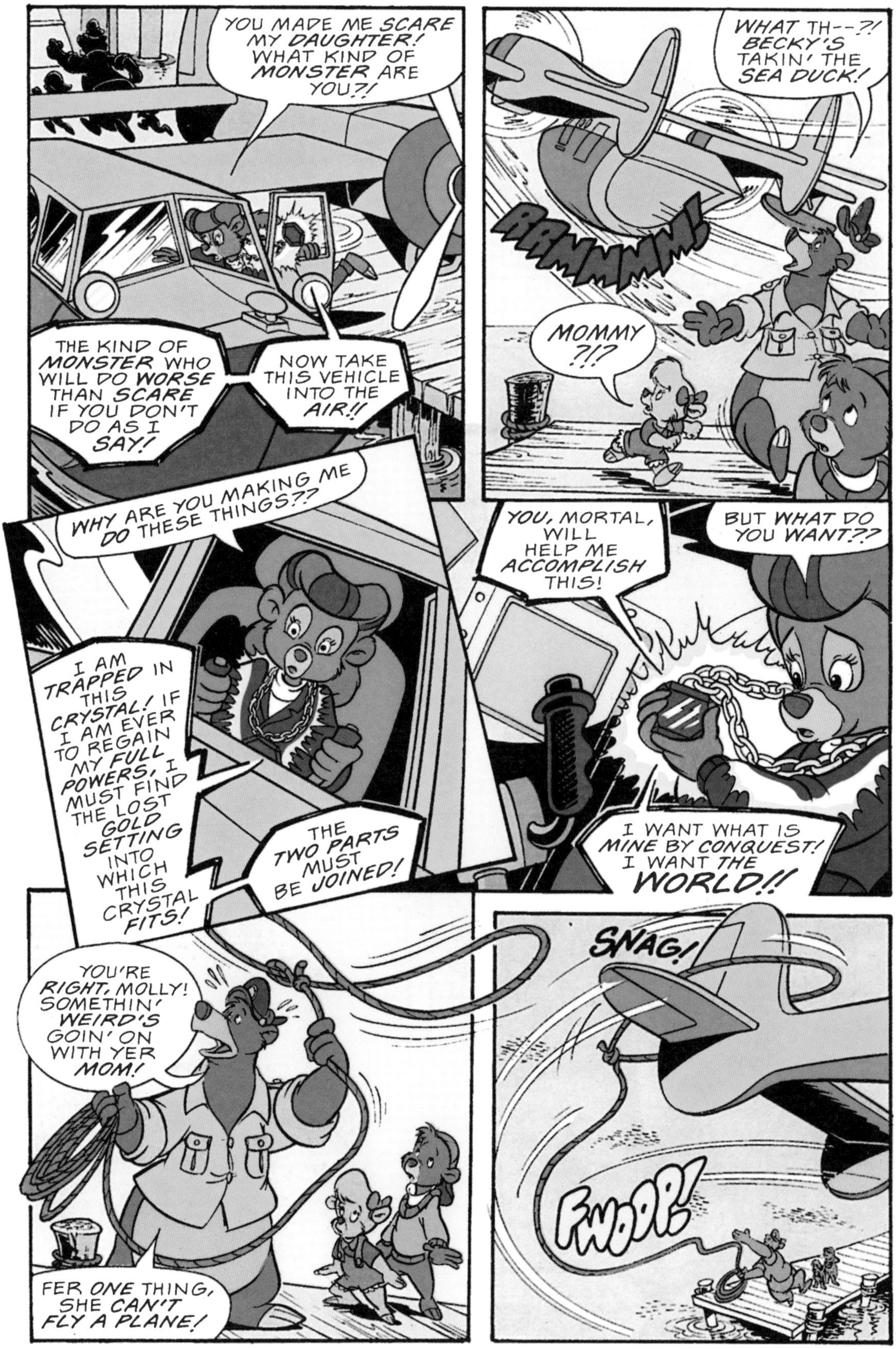
YOU MADE ME SCARE MY DAUGHTER! WHAT KIND OF MONSTER ARE YOU?!
THE KIND OF MONSTER WHO WILL DO WORSE THAN SCARE IF YOU DON'T DO AS I SAY!
NOW TAKE THIS VEHICLE INTO THE AIR!!
WHAT TH--?! BECKY'S TAKIN' THE SEA DUCK!
RRNMMMM!
MOMMY ?!?
WHY ARE YOU MAKING ME DO THESE THINGS??
I AM TRAPPED IN THIS CRYSTAL! IF I AM EVER TO REGAIN MY FULL POWERS, I MUST FIND THE LOST GOLD SETTING INTO WHICH THIS CRYSTAL FITS!
THE TWO PARTS MUST BE JOINED!
YOU, MORTAL, WILL HELP ME ACCOMPLISH THIS!
BUT WHAT DO YOU WANT??
I WANT WHAT IS MINE BY CONQUEST! I WANT THE WORLD!!
YOU'RE RIGHT, MOLLY! SOMETHIN' WEIRD'S GOIN' ON WITH YER MOM!
FER ONE THING, SHE CAN'T FLY A PLANE!
SNAG!
FWOOP!

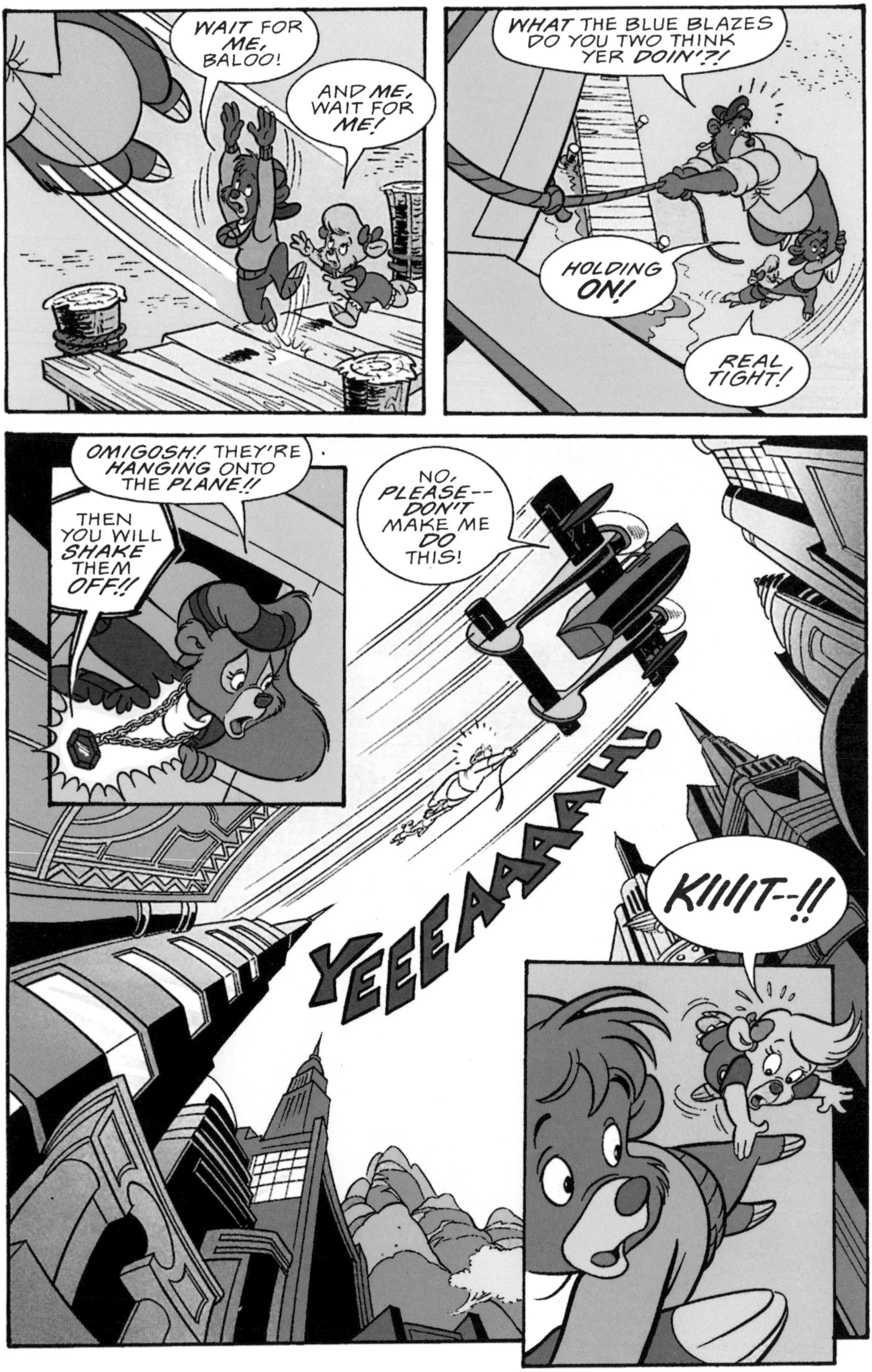
WAIT FOR ME, BALOO!
AND ME, WAIT FOR ME!
WHAT THE BLUE BLAZES DO YOU TWO THINK YER DOIN'?!
HOLDING ON!
REAL TIGHT!
OMIGOSH! THEY'RE HANGING ONTO THE PLANE!!
THEN YOU WILL SHAKE THEM OFF!!
NO, PLEASE-- DON'T MAKE ME DO THIS!
YEEEAAAAAH!
KIIIIT--!!

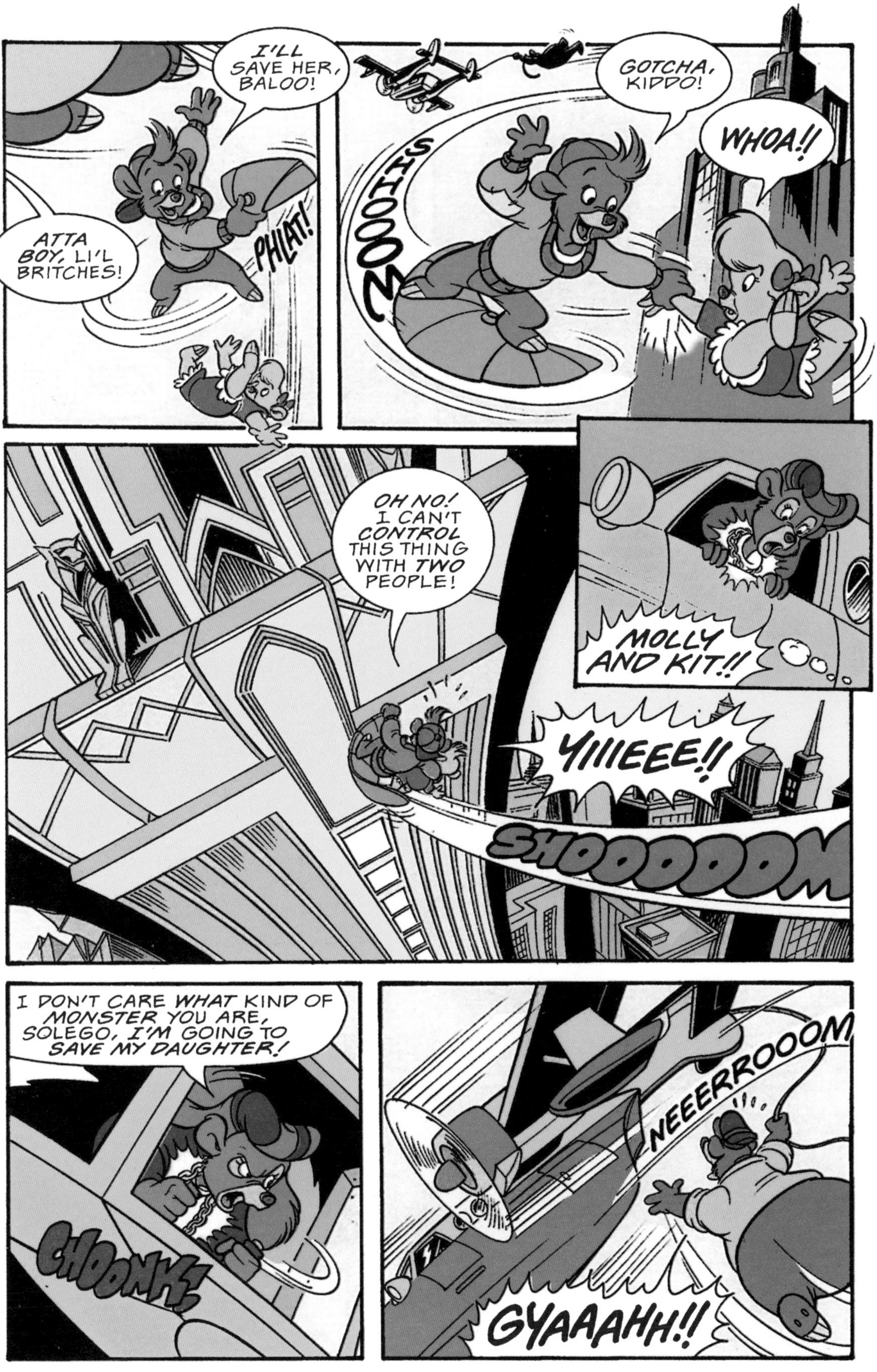
I'LL SAVE HER, BALOO!
ATTA BOY, LI'L BRITCHES!
PHLAT!
GOTCHA, KIDDO!
SHHOOOOM
WHOA!!
MOLLY AND KIT!!
OH NO! I CAN'T CONTROL THIS THING WITH TWO PEOPLE!
YIIIEEE!!
SHOOOOOOM
I DON'T CARE WHAT KIND OF MONSTER YOU ARE, SOLEGO, I'M GOING TO SAVE MY DAUGHTER!
CHOONK!
NEEERROOOM
GYAAAHH!!

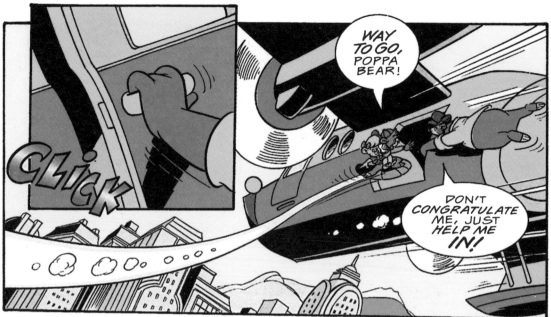

WAY TO GO, POPPA BEAR!

DON'T CONGRATULATE ME, JUST HELP ME IN!

HOO-WEEE, THAT WAS CLOSE! NOW LET'S FIND OUT WHAT'S GOIN' ON WITH BECKY!

THERE IS NO BECKY!

I AM SOLEGO, THE CHAOS GOD!!

NO ≥GASP!≤ I AM REBECCA CUNNINGHAM ≥GASP!≤ AND I WANT MY LIFE BACK, YOU BEAST!

IT'S THAT NECKLACE, BALOO!

MOLLY, DON'T TOUCH IT!

BISK TOLD ME ALL ABOUT YOU, YOU BAD MEANIE! GIVE ME MY MOMMY BACK!!

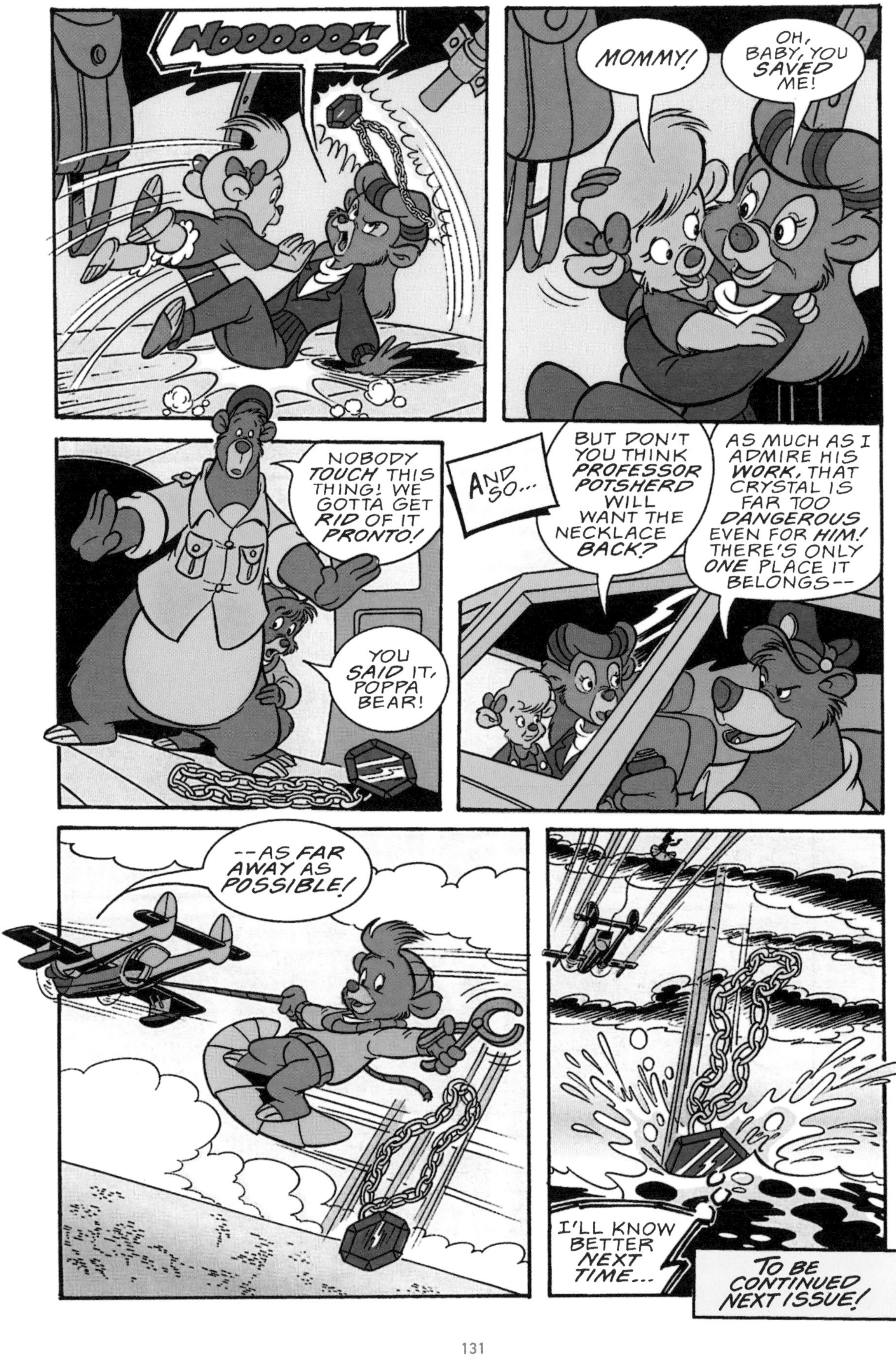
NOOOOO!!
MOMMY!
OH, BABY, YOU SAVED ME!
NOBODY TOUCH THIS THING! WE GOTTA GET RID OF IT PRONTO!
YOU SAID IT, POPPA BEAR!
AND SO...
BUT DON'T YOU THINK HIS PROFESSOR POTSHERD WILL WANT THE NECKLACE BACK?
AS MUCH AS I ADMIRE HIS WORK, THAT CRYSTAL IS FAR TOO DANGEROUS EVEN FOR HIM! THERE'S ONLY ONE PLACE IT BELONGS--
--AS FAR AWAY AS POSSIBLE!
I'LL KNOW BETTER NEXT TIME...
TO BE CONTINUED NEXT ISSUE!

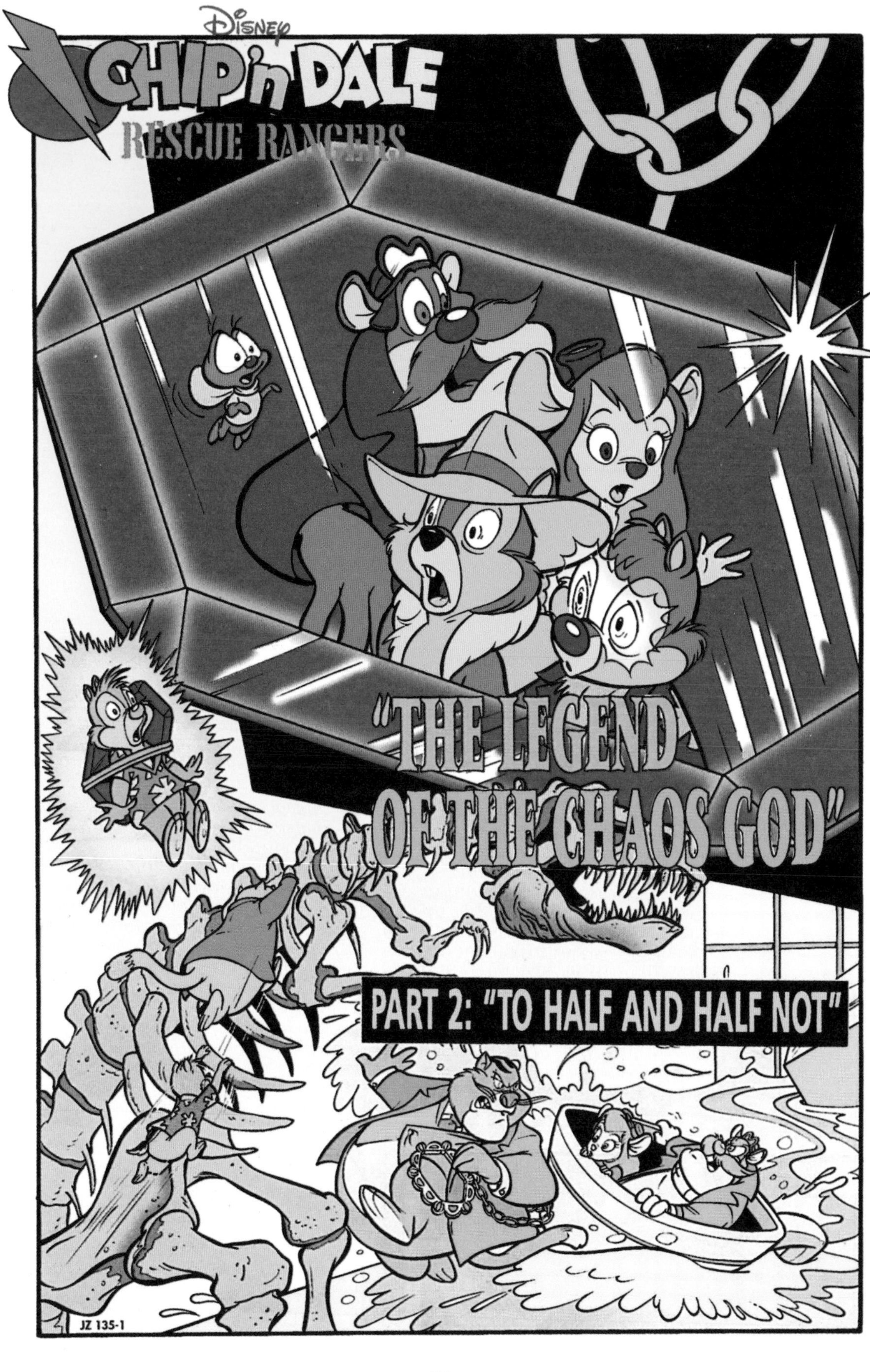
Disney
CHIP 'n DALE
RESCUE RANGERS
"THE LEGEND OF THE CHAOS GOD"
PART 2: "TO HALF AND HALF NOT"
JZ 135-1

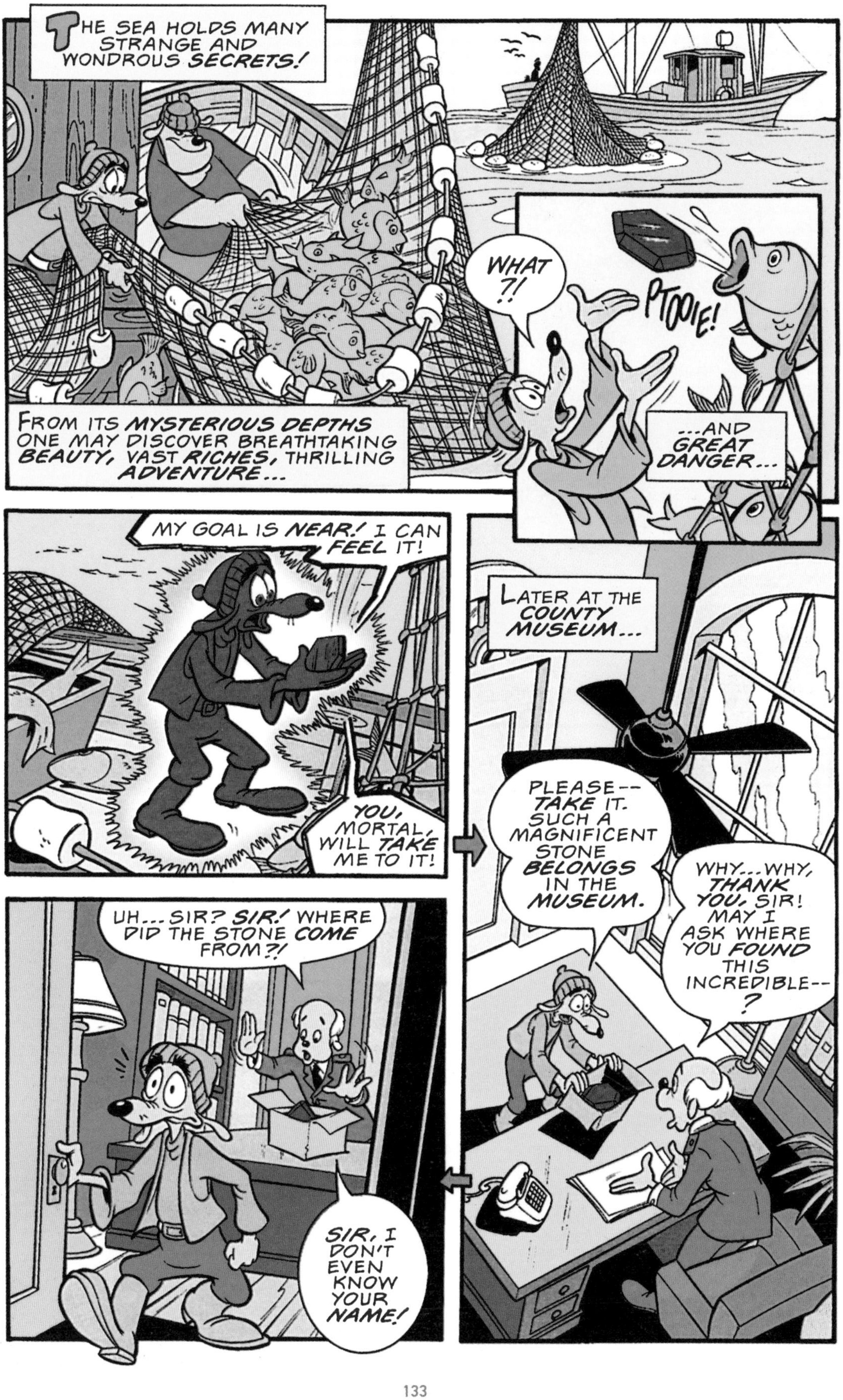
THE SEA HOLDS MANY STRANGE AND WONDROUS SECRETS!
FROM ITS MYSTERIOUS DEPTHS ONE MAY DISCOVER BREATHTAKING BEAUTY, VAST RICHES, THRILLING ADVENTURE...
WHAT ?!
PTOOIE!
...AND GREAT DANGER...
MY GOAL IS NEAR! I CAN FEEL IT!
YOU, MORTAL, WILL TAKE ME TO IT!
LATER AT THE COUNTY MUSEUM...
PLEASE-- TAKE IT. SUCH A MAGNIFICENT STONE BELONGS IN THE MUSEUM.
WHY...WHY, THANK YOU, SIR! MAY I ASK WHERE YOU FOUND THIS INCREDIBLE-- ?
UH...SIR? SIR! WHERE DID THE STONE COME FROM?!
SIR, I DON'T EVEN KNOW YOUR NAME!

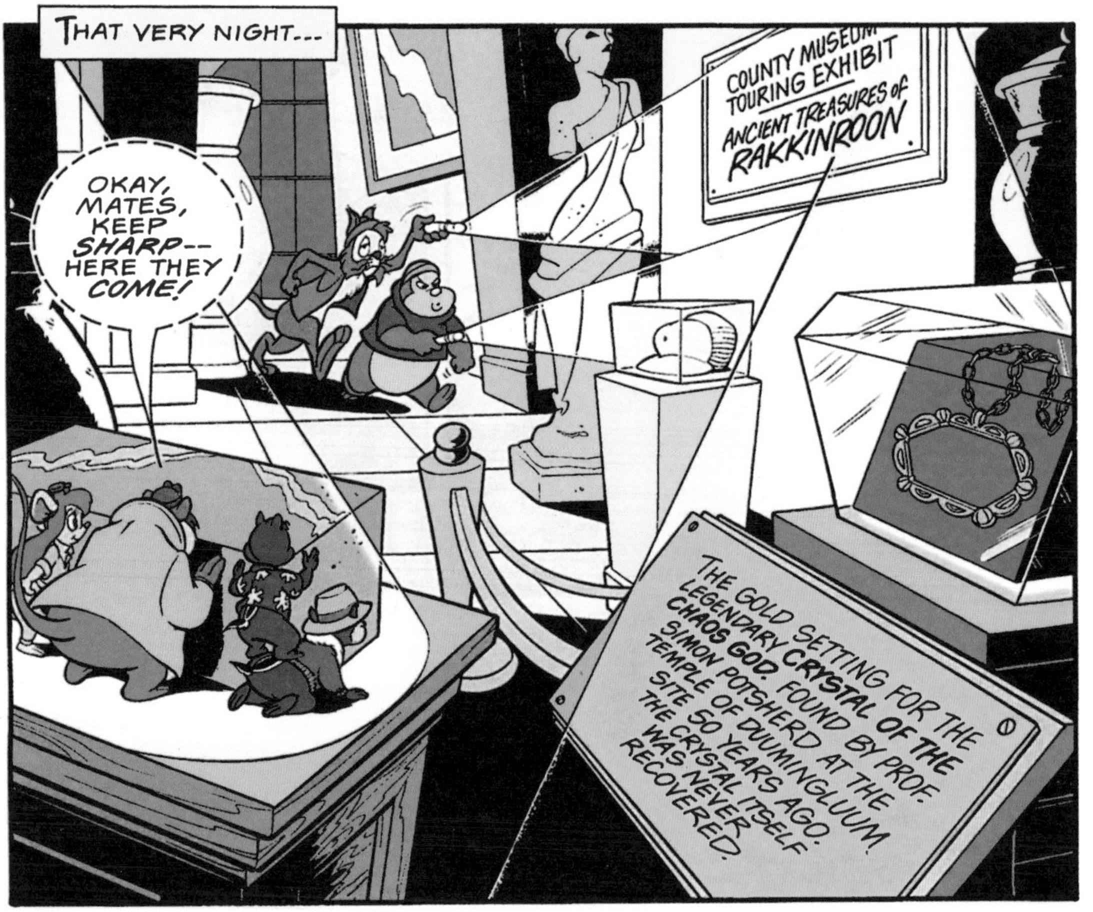
THAT VERY NIGHT...
COUNTY MUSEUM TOURING EXHIBIT
ANCIENT TREASURES OF RAKKINROON
OKAY, MATES, KEEP SHARP-- HERE THEY COME!
THE GOLD SETTING FOR THE LEGENDARY CRYSTAL OF THE CHAOS GOD. FOUND BY PROF. SIMON POTSHERD AT THE TEMPLE OF DUUMINGLUUM SITE 50 YEARS AGO. THE CRYSTAL ITSELF WAS NEVER RECOVERED.

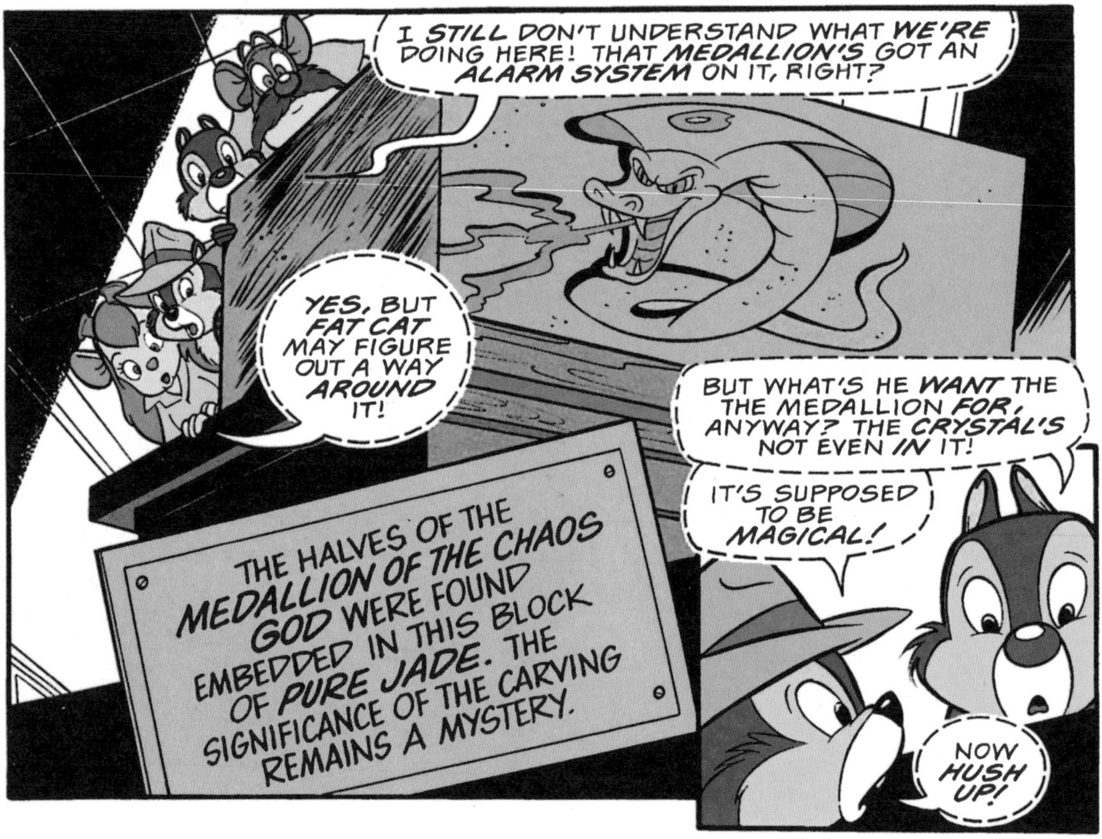
I STILL DON'T UNDERSTAND WHAT WE'RE DOING HERE! THAT MEDALLION'S GOT AN ALARM SYSTEM ON IT, RIGHT?
YES, BUT FAT CAT MAY FIGURE OUT A WAY AROUND IT!
BUT WHAT'S HE WANT THE THE MEDALLION FOR, ANYWAY? THE CRYSTAL'S NOT EVEN IN IT!
IT'S SUPPOSED TO BE MAGICAL!
THE HALVES OF THE MEDALLION OF THE CHAOS GOD WERE FOUND EMBEDDED IN THIS BLOCK OF PURE JADE. THE SIGNIFICANCE OF THE CARVING REMAINS A MYSTERY.
NOW HUSH UP!

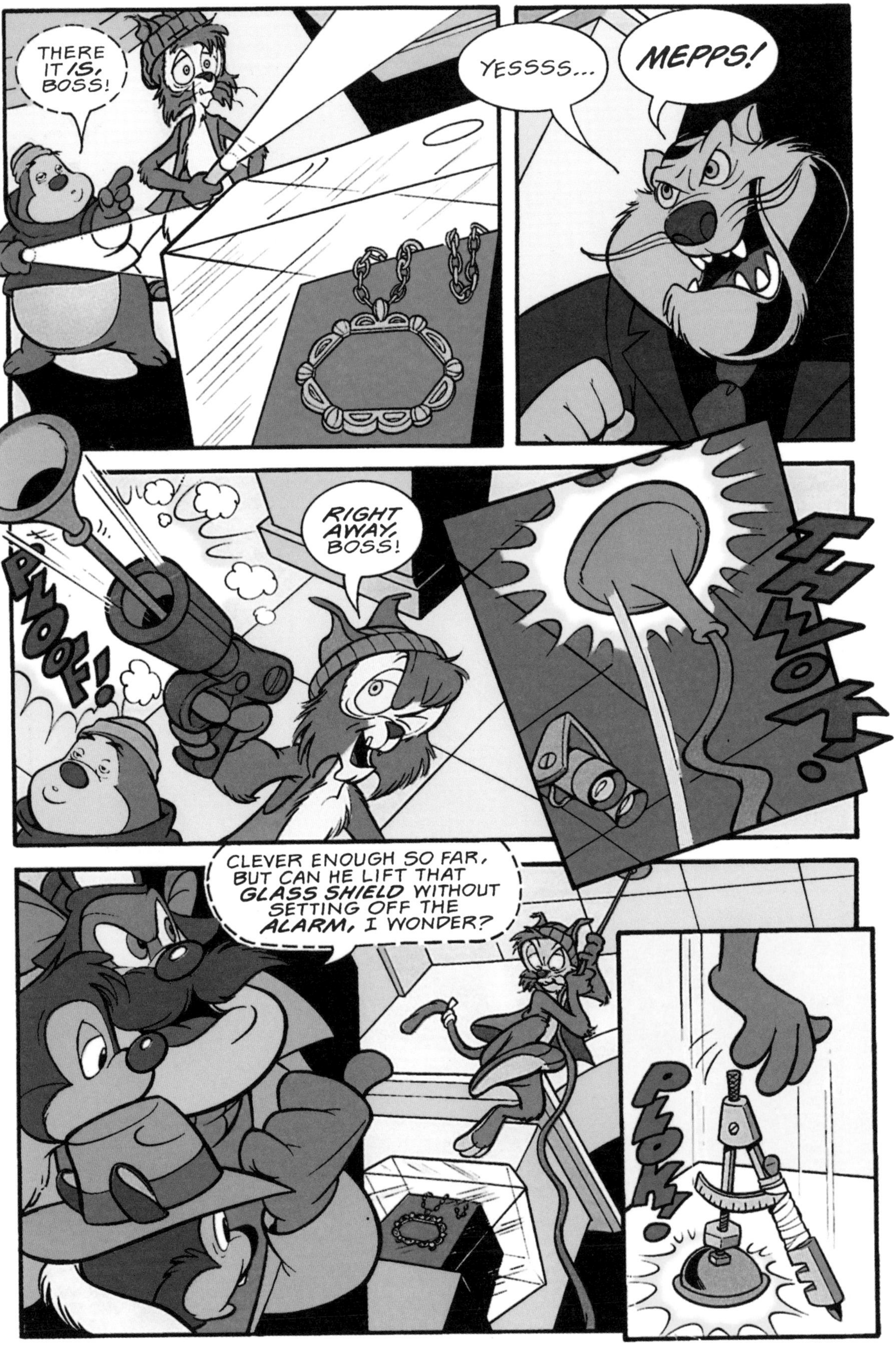
THERE IT IS, BOSS!
YESSSS...
MEPPS!
PWOOF!!
RIGHT AWAY, BOSS!
THWOK!
CLEVER ENOUGH SO FAR, BUT CAN HE LIFT THAT GLASS SHIELD WITHOUT SETTING OFF THE ALARM, I WONDER?
PLOK!

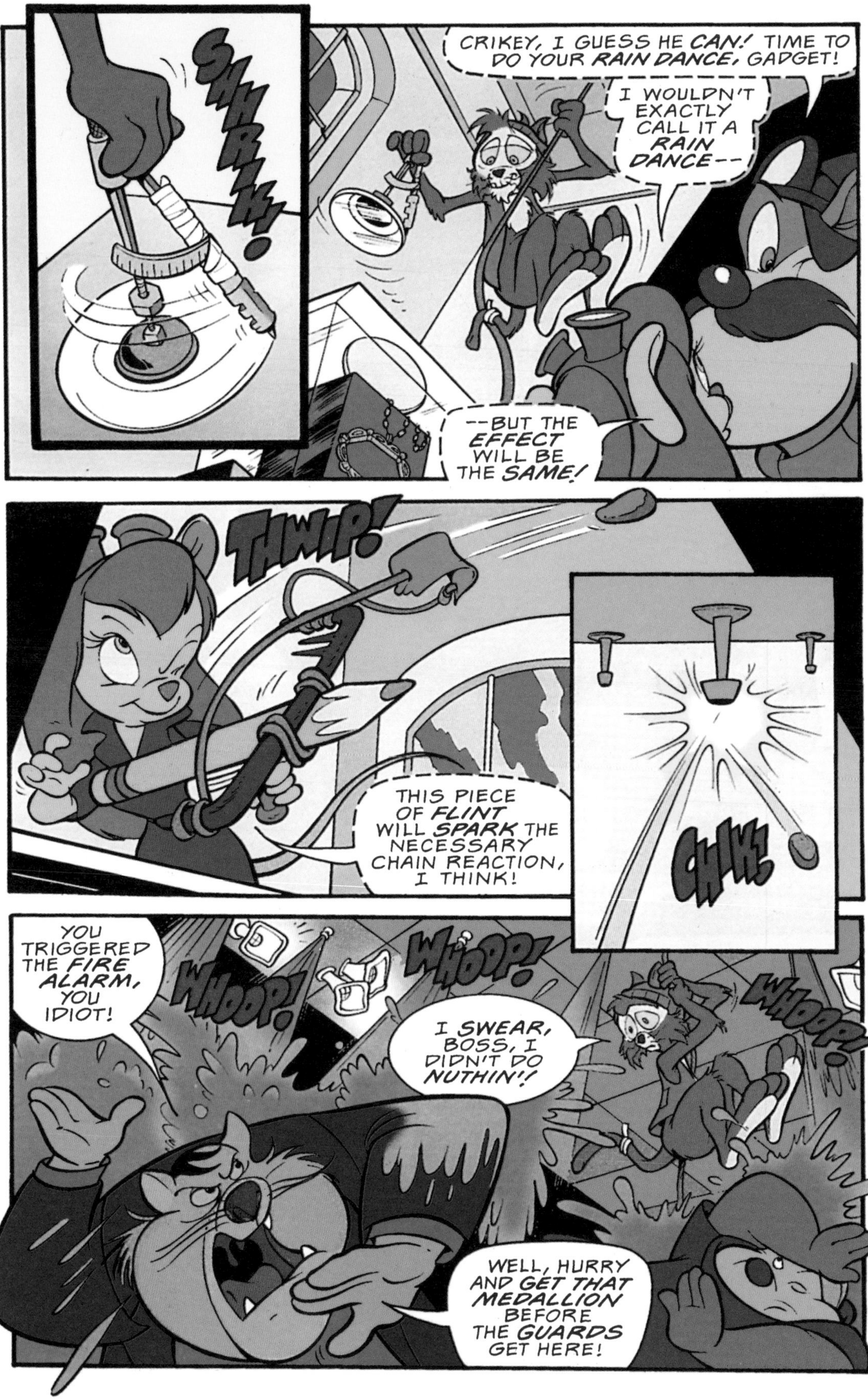
SHHRIKK!
CRIKEY, I GUESS HE CAN! TIME TO DO YOUR RAIN DANCE, GADGET!
I WOULDN'T EXACTLY CALL IT A RAIN DANCE--
--BUT THE EFFECT WILL BE THE SAME!
THWIP!
THIS PIECE OF FLINT WILL SPARK THE NECESSARY CHAIN REACTION, I THINK!
CHIK!
YOU TRIGGERED THE FIRE ALARM, YOU IDIOT!
WHOOP!
WHOOP!
WHOOP!
I SWEAR, BOSS, I DIDN'T DO NUTHIN'!
WELL, HURRY AND GET THAT MEDALLION BEFORE THE GUARDS GET HERE!

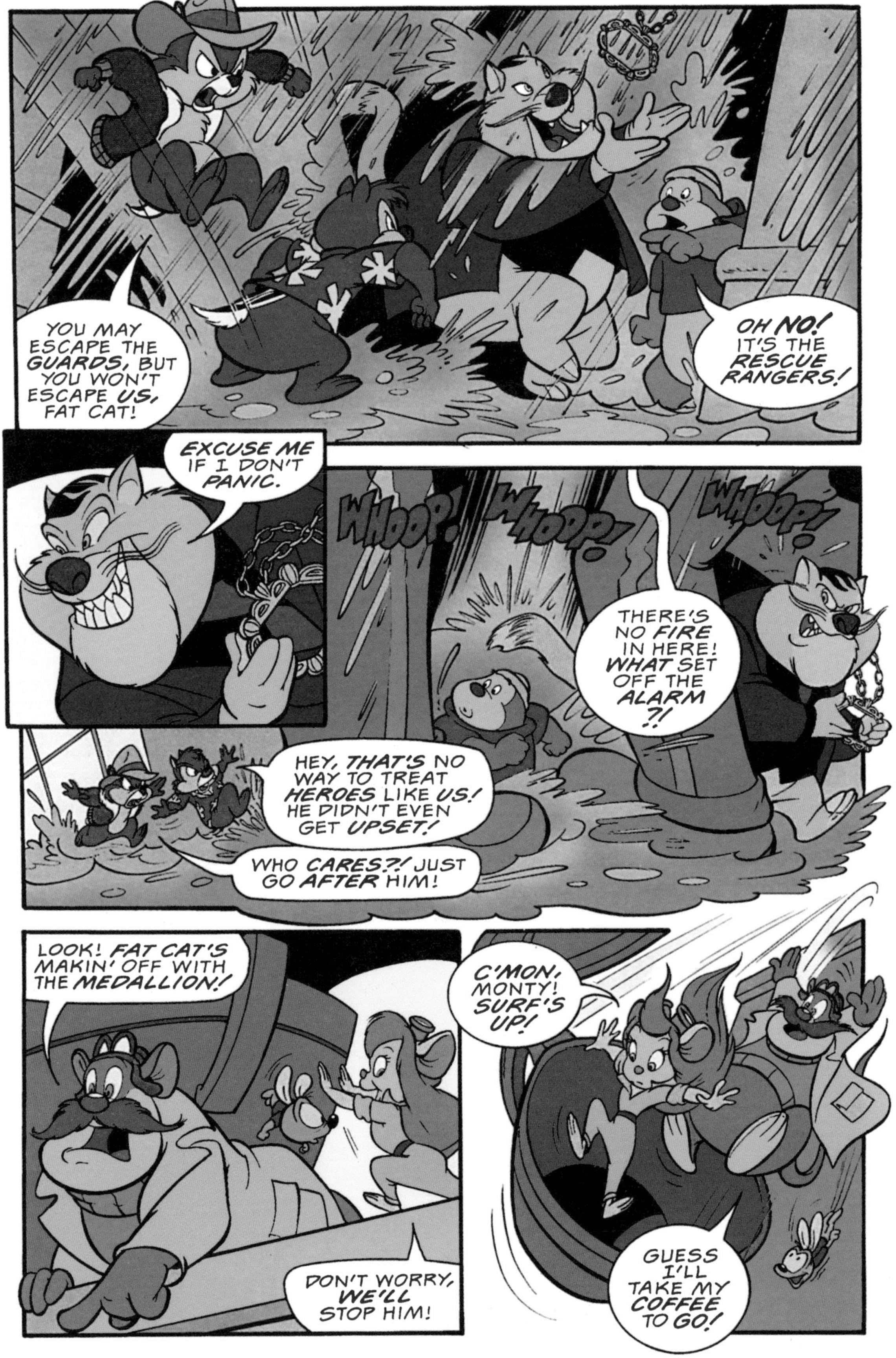
YOU MAY ESCAPE THE GUARDS, BUT YOU WON'T ESCAPE US, FAT CAT!
OH NO! IT'S THE RESCUE RANGERS!
EXCUSE ME IF I DON'T PANIC.
WHOOP! WHOOP! WHOOP!
THERE'S NO FIRE IN HERE! WHAT SET OFF THE ALARM ?!
HEY, THAT'S NO WAY TO TREAT HEROES LIKE US! HE DIDN'T EVEN GET UPSET!
WHO CARES?! JUST GO AFTER HIM!
LOOK! FAT CAT'S MAKIN' OFF WITH THE MEDALLION!
DON'T WORRY, WE'LL STOP HIM!
C'MON, MONTY! SURF'S UP!
GUESS I'LL TAKE MY COFFEE TO GO!

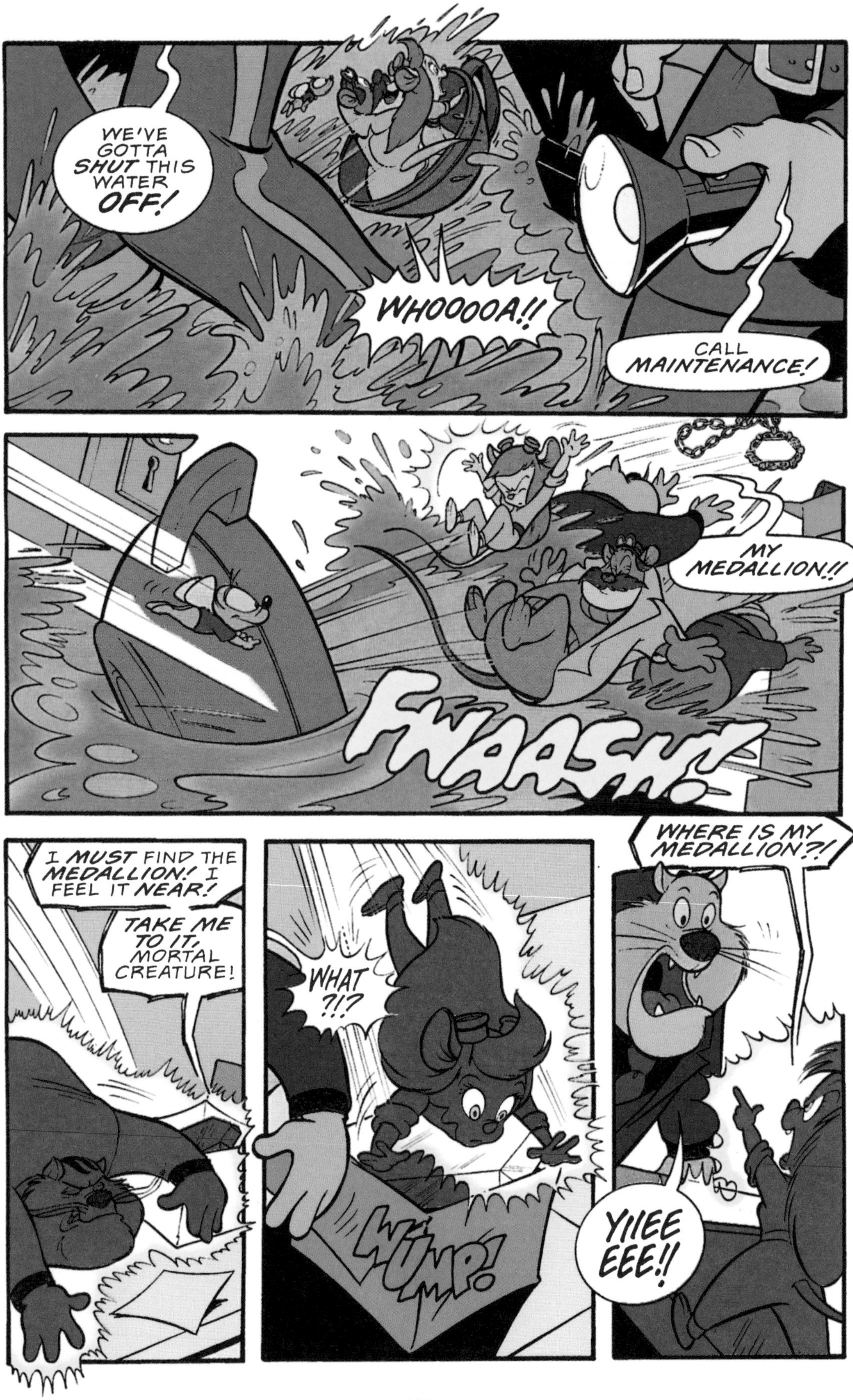

WE'VE GOTTA SHUT THIS WATER OFF!
WHOOOOA!!
CALL MAINTENANCE!
MY MEDALLION!!
FWAASH!
I MUST FIND THE MEDALLION! I FEEL IT NEAR!
TAKE ME TO IT, MORTAL CREATURE!
WHAT ?!?
WUMP!
WHERE IS MY MEDALLION?!
YIIEE EEE!!

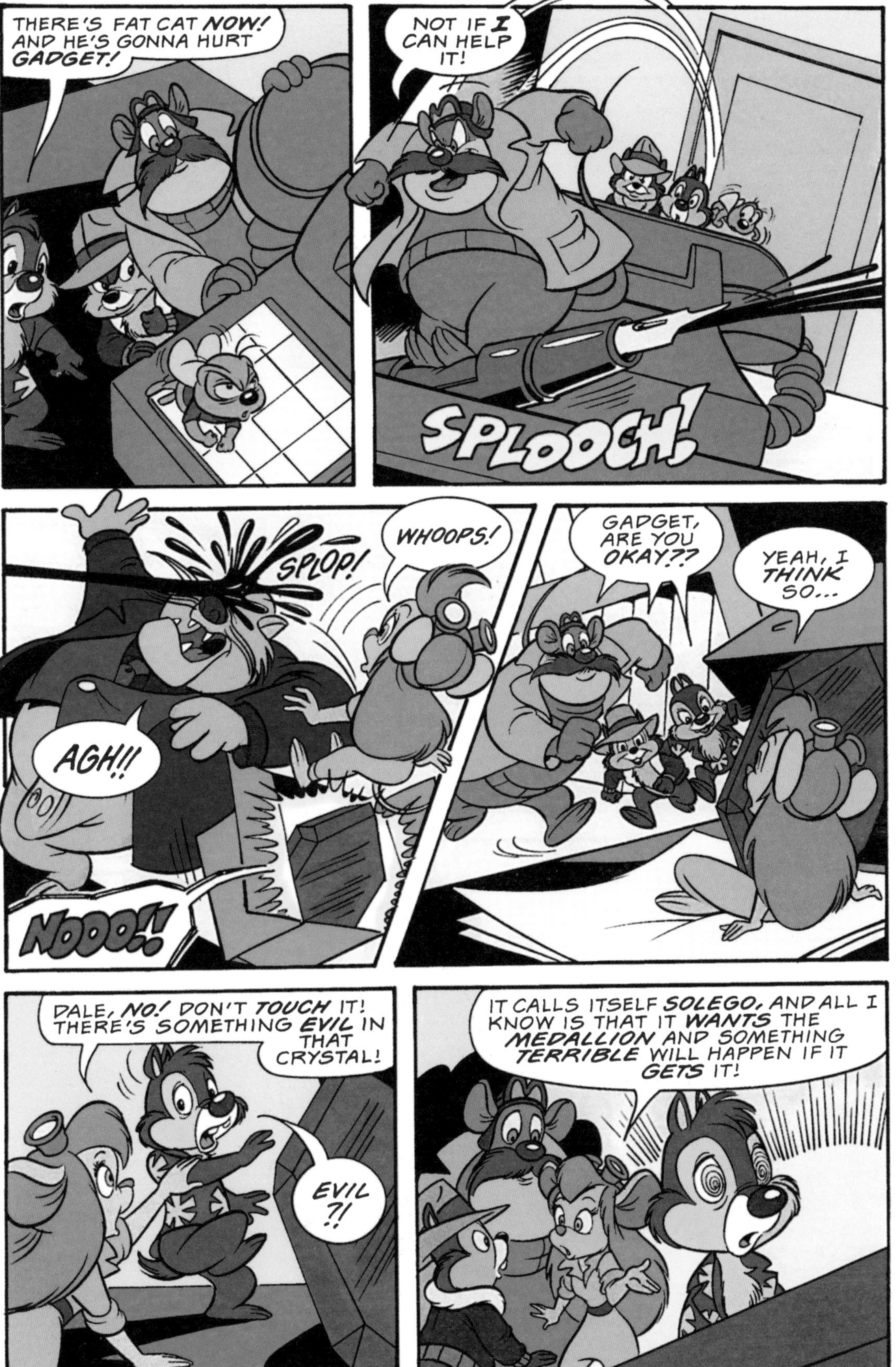
THERE'S FAT CAT NOW! AND HE'S GONNA HURT GADGET!
NOT IF I CAN HELP IT!
SPLOOCH!
SPLOP!
WHOOPS!
AGH!!
NOOO!!
GADGET, ARE YOU OKAY??
YEAH, I THINK SO...
DALE, NO! DON'T TOUCH IT! THERE'S SOMETHING EVIL IN THAT CRYSTAL!
EVIL ?!
IT CALLS ITSELF SOLEGO, AND ALL I KNOW IS THAT IT WANTS THE MEDALLION AND SOMETHING TERRIBLE WILL HAPPEN IF IT GETS IT!

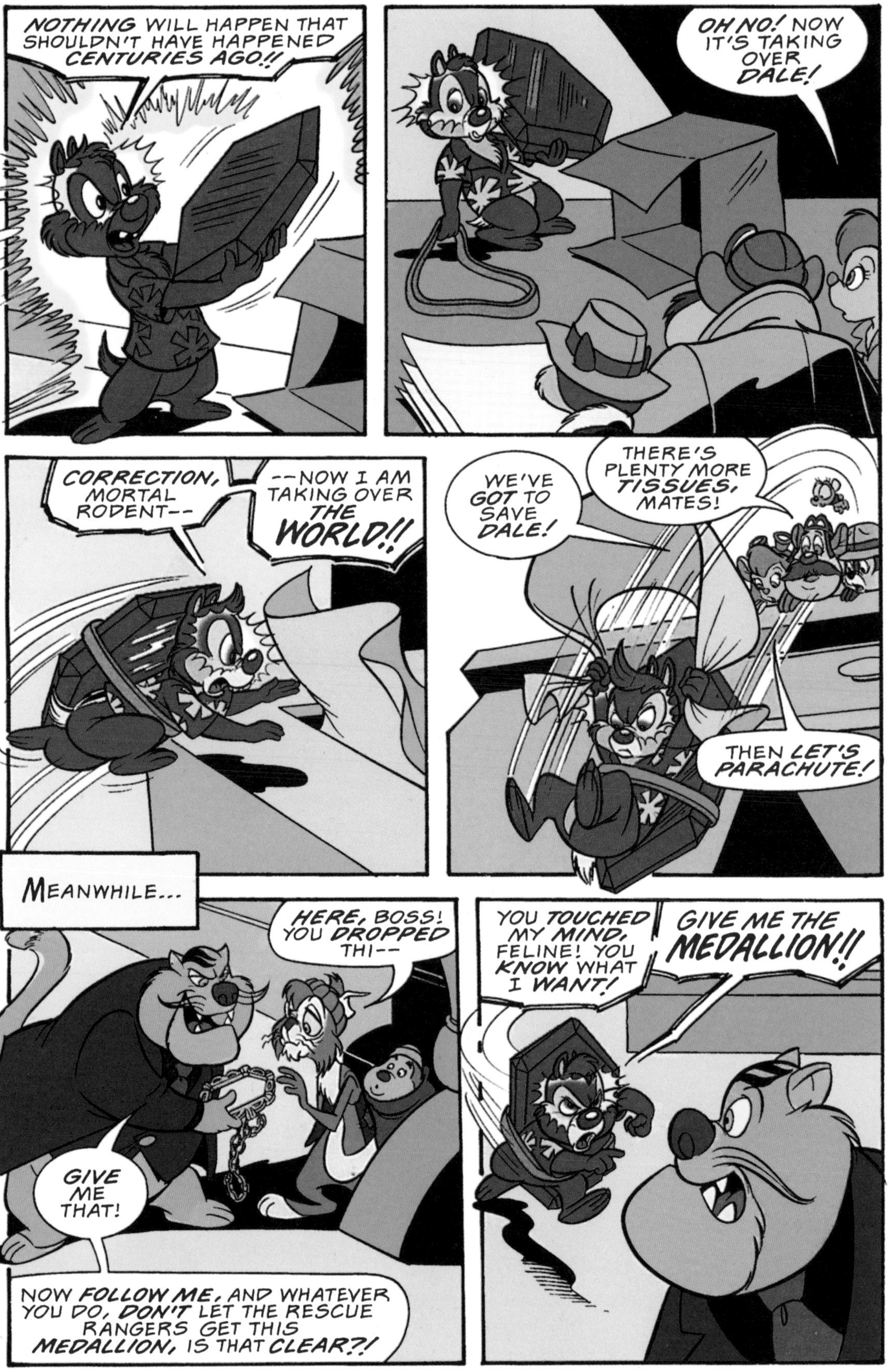
NOTHING WILL HAPPEN THAT SHOULDN'T HAVE HAPPENED CENTURIES AGO!!
OH NO! NOW IT'S TAKING OVER DALE!
CORRECTION, MORTAL RODENT--
--NOW I AM TAKING OVER THE WORLD!!
WE'VE GOT TO SAVE DALE!
THERE'S PLENTY MORE TISSUES, MATES!
THEN LET'S PARACHUTE!
MEANWHILE...
HERE, BOSS! YOU DROPPED THI--
GIVE ME THAT!
NOW FOLLOW ME, AND WHATEVER YOU DO, DON'T LET THE RESCUE RANGERS GET THIS MEDALLION, IS THAT CLEAR?!
YOU TOUCHED MY MIND, FELINE! YOU KNOW WHAT I WANT!
GIVE ME THE MEDALLION!!

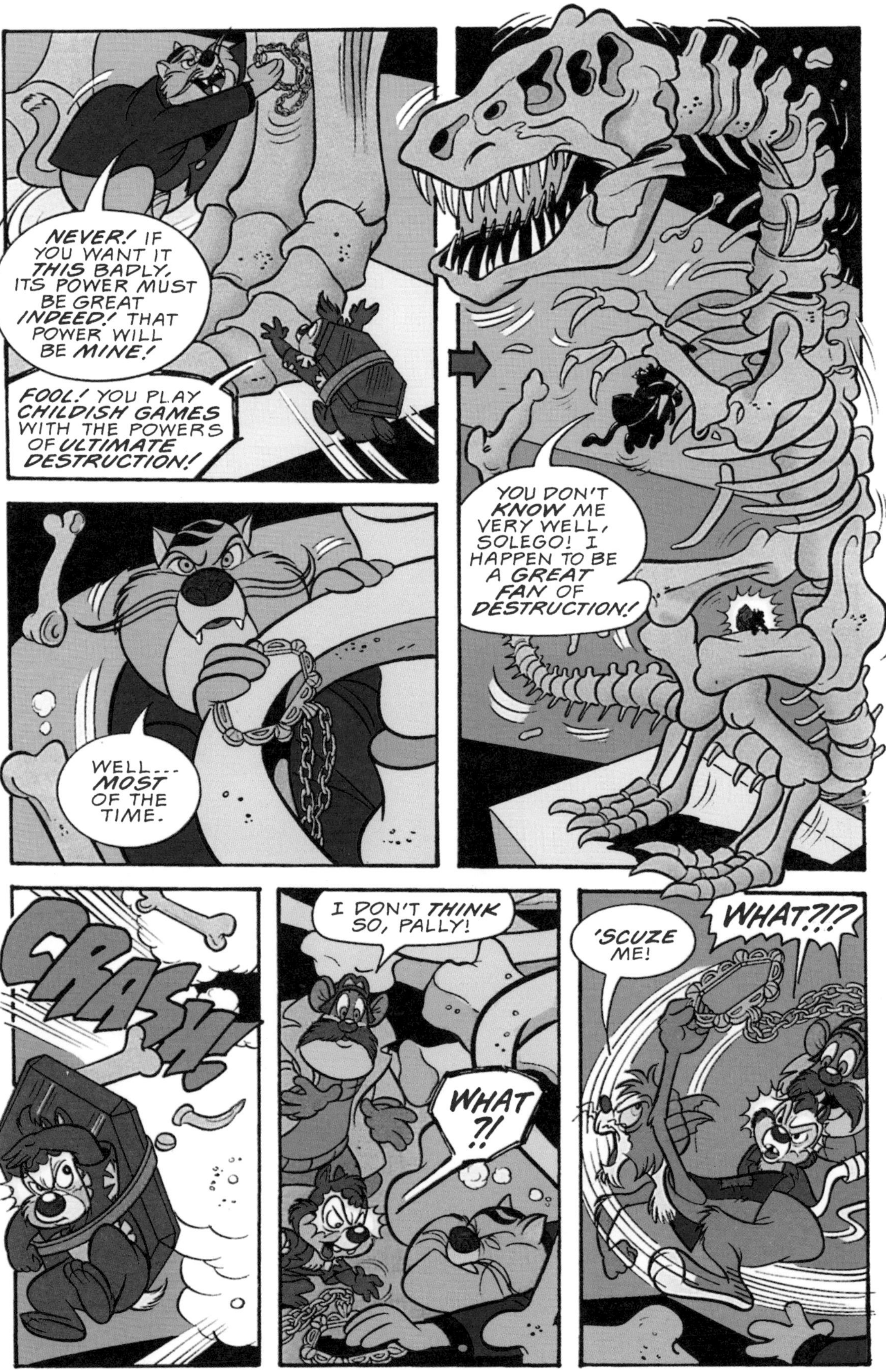
NEVER! IF YOU WANT IT THIS BADLY, ITS POWER MUST BE GREAT INDEED! THAT POWER WILL BE MINE!
FOOL! YOU PLAY CHILDISH GAMES WITH THE POWERS OF ULTIMATE DESTRUCTION!
YOU DON'T KNOW ME VERY WELL, SOLEGO! I HAPPEN TO BE A GREAT FAN OF DESTRUCTION!
WELL... MOST OF THE TIME.
CRASH!
I DON'T THINK SO, PALLY!
WHAT ?!
'SCUZE ME!
WHAT?!?

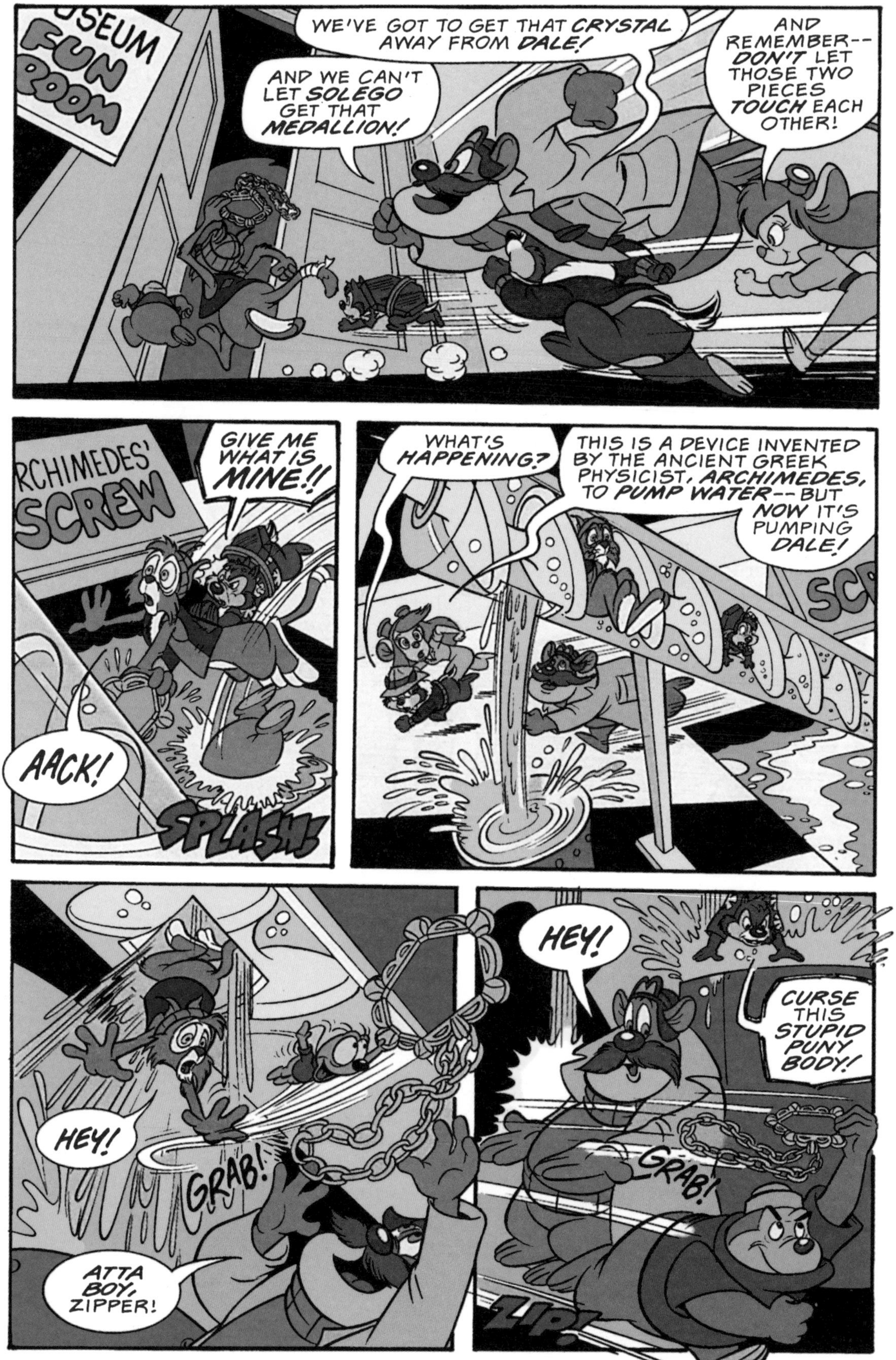
MUSEUM FUN ROOM
WE'VE GOT TO GET THAT CRYSTAL AWAY FROM DALE!
AND WE CAN'T LET SOLEGO GET THAT MEDALLION!
AND REMEMBER-- DON'T LET THOSE TWO PIECES TOUCH EACH OTHER!
ARCHIMEDES' SCREW
GIVE ME WHAT IS MINE!!
AACK!
SPLASH!
WHAT'S HAPPENING?
THIS IS A DEVICE INVENTED BY THE ANCIENT GREEK PHYSICIST, ARCHIMEDES, TO PUMP WATER-- BUT NOW IT'S PUMPING DALE!
HEY!
GRAB!
ATTA BOY, ZIPPER!
HEY!
CURSE THIS STUPID PUNY BODY!
GRAB!
ZIP!

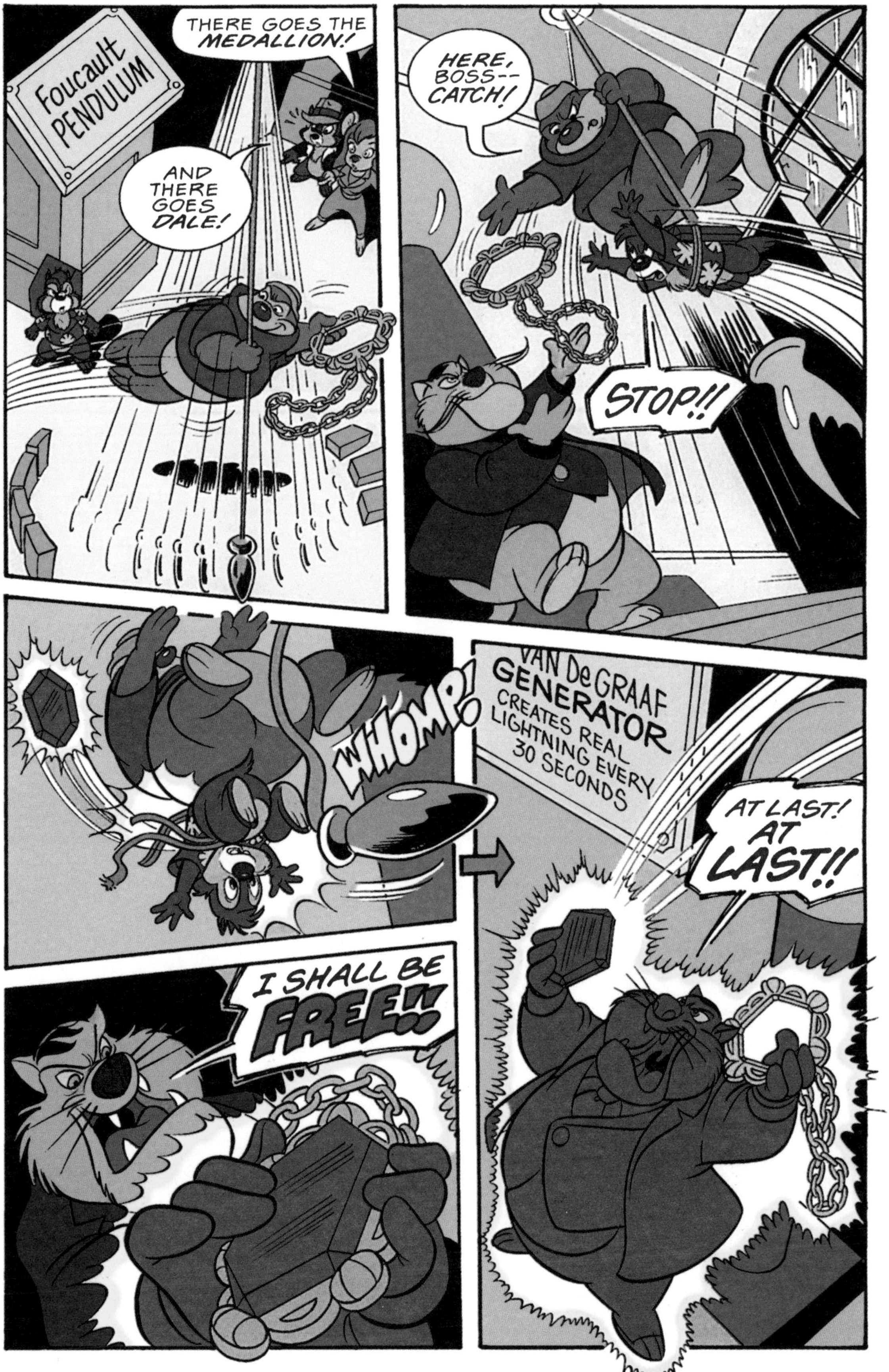
Foucault PENDULUM
THERE GOES THE MEDALLION!
AND THERE GOES DALE!
HERE, BOSS--CATCH!
STOP!!
WHOMP!
VAN DeGRAAF GENERATOR CREATES REAL LIGHTNING EVERY 30 SECONDS
AT LAST! AT LAST!!
I SHALL BE FREE!!

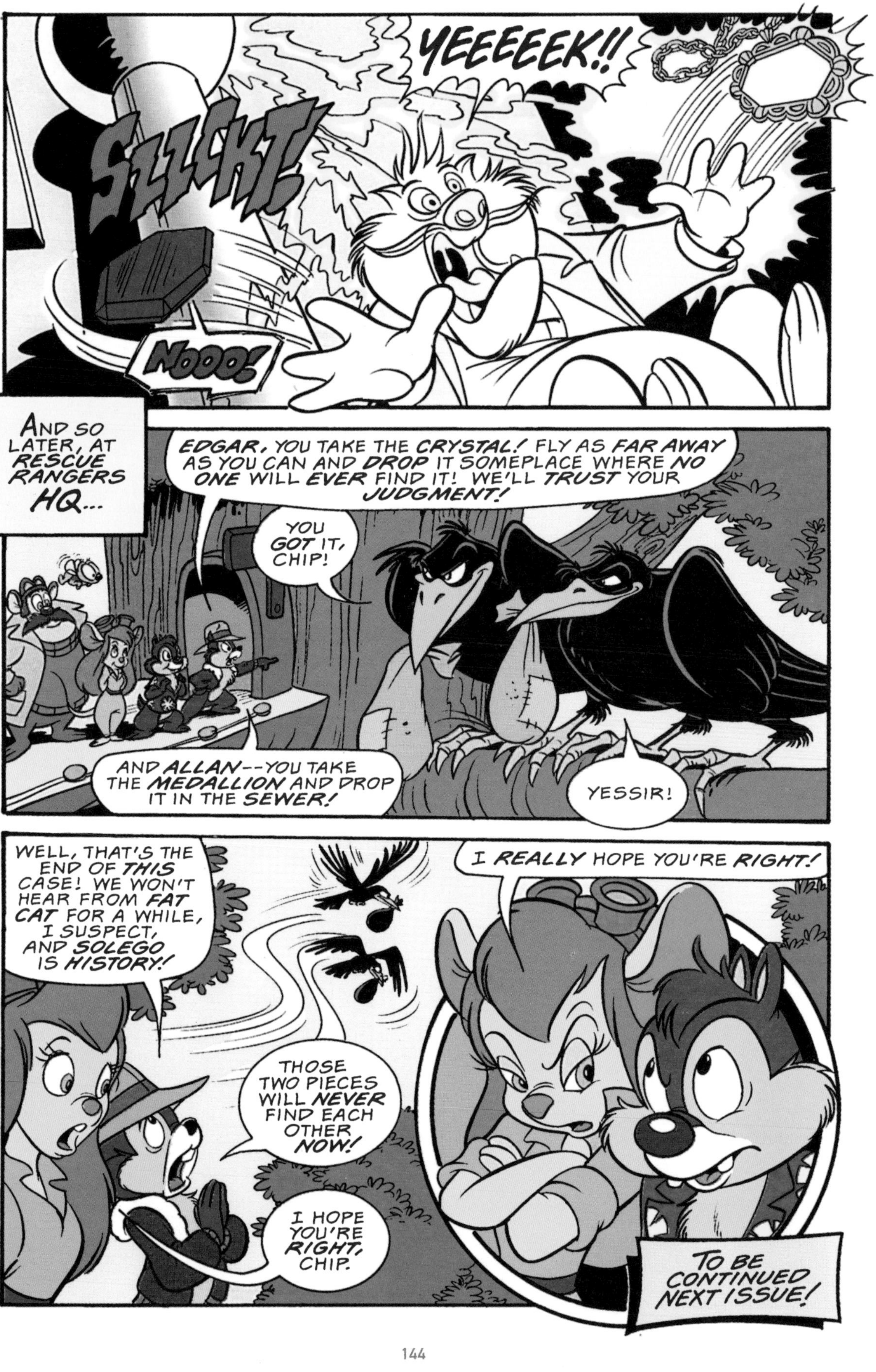
YEEEEEK!!
SZZCKT!
NOOOO!
AND SO LATER, AT RESCUE RANGERS HQ...
EDGAR, YOU TAKE THE CRYSTAL! FLY AS FAR AWAY AS YOU CAN AND DROP IT SOMEPLACE WHERE NO ONE WILL EVER FIND IT! WE'LL TRUST YOUR JUDGMENT!
YOU GOT IT, CHIP!
AND ALLAN--YOU TAKE THE MEDALLION AND DROP IT IN THE SEWER!
YESSIR!
WELL, THAT'S THE END OF THIS CASE! WE WON'T HEAR FROM FAT CAT FOR A WHILE, I SUSPECT, AND SOLEGO IS HISTORY!
THOSE TWO PIECES WILL NEVER FIND EACH OTHER NOW!
I HOPE YOU'RE RIGHT, CHIP.
I REALLY HOPE YOU'RE RIGHT!
TO BE CONTINUED NEXT ISSUE!

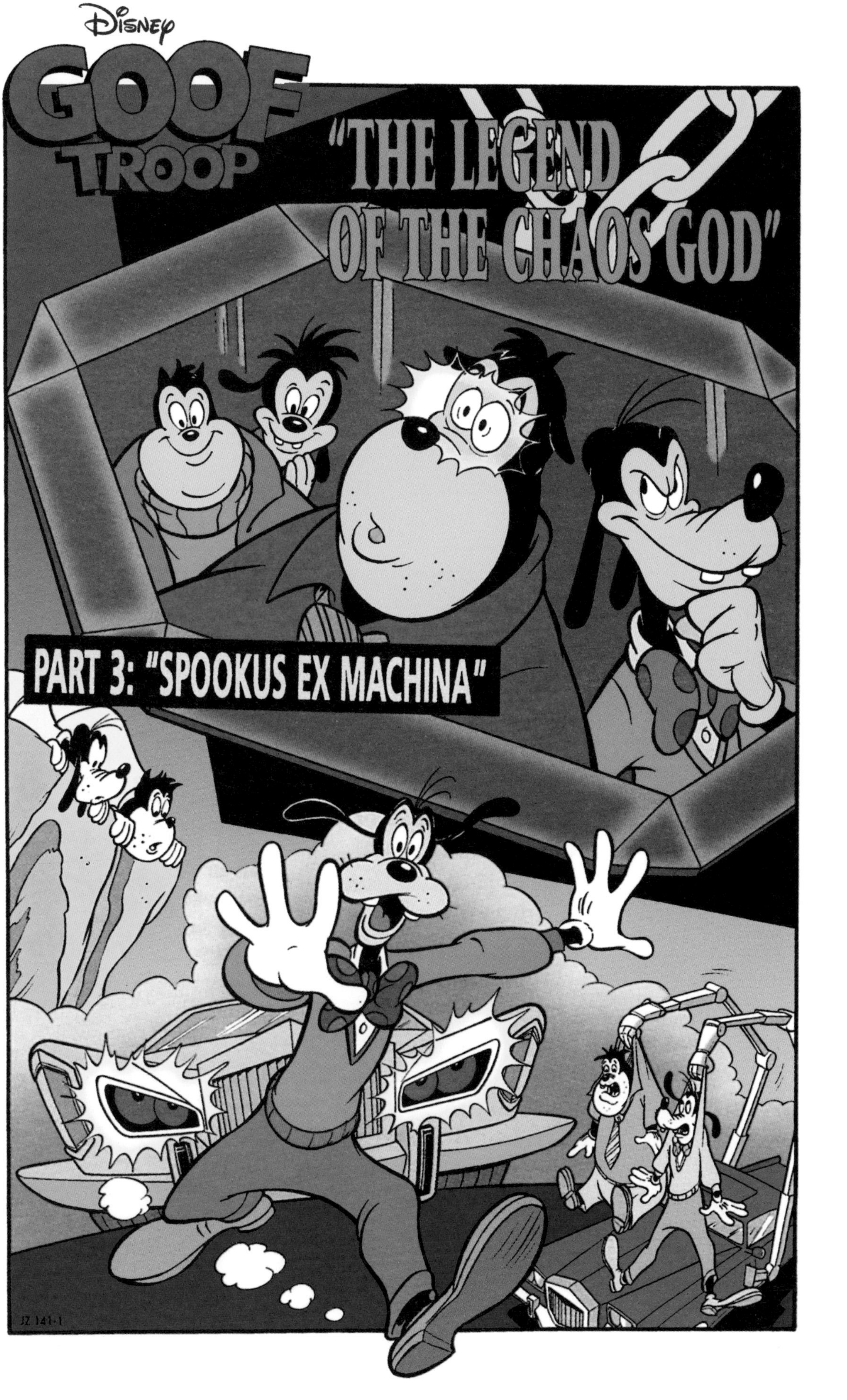
DISNEY
GOOF TROOP
"THE LEGEND OF THE CHAOS GOD"
PART 3: "SPOOKUS EX MACHINA"
JZ 141-1

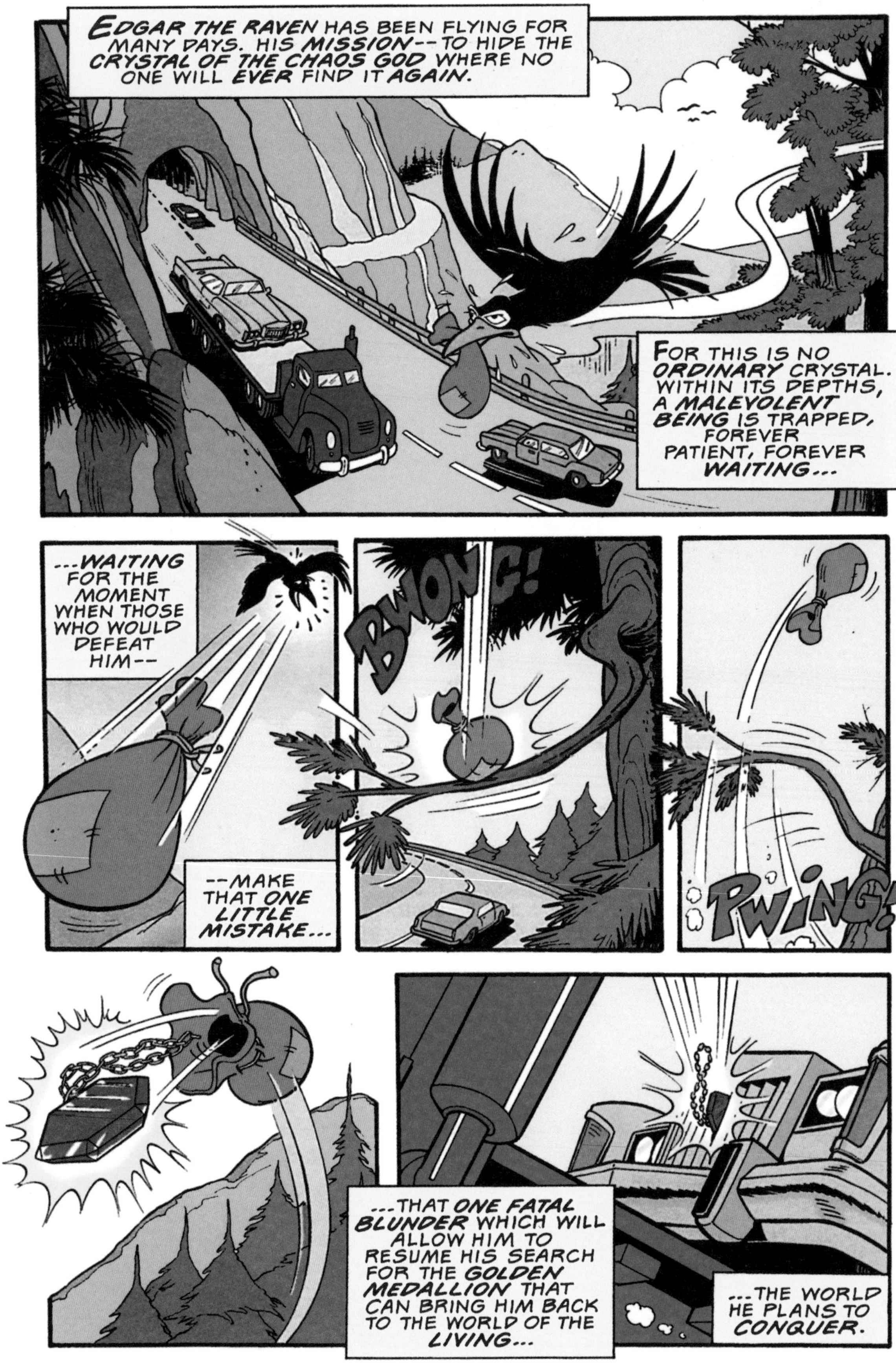
EDGAR THE RAVEN HAS BEEN FLYING FOR MANY DAYS. HIS MISSION--TO HIDE THE CRYSTAL OF THE CHAOS GOD WHERE NO ONE WILL EVER FIND IT AGAIN.
FOR THIS IS NO ORDINARY CRYSTAL. WITHIN ITS DEPTHS, A MALEVOLENT BEING IS TRAPPED, FOREVER PATIENT, FOREVER WAITING...
...WAITING FOR THE MOMENT WHEN THOSE WHO WOULD DEFEAT HIM--
--MAKE THAT ONE LITTLE MISTAKE...
BWONG!
PWING!
...THAT ONE FATAL BLUNDER WHICH WILL ALLOW HIM TO RESUME HIS SEARCH FOR THE GOLDEN MEDALLION THAT CAN BRING HIM BACK TO THE WORLD OF THE LIVING...
...THE WORLD HE PLANS TO CONQUER.

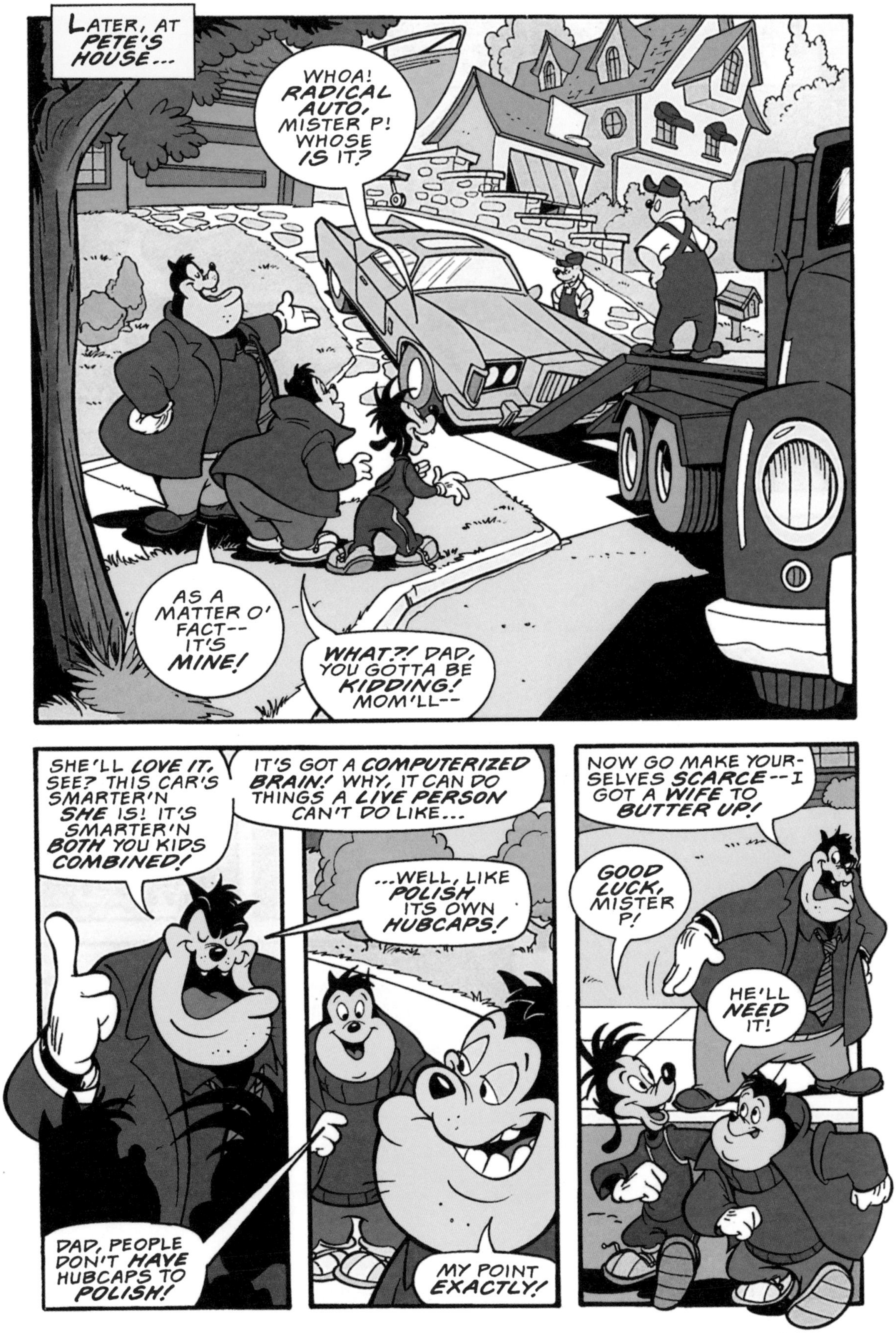

LATER, AT PETE'S HOUSE...
WHOA! RADICAL AUTO, MISTER P! WHOSE IS IT?
AS A MATTER O' FACT-- IT'S MINE!
WHAT?! DAD, YOU GOTTA BE KIDDING! MOM'LL--
SHE'LL LOVE IT, SEE? THIS CAR'S SMARTER'N SHE IS! IT'S SMARTER'N BOTH YOU KIDS COMBINED!
IT'S GOT A COMPUTERIZED BRAIN! WHY, IT CAN DO THINGS A LIVE PERSON CAN'T DO LIKE...
...WELL, LIKE POLISH ITS OWN HUBCAPS!
DAD, PEOPLE DON'T HAVE HUBCAPS TO POLISH!
MY POINT EXACTLY!
NOW GO MAKE YOURSELVES SCARCE--I GOT A WIFE TO BUTTER UP!
GOOD LUCK, MISTER P!
HE'LL NEED IT!

GAWRSH, PETIE, WHO LEFT THE *FANCY* CAR IN YER *DRIVEWAY?*

THAT'S *MY* FANCY CAR, AN' GO AWAY, I'M *BUSY!*

OH, *SNOOKY-WOOKUMS!* I HAVE SOMETHING TO *SHOOOOW* YOU!

BROTHER, DO I KNOW *THAT* TONE OF VOICE!

ALL RIGHT, WHAT DID YOU BUY *THIS* TIME?!

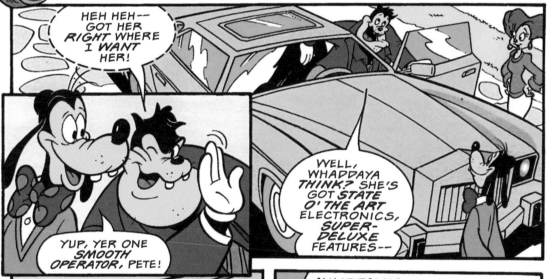

HEH HEH-- GOT HER *RIGHT* WHERE I *WANT* HER!

YUP, YER ONE *SMOOTH OPERATOR,* PETE!

WELL, WHADDAYA *THINK?* SHE'S GOT *STATE O' THE ART* ELECTRONICS, *SUPER-DELUXE* FEATURES--

--AN' JUST *LISTEN* TO THAT ENGINE *PURR!*

RRRMMM

HUH-- ?!

AN' IT *TALKS* TO YA, TOO! IT TELLS YOU WHEN YER *DOOR* IS *OPEN!* GOOD *SAFETY* FEATURE FOR THE *KIDS,* EH?

CLOSE THAT DOOR!!

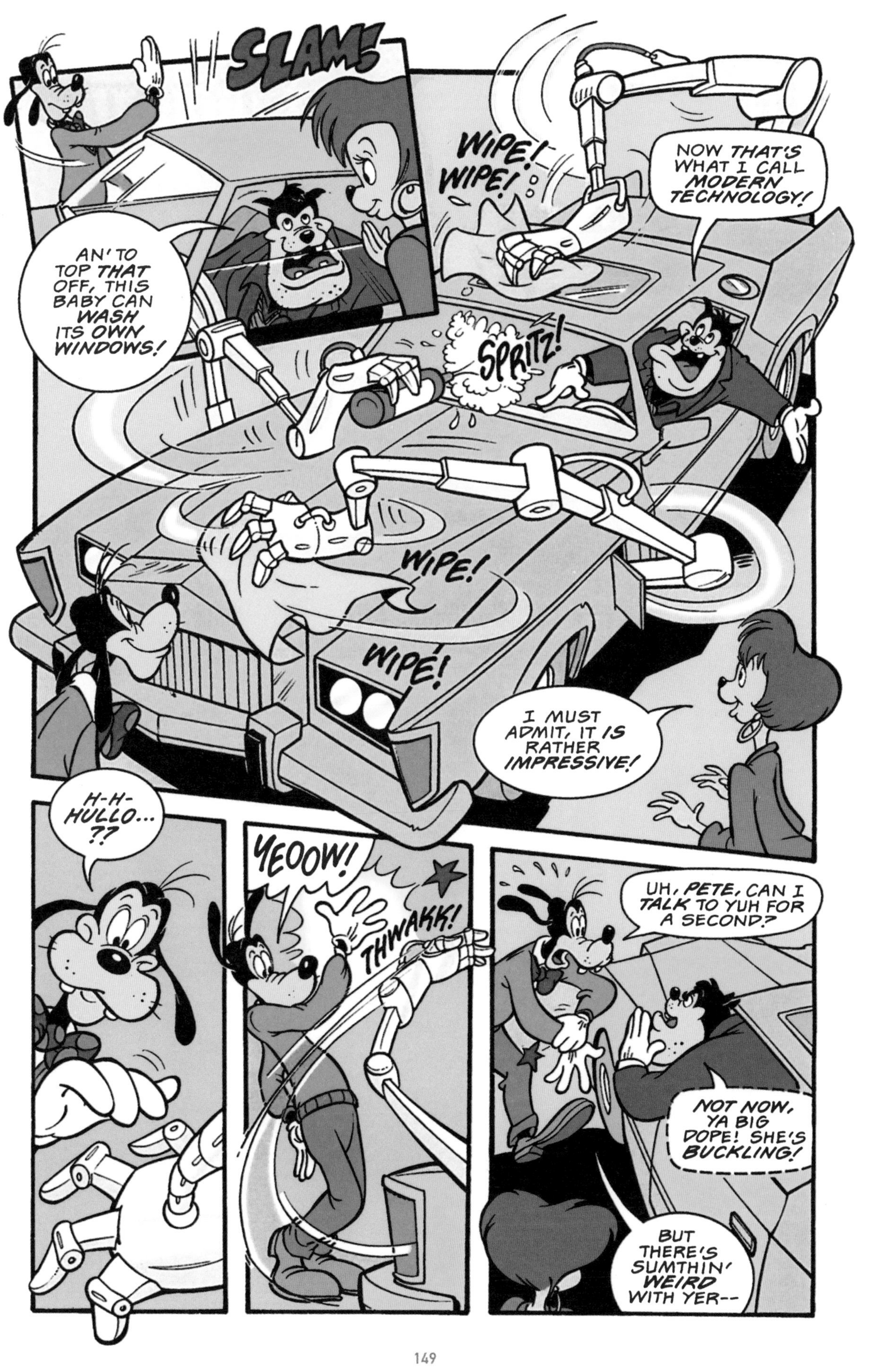
SLAM!
AN' TO TOP THAT OFF, THIS BABY CAN WASH ITS OWN WINDOWS!
WIPE! WIPE!
NOW THAT'S WHAT I CALL MODERN TECHNOLOGY!
SPRITZ!
WIPE!
WIPE!
I MUST ADMIT, IT IS RATHER IMPRESSIVE!
H-H-HULLO... ??
YEOOW!
THWAKK!
UH, PETE, CAN I TALK TO YUH FOR A SECOND?
NOT NOW, YA BIG DOPE! SHE'S BUCKLING!
BUT THERE'S SUMTHIN' WEIRD WITH YER--

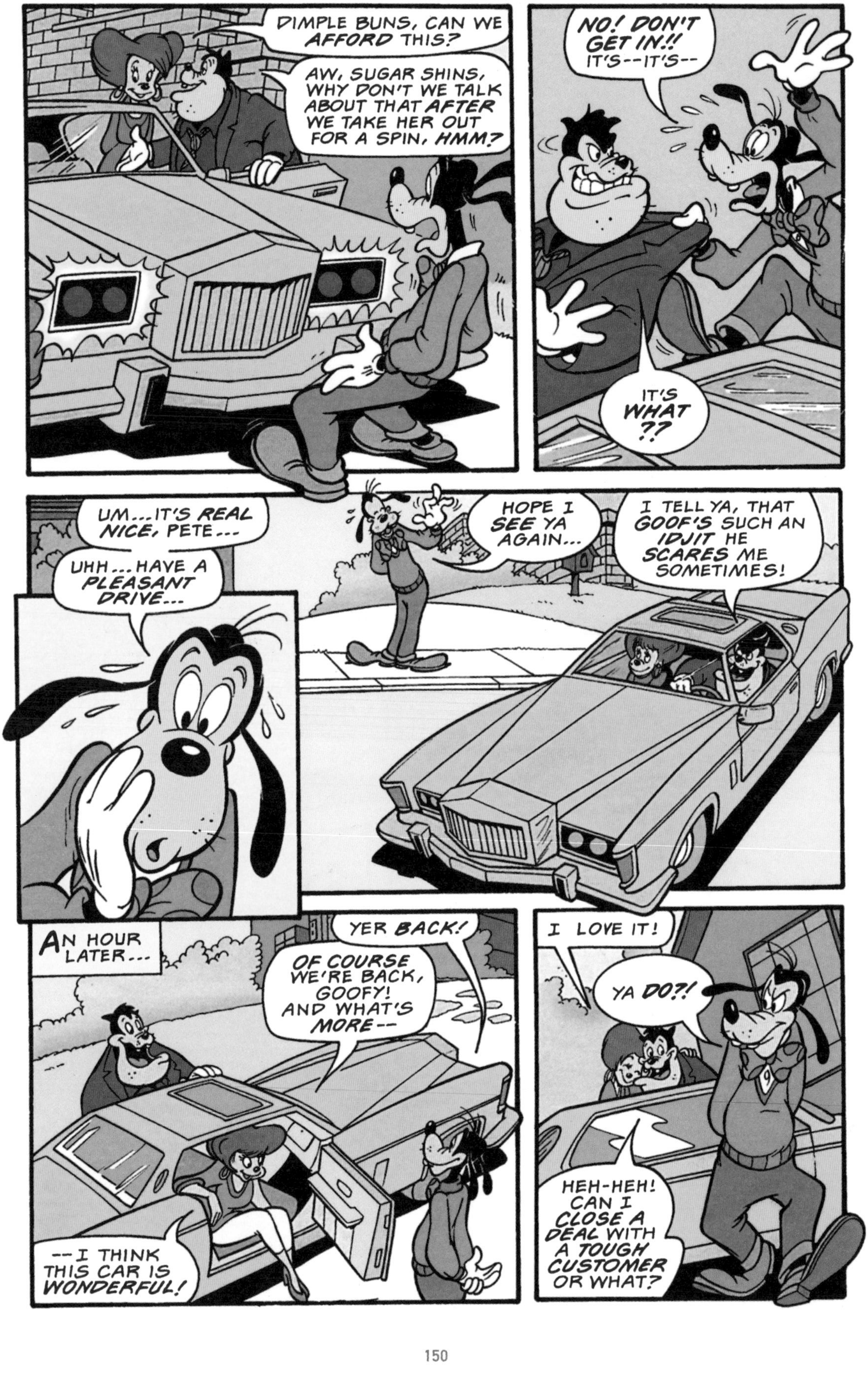
DIMPLE BUNS, CAN WE AFFORD THIS?
AW, SUGAR SHINS, WHY DON'T WE TALK ABOUT THAT AFTER WE TAKE HER OUT FOR A SPIN, HMM?
NO! DON'T GET IN!! IT'S--IT'S--
IT'S WHAT??
UM...IT'S REAL NICE, PETE...
UHH...HAVE A PLEASANT DRIVE...
HOPE I SEE YA AGAIN...
I TELL YA, THAT GOOF'S SUCH AN IDJIT HE SCARES ME SOMETIMES!
AN HOUR LATER...
YER BACK!
OF COURSE WE'RE BACK, GOOFY! AND WHAT'S MORE--
--I THINK THIS CAR IS WONDERFUL!
I LOVE IT!
YA DO?!
HEH-HEH! CAN I CLOSE A DEAL WITH A TOUGH CUSTOMER OR WHAT?

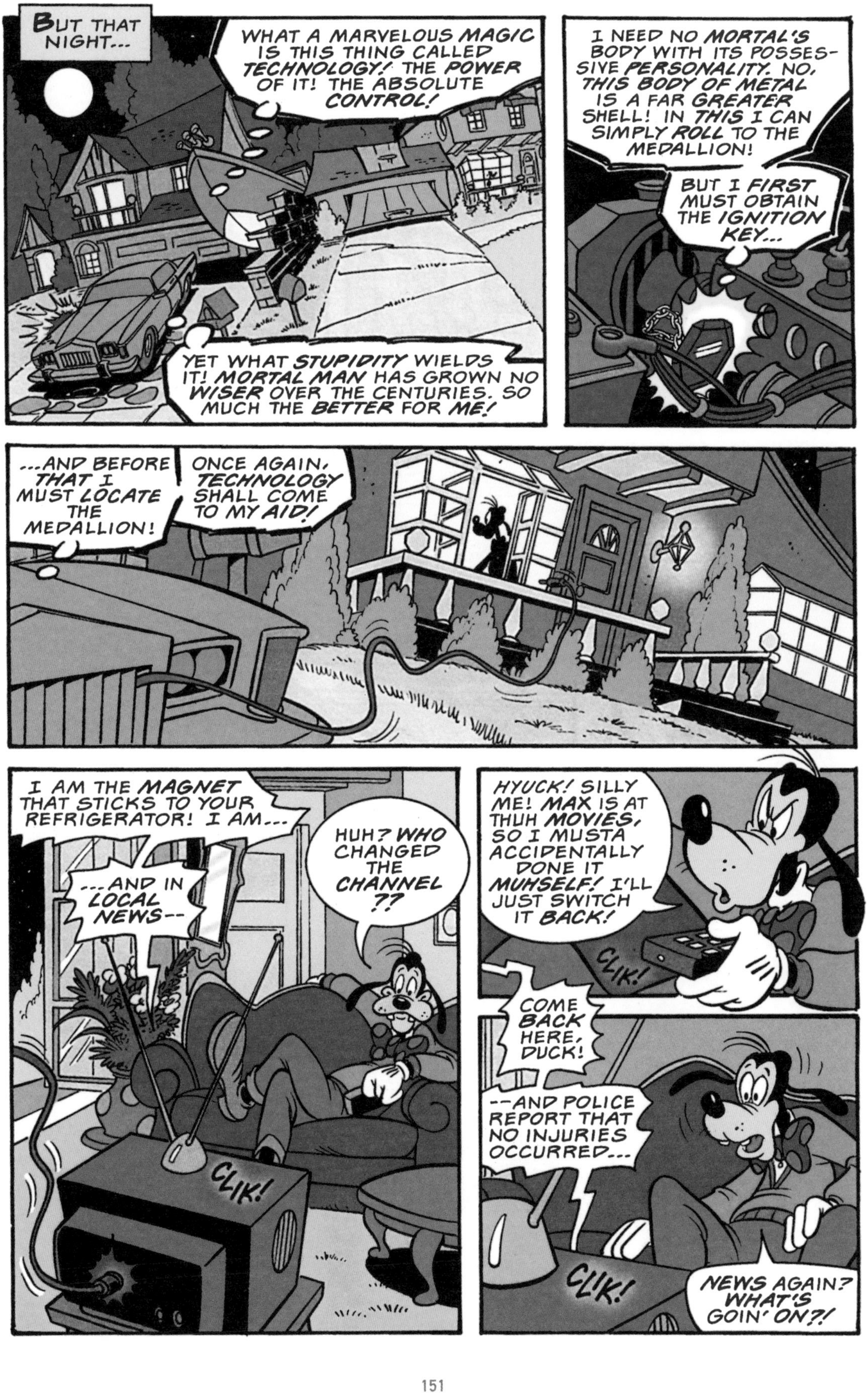
BUT THAT NIGHT...
WHAT A MARVELOUS MAGIC IS THIS THING CALLED TECHNOLOGY! THE POWER OF IT! THE ABSOLUTE CONTROL!
YET WHAT STUPIDITY WIELDS IT! MORTAL MAN HAS GROWN NO WISER OVER THE CENTURIES. SO MUCH THE BETTER FOR ME!
I NEED NO MORTAL'S BODY WITH ITS POSSESSIVE PERSONALITY. NO, THIS BODY OF METAL IS A FAR GREATER SHELL! IN THIS I CAN SIMPLY ROLL TO THE MEDALLION!
BUT I FIRST MUST OBTAIN THE IGNITION KEY...
...AND BEFORE THAT I MUST LOCATE THE MEDALLION!
ONCE AGAIN, TECHNOLOGY SHALL COME TO MY AID!
I AM THE MAGNET THAT STICKS TO YOUR REFRIGERATOR! I AM...
...AND IN LOCAL NEWS--
HUH? WHO CHANGED THE CHANNEL ??
CLIK!
HYUCK! SILLY ME! MAX IS AT THUH MOVIES, SO I MUSTA ACCIDENTALLY DONE IT MUHSELF! I'LL JUST SWITCH IT BACK!
CLIK!
COME BACK HERE, DUCK!
--AND POLICE REPORT THAT NO INJURIES OCCURRED...
CLIK!
NEWS AGAIN? WHAT'S GOIN' ON?!

IN OTHER NEWS, THE MYSTERIOUS DISAPPEARANCE OF THE *CHAOS GOD MEDALLION* HAS BEEN *SOLVED,* AT LEAST IN *PART!*

WHATSA *MATTER* WITH THIS DERNED THING?!

SCROOGE McDUCK, OWNER OF THE RELIC WHO HAD GENEROUSLY ALLOWED IT TO BE INCLUDED IN THE *"ANCIENT TREASURES OF RAKKINROON"* MUSEUM TOUR, FOUND IT TODAY, IN OF ALL PLACES, A *PAWN-SHOP!*

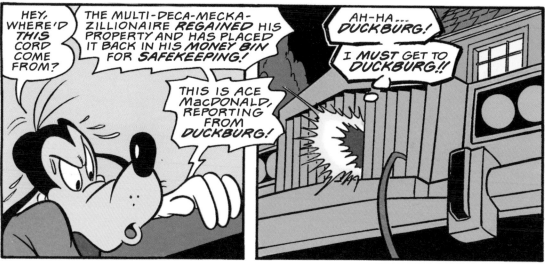

HEY, WHERE'D *THIS CORD* COME FROM?

THE MULTI-DECA-MECKA-ZILLIONAIRE *REGAINED* HIS PROPERTY AND HAS PLACED IT BACK IN HIS *MONEY BIN* FOR *SAFEKEEPING!*

THIS IS ACE MacDONALD, REPORTING FROM *DUCKBURG!*

AH-HA... *DUCKBURG!*

I MUST GET TO *DUCKBURG!!*

OMIGOSH! PETE'S CAR ISN'T HAUNTED--

--IT'S *ALIVE !!*

ZIP!

PETE! OPEN UP!!

BAM! BAM!

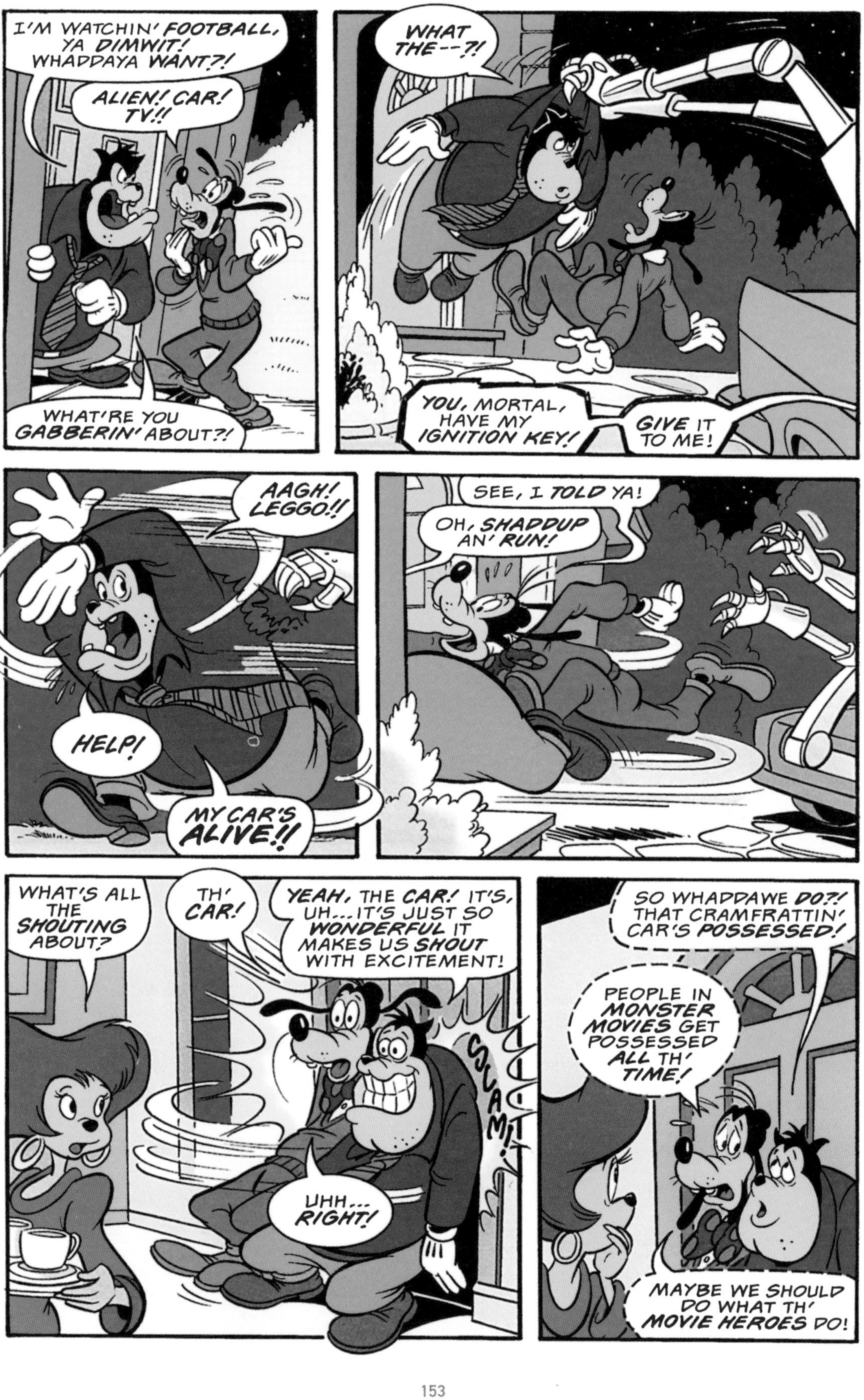
I'M WATCHIN' FOOTBALL, YA DIMWIT! WHADDAYA WANT?!
ALIEN! CAR! TV!!
WHAT'RE YOU GABBERIN' ABOUT?!
WHAT THE--?!
YOU, MORTAL, HAVE MY IGNITION KEY!
GIVE IT TO ME!
AAGH! LEGGO!!
HELP!
MY CAR'S ALIVE!!
SEE, I TOLD YA!
OH, SHADDUP AN' RUN!
WHAT'S ALL THE SHOUTING ABOUT?
TH' CAR!
YEAH, THE CAR! IT'S, UH... IT'S JUST SO WONDERFUL IT MAKES US SHOUT WITH EXCITEMENT!
SSLAM!
UHH... RIGHT!
SO WHADDAWE DO?! THAT CRAMFRATTIN' CAR'S POSSESSED!
PEOPLE IN MONSTER MOVIES GET POSSESSED ALL TH' TIME!
MAYBE WE SHOULD DO WHAT TH' MOVIE HEROES DO!

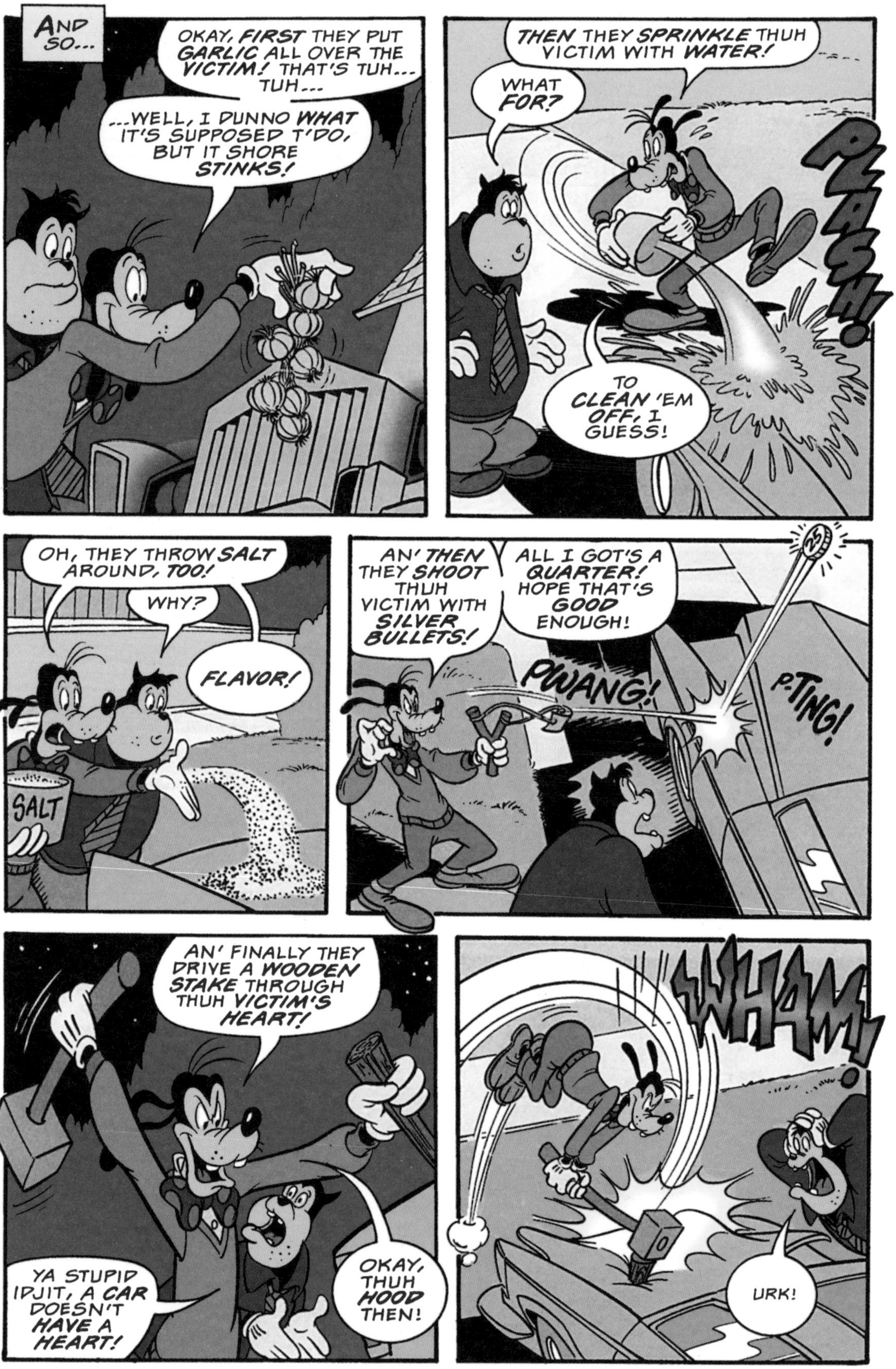
AND SO...
OKAY, FIRST THEY PUT GARLIC ALL OVER THE VICTIM! THAT'S TUH... TUH...
...WELL, I DUNNO WHAT IT'S SUPPOSED T'DO, BUT IT SHORE STINKS!
THEN THEY SPRINKLE THUH VICTIM WITH WATER!
WHAT FOR?
PLASH!
TO CLEAN 'EM OFF, I GUESS!
OH, THEY THROW SALT AROUND, TOO!
WHY?
FLAVOR!
SALT
AN' THEN THEY SHOOT THUH VICTIM WITH SILVER BULLETS!
ALL I GOT'S A QUARTER! HOPE THAT'S GOOD ENOUGH!
PWANG!
P-TING!
AN' FINALLY THEY DRIVE A WOODEN STAKE THROUGH THUH VICTIM'S HEART!
YA STUPID IDJIT, A CAR DOESN'T HAVE A HEART!
OKAY, THUH HOOD THEN!
WHAM!
URK!

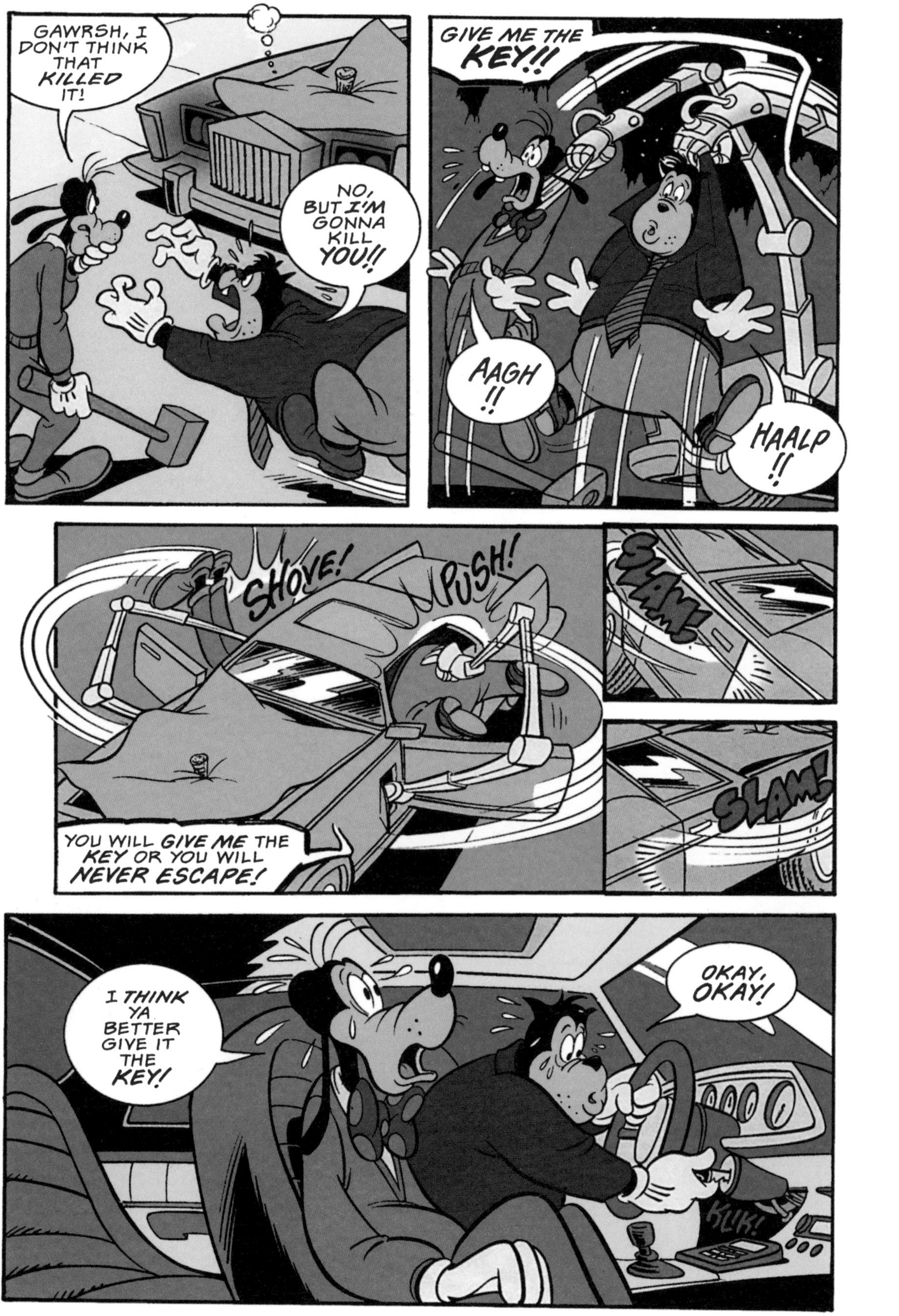
GAWRSH, I DON'T THINK THAT KILLED IT!
NO, BUT I'M GONNA KILL YOU!!
GIVE ME THE KEY!!
AAGH !!
HAALP !!
SHOVE!
PUSH!
SLAM!
YOU WILL GIVE ME THE KEY OR YOU WILL NEVER ESCAPE!
SLAM!
I THINK YA BETTER GIVE IT THE KEY!
OKAY, OKAY!
KLIK!

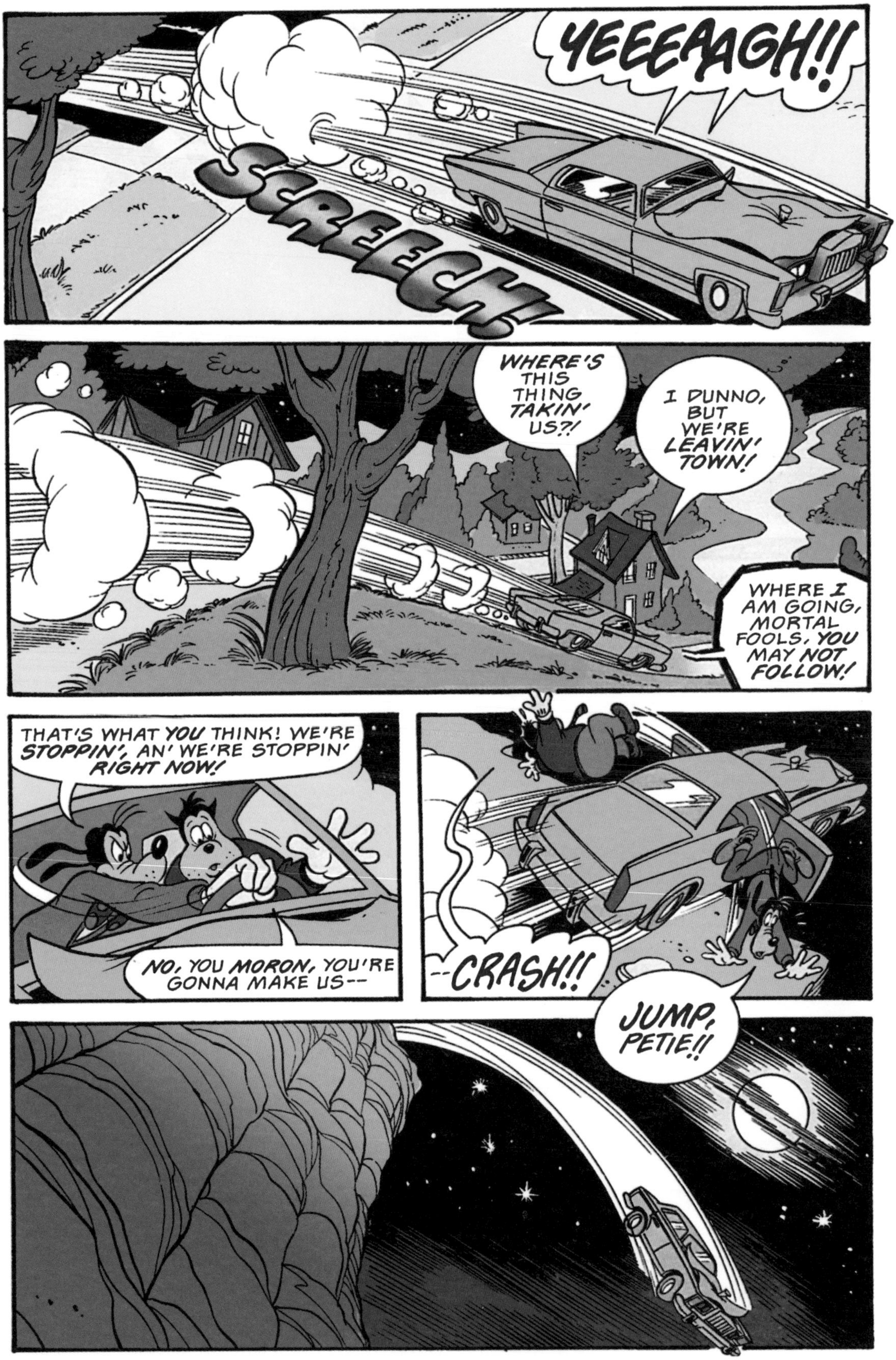

YEEEAAAGH!!
SCREECH!!
WHERE'S THIS THING TAKIN' US?!
I DUNNO, BUT WE'RE LEAVIN' TOWN!
WHERE I AM GOING, MORTAL FOOLS, YOU MAY NOT FOLLOW!
THAT'S WHAT YOU THINK! WE'RE STOPPIN', AN' WE'RE STOPPIN' RIGHT NOW!
NO, YOU MORON, YOU'RE GONNA MAKE US--
--CRASH!!
JUMP, PETIE!!

IT CRASHED.

NO KIDDIN'.

GONE...MY CAR...POSSESSED AND NOW GONE...

AND IT'S STILL GONNA COST ME A FORTUNE!!

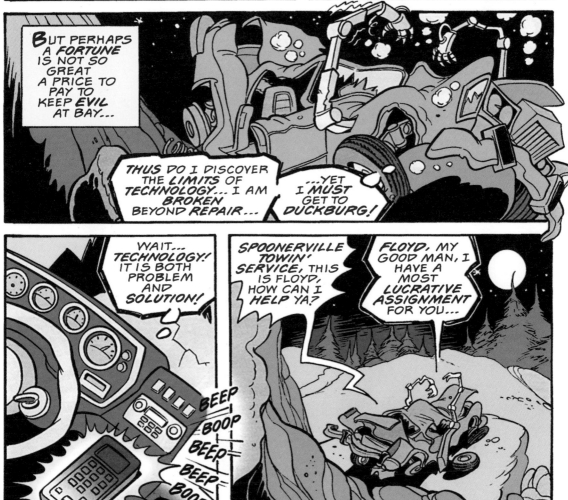

BUT PERHAPS A FORTUNE IS NOT SO GREAT A PRICE TO PAY TO KEEP EVIL AT BAY...

THUS DO I DISCOVER THE LIMITS OF TECHNOLOGY... I AM BROKEN BEYOND REPAIR...

...YET I MUST GET TO DUCKBURG!

WAIT... TECHNOLOGY! IT IS BOTH PROBLEM AND SOLUTION!

BEEP BOOP BEEP BEEP BOOP

SPOONERVILLE TOWIN' SERVICE, THIS IS FLOYD, HOW CAN I HELP YA?

FLOYD, MY GOOD MAN, I HAVE A MOST LUCRATIVE ASSIGNMENT FOR YOU...

TO BE CONTINUED NEXT ISSUE!

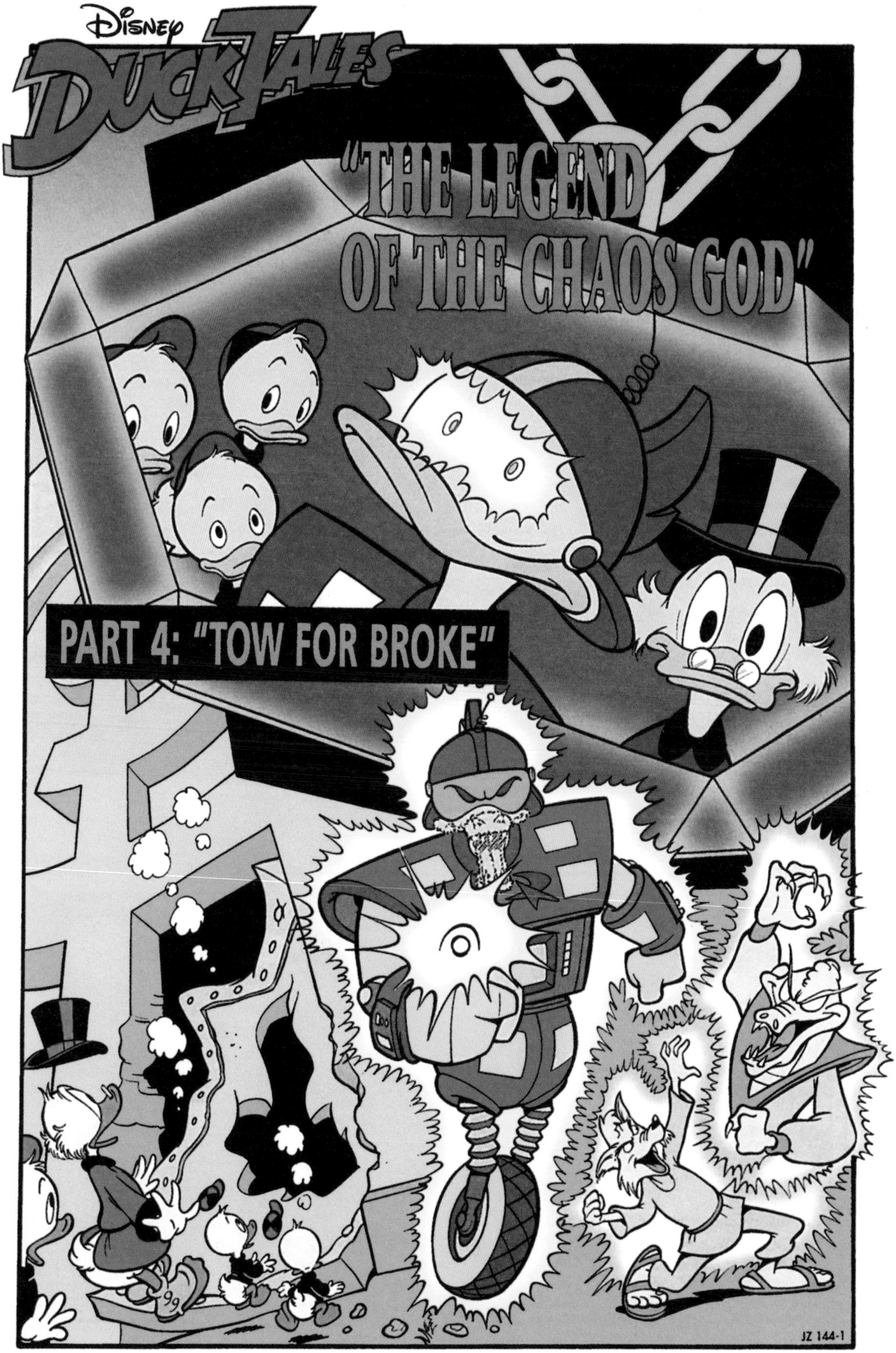
Disney
DuckTales
"THE LEGEND OF THE CHAOS GOD"
PART 4: "TOW FOR BROKE"
JZ 144-1

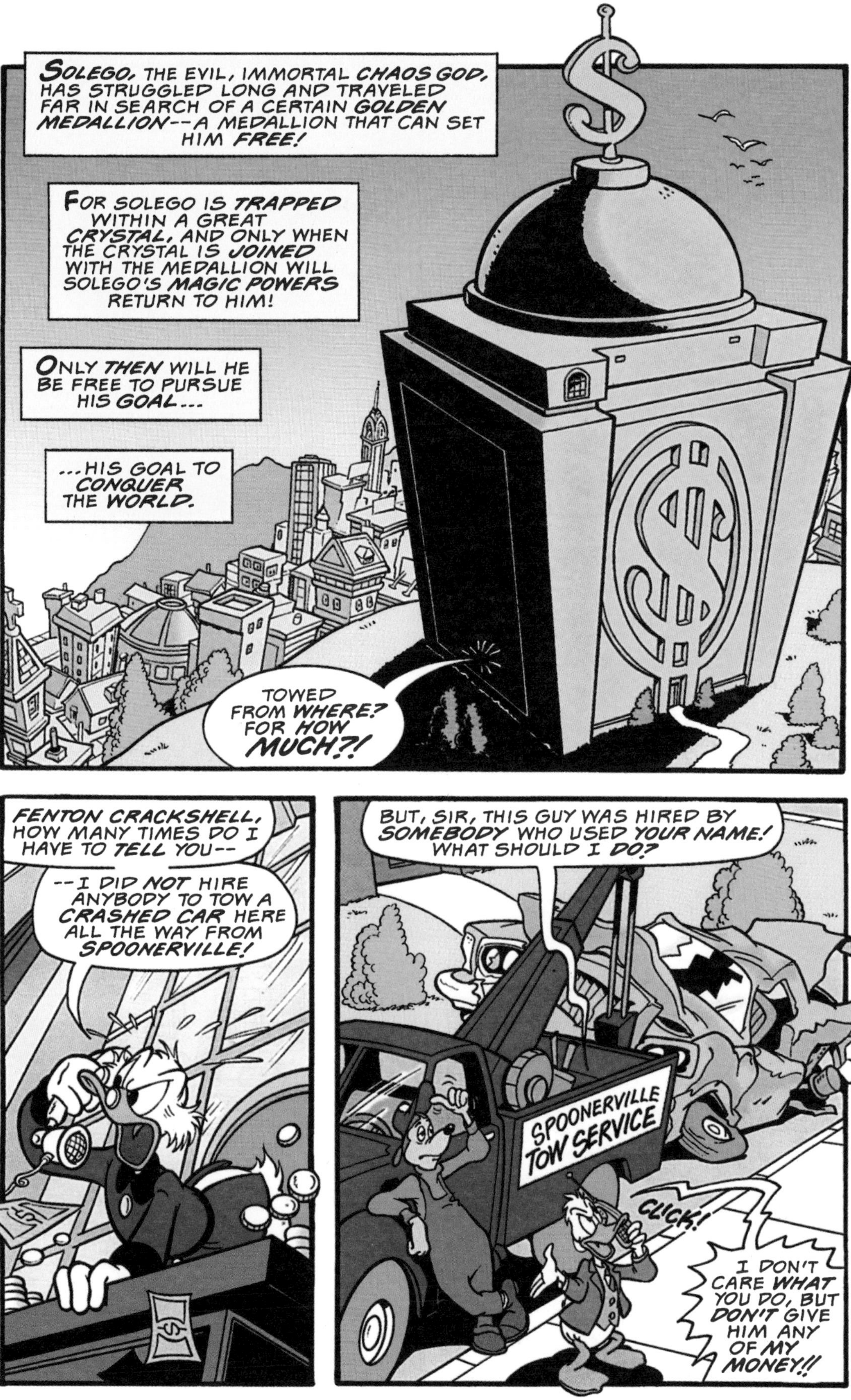
SOLEGO, THE EVIL, IMMORTAL CHAOS GOD, HAS STRUGGLED LONG AND TRAVELED FAR IN SEARCH OF A CERTAIN GOLDEN MEDALLION--A MEDALLION THAT CAN SET HIM FREE!
FOR SOLEGO IS TRAPPED WITHIN A GREAT CRYSTAL, AND ONLY WHEN THE CRYSTAL IS JOINED WITH THE MEDALLION WILL SOLEGO'S MAGIC POWERS RETURN TO HIM!
ONLY THEN WILL HE BE FREE TO PURSUE HIS GOAL...
...HIS GOAL TO CONQUER THE WORLD.
TOWED FROM WHERE? FOR HOW MUCH?!
FENTON CRACKSHELL, HOW MANY TIMES DO I HAVE TO TELL YOU--
--I DID NOT HIRE ANYBODY TO TOW A CRASHED CAR HERE ALL THE WAY FROM SPOONERVILLE!
BUT, SIR, THIS GUY WAS HIRED BY SOMEBODY WHO USED YOUR NAME! WHAT SHOULD I DO?
SPOONERVILLE TOW SERVICE
CLICK!
I DON'T CARE WHAT YOU DO, BUT DON'T GIVE HIM ANY OF MY MONEY!!

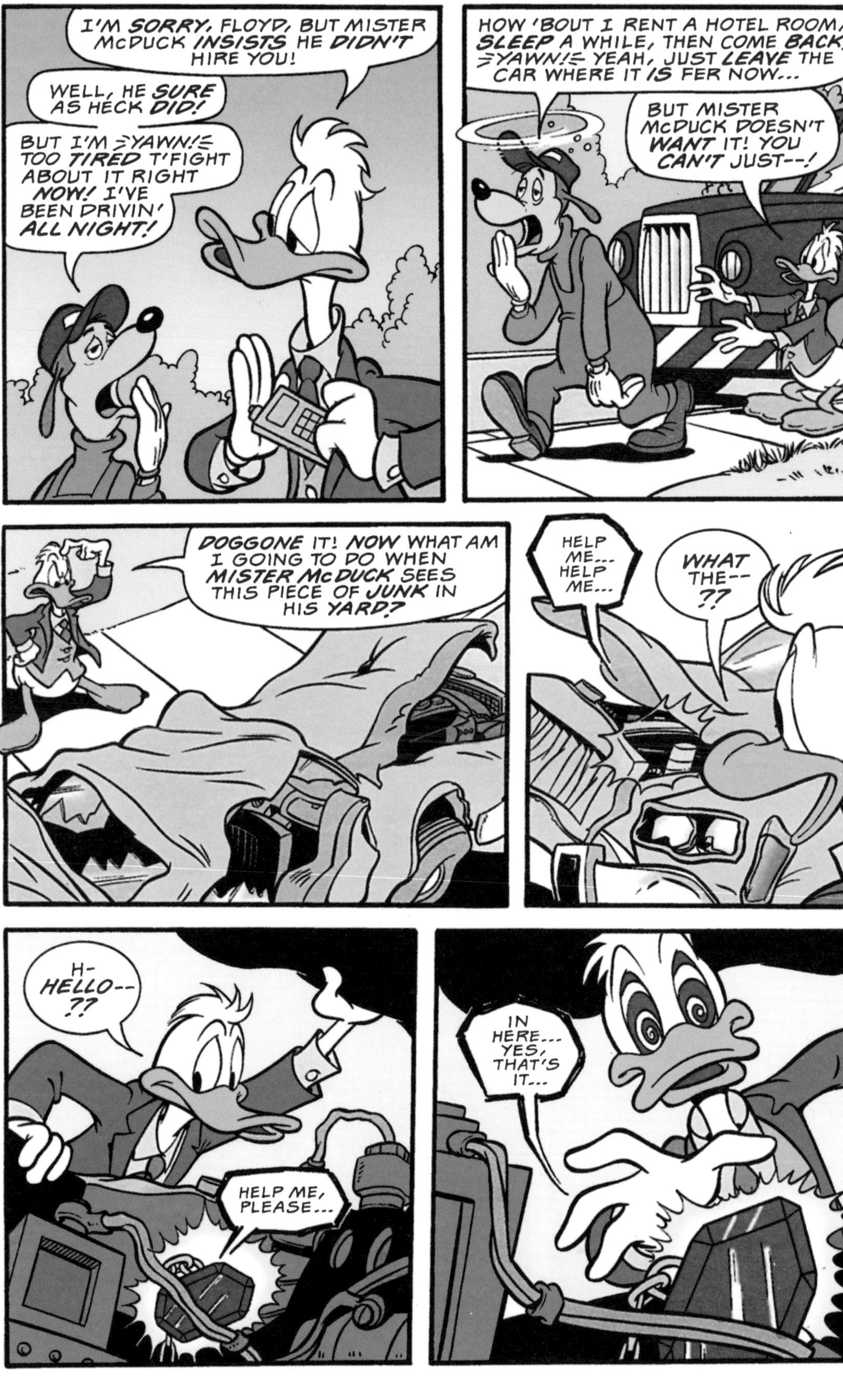

I'M SORRY, FLOYD, BUT MISTER McDUCK INSISTS HE DIDN'T HIRE YOU!
WELL, HE SURE AS HECK DID!
BUT I'M =YAWN!= TOO TIRED T'FIGHT ABOUT IT RIGHT NOW! I'VE BEEN DRIVIN' ALL NIGHT!
HOW 'BOUT I RENT A HOTEL ROOM, SLEEP A WHILE, THEN COME BACK? =YAWN!= YEAH, JUST LEAVE THE CAR WHERE IT IS FER NOW...
BUT MISTER McDUCK DOESN'T WANT IT! YOU CAN'T JUST--!
DOGGONE IT! NOW WHAT AM I GOING TO DO WHEN MISTER McDUCK SEES THIS PIECE OF JUNK IN HIS YARD?
HELP ME... HELP ME...
WHAT THE-- ??
H-HELLO-- ??
HELP ME, PLEASE...
IN HERE... YES, THAT'S IT...

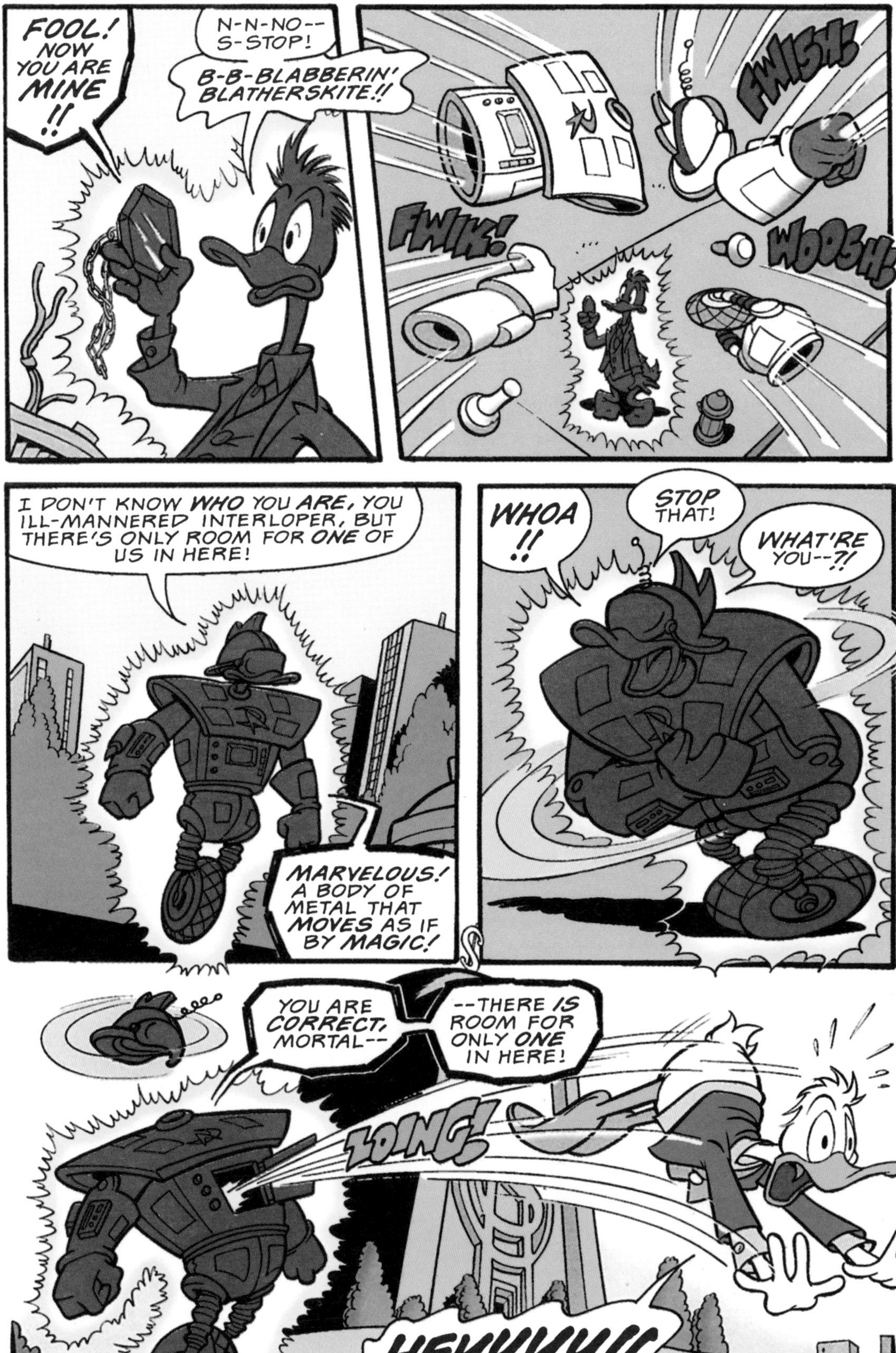
FOOL! NOW YOU ARE MINE !!
N-N-NO-- S-STOP!
B-B-BLABBERIN' BLATHERSKITE!!
FWISH!
FWIK!
WOOSH!
I DON'T KNOW WHO YOU ARE, YOU ILL-MANNERED INTERLOPER, BUT THERE'S ONLY ROOM FOR ONE OF US IN HERE!
MARVELOUS! A BODY OF METAL THAT MOVES AS IF BY MAGIC!
WHOA !!
STOP THAT!
WHAT'RE YOU--?!
YOU ARE CORRECT, MORTAL--
--THERE IS ROOM FOR ONLY ONE IN HERE!
ZOING!
HEYYYY!!

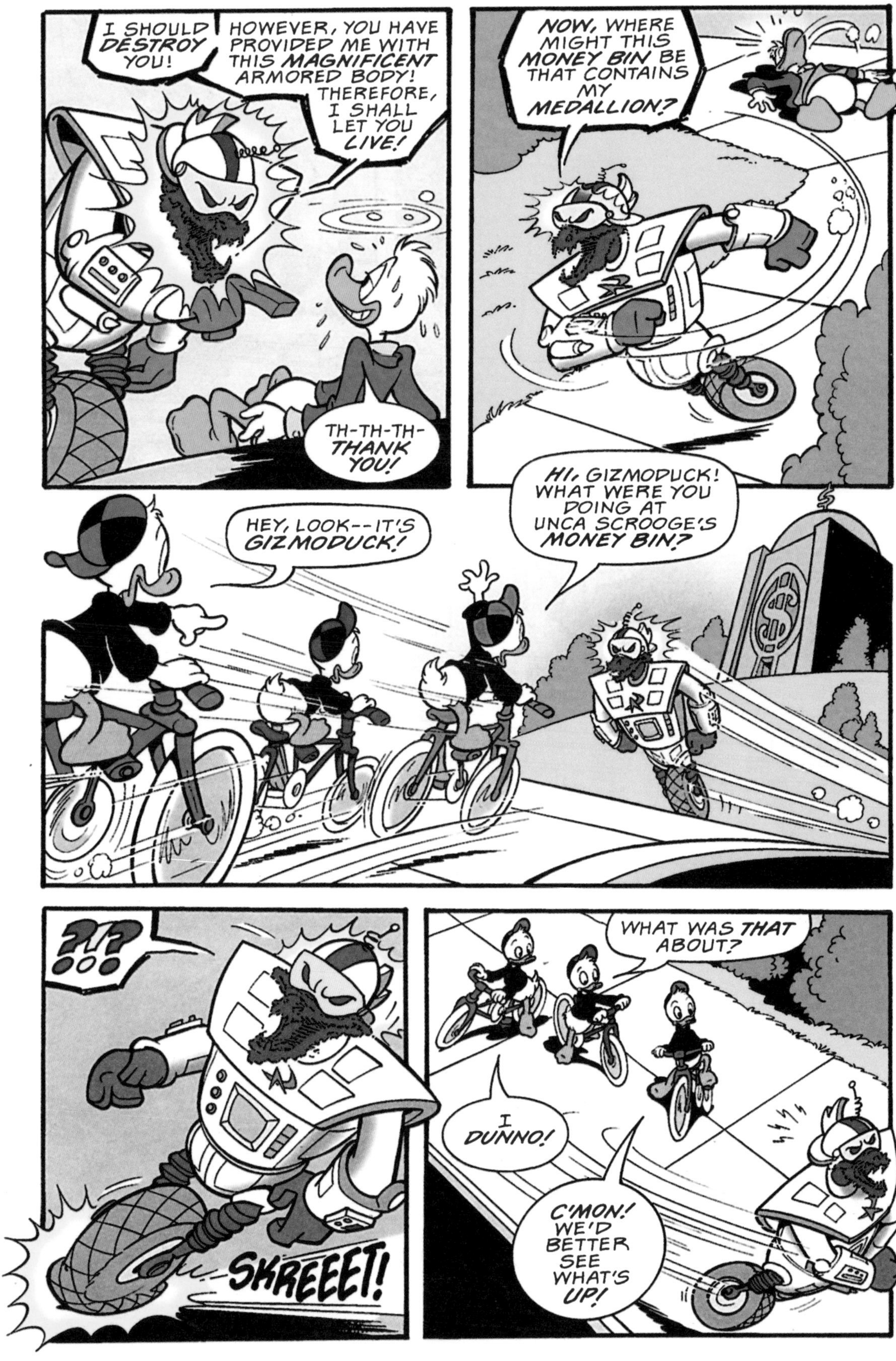
I SHOULD DESTROY YOU!
HOWEVER, YOU HAVE PROVIDED ME WITH THIS MAGNIFICENT ARMORED BODY! THEREFORE, I SHALL LET YOU LIVE!
TH-TH-TH-THANK YOU!
NOW, WHERE MIGHT THIS MONEY BIN BE THAT CONTAINS MY MEDALLION?
HEY, LOOK--IT'S GIZMODUCK!
HI, GIZMODUCK! WHAT WERE YOU DOING AT UNCA SCROOGE'S MONEY BIN?
?!?
SKREEET!
WHAT WAS THAT ABOUT?
I DUNNO!
C'MON! WE'D BETTER SEE WHAT'S UP!

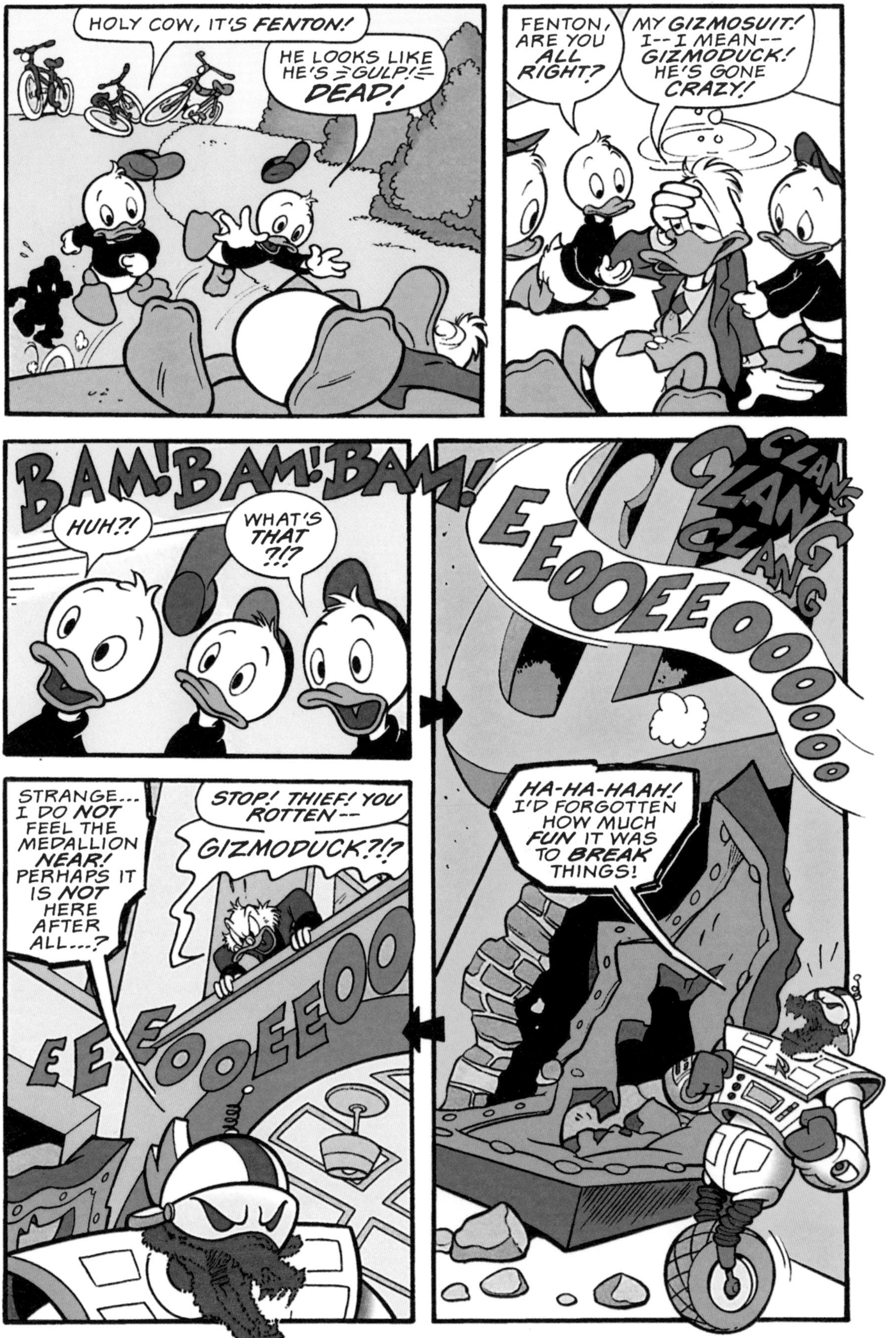
HOLY COW, IT'S FENTON!
HE LOOKS LIKE HE'S =GULP!= DEAD!
FENTON, ARE YOU ALL RIGHT?
MY GIZMOSUIT! I-- I MEAN-- GIZMODUCK! HE'S GONE CRAZY!
BAM! BAM! BAM!
HUH?!
WHAT'S THAT ?!?
CLANG CLANG CLANG
EEOOEEOOOOOOO
STRANGE... I DO NOT FEEL THE MEDALLION NEAR! PERHAPS IT IS NOT HERE AFTER ALL...?
STOP! THIEF! YOU ROTTEN --
GIZMODUCK?!?
EEOOEEOO
HA-HA-HAAH! I'D FORGOTTEN HOW MUCH FUN IT WAS TO BREAK THINGS!

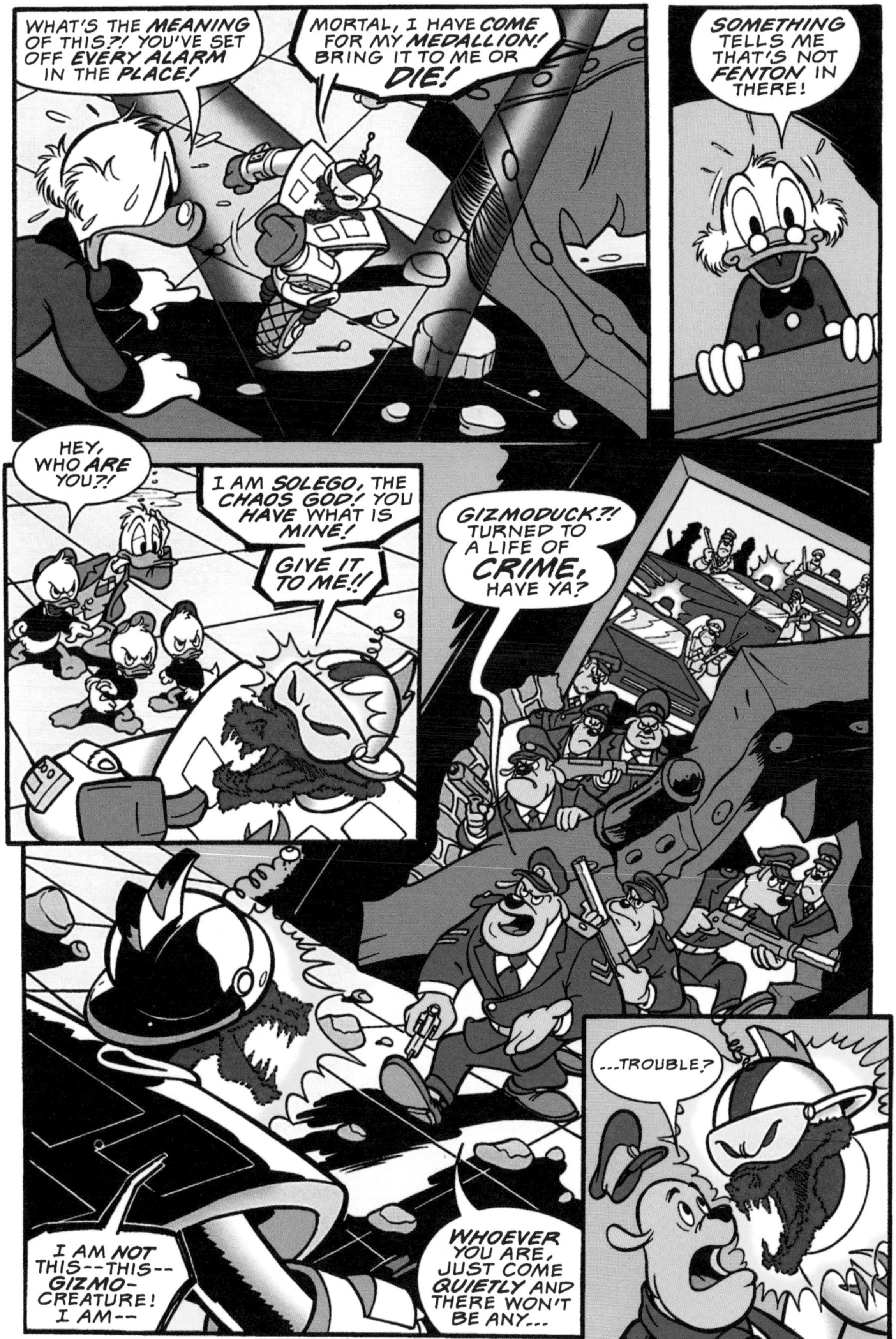
WHAT'S THE MEANING OF THIS?! YOU'VE SET OFF EVERY ALARM IN THE PLACE!
MORTAL, I HAVE COME FOR MY MEDALLION! BRING IT TO ME OR DIE!
SOMETHING TELLS ME THAT'S NOT FENTON IN THERE!
HEY, WHO ARE YOU?!
I AM SOLEGO, THE CHAOS GOD! YOU HAVE WHAT IS MINE!
GIVE IT TO ME!!
GIZMODUCK?! TURNED TO A LIFE OF CRIME, HAVE YA?
I AM NOT THIS--THIS--GIZMO-CREATURE! I AM--
WHOEVER YOU ARE, JUST COME QUIETLY AND THERE WON'T BE ANY...
...TROUBLE?

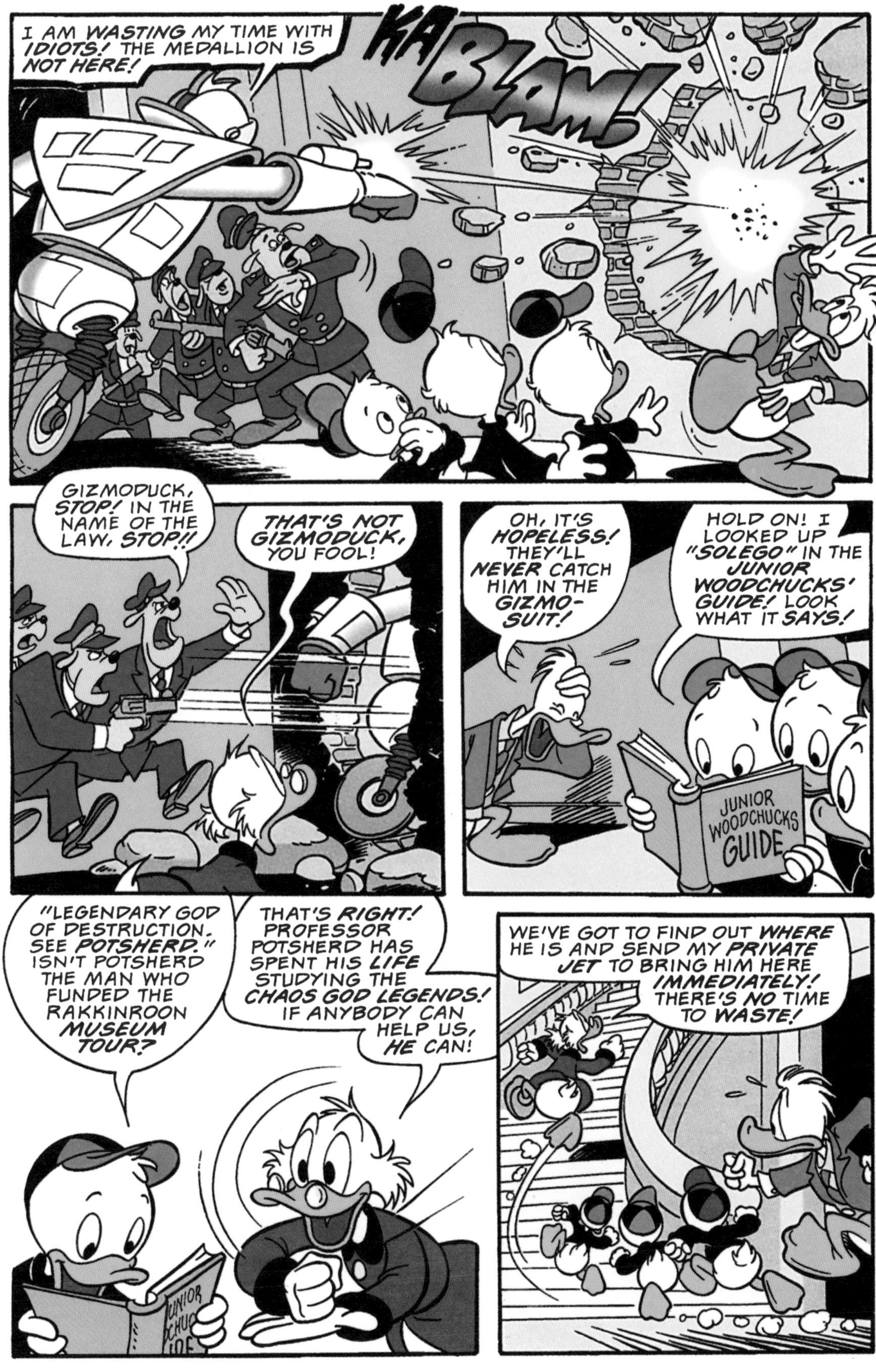
KA BLAM!
I AM WASTING MY TIME WITH IDIOTS! THE MEDALLION IS NOT HERE!
GIZMODUCK, STOP! IN THE NAME OF THE LAW, STOP!!
THAT'S NOT GIZMODUCK, YOU FOOL!
OH, IT'S HOPELESS! THEY'LL NEVER CATCH HIM IN THE GIZMO-SUIT!
HOLD ON! I LOOKED UP "SOLEGO" IN THE JUNIOR WOODCHUCKS' GUIDE! LOOK WHAT IT SAYS!
JUNIOR WOODCHUCKS GUIDE
"LEGENDARY GOD OF DESTRUCTION. SEE POTSHERD." ISN'T POTSHERD THE MAN WHO FUNDED THE RAKKINROON MUSEUM TOUR?
THAT'S RIGHT! PROFESSOR POTSHERD HAS SPENT HIS LIFE STUDYING THE CHAOS GOD LEGENDS! IF ANYBODY CAN HELP US, HE CAN!
WE'VE GOT TO FIND OUT WHERE HE IS AND SEND MY PRIVATE JET TO BRING HIM HERE IMMEDIATELY! THERE'S NO TIME TO WASTE!

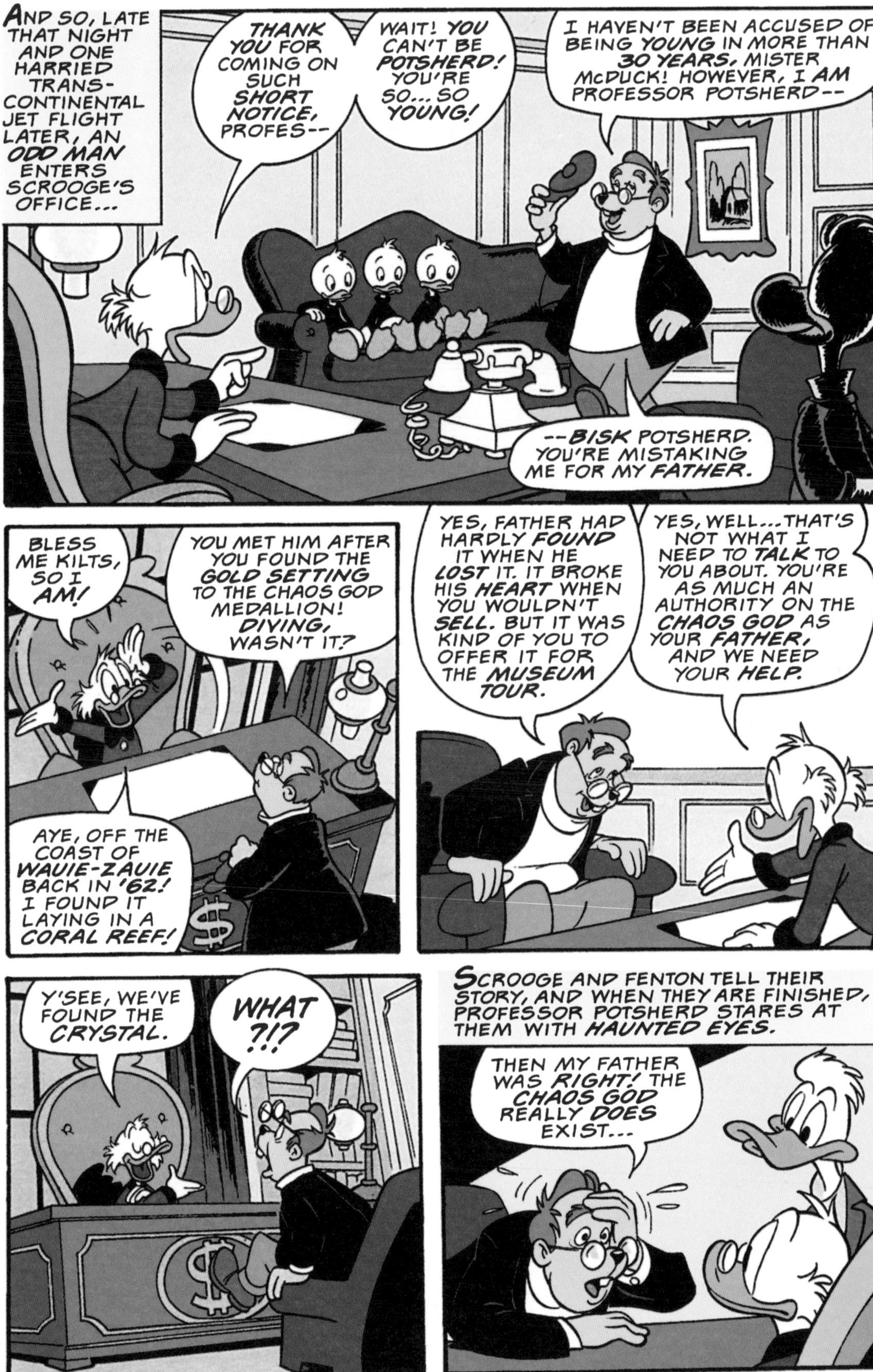

AND SO, LATE THAT NIGHT AND ONE HARRIED TRANS-CONTINENTAL JET FLIGHT LATER, AN ODD MAN ENTERS SCROOGE'S OFFICE...
THANK YOU FOR COMING ON SUCH SHORT NOTICE, PROFES--
WAIT! YOU CAN'T BE POTSHERD! YOU'RE SO... SO YOUNG!
I HAVEN'T BEEN ACCUSED OF BEING YOUNG IN MORE THAN 30 YEARS, MISTER McDUCK! HOWEVER, I AM PROFESSOR POTSHERD--
--BISK POTSHERD. YOU'RE MISTAKING ME FOR MY FATHER.
BLESS ME KILTS, SO I AM!
YOU MET HIM AFTER YOU FOUND THE GOLD SETTING TO THE CHAOS GOD MEDALLION! DIVING, WASN'T IT?
AYE, OFF THE COAST OF WAUIE-ZAUIE BACK IN '62! I FOUND IT LAYING IN A CORAL REEF!
YES, FATHER HAD HARDLY FOUND IT WHEN HE LOST IT. IT BROKE HIS HEART WHEN YOU WOULDN'T SELL. BUT IT WAS KIND OF YOU TO OFFER IT FOR THE MUSEUM TOUR.
YES, WELL... THAT'S NOT WHAT I NEED TO TALK TO YOU ABOUT. YOU'RE AS MUCH AN AUTHORITY ON THE CHAOS GOD AS YOUR FATHER, AND WE NEED YOUR HELP.
Y'SEE, WE'VE FOUND THE CRYSTAL.
WHAT ?!?
SCROOGE AND FENTON TELL THEIR STORY, AND WHEN THEY ARE FINISHED, PROFESSOR POTSHERD STARES AT THEM WITH HAUNTED EYES.
THEN MY FATHER WAS RIGHT! THE CHAOS GOD REALLY DOES EXIST...

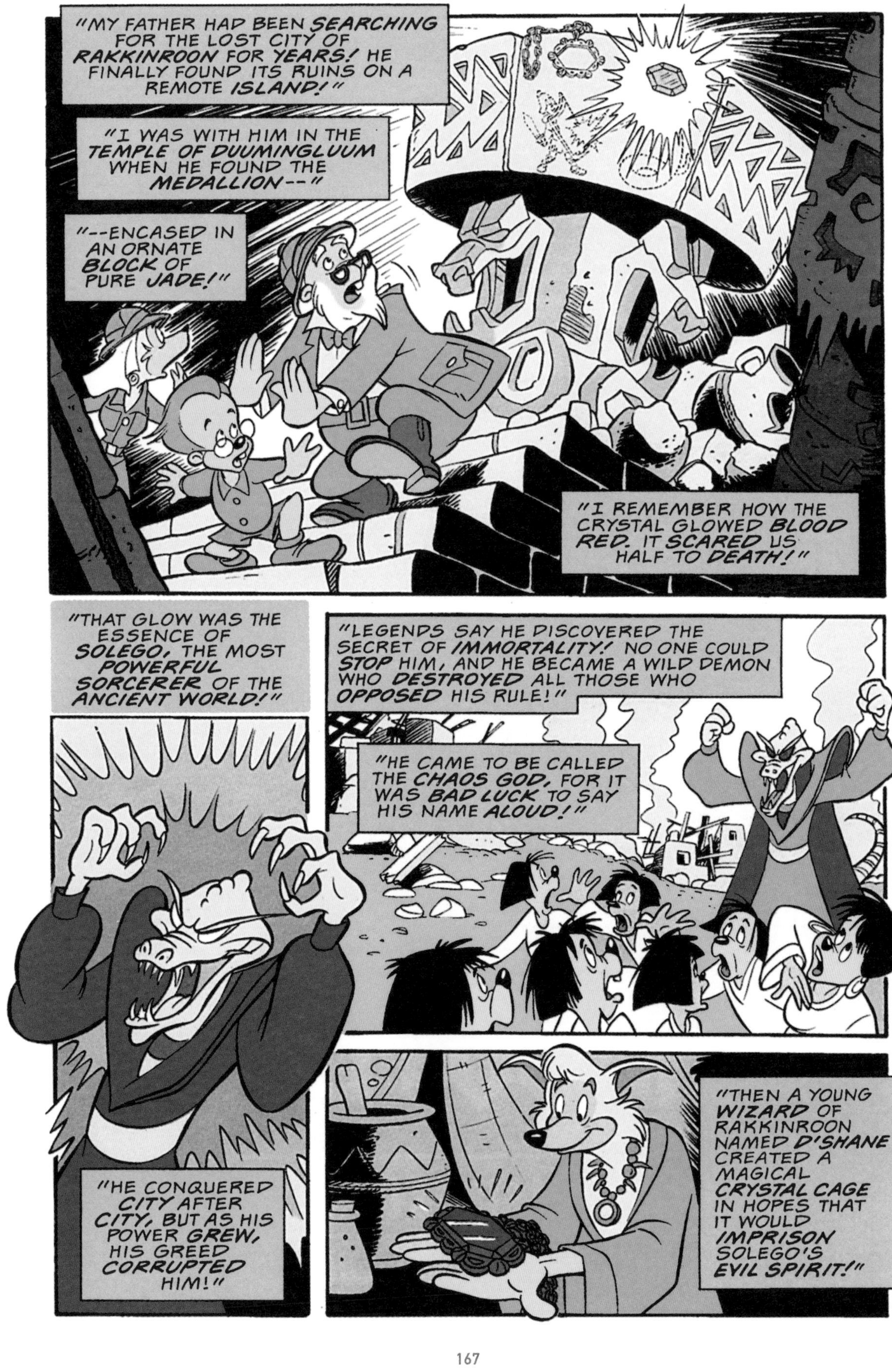
"MY FATHER HAD BEEN SEARCHING FOR THE LOST CITY OF RAKKINROON FOR YEARS! HE FINALLY FOUND ITS RUINS ON A REMOTE ISLAND!"
"I WAS WITH HIM IN THE TEMPLE OF DUUMINGLUUM WHEN HE FOUND THE MEDALLION--"
"--ENCASED IN AN ORNATE BLOCK OF PURE JADE!"
"I REMEMBER HOW THE CRYSTAL GLOWED BLOOD RED. IT SCARED US HALF TO DEATH!"
"THAT GLOW WAS THE ESSENCE OF SOLEGO, THE MOST POWERFUL SORCERER OF THE ANCIENT WORLD!"
"LEGENDS SAY HE DISCOVERED THE SECRET OF IMMORTALITY! NO ONE COULD STOP HIM, AND HE BECAME A WILD DEMON WHO DESTROYED ALL THOSE WHO OPPOSED HIS RULE!"
"HE CAME TO BE CALLED THE CHAOS GOD, FOR IT WAS BAD LUCK TO SAY HIS NAME ALOUD!"
"HE CONQUERED CITY AFTER CITY, BUT AS HIS POWER GREW, HIS GREED CORRUPTED HIM!"
"THEN A YOUNG WIZARD OF RAKKINROON NAMED D'SHANE CREATED A MAGICAL CRYSTAL CAGE IN HOPES THAT IT WOULD IMPRISON SOLEGO'S EVIL SPIRIT!"

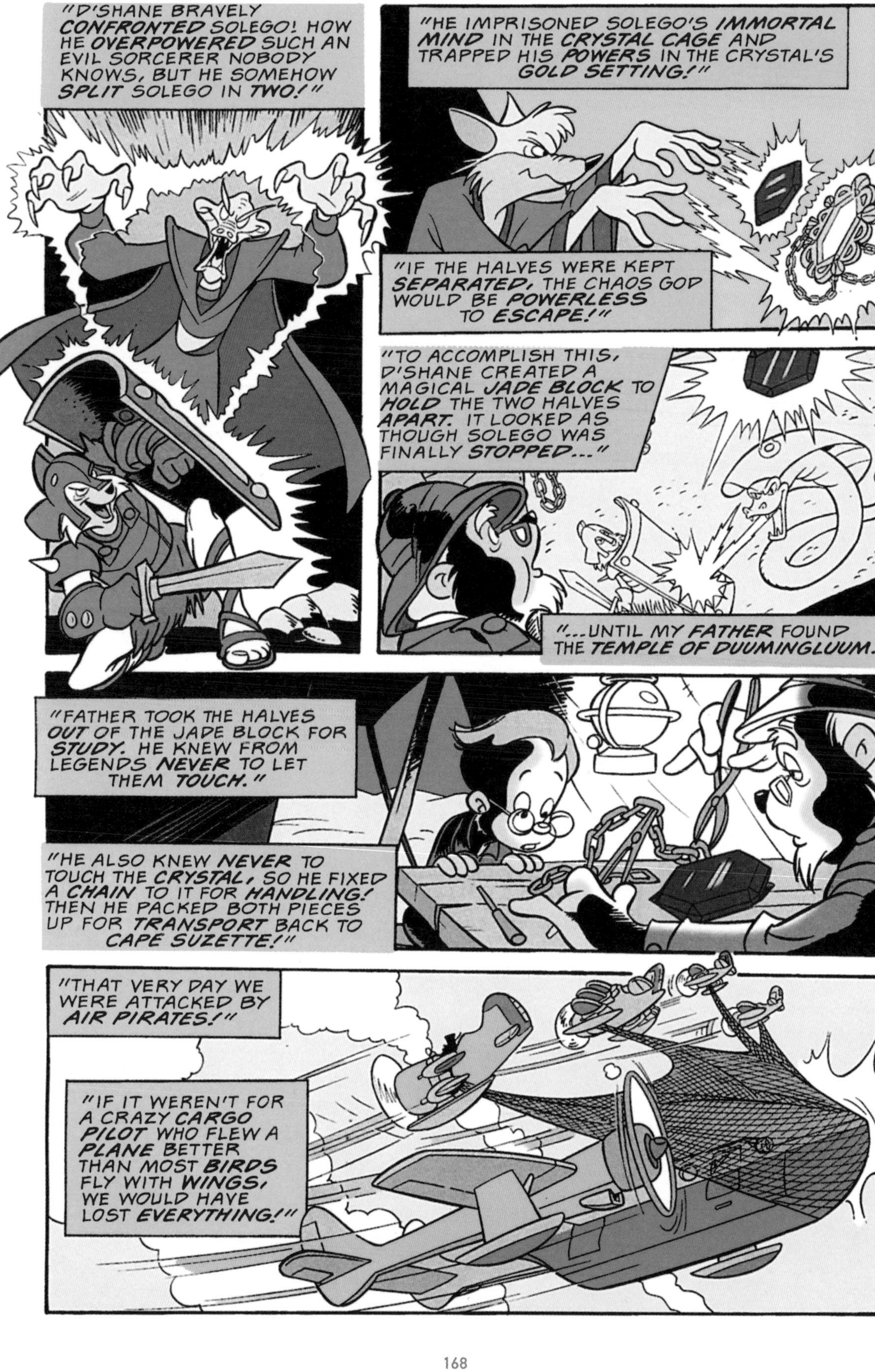
"D'SHANE BRAVELY CONFRONTED SOLEGO! HOW HE OVERPOWERED SUCH AN EVIL SORCERER NOBODY KNOWS, BUT HE SOMEHOW SPLIT SOLEGO IN TWO!"
"HE IMPRISONED SOLEGO'S IMMORTAL MIND IN THE CRYSTAL CAGE AND TRAPPED HIS POWERS IN THE CRYSTAL'S GOLD SETTING!"
"IF THE HALVES WERE KEPT SEPARATED, THE CHAOS GOD WOULD BE POWERLESS TO ESCAPE!"
"TO ACCOMPLISH THIS, D'SHANE CREATED A MAGICAL JADE BLOCK TO HOLD THE TWO HALVES APART. IT LOOKED AS THOUGH SOLEGO WAS FINALLY STOPPED..."
"...UNTIL MY FATHER FOUND THE TEMPLE OF DUUMINGLUUM."
"FATHER TOOK THE HALVES OUT OF THE JADE BLOCK FOR STUDY. HE KNEW FROM LEGENDS NEVER TO LET THEM TOUCH."
"HE ALSO KNEW NEVER TO TOUCH THE CRYSTAL, SO HE FIXED A CHAIN TO IT FOR HANDLING! THEN HE PACKED BOTH PIECES UP FOR TRANSPORT BACK TO CAPE SUZETTE!"
"THAT VERY DAY WE WERE ATTACKED BY AIR PIRATES!"
"IF IT WEREN'T FOR A CRAZY CARGO PILOT WHO FLEW A PLANE BETTER THAN MOST BIRDS FLY WITH WINGS, WE WOULD HAVE LOST EVERYTHING!"

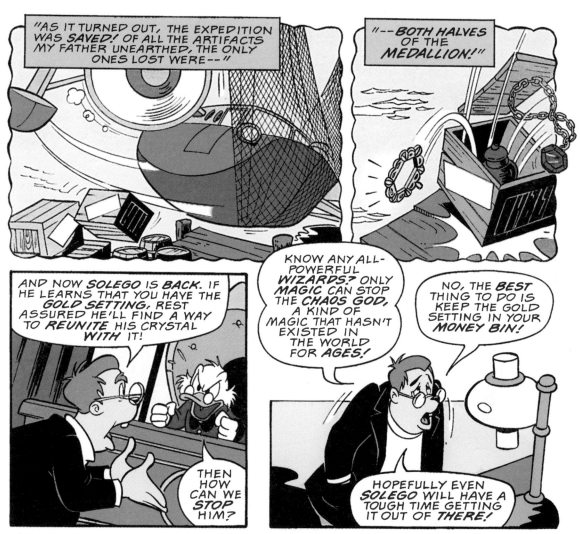

"AS IT TURNED OUT, THE EXPEDITION WAS *SAVED!* OF ALL THE ARTIFACTS MY FATHER UNEARTHED, THE ONLY ONES LOST WERE--"

"--BOTH HALVES OF THE *MEDALLION!*"

AND NOW *SOLEGO* IS *BACK.* IF HE LEARNS THAT YOU HAVE THE *GOLD SETTING,* REST ASSURED HE'LL FIND A WAY TO *REUNITE* HIS CRYSTAL *WITH* IT!

KNOW ANY ALL-POWERFUL *WIZARDS?* ONLY *MAGIC* CAN STOP THE *CHAOS GOD,* A KIND OF MAGIC THAT HASN'T EXISTED IN THE WORLD FOR *AGES!*

NO, THE *BEST* THING TO DO IS KEEP THE GOLD SETTING IN YOUR *MONEY BIN!*

THEN HOW CAN WE *STOP* HIM?

HOPEFULLY EVEN *SOLEGO* WILL HAVE A TOUGH TIME GETTING IT OUT OF *THERE!*

MONEY BIN...?? IT'S NOT *IN* MY MONEY BIN! I SENT IT TO MY JEWELER'S SHOP IN *ST. CANARD* TO BE *CLEANED!*

MEANWHILE AND ELSE-WHERE IN DUCKBURG, AS THE SUN OF A *NEW DAY* BEGINS TO *RISE...*

THIS MAGIC CALLED *TECHNOLOGY* NEVER CEASES TO *AMAZE* ME! WEAPONRY, TOOLS, ARMOR-- ALL HERE IN ONE BODY!

ONCE I REGAIN MY *FULL* POWERS, I SHALL COMBINE THEM WITH *TECHNOLOGY* AND BE *MORE* POWERFUL THAN *EVER!*

SHOOP!

WHIP! SHWIP!

ZIP!

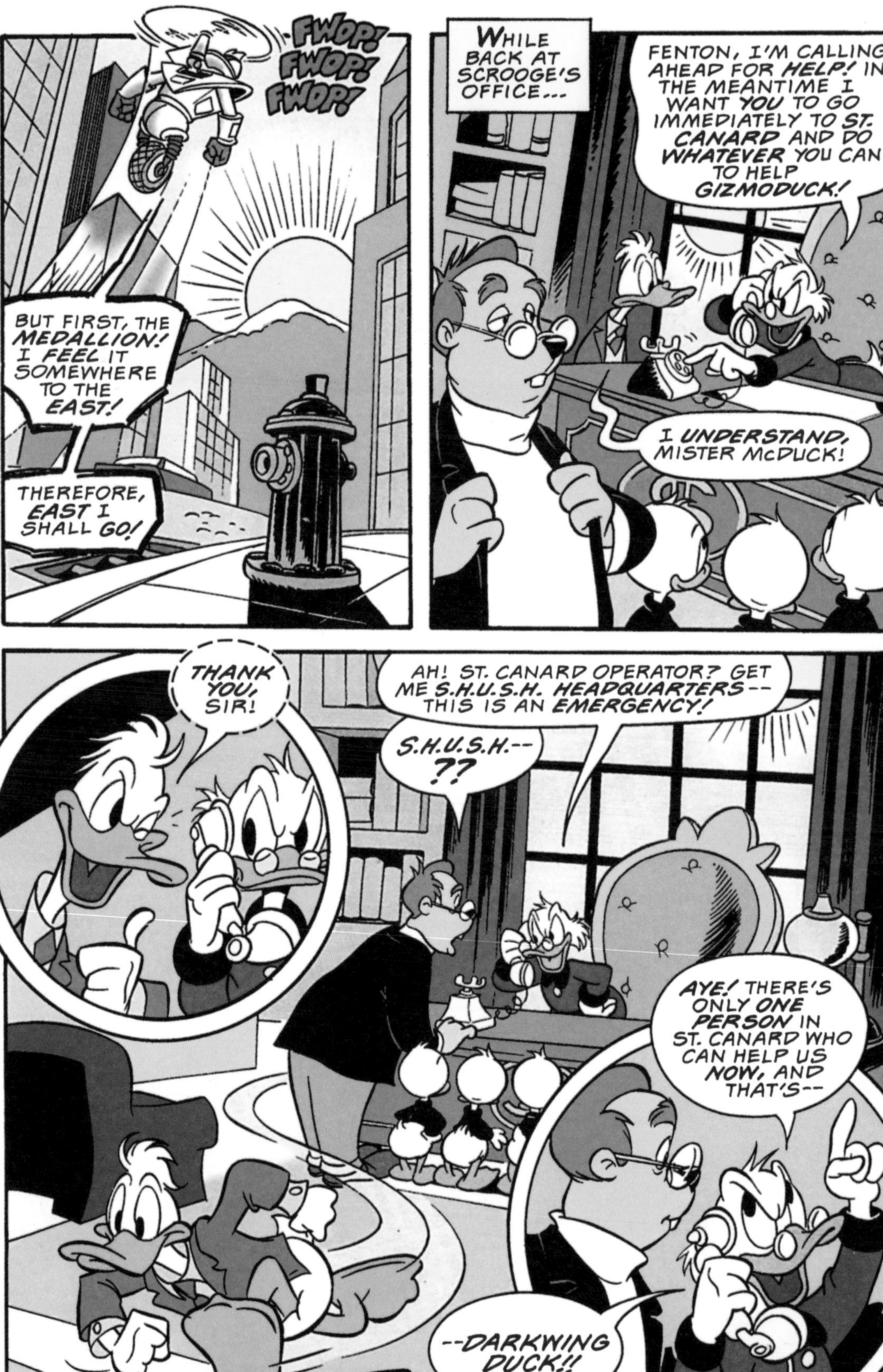
FWOP! FWOP! FWOP!
BUT FIRST, THE MEDALLION! I FEEL IT SOMEWHERE TO THE EAST!
THEREFORE, EAST I SHALL GO!
WHILE BACK AT SCROOGE'S OFFICE...
FENTON, I'M CALLING AHEAD FOR HELP! IN THE MEANTIME I WANT YOU TO GO IMMEDIATELY TO ST. CANARD AND DO WHATEVER YOU CAN TO HELP GIZMODUCK!
I UNDERSTAND, MISTER McDUCK!
THANK YOU, SIR!
AH! ST. CANARD OPERATOR? GET ME S.H.U.S.H. HEADQUARTERS -- THIS IS AN EMERGENCY!
S.H.U.S.H.-- ??
AYE! THERE'S ONLY ONE PERSON IN ST. CANARD WHO CAN HELP US NOW, AND THAT'S--
--DARKWING DUCK!!
TO BE CONCLUDED NEXT ISSUE!

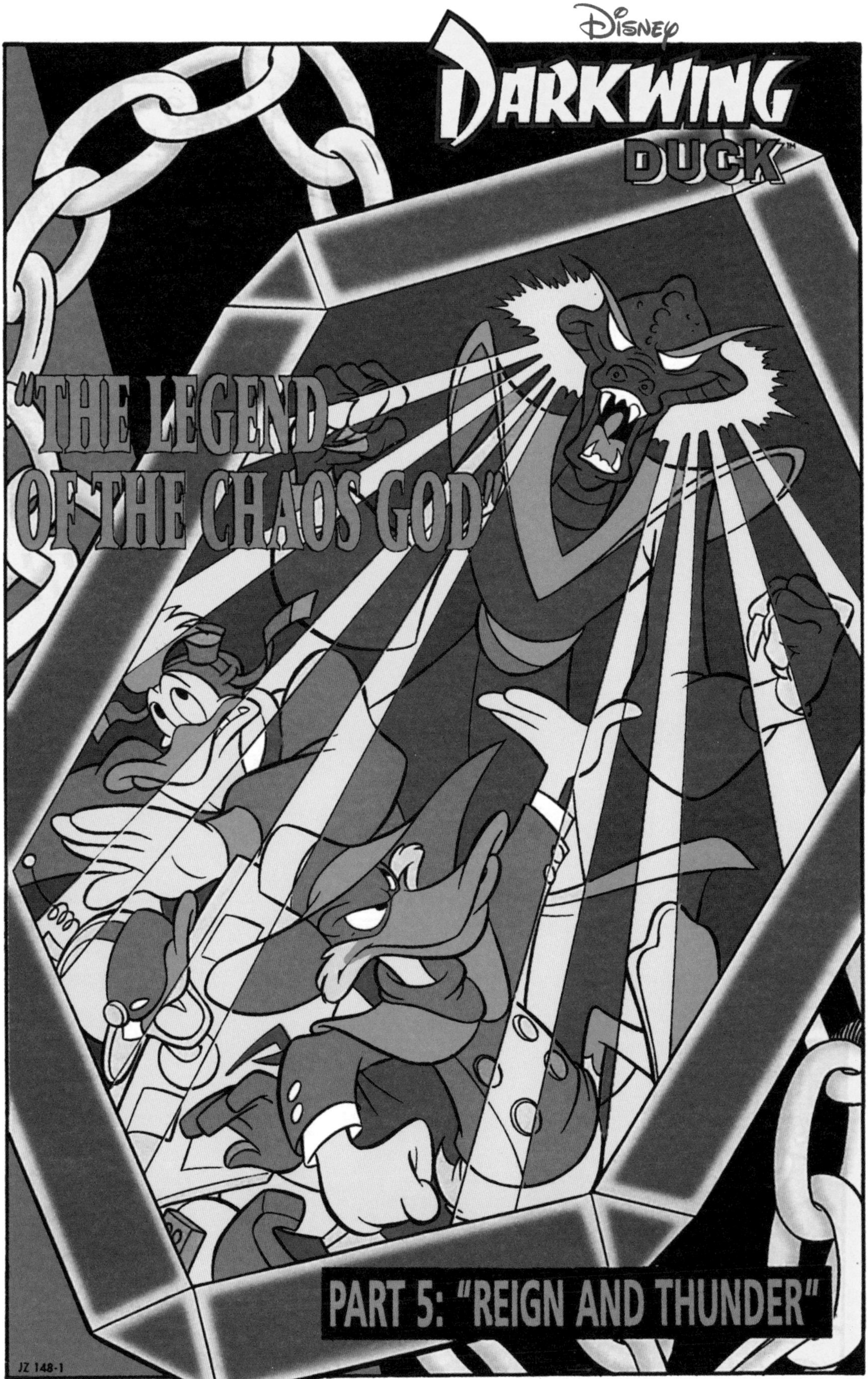
Disney
DARKWING DUCK™
"THE LEGEND OF THE CHAOS GOD"
PART 5: "REIGN AND THUNDER"
JZ 148-1

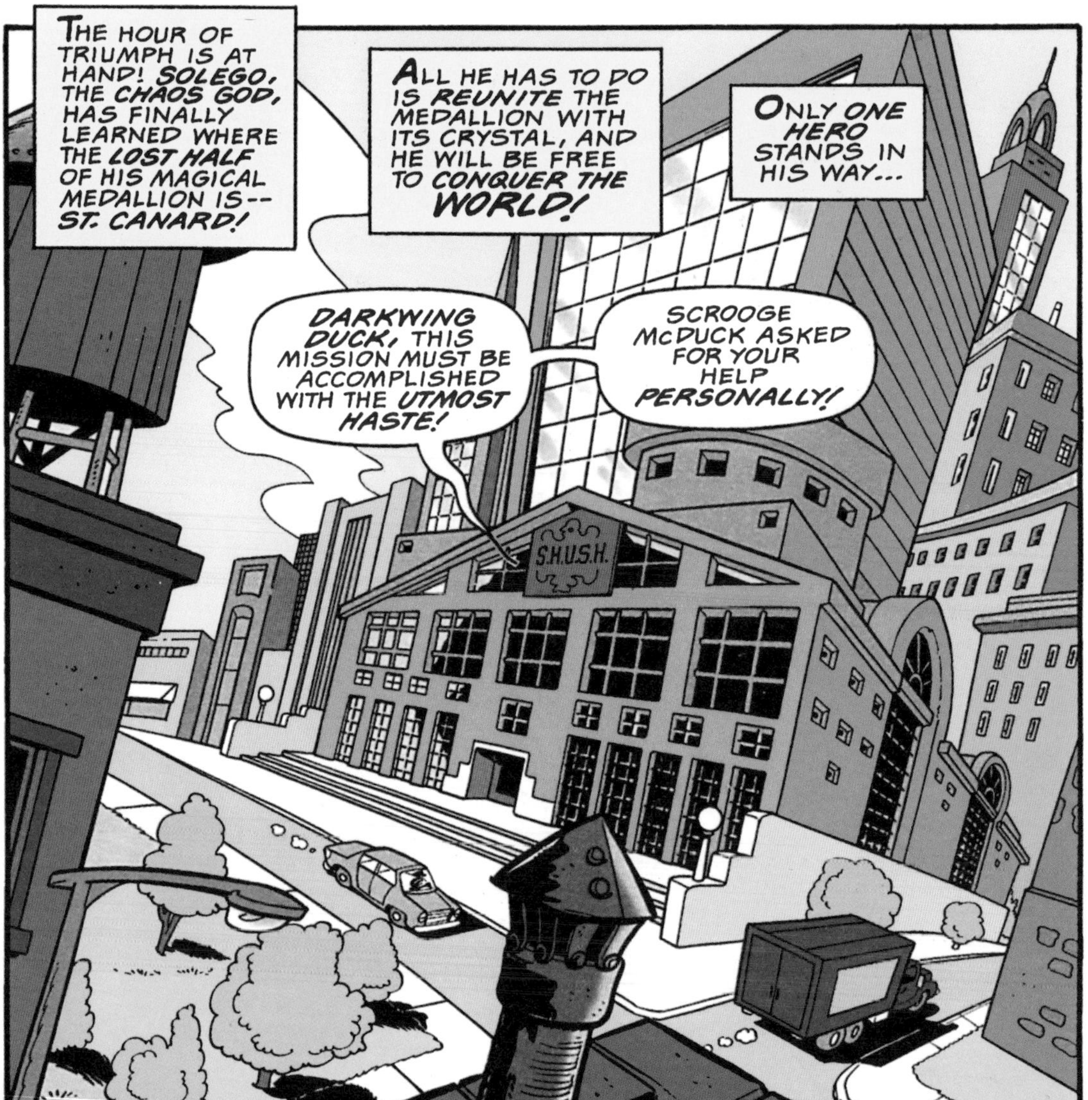
THE HOUR OF TRIUMPH IS AT HAND! SOLEGO, THE CHAOS GOD, HAS FINALLY LEARNED WHERE THE LOST HALF OF HIS MAGICAL MEDALLION IS-- ST. CANARD!
ALL HE HAS TO DO IS REUNITE THE MEDALLION WITH ITS CRYSTAL, AND HE WILL BE FREE TO CONQUER THE WORLD!
ONLY ONE HERO STANDS IN HIS WAY...
DARKWING DUCK, THIS MISSION MUST BE ACCOMPLISHED WITH THE UTMOST HASTE!
SCROOGE McDUCK ASKED FOR YOUR HELP PERSONALLY!
S.H.U.S.H.

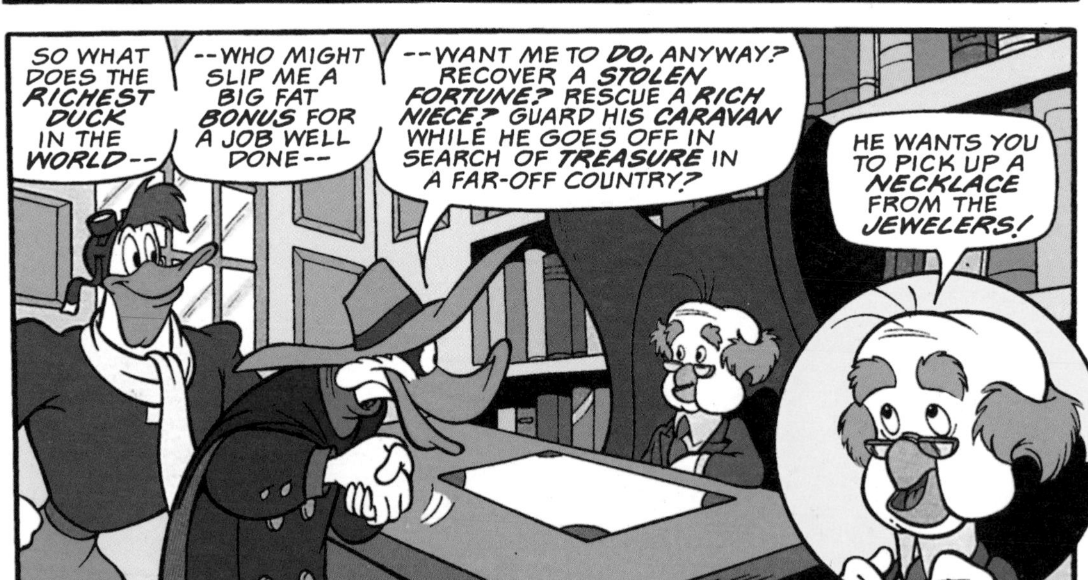
SO WHAT DOES THE RICHEST DUCK IN THE WORLD--
--WHO MIGHT SLIP ME A BIG FAT BONUS FOR A JOB WELL DONE--
--WANT ME TO DO, ANYWAY? RECOVER A STOLEN FORTUNE? RESCUE A RICH NIECE? GUARD HIS CARAVAN WHILE HE GOES OFF IN SEARCH OF TREASURE IN A FAR-OFF COUNTRY?
HE WANTS YOU TO PICK UP A NECKLACE FROM THE JEWELERS!

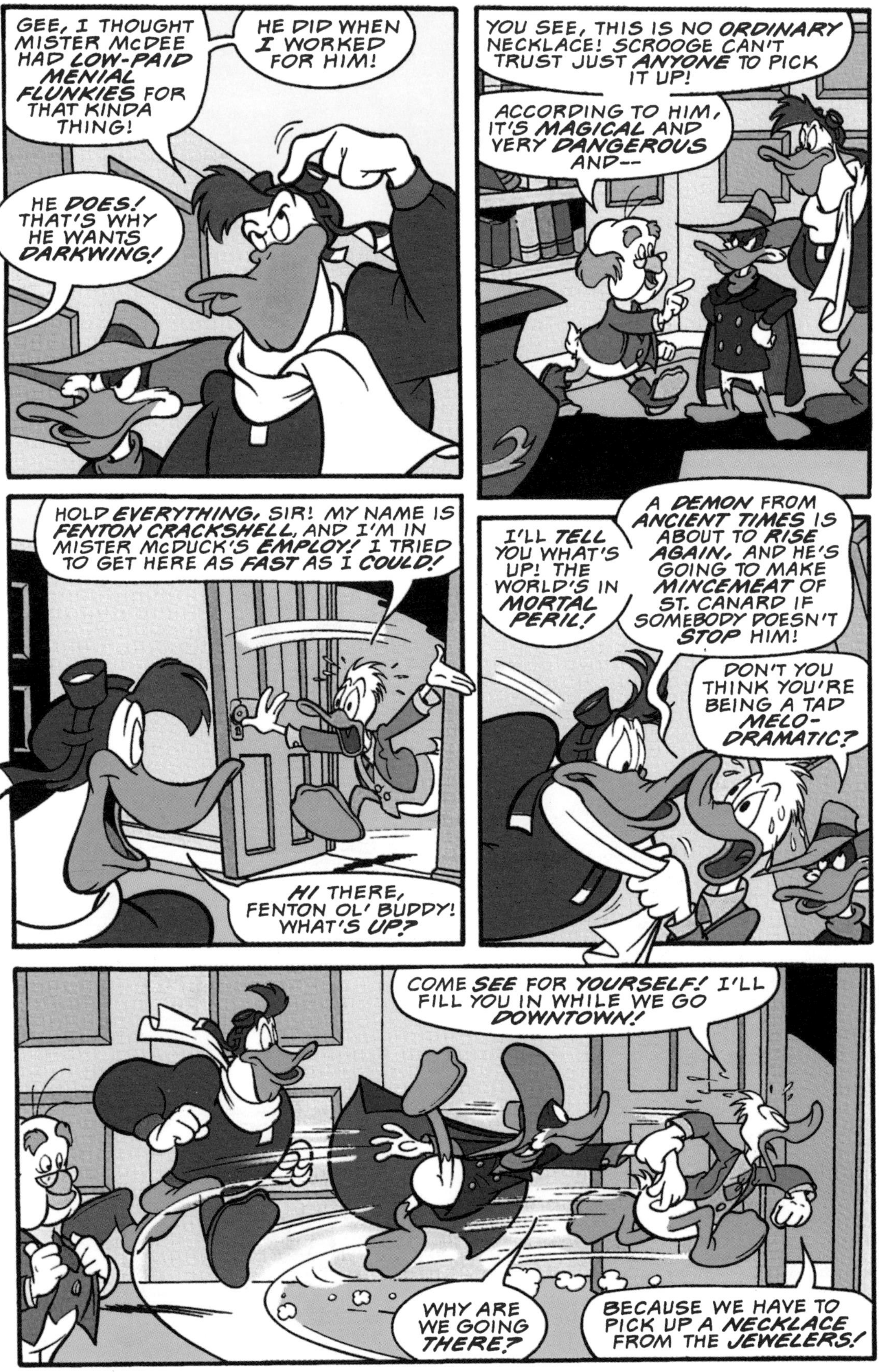
GEE, I THOUGHT MISTER McDEE HAD LOW-PAID MENIAL FLUNKIES FOR THAT KINDA THING!
HE DID WHEN I WORKED FOR HIM!
HE DOES! THAT'S WHY HE WANTS DARKWING!
YOU SEE, THIS IS NO ORDINARY NECKLACE! SCROOGE CAN'T TRUST JUST ANYONE TO PICK IT UP!
ACCORDING TO HIM, IT'S MAGICAL AND VERY DANGEROUS AND--
HOLD EVERYTHING, SIR! MY NAME IS FENTON CRACKSHELL, AND I'M IN MISTER McDUCK'S EMPLOY! I TRIED TO GET HERE AS FAST AS I COULD!
HI THERE, FENTON OL' BUDDY! WHAT'S UP?
I'LL TELL YOU WHAT'S UP! THE WORLD'S IN MORTAL PERIL!
A DEMON FROM ANCIENT TIMES IS ABOUT TO RISE AGAIN, AND HE'S GOING TO MAKE MINCEMEAT OF ST. CANARD IF SOMEBODY DOESN'T STOP HIM!
DON'T YOU THINK YOU'RE BEING A TAD MELO-DRAMATIC?
COME SEE FOR YOURSELF! I'LL FILL YOU IN WHILE WE GO DOWNTOWN!
WHY ARE WE GOING THERE?
BECAUSE WE HAVE TO PICK UP A NECKLACE FROM THE JEWELERS!

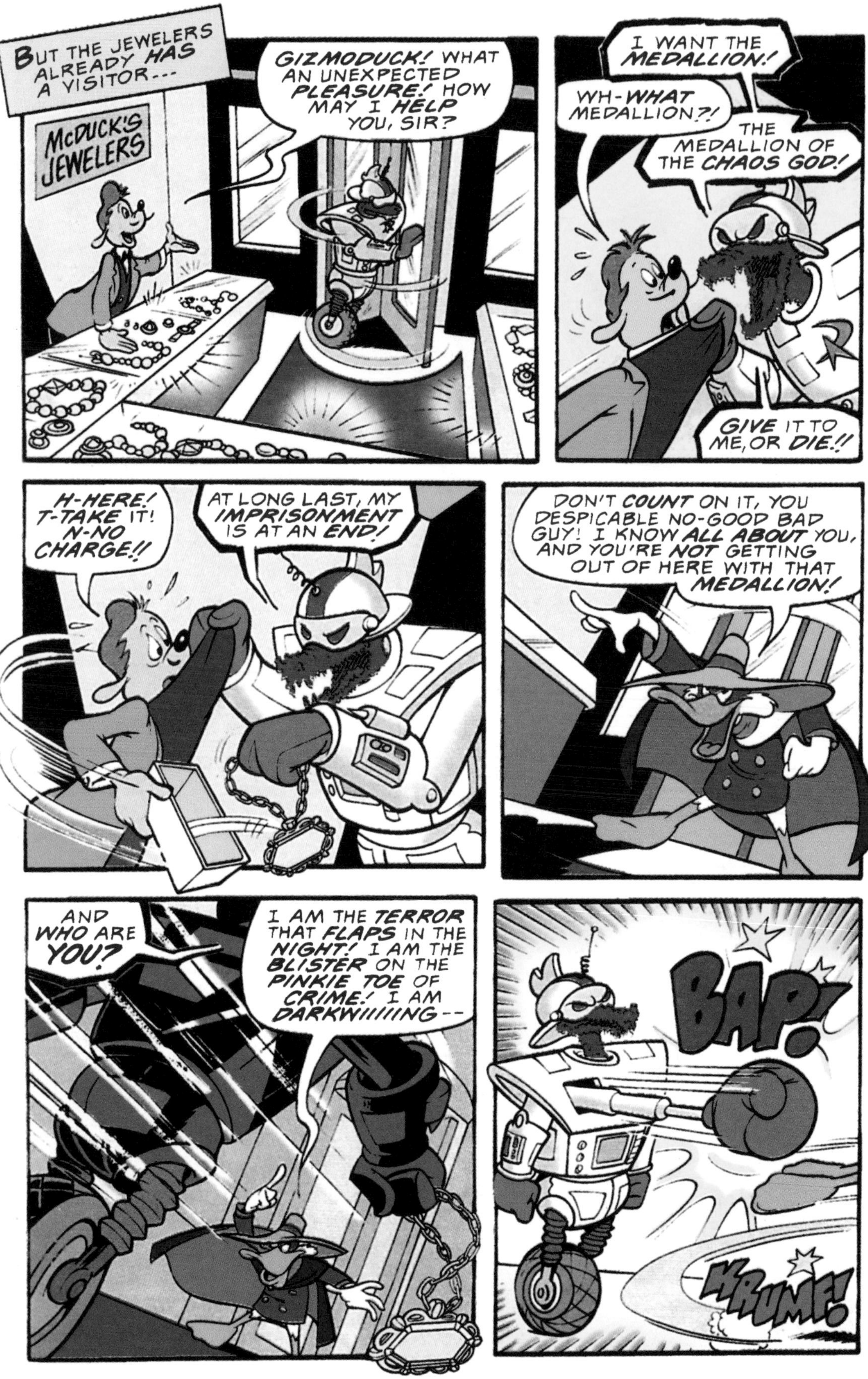
BUT THE JEWELERS ALREADY HAS A VISITOR---
McDUCK'S JEWELERS
GIZMODUCK! WHAT AN UNEXPECTED PLEASURE! HOW MAY I HELP YOU, SIR?
I WANT THE MEDALLION!
WH-WHAT MEDALLION?!
THE MEDALLION OF THE CHAOS GOD!
GIVE IT TO ME, OR DIE!!
H-HERE! T-TAKE IT! N-NO CHARGE!!
AT LONG LAST, MY IMPRISONMENT IS AT AN END!
DON'T COUNT ON IT, YOU DESPICABLE NO-GOOD BAD GUY! I KNOW ALL ABOUT YOU, AND YOU'RE NOT GETTING OUT OF HERE WITH THAT MEDALLION!
AND WHO ARE YOU?
I AM THE TERROR THAT FLAPS IN THE NIGHT! I AM THE BLISTER ON THE PINKIE TOE OF CRIME! I AM DARKWIIIIIING--
BAP!
KRUMF!

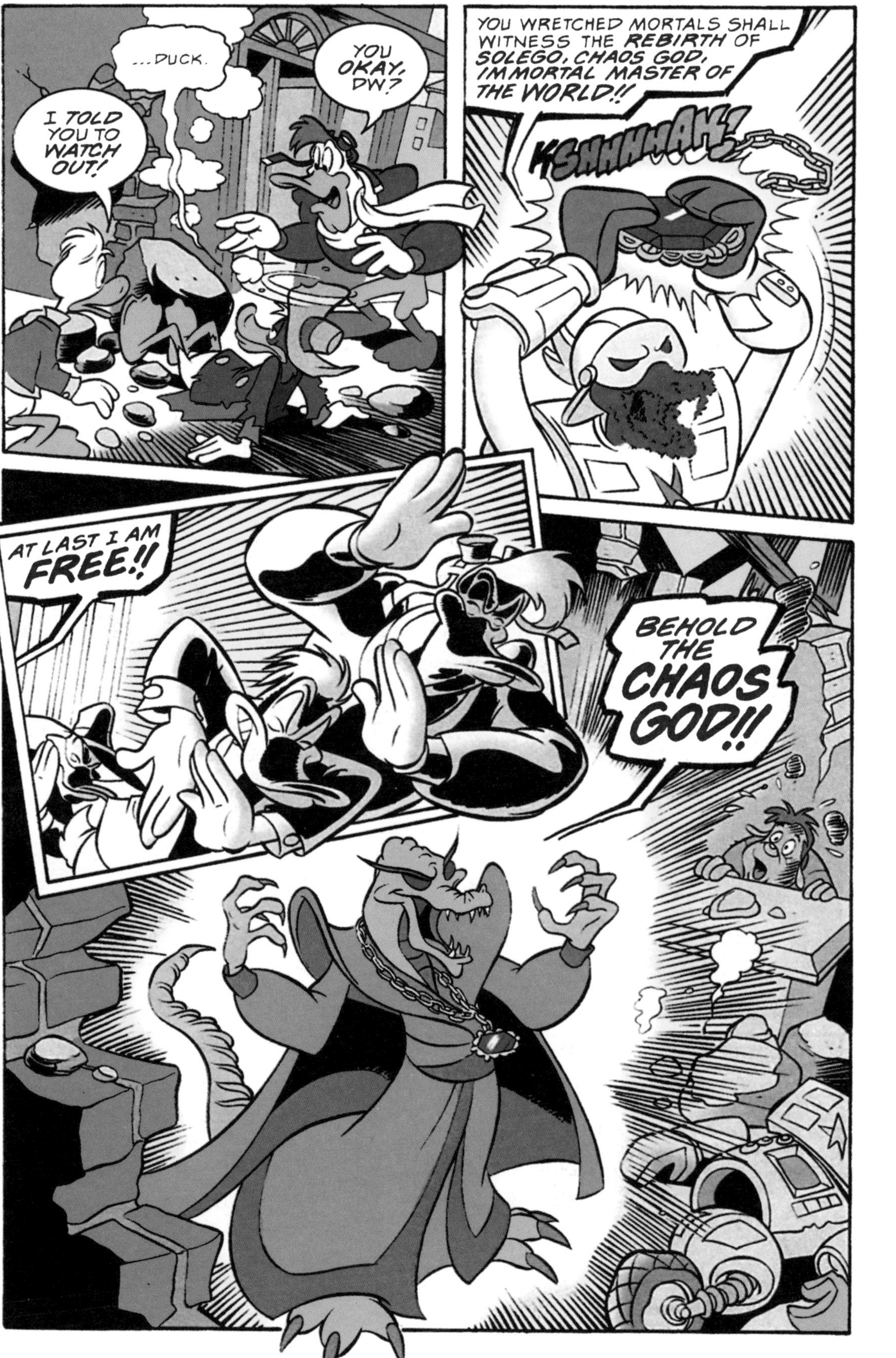

I TOLD YOU TO WATCH OUT!
...DUCK.
YOU OKAY, DW?
YOU WRETCHED MORTALS SHALL WITNESS THE REBIRTH OF SOLEGO, CHAOS GOD, IMMORTAL MASTER OF THE WORLD!!
K-SHHHHAH!
AT LAST I AM FREE!!
BEHOLD THE CHAOS GOD!!

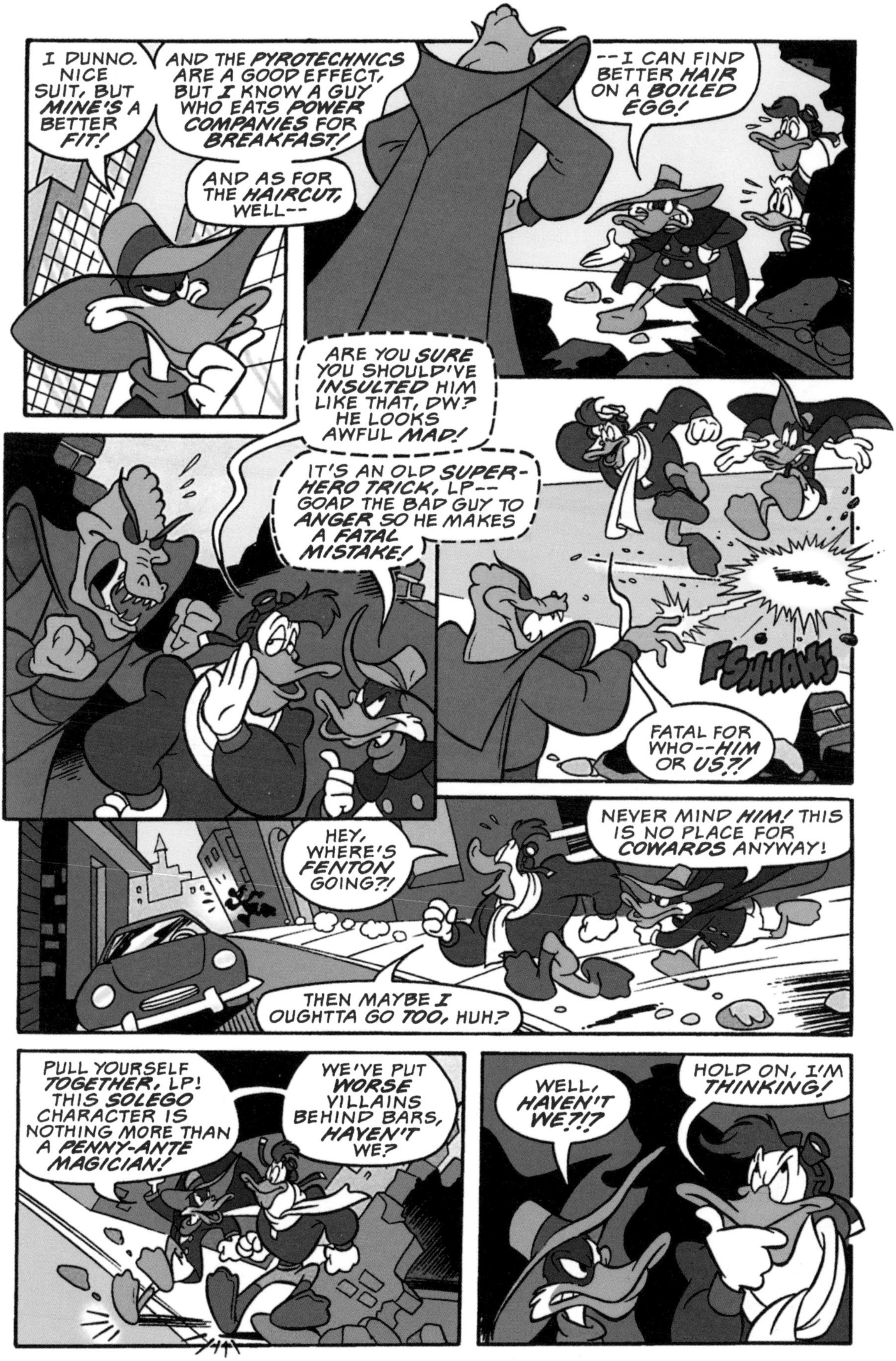
I DUNNO. NICE SUIT, BUT MINE'S A BETTER FIT!
AND THE PYROTECHNICS ARE A GOOD EFFECT, BUT I KNOW A GUY WHO EATS POWER COMPANIES FOR BREAKFAST!
AND AS FOR THE HAIRCUT, WELL--
--I CAN FIND BETTER HAIR ON A BOILED EGG!
ARE YOU SURE YOU SHOULD'VE INSULTED HIM LIKE THAT, DW? HE LOOKS AWFUL MAD!
IT'S AN OLD SUPER-HERO TRICK, LP-- GOAD THE BAD GUY TO ANGER SO HE MAKES A FATAL MISTAKE!
FSHHAWW
FATAL FOR WHO--HIM OR US?!
HEY, WHERE'S FENTON GOING?!
NEVER MIND HIM! THIS IS NO PLACE FOR COWARDS ANYWAY!
THEN MAYBE I OUGHTTA GO TOO, HUH?
PULL YOURSELF TOGETHER, LP! THIS SOLEGO CHARACTER IS NOTHING MORE THAN A PENNY-ANTE MAGICIAN!
WE'VE PUT WORSE VILLAINS BEHIND BARS, HAVEN'T WE?
WELL, HAVEN'T WE?!?
HOLD ON, I'M THINKING!

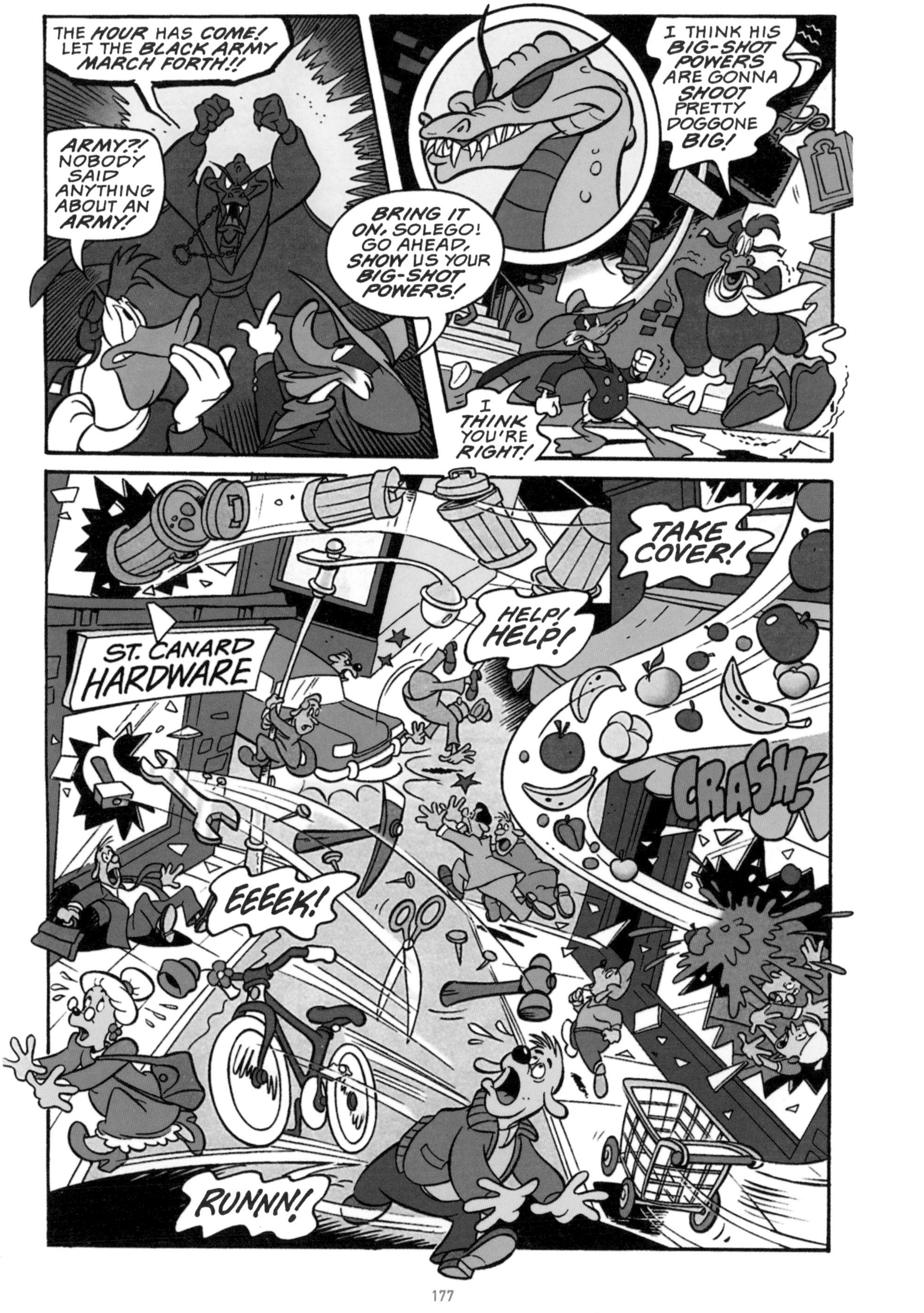
THE HOUR HAS COME! LET THE BLACK ARMY MARCH FORTH!!
ARMY?! NOBODY SAID ANYTHING ABOUT AN ARMY!
BRING IT ON, SOLEGO! GO AHEAD, SHOW US YOUR BIG-SHOT POWERS!
I THINK HIS BIG-SHOT POWERS ARE GONNA SHOOT PRETTY DOGGONE BIG!
I THINK YOU'RE RIGHT!
TAKE COVER!
HELP! HELP!
ST. CANARD HARDWARE
CRASH!
EEEEK!
RUNNN!

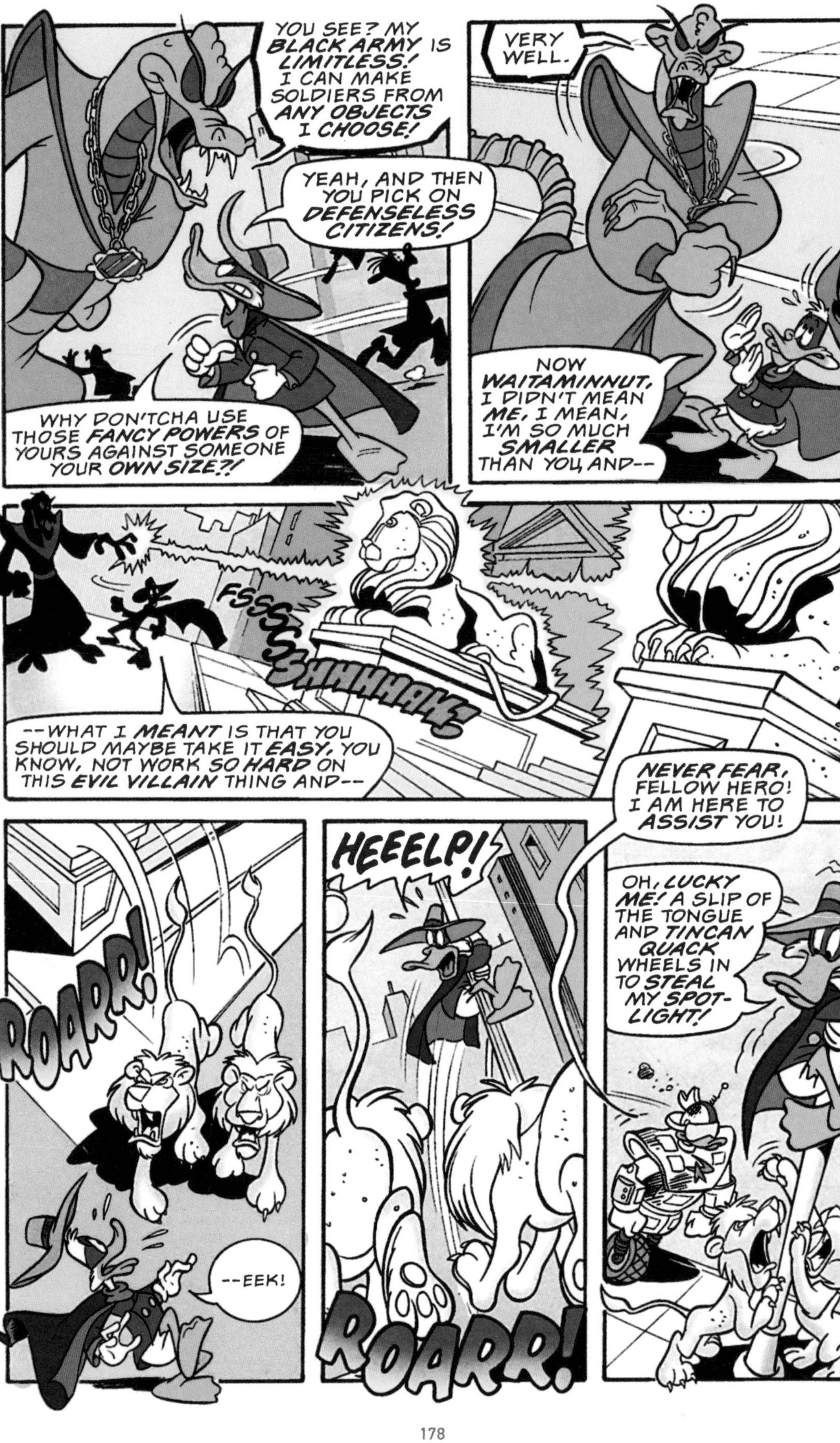
YOU SEE? MY BLACK ARMY IS LIMITLESS! I CAN MAKE SOLDIERS FROM ANY OBJECTS I CHOOSE!
YEAH, AND THEN YOU PICK ON DEFENSELESS CITIZENS!
WHY DON'TCHA USE THOSE FANCY POWERS OF YOURS AGAINST SOMEONE YOUR OWN SIZE?!
VERY WELL.
NOW WAITAMINNUT, I DIDN'T MEAN ME, I MEAN, I'M SO MUCH SMALLER THAN YOU, AND--
FSSSSSSHHHHHAK!
--WHAT I MEANT IS THAT YOU SHOULD MAYBE TAKE IT EASY. YOU KNOW, NOT WORK SO HARD ON THIS EVIL VILLAIN THING AND--
ROARR!
--EEK!
HEEELP!
ROARR!
NEVER FEAR, FELLOW HERO! I AM HERE TO ASSIST YOU!
OH, LUCKY ME! A SLIP OF THE TONGUE AND TINCAN QUACK WHEELS IN TO STEAL MY SPOT-LIGHT!

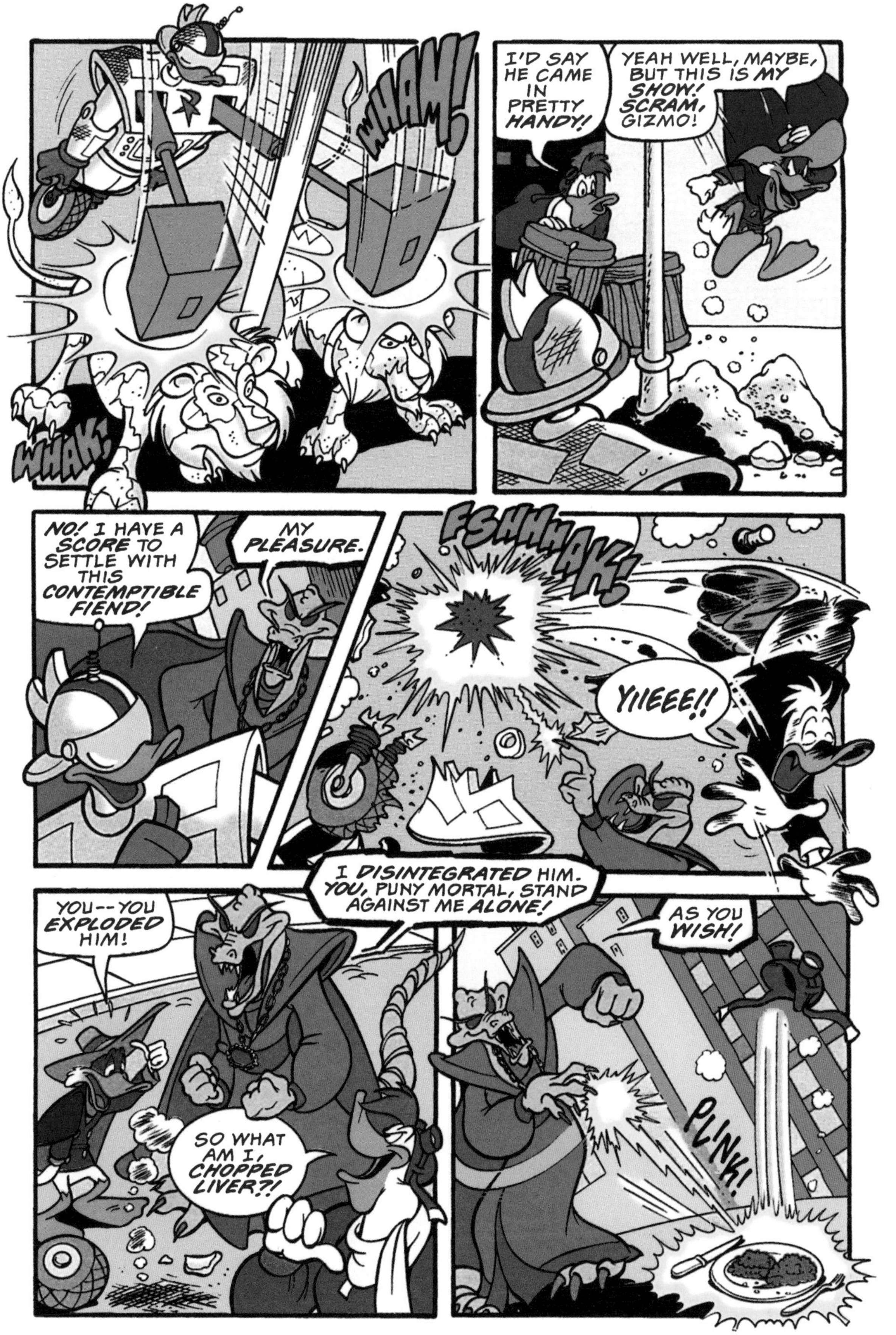
WHAM!
WHAK!
I'D SAY HE CAME IN PRETTY HANDY!
YEAH WELL, MAYBE, BUT THIS IS MY SHOW! SCRAM, GIZMO!
NO! I HAVE A SCORE TO SETTLE WITH THIS CONTEMPTIBLE FIEND!
MY PLEASURE.
FSHHHAK!
YIIEEE!!
YOU--YOU EXPLODED HIM!
I DISINTEGRATED HIM. YOU, PUNY MORTAL, STAND AGAINST ME ALONE!
SO WHAT AM I, CHOPPED LIVER?!
AS YOU WISH!
PLINK!

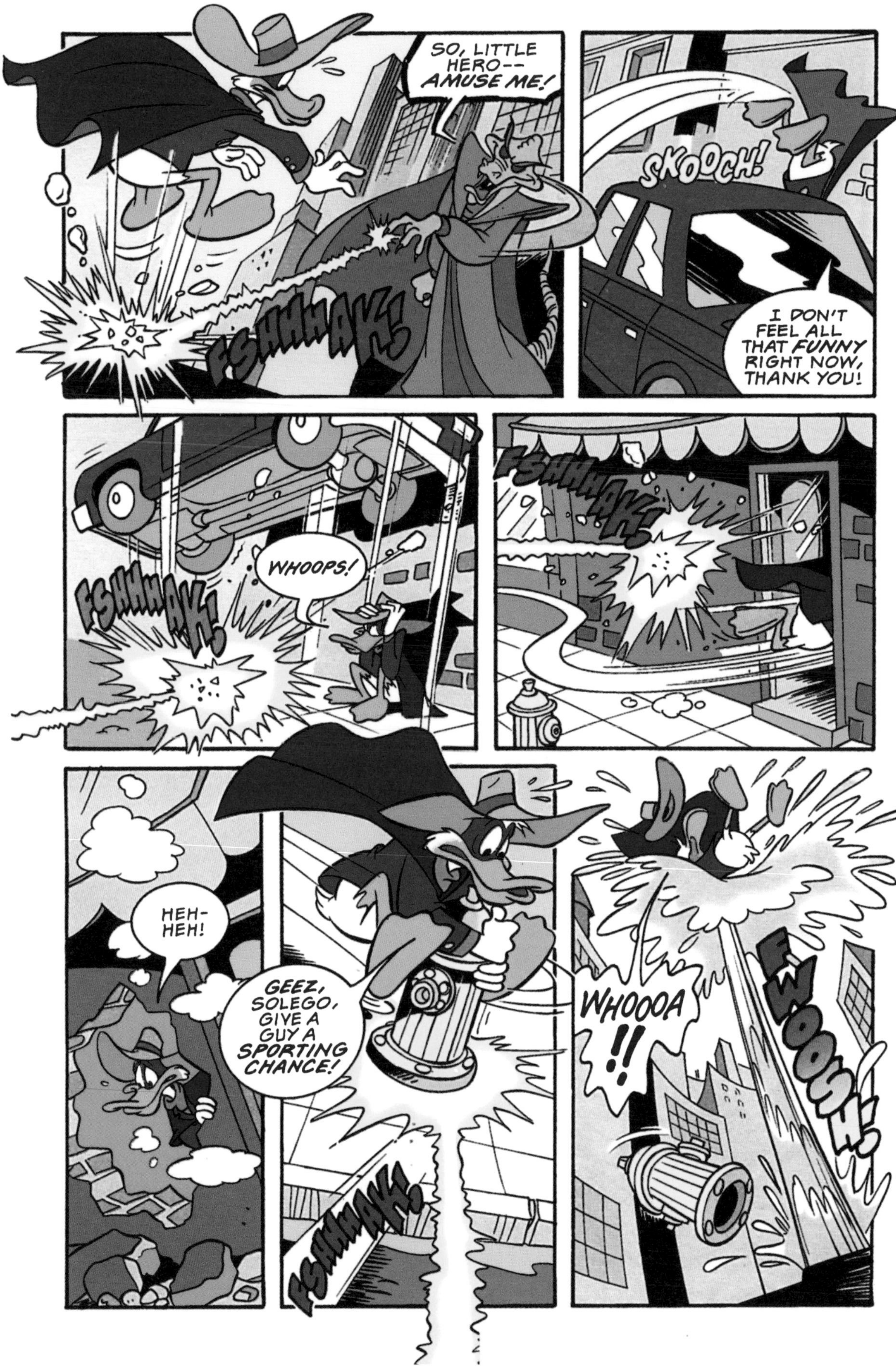

SO, LITTLE HERO-- AMUSE ME!
FSHHHAK!
SKOOCH!
I DON'T FEEL ALL THAT FUNNY RIGHT NOW, THANK YOU!
FSHHHAK!
WHOOPS!
FSHHHAK!
HEH-HEH!
GEEZ, SOLEGO, GIVE A GUY A SPORTING CHANCE!
FSHHHAK!
WHOOOA!!
FWOOSH!

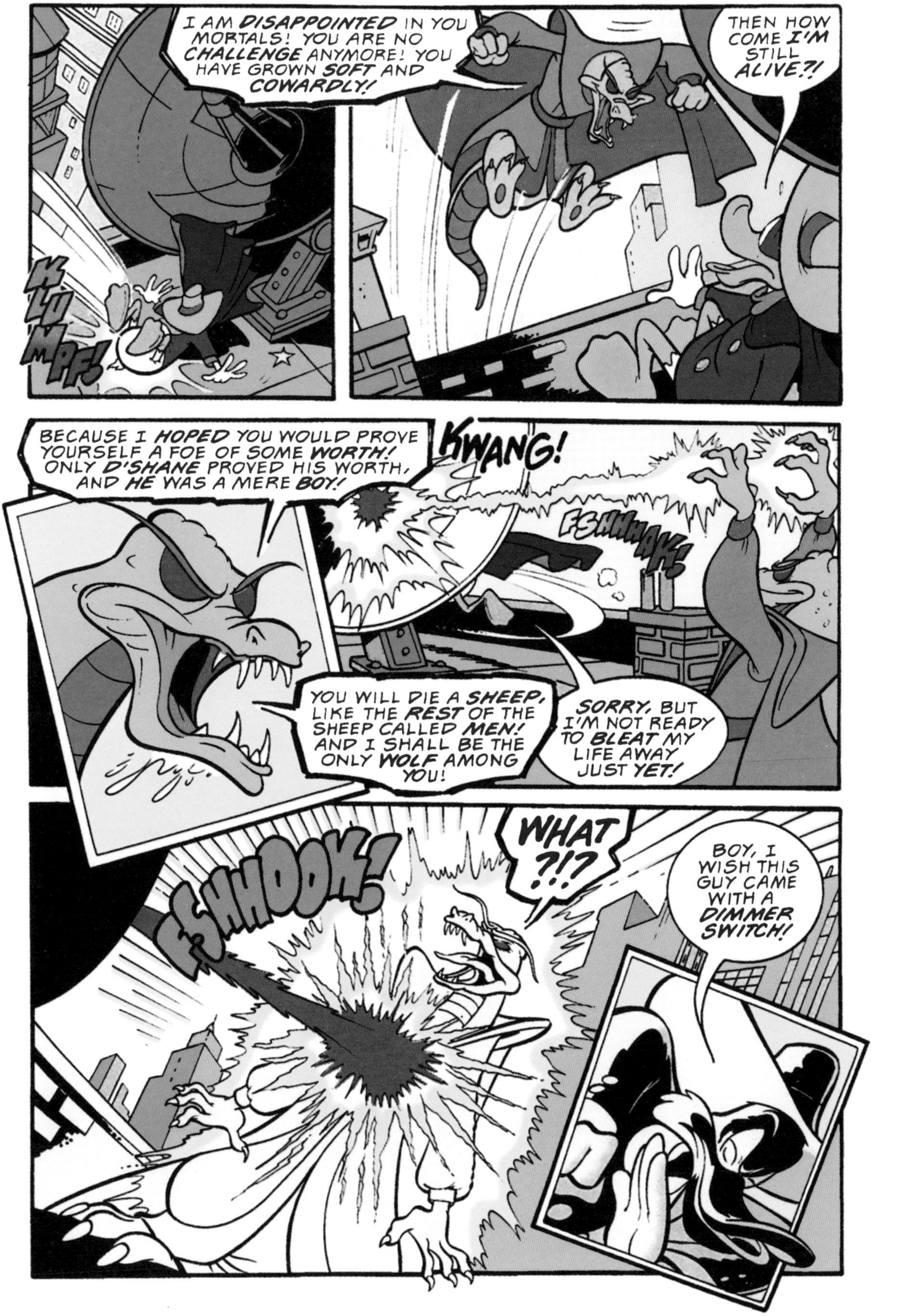

I AM DISAPPOINTED IN YOU MORTALS! YOU ARE NO CHALLENGE ANYMORE! YOU HAVE GROWN SOFT AND COWARDLY!
KLUMPF!
THEN HOW COME I'M STILL ALIVE?!
BECAUSE I HOPED YOU WOULD PROVE YOURSELF A FOE OF SOME WORTH! ONLY D'SHANE PROVED HIS WORTH, AND HE WAS A MERE BOY!
KWANG!
FSHHHAK!
YOU WILL DIE A SHEEP, LIKE THE REST OF THE SHEEP CALLED MEN! AND I SHALL BE THE ONLY WOLF AMONG YOU!
SORRY, BUT I'M NOT READY TO BLEAT MY LIFE AWAY JUST YET!
FSHHOOK!
WHAT ?!?
BOY, I WISH THIS GUY CAME WITH A DIMMER SWITCH!

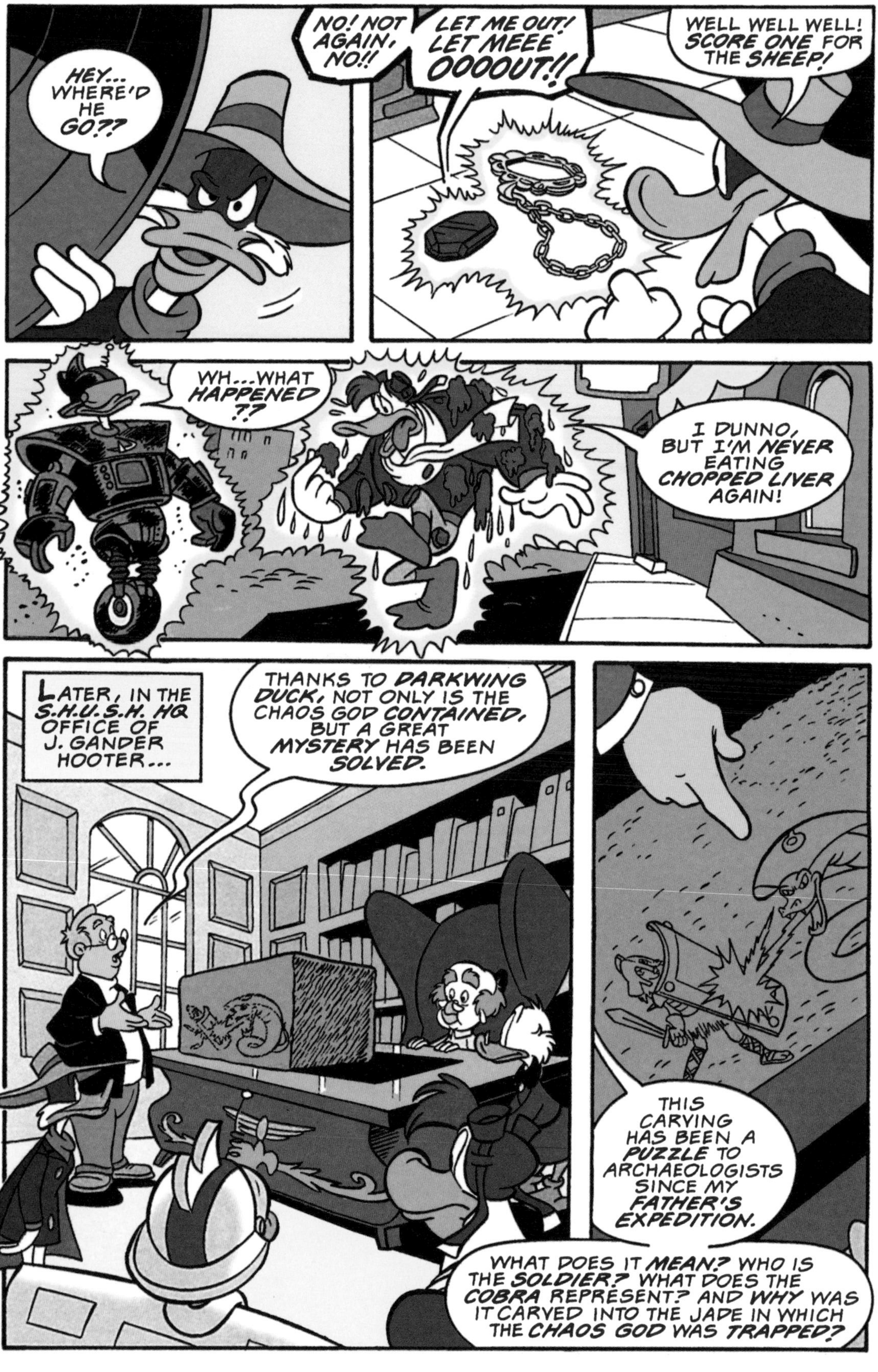
HEY... WHERE'D HE GO??
NO! NOT AGAIN, NO!!
LET ME OUT! LET MEEE OOOOUT!!
WELL WELL WELL! SCORE ONE FOR THE SHEEP!
WH...WHAT HAPPENED??
I DUNNO, BUT I'M NEVER EATING CHOPPED LIVER AGAIN!
LATER, IN THE S.H.U.S.H. HQ OFFICE OF J. GANDER HOOTER...
THANKS TO DARKWING DUCK, NOT ONLY IS THE CHAOS GOD CONTAINED, BUT A GREAT MYSTERY HAS BEEN SOLVED.
THIS CARVING HAS BEEN A PUZZLE TO ARCHAEOLOGISTS SINCE MY FATHER'S EXPEDITION.
WHAT DOES IT MEAN? WHO IS THE SOLDIER? WHAT DOES THE COBRA REPRESENT? AND WHY WAS IT CARVED INTO THE JADE IN WHICH THE CHAOS GOD WAS TRAPPED?

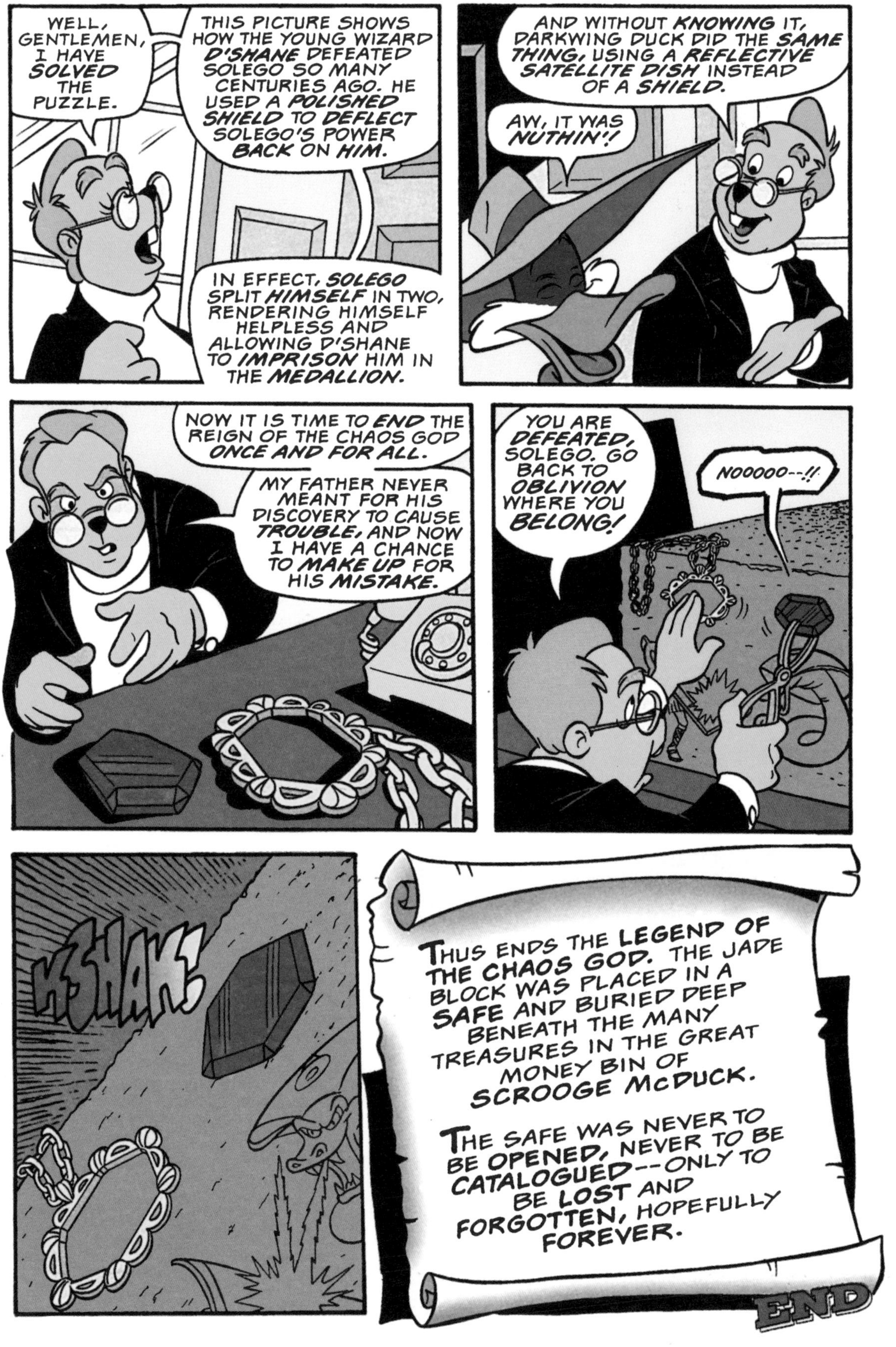

WELL, GENTLEMEN, I HAVE SOLVED THE PUZZLE.
THIS PICTURE SHOWS HOW THE YOUNG WIZARD D'SHANE DEFEATED SOLEGO SO MANY CENTURIES AGO. HE USED A POLISHED SHIELD TO DEFLECT SOLEGO'S POWER BACK ON HIM.
IN EFFECT, SOLEGO SPLIT HIMSELF IN TWO, RENDERING HIMSELF HELPLESS AND ALLOWING D'SHANE TO IMPRISON HIM IN THE MEDALLION.
AND WITHOUT KNOWING IT, DARKWING DUCK DID THE SAME THING, USING A REFLECTIVE SATELLITE DISH INSTEAD OF A SHIELD.
AW, IT WAS NUTHIN'!
NOW IT IS TIME TO END THE REIGN OF THE CHAOS GOD ONCE AND FOR ALL.
MY FATHER NEVER MEANT FOR HIS DISCOVERY TO CAUSE TROUBLE, AND NOW I HAVE A CHANCE TO MAKE UP FOR HIS MISTAKE.
YOU ARE DEFEATED, SOLEGO. GO BACK TO OBLIVION WHERE YOU BELONG!
NOOOOO--!!
K-SHAK!
THUS ENDS THE LEGEND OF THE CHAOS GOD. THE JADE BLOCK WAS PLACED IN A SAFE AND BURIED DEEP BENEATH THE MANY TREASURES IN THE GREAT MONEY BIN OF SCROOGE McDUCK.
THE SAFE WAS NEVER TO BE OPENED, NEVER TO BE CATALOGUED--ONLY TO BE LOST AND FORGOTTEN, HOPEFULLY FOREVER.
END

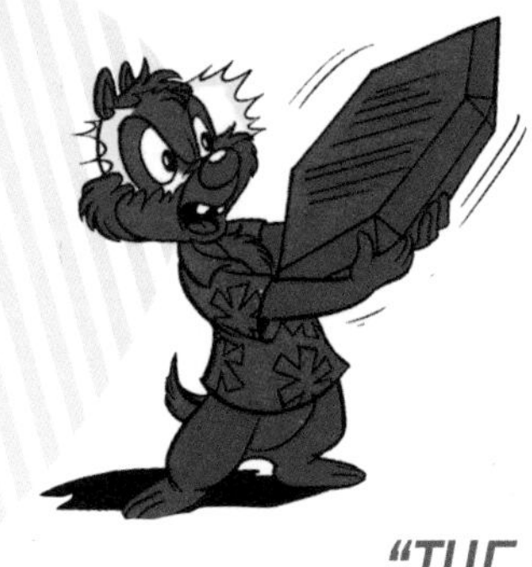

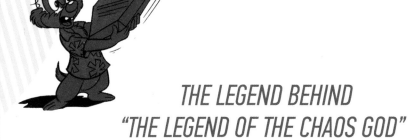

THE LEGEND BEHIND "THE LEGEND OF THE CHAOS GOD"

BY DAVID CODY WEISS

In the early 1990s, the five-show *Disney Afternoon* TV animation block was riding high on the airwaves—and every month, Disney Publishing Worldwide's own *Disney Adventures* digest magazine featured comics spin-off stories, many of which my wife and colleague, Bobbi JG Weiss, and I were honored to write.

In 1994, word came down from on high to the *Disney Adventures* crew: create a serialized, extended-length comic story to support all five of the then-current *Disney Afternoon* shows... at once! The shows—*TaleSpin*, *Chip 'n' Dale Rescue Rangers*, *Goof Troop*, *DuckTales* and *Darkwing Duck*—were a company-wide hit, and we had to do our bit. *Disney Adventures* editor Marv Wolfman tapped Bobbi for the script after she and I came up with a plot to tie all the contrasting elements together.

Those contrasts were significant. Each of the five shows inhabited separate worlds which had their own universes, histories, and different art styles. Up until that point, no Disney story had ever combined the franchises, in effect breaking those barriers. We had a deep respect for that precedence, but that set us up with an impossible challenge—how to cross over five shows without actually crossing anything over.

If we couldn't cross the shows, we needed something that could be passed *from* show to show—a metaphorical football we could hand off to each of the five animated teams to battle with on their home turf. Something magical, obviously, and possessed by a terrible evil that could take over even the most innocent players. So we created Solego and the Chaos Crystal. (Trivia note: we named the villain after his basic trait—a *sole ego.*)

Once we solved the impossible crossover challenge, it was business as usual in crafting the individual chapters that made up the saga. Each incursion made by Solego and his crystal into the five shows worked as an episode of that show. That was the most important question for Bobbi and myself as players in other peoples' universes—could we write a story that would make a good episode, or maybe enter the canon someday?

This volume's editor, David Gerstein, informs me that Solego—with a slight overhaul to his backstory—was actually described and shown in "Let's Get Dangerous," a Darkwing Duck-themed episode of 2017's rebooted *DuckTales* series. Hey, we *did* enter the canon! •

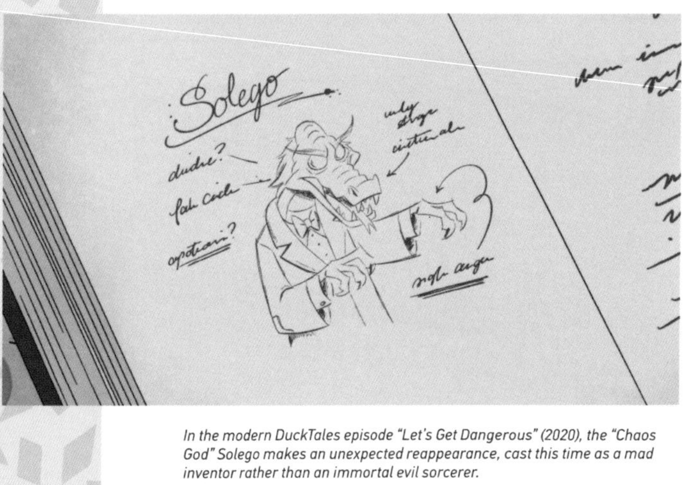
Solego

In the modern DuckTales episode "Let's Get Dangerous" (2020), the "Chaos God" Solego makes an unexpected reappearance, cast this time as a mad inventor rather than an immortal evil sorcerer.

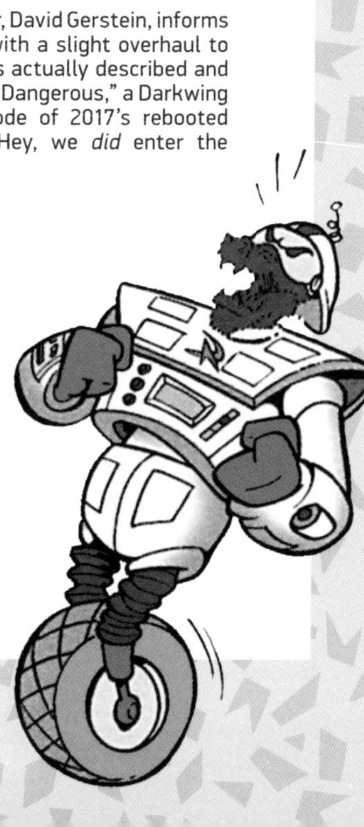

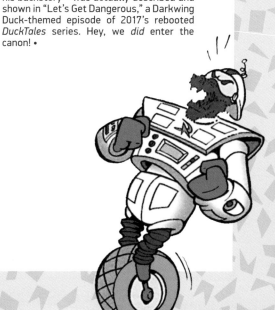

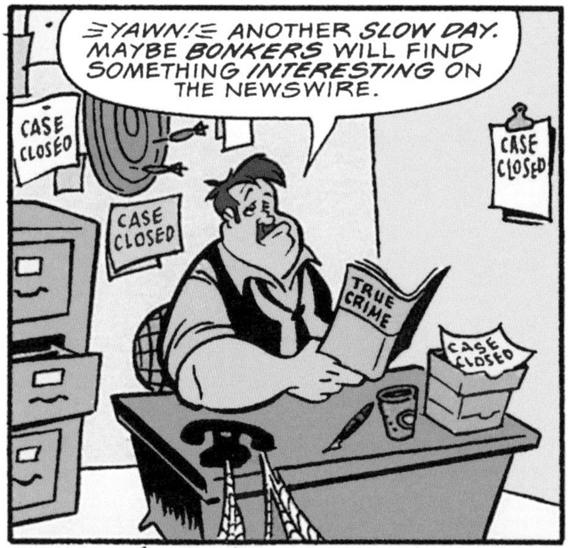
=YAWN!= ANOTHER SLOW DAY. MAYBE BONKERS WILL FIND SOMETHING INTERESTING ON THE NEWSWIRE.
CASE CLOSED
CASE CLOSED
CASE CLOSED
TRUE CRIME
CASE CLOSED

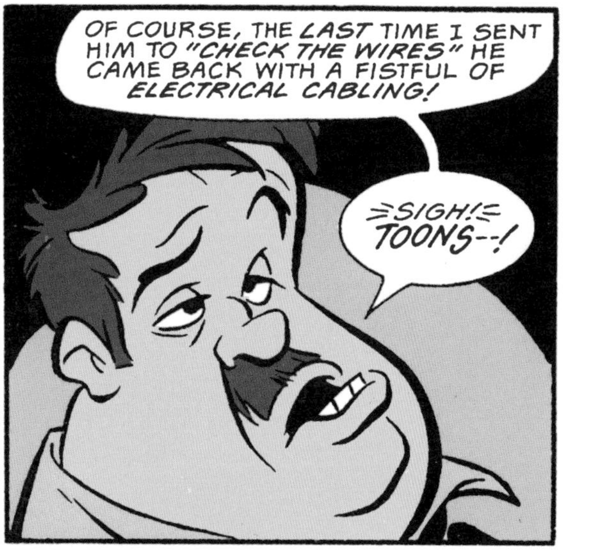
OF COURSE, THE LAST TIME I SENT HIM TO "CHECK THE WIRES" HE CAME BACK WITH A FISTFUL OF ELECTRICAL CABLING!
=SIGH!= TOONS--!

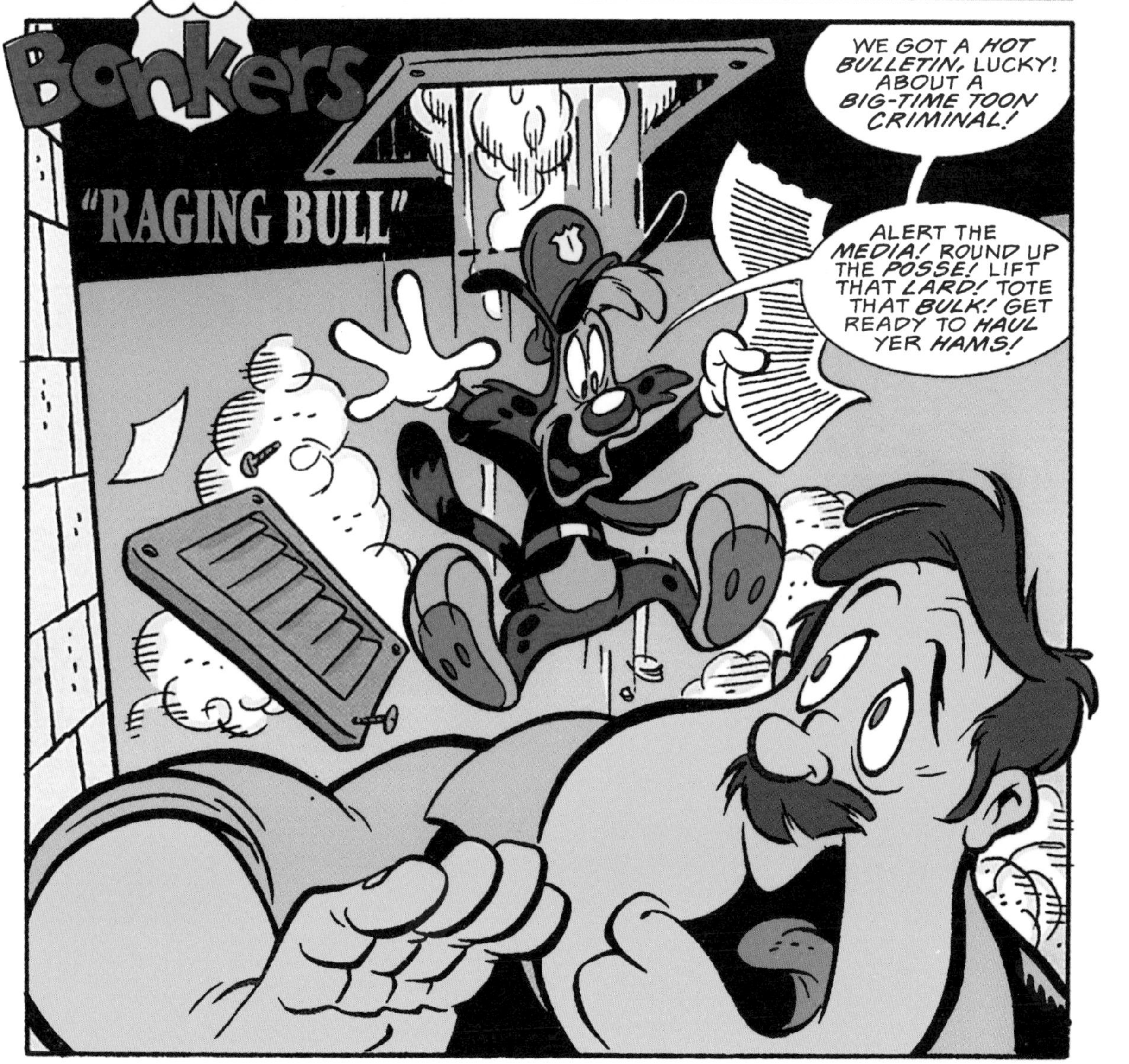
Bonkers
"RAGING BULL"
WE GOT A HOT BULLETIN, LUCKY! ABOUT A BIG-TIME TOON CRIMINAL!
ALERT THE MEDIA! ROUND UP THE POSSE! LIFT THAT LARD! TOTE THAT BULK! GET READY TO HAUL YER HAMS!

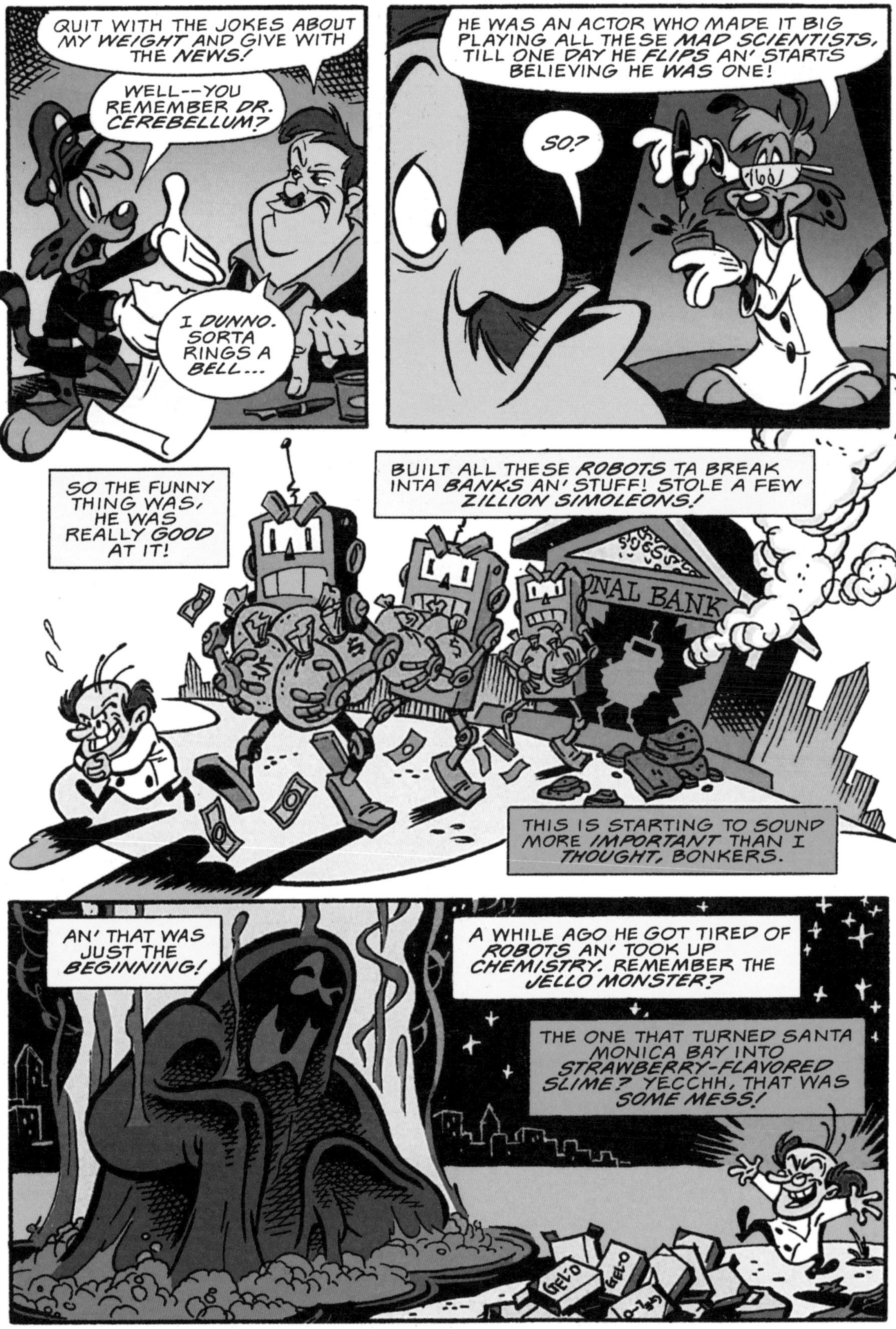
QUIT WITH THE JOKES ABOUT MY WEIGHT AND GIVE WITH THE NEWS!
WELL--YOU REMEMBER DR. CEREBELLUM?
I DUNNO. SORTA RINGS A BELL...
HE WAS AN ACTOR WHO MADE IT BIG PLAYING ALL THESE MAD SCIENTISTS, TILL ONE DAY HE FLIPS AN' STARTS BELIEVING HE WAS ONE!
SO?
SO THE FUNNY THING WAS, HE WAS REALLY GOOD AT IT!
BUILT ALL THESE ROBOTS TA BREAK INTA BANKS AN' STUFF! STOLE A FEW ZILLION SIMOLEONS!
NAL BANK
THIS IS STARTING TO SOUND MORE IMPORTANT THAN I THOUGHT, BONKERS.
AN' THAT WAS JUST THE BEGINNING!
A WHILE AGO HE GOT TIRED OF ROBOTS AN' TOOK UP CHEMISTRY. REMEMBER THE JELLO MONSTER?
THE ONE THAT TURNED SANTA MONICA BAY INTO STRAWBERRY-FLAVORED SLIME? YECCHH, THAT WAS SOME MESS!
GEL-O
GEL-O

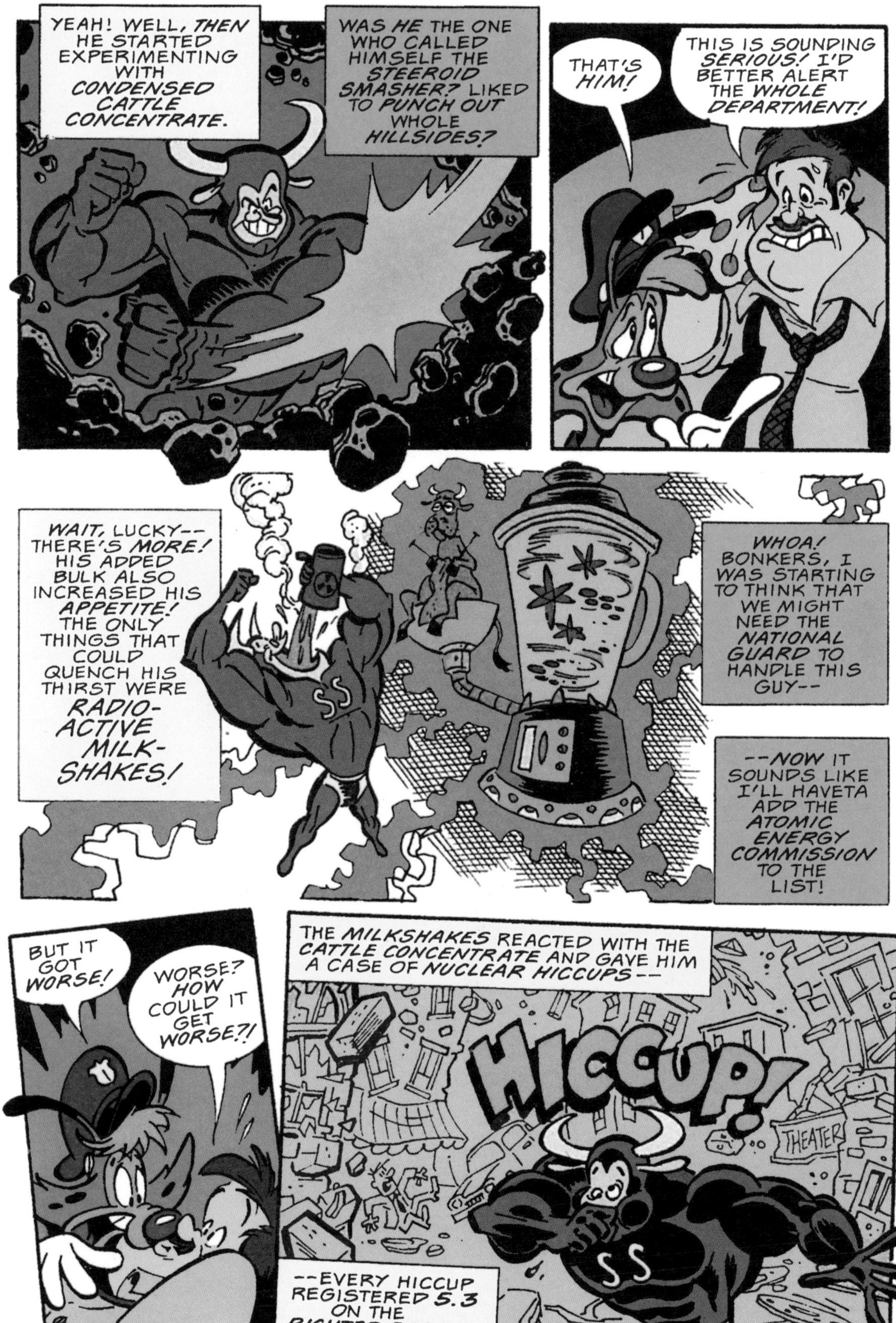
YEAH! WELL, THEN HE STARTED EXPERIMENTING WITH CONDENSED CATTLE CONCENTRATE.
WAS HE THE ONE WHO CALLED HIMSELF THE STEEROID SMASHER? LIKED TO PUNCH OUT WHOLE HILLSIDES?
THAT'S HIM!
THIS IS SOUNDING SERIOUS! I'D BETTER ALERT THE WHOLE DEPARTMENT!
WAIT, LUCKY-- THERE'S MORE! HIS ADDED BULK ALSO INCREASED HIS APPETITE! THE ONLY THINGS THAT COULD QUENCH HIS THIRST WERE RADIO-ACTIVE MILK-SHAKES!
WHOA! BONKERS, I WAS STARTING TO THINK THAT WE MIGHT NEED THE NATIONAL GUARD TO HANDLE THIS GUY--
--NOW IT SOUNDS LIKE I'LL HAVETA ADD THE ATOMIC ENERGY COMMISSION TO THE LIST!
BUT IT GOT WORSE!
WORSE? HOW COULD IT GET WORSE?!
THE MILKSHAKES REACTED WITH THE CATTLE CONCENTRATE AND GAVE HIM A CASE OF NUCLEAR HICCUPS--
HICCUP!
THEATER
--EVERY HICCUP REGISTERED 5.3 ON THE RICHTER SCALE...

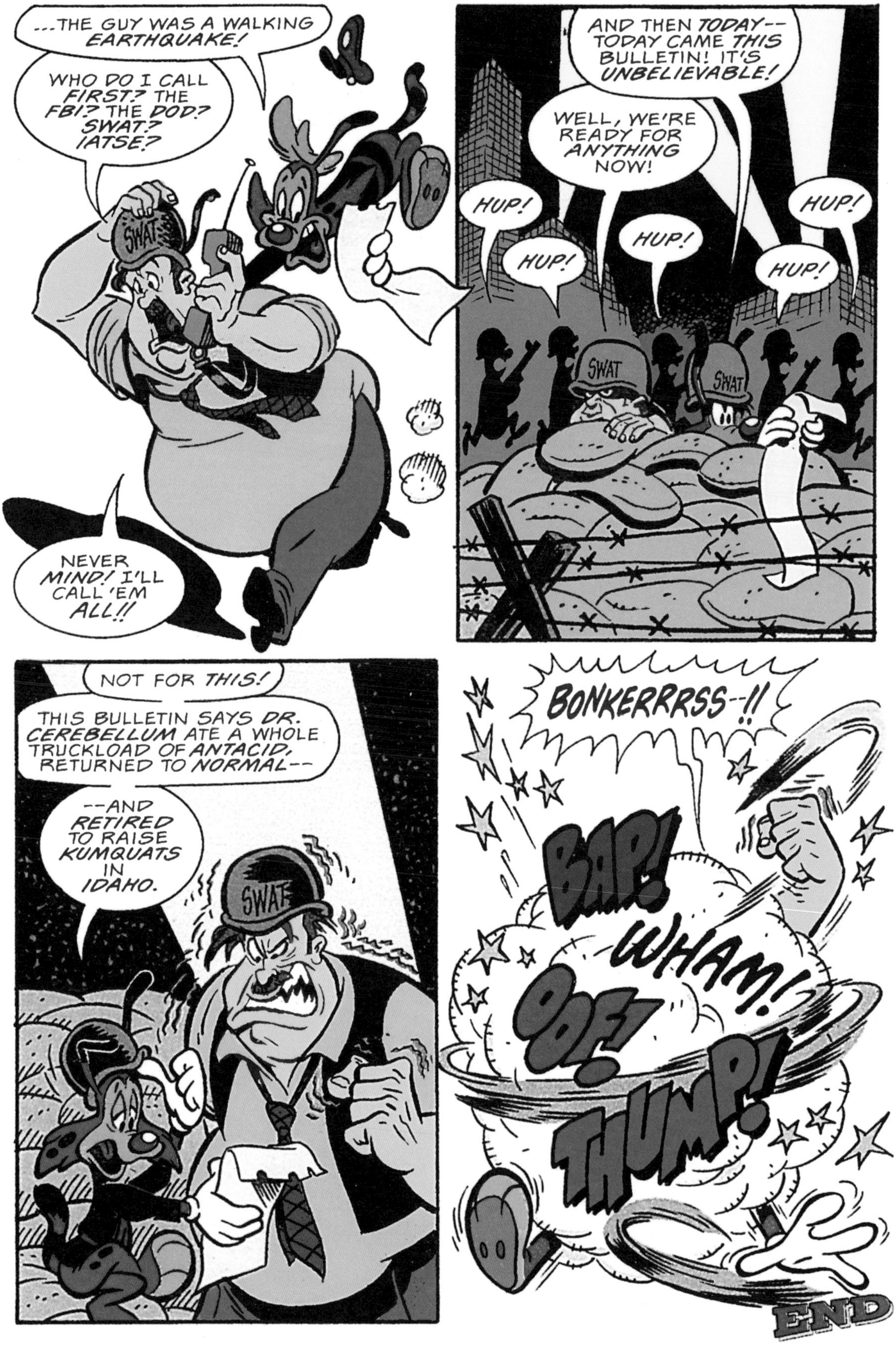
...THE GUY WAS A WALKING EARTHQUAKE!
WHO DO I CALL FIRST? THE FBI? THE DOD? SWAT? IATSE?
SWAT
NEVER MIND! I'LL CALL 'EM ALL!!
AND THEN TODAY-- TODAY CAME THIS BULLETIN! IT'S UNBELIEVABLE!
WELL, WE'RE READY FOR ANYTHING NOW!
HUP!
HUP!
HUP!
HUP!
HUP!
SWAT
SWAT
NOT FOR THIS!
THIS BULLETIN SAYS DR. CEREBELLUM ATE A WHOLE TRUCKLOAD OF ANTACID, RETURNED TO NORMAL--
--AND RETIRED TO RAISE KUMQUATS IN IDAHO.
SWAT
BONKERRRSS--!!
BAP!
WHAM!
OOF!
THUMP!
END

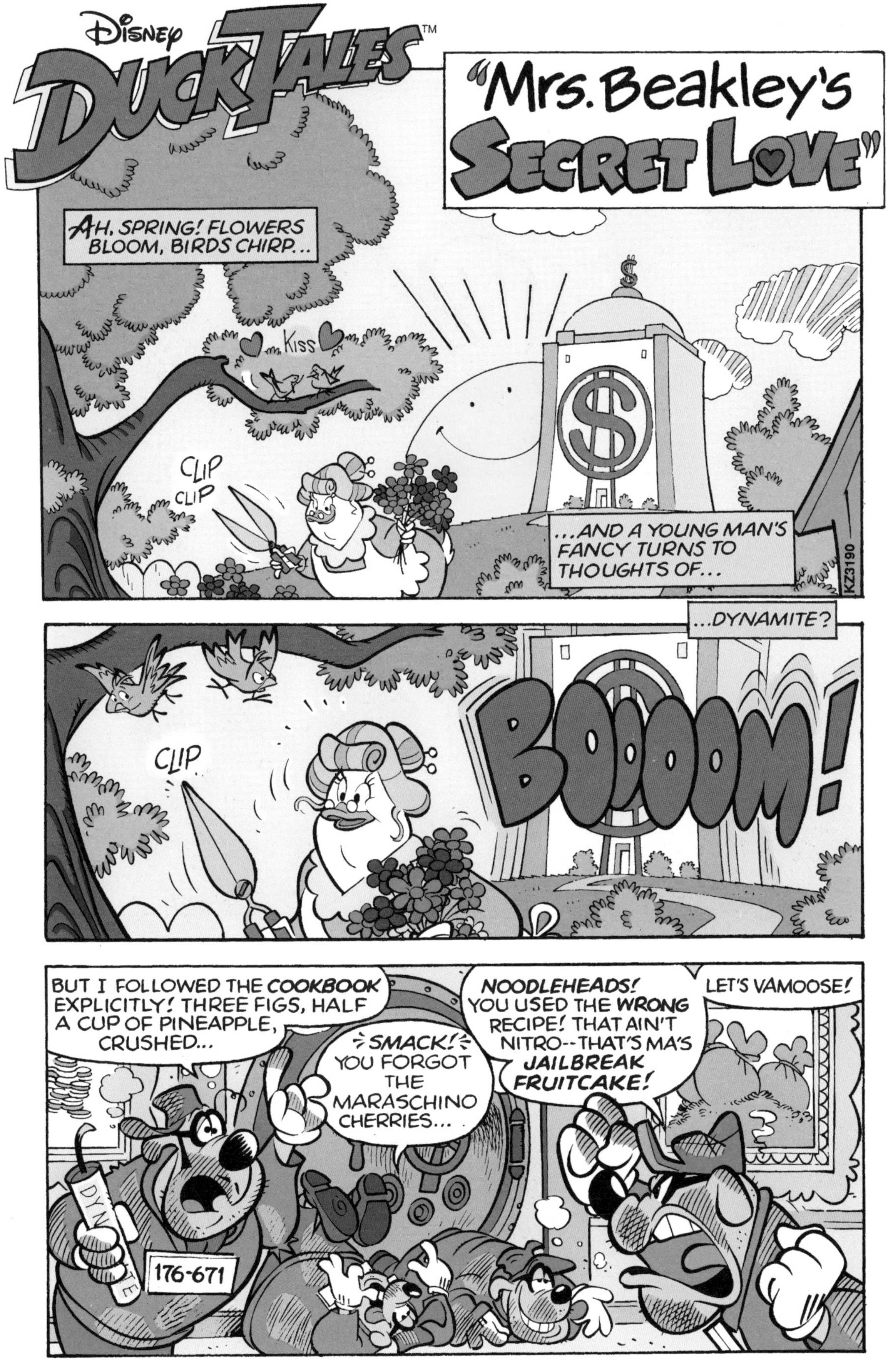
Disney DuckTales™
"Mrs. Beakley's Secret Love"
AH, SPRING! FLOWERS BLOOM, BIRDS CHIRP...
KISS
CLIP CLIP
...AND A YOUNG MAN'S FANCY TURNS TO THOUGHTS OF...
KZ3190
...DYNAMITE?
CLIP
BOOOOM!
BUT I FOLLOWED THE COOKBOOK EXPLICITLY! THREE FIGS, HALF A CUP OF PINEAPPLE, CRUSHED...
SMACK! YOU FORGOT THE MARASCHINO CHERRIES...
NOODLEHEADS! YOU USED THE WRONG RECIPE! THAT AIN'T NITRO--THAT'S MA'S JAILBREAK FRUITCAKE!
LET'S VAMOOSE!
176-671

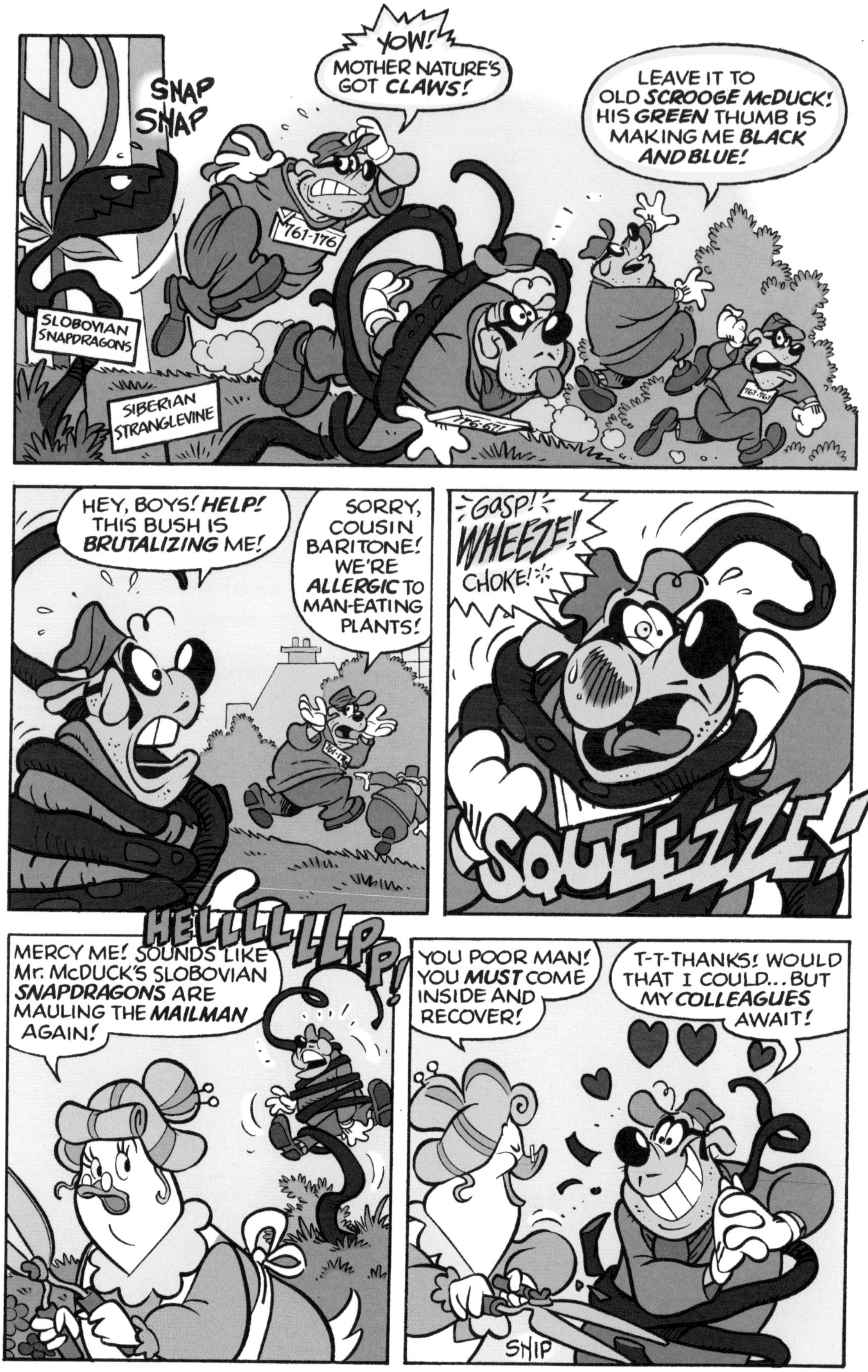
SNAP SNAP
YOW! MOTHER NATURE'S GOT CLAWS!
LEAVE IT TO OLD SCROOGE McDUCK! HIS GREEN THUMB IS MAKING ME BLACK AND BLUE!
761-176
SLOBOVIAN SNAPDRAGONS
SIBERIAN STRANGLEVINE
HEY, BOYS! HELP! THIS BUSH IS BRUTALIZING ME!
SORRY, COUSIN BARITONE! WE'RE ALLERGIC TO MAN-EATING PLANTS!
Gasp! WHEEZE! CHOKE!
SQUEEZZE!
HELLLLLLLPPP!
MERCY ME! SOUNDS LIKE Mr. McDUCK'S SLOBOVIAN SNAPDRAGONS ARE MAULING THE MAILMAN AGAIN!
YOU POOR MAN! YOU MUST COME INSIDE AND RECOVER!
T-T-THANKS! WOULD THAT I COULD... BUT MY COLLEAGUES AWAIT!
SNIP

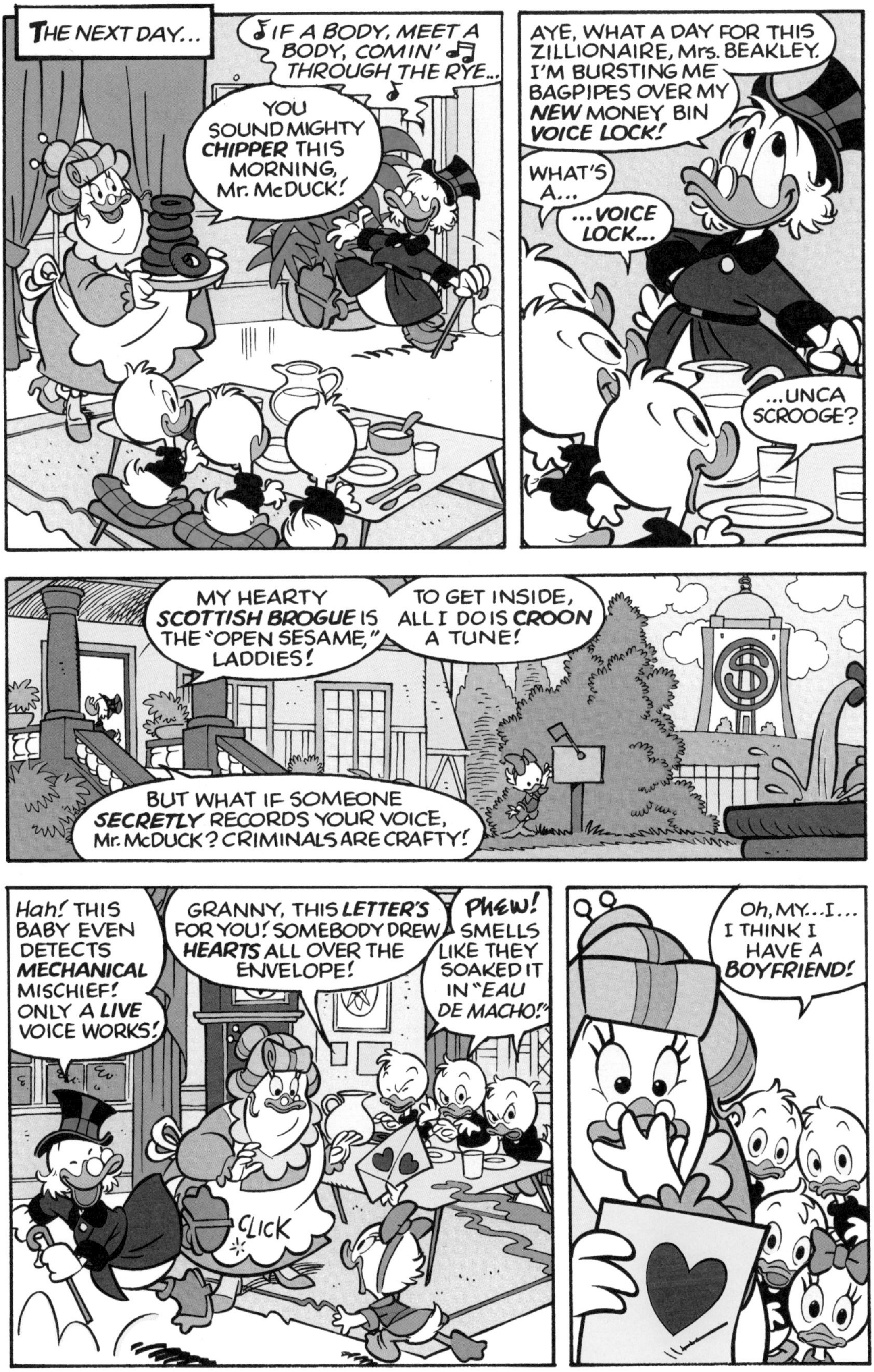
THE NEXT DAY...
IF A BODY, MEET A BODY, COMIN' THROUGH THE RYE...
YOU SOUND MIGHTY CHIPPER THIS MORNING, Mr. McDUCK!
AYE, WHAT A DAY FOR THIS ZILLIONAIRE, Mrs. BEAKLEY. I'M BURSTING ME BAGPIPES OVER MY NEW MONEY BIN VOICE LOCK!
WHAT'S A...
...VOICE LOCK...
...UNCA SCROOGE?
MY HEARTY SCOTTISH BROGUE IS THE "OPEN SESAME," LADDIES!
TO GET INSIDE, ALL I DO IS CROON A TUNE!
BUT WHAT IF SOMEONE SECRETLY RECORDS YOUR VOICE, Mr. McDUCK? CRIMINALS ARE CRAFTY!
Hah! THIS BABY EVEN DETECTS MECHANICAL MISCHIEF! ONLY A LIVE VOICE WORKS!
GRANNY, THIS LETTER'S FOR YOU! SOMEBODY DREW HEARTS ALL OVER THE ENVELOPE!
PHEW! SMELLS LIKE THEY SOAKED IT IN "EAU DE MACHO!"
CLICK
Oh, MY...I... I THINK I HAVE A BOYFRIEND!

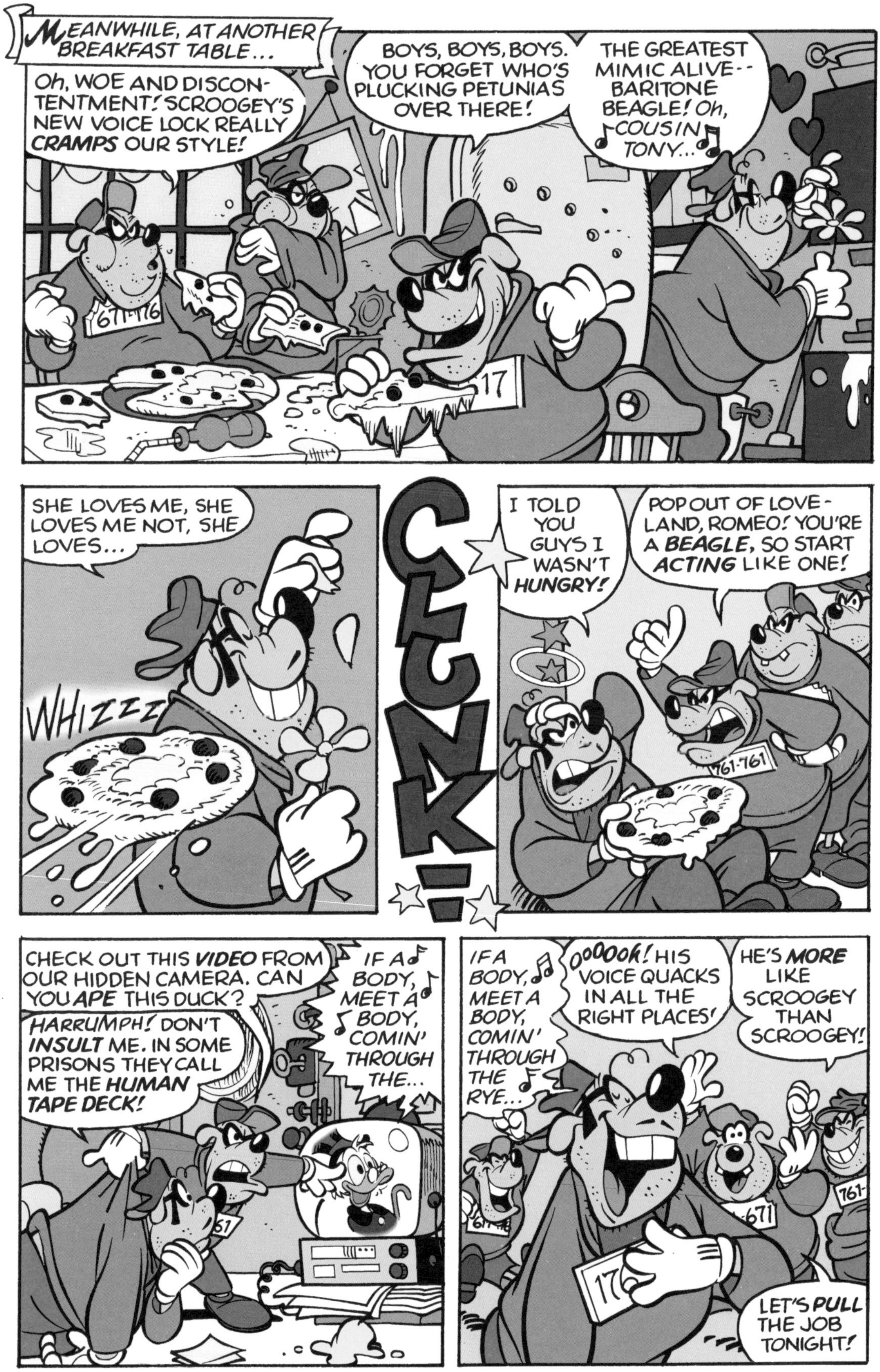
MEANWHILE, AT ANOTHER BREAKFAST TABLE...
Oh, WOE AND DISCONTENTMENT! SCROOGEY'S NEW VOICE LOCK REALLY CRAMPS OUR STYLE!
BOYS, BOYS, BOYS. YOU FORGET WHO'S PLUCKING PETUNIAS OVER THERE!
THE GREATEST MIMIC ALIVE-- BARITONE BEAGLE! Oh, COUSIN TONY...
671-176
176
SHE LOVES ME, SHE LOVES ME NOT, SHE LOVES...
WHIZZZ
CLUNK!
I TOLD YOU GUYS I WASN'T HUNGRY!
POP OUT OF LOVE-LAND, ROMEO! YOU'RE A BEAGLE, SO START ACTING LIKE ONE!
761-761
CHECK OUT THIS VIDEO FROM OUR HIDDEN CAMERA. CAN YOU APE THIS DUCK?
HARRUMPH! DON'T INSULT ME. IN SOME PRISONS THEY CALL ME THE HUMAN TAPE DECK!
IF A BODY, MEET A BODY, COMIN' THROUGH THE...
IF A BODY, MEET A BODY, COMIN' THROUGH THE RYE...
OOOOOK! HIS VOICE QUACKS IN ALL THE RIGHT PLACES!
HE'S MORE LIKE SCROOGEY THAN SCROOGEY!
LET'S PULL THE JOB TONIGHT!

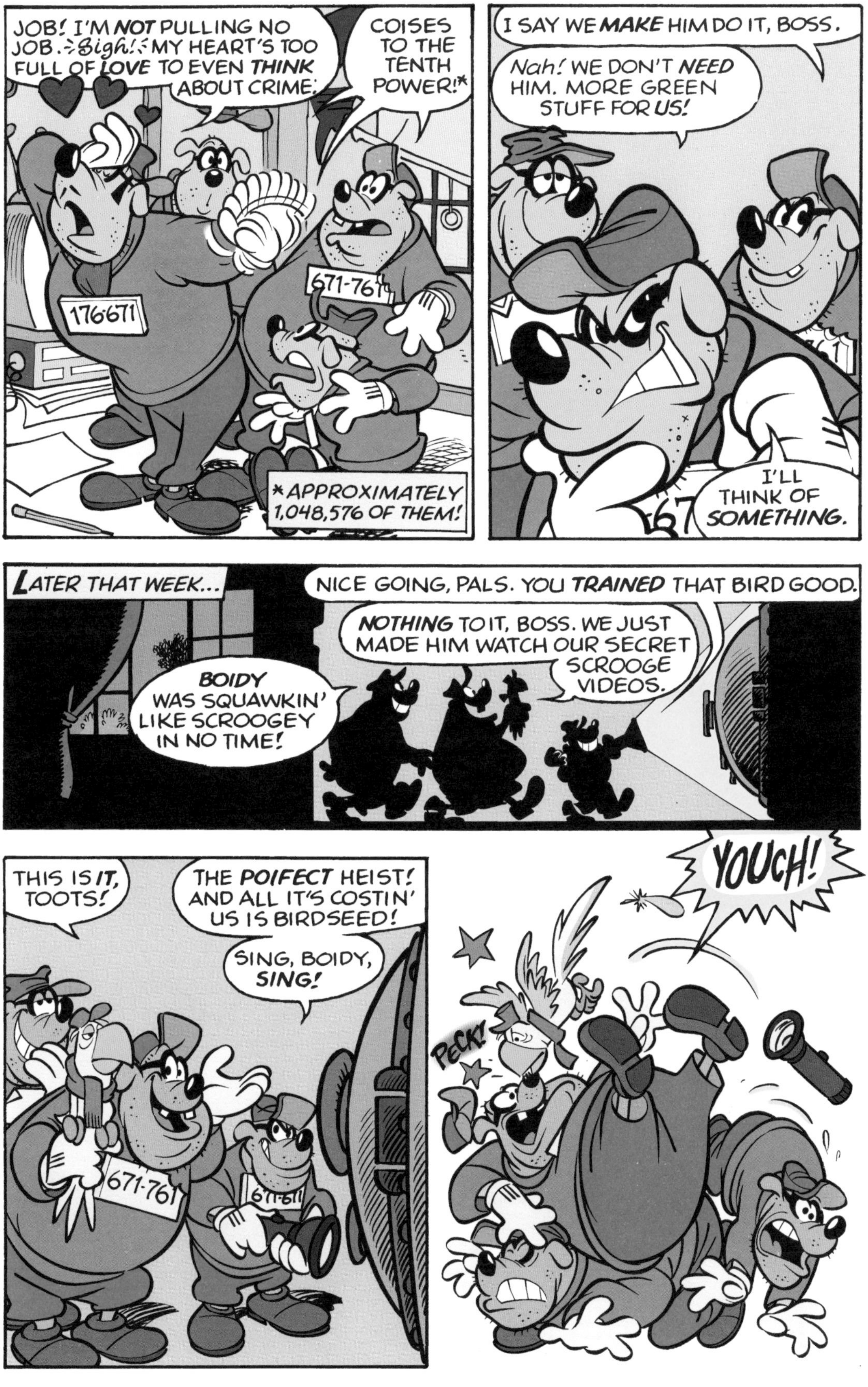
JOB! I'M NOT PULLING NO JOB. Sigh! MY HEART'S TOO FULL OF LOVE TO EVEN THINK ABOUT CRIME.
COISES TO THE TENTH POWER!*
176-671
671-761
*APPROXIMATELY 1,048,576 OF THEM!
I SAY WE MAKE HIM DO IT, BOSS.
Nah! WE DON'T NEED HIM. MORE GREEN STUFF FOR US!
I'LL THINK OF SOMETHING.
LATER THAT WEEK...
NICE GOING, PALS. YOU TRAINED THAT BIRD GOOD.
NOTHING TO IT, BOSS. WE JUST MADE HIM WATCH OUR SECRET SCROOGE VIDEOS.
BOIDY WAS SQUAWKIN' LIKE SCROOGEY IN NO TIME!
THIS IS IT, TOOTS!
THE POIFECT HEIST! AND ALL IT'S COSTIN' US IS BIRDSEED!
SING, BOIDY, SING!
671-761
671-611
YOUCH!
PECK!

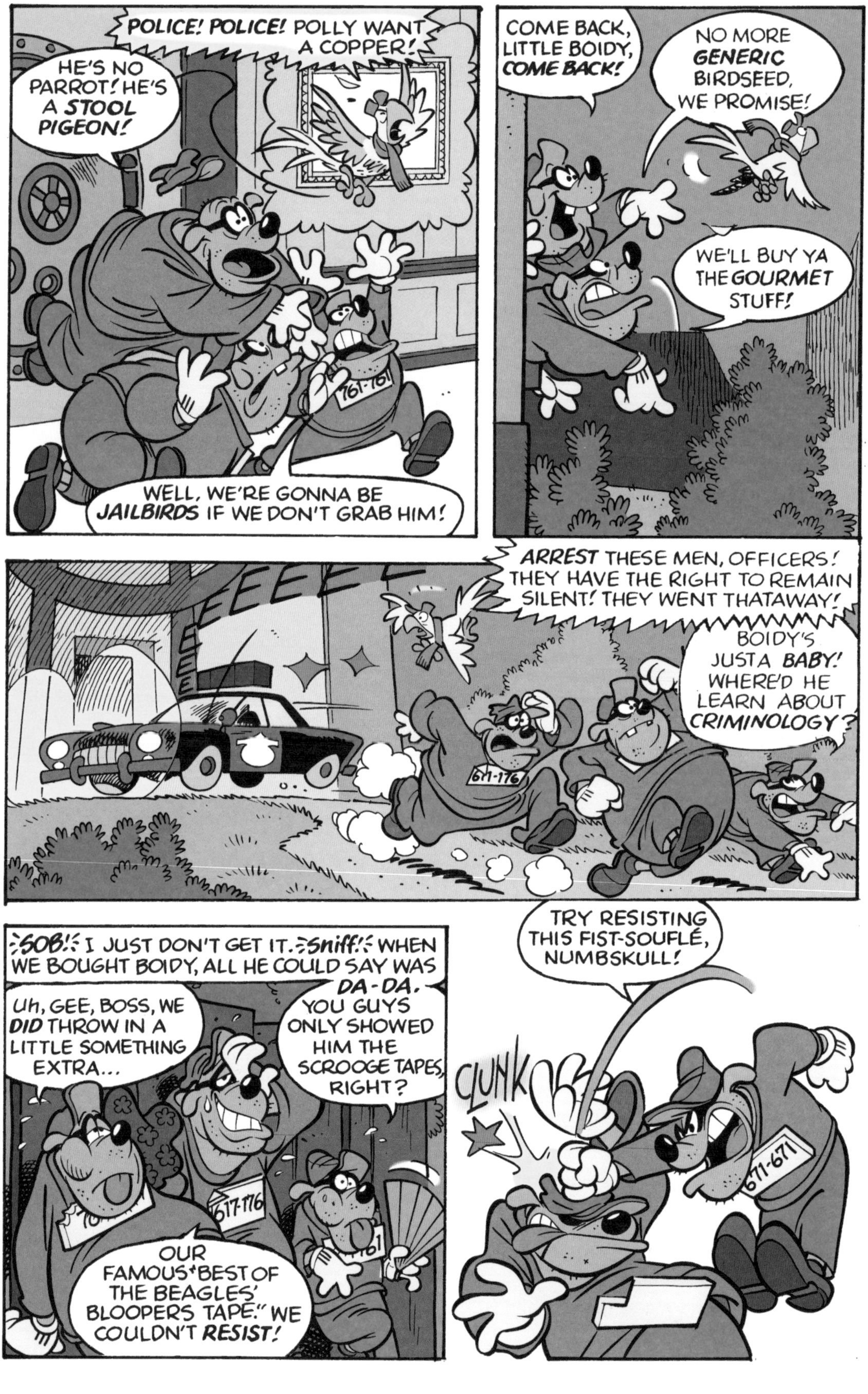
POLICE! POLICE! POLLY WANT A COPPER!
HE'S NO PARROT! HE'S A STOOL PIGEON!
WELL, WE'RE GONNA BE JAILBIRDS IF WE DON'T GRAB HIM!
761-761
COME BACK, LITTLE BOIDY, COME BACK!
NO MORE GENERIC BIRDSEED, WE PROMISE!
WE'LL BUY YA THE GOURMET STUFF!
EEEEEE
ARREST THESE MEN, OFFICERS! THEY HAVE THE RIGHT TO REMAIN SILENT! THEY WENT THATAWAY!
BOIDY'S JUSTA BABY! WHERE'D HE LEARN ABOUT CRIMINOLOGY?
671-176
SOB! I JUST DON'T GET IT. Sniff! WHEN WE BOUGHT BOIDY, ALL HE COULD SAY WAS DA-DA.
Uh, GEE, BOSS, WE DID THROW IN A LITTLE SOMETHING EXTRA...
YOU GUYS ONLY SHOWED HIM THE SCROOGE TAPES, RIGHT?
617-176
OUR FAMOUS "BEST OF THE BEAGLES' BLOOPERS TAPE." WE COULDN'T RESIST!
TRY RESISTING THIS FIST-SOUFLÉ, NUMBSKULL!
CLUNK
671-671

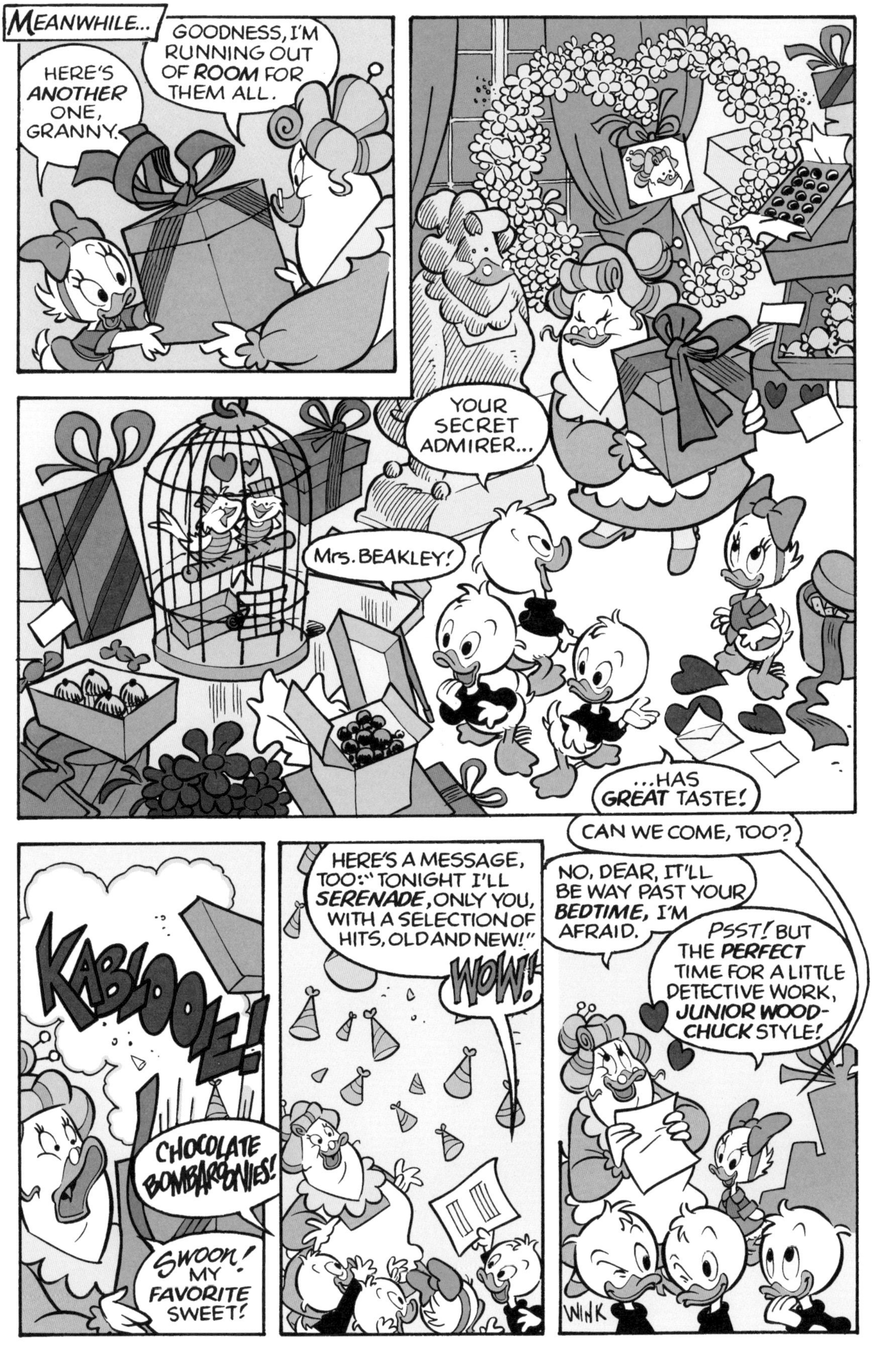
MEANWHILE...
HERE'S ANOTHER ONE, GRANNY.
GOODNESS, I'M RUNNING OUT OF ROOM FOR THEM ALL.
YOUR SECRET ADMIRER...
Mrs. BEAKLEY!
...HAS GREAT TASTE!
KABLOOIE!
CHOCOLATE BOMBARONIES!
SWOON! MY FAVORITE SWEET!
HERE'S A MESSAGE, TOO: "TONIGHT I'LL SERENADE, ONLY YOU, WITH A SELECTION OF HITS, OLD AND NEW!"
WOW!
CAN WE COME, TOO?
NO, DEAR, IT'LL BE WAY PAST YOUR BEDTIME, I'M AFRAID.
PSST! BUT THE PERFECT TIME FOR A LITTLE DETECTIVE WORK, JUNIOR WOODCHUCK STYLE!
WINK

THAT NIGHT...

WHAT LIGHT THROUGH THAT THERE WINDOW BREAKS? IT IS THE MOON, AND YOU ARE THE SUN, OR STAR, OR SOMETHING LIKE THAT.

SORRY, MY SHAKESPEARE'S RUSTY.

OH! WHO'S THERE?

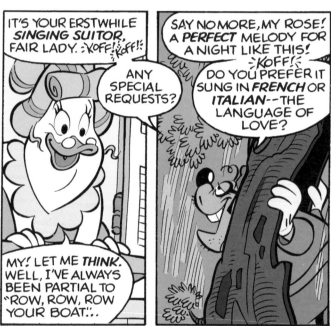

IT'S YOUR ERSTWHILE *SINGING SUITOR*, FAIR LADY. :KOFF! KOFF!:

ANY SPECIAL REQUESTS?

MY! LET ME *THINK*. WELL, I'VE ALWAYS BEEN PARTIAL TO "ROW, ROW, ROW YOUR BOAT."..

SAY NO MORE, MY ROSE! A *PERFECT* MELODY FOR A NIGHT LIKE THIS! :KOFF!: DO YOU PREFER IT SUNG IN *FRENCH* OR *ITALIAN*--THE LANGUAGE OF LOVE?

DEAR ME, YOU SOUND SO... *CONTINENTAL!*

AHEM! ♪ ROW, ROW, ROW YOUR BOAT, ♫ GENTLY DOWN DOWN THE...

176-671

THREE HOURS LATER...

GOOD NIGHT, MY *PASSION FLOWER!* PARTING IS SUCH-- :KOFF: SWEET SORROW! A-A-A-*CHOOO!*

?

196

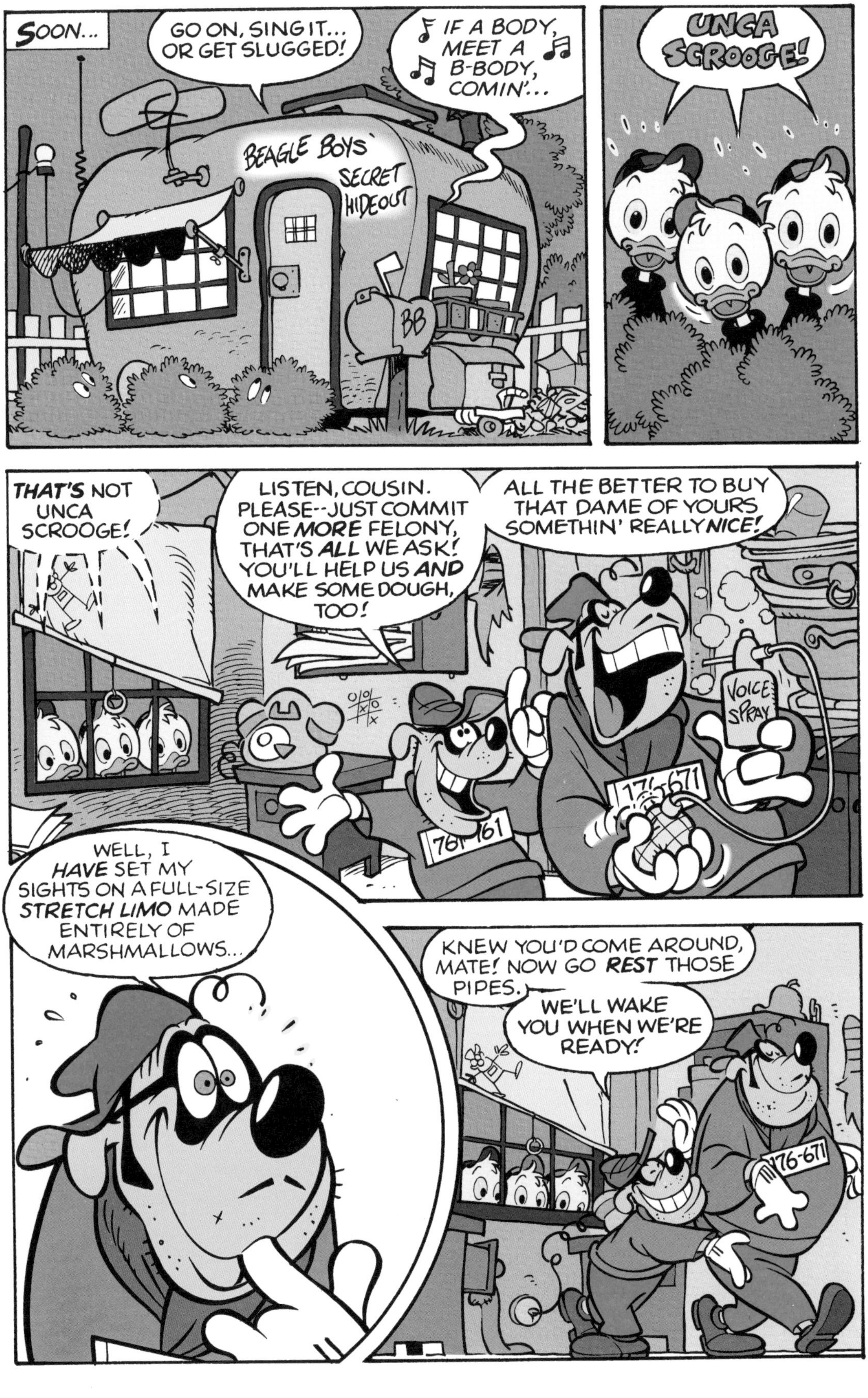
SOON...
GO ON, SING IT... OR GET SLUGGED!
IF A BODY, MEET A B-BODY, COMIN'...
BEAGLE BOYS' SECRET HIDEOUT
BB
UNCA SCROOGE!
THAT'S NOT UNCA SCROOGE!
LISTEN, COUSIN. PLEASE--JUST COMMIT ONE MORE FELONY, THAT'S ALL WE ASK! YOU'LL HELP US AND MAKE SOME DOUGH, TOO!
ALL THE BETTER TO BUY THAT DAME OF YOURS SOMETHIN' REALLY NICE!
VOICE SPRAY
176-671
761-161
WELL, I HAVE SET MY SIGHTS ON A FULL-SIZE STRETCH LIMO MADE ENTIRELY OF MARSHMALLOWS...
KNEW YOU'D COME AROUND, MATE! NOW GO REST THOSE PIPES.
WE'LL WAKE YOU WHEN WE'RE READY!
176-671

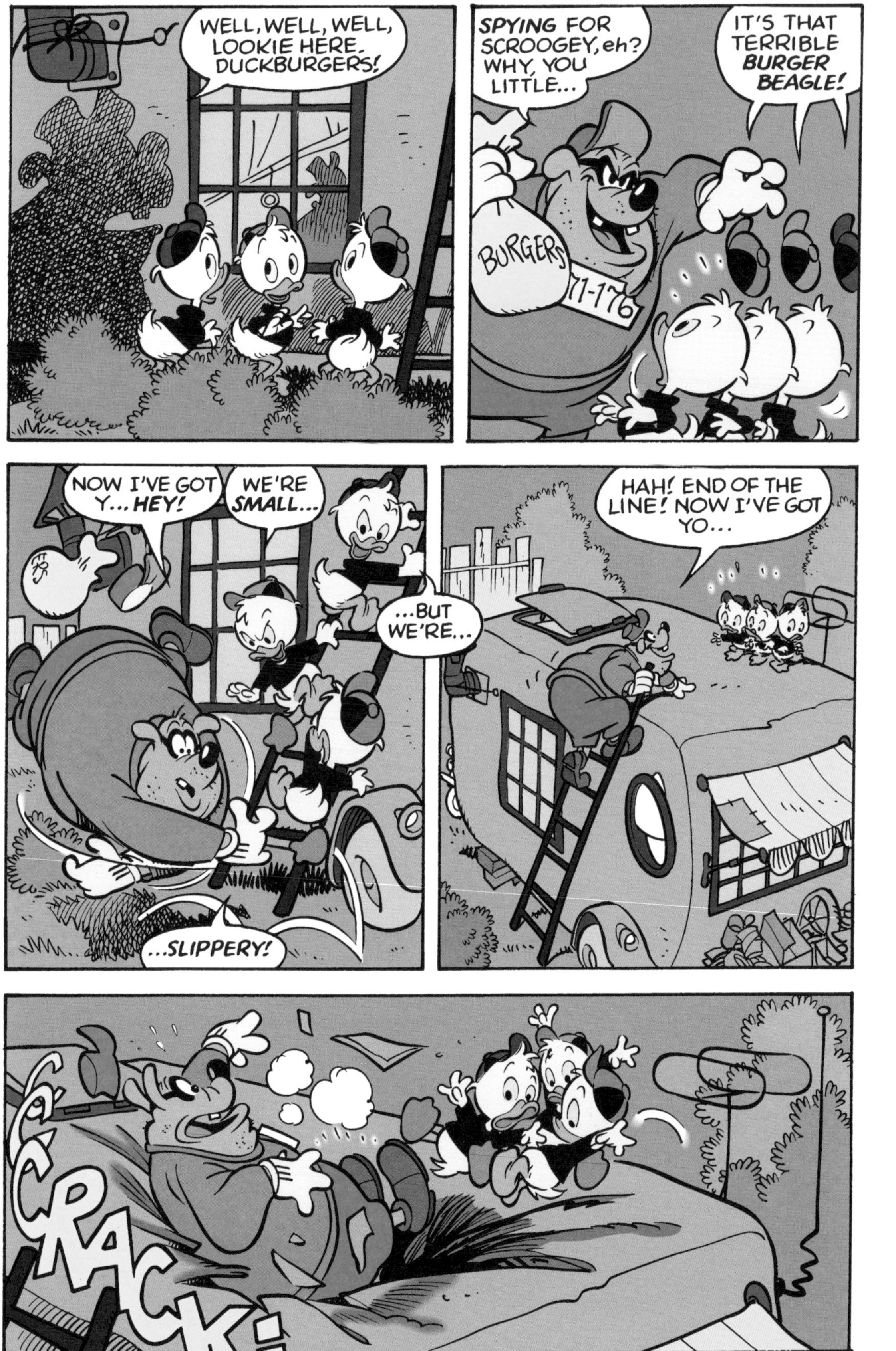
WELL, WELL, WELL, LOOKIE HERE. DUCKBURGERS!
SPYING FOR SCROOGEY, eh? WHY, YOU LITTLE...
IT'S THAT TERRIBLE BURGER BEAGLE!
BURGERS
71-176
NOW I'VE GOT Y... HEY!
WE'RE SMALL...
...BUT WE'RE...
...SLIPPERY!
HAH! END OF THE LINE! NOW I'VE GOT YO...
CRACK!

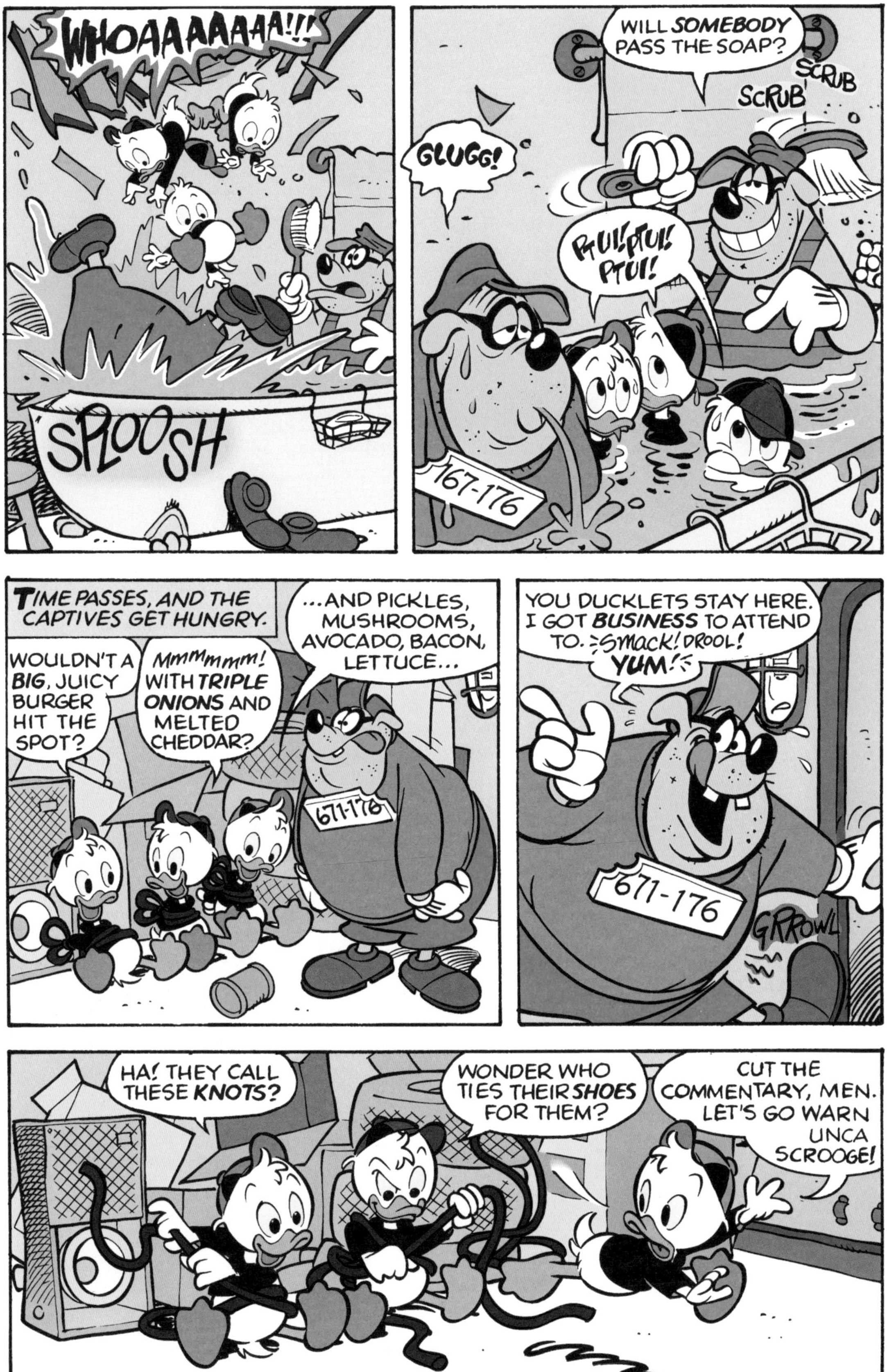
WHOAAAAAAA!!!
SPLOOSH
WILL SOMEBODY PASS THE SOAP?
SCRUB
SCRUB
GLUGG!
PTUI! PTUI! PTUI!
167-176
TIME PASSES, AND THE CAPTIVES GET HUNGRY.
WOULDN'T A BIG, JUICY BURGER HIT THE SPOT?
Mmmmmm! WITH TRIPLE ONIONS AND MELTED CHEDDAR?
...AND PICKLES, MUSHROOMS, AVOCADO, BACON, LETTUCE...
671-176
YOU DUCKLETS STAY HERE. I GOT BUSINESS TO ATTEND TO. Smack! DROOL! YUM!
671-176
GRROWL
HA! THEY CALL THESE KNOTS?
WONDER WHO TIES THEIR SHOES FOR THEM?
CUT THE COMMENTARY, MEN. LET'S GO WARN UNCA SCROOGE!

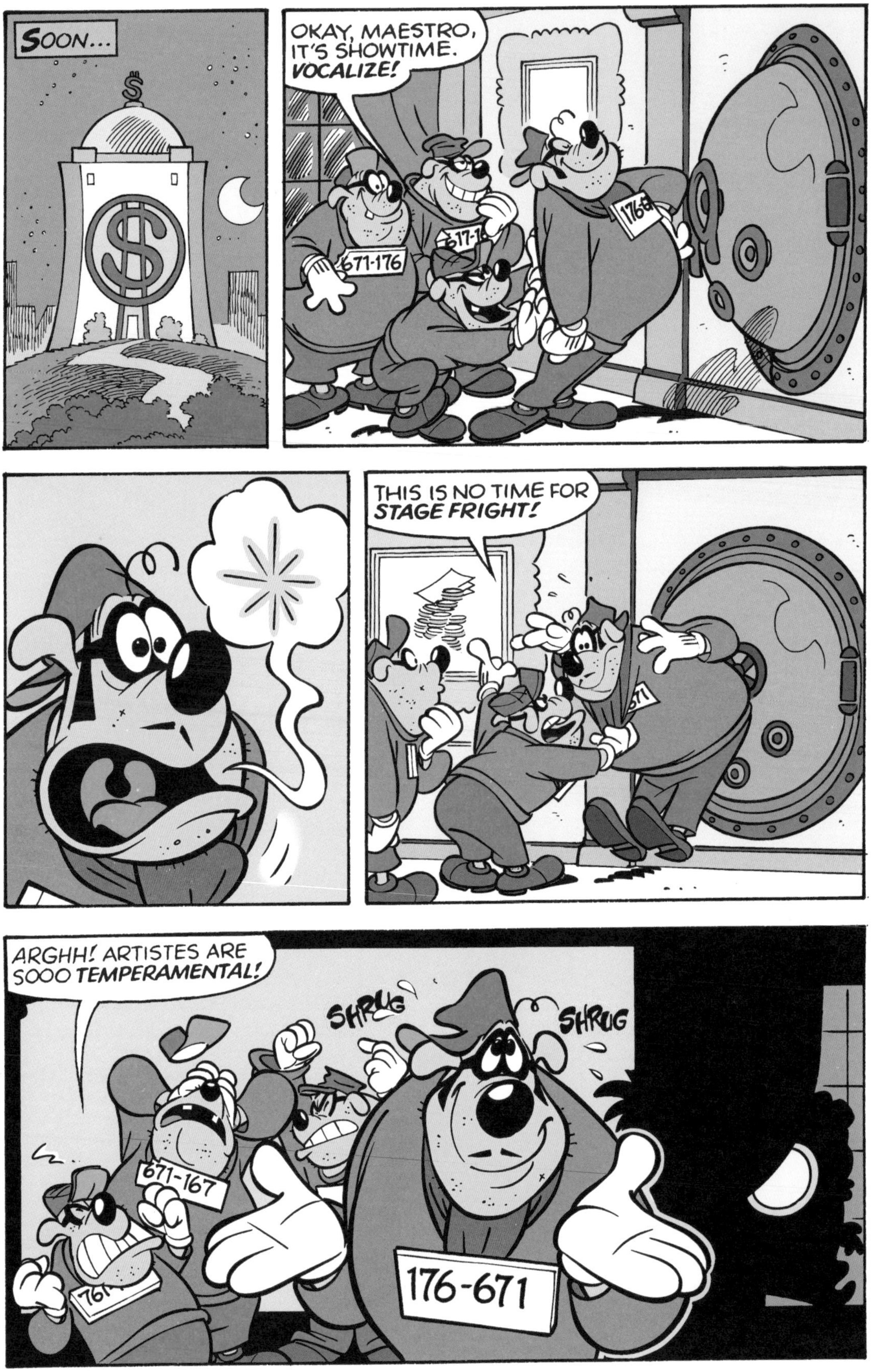
SOON...
OKAY, MAESTRO, IT'S SHOWTIME. VOCALIZE!
671-176
176-671
THIS IS NO TIME FOR STAGE FRIGHT!
ARGHH! ARTISTES ARE SOOO TEMPERAMENTAL!
SHRUG
SHRUG
671-167
176-671

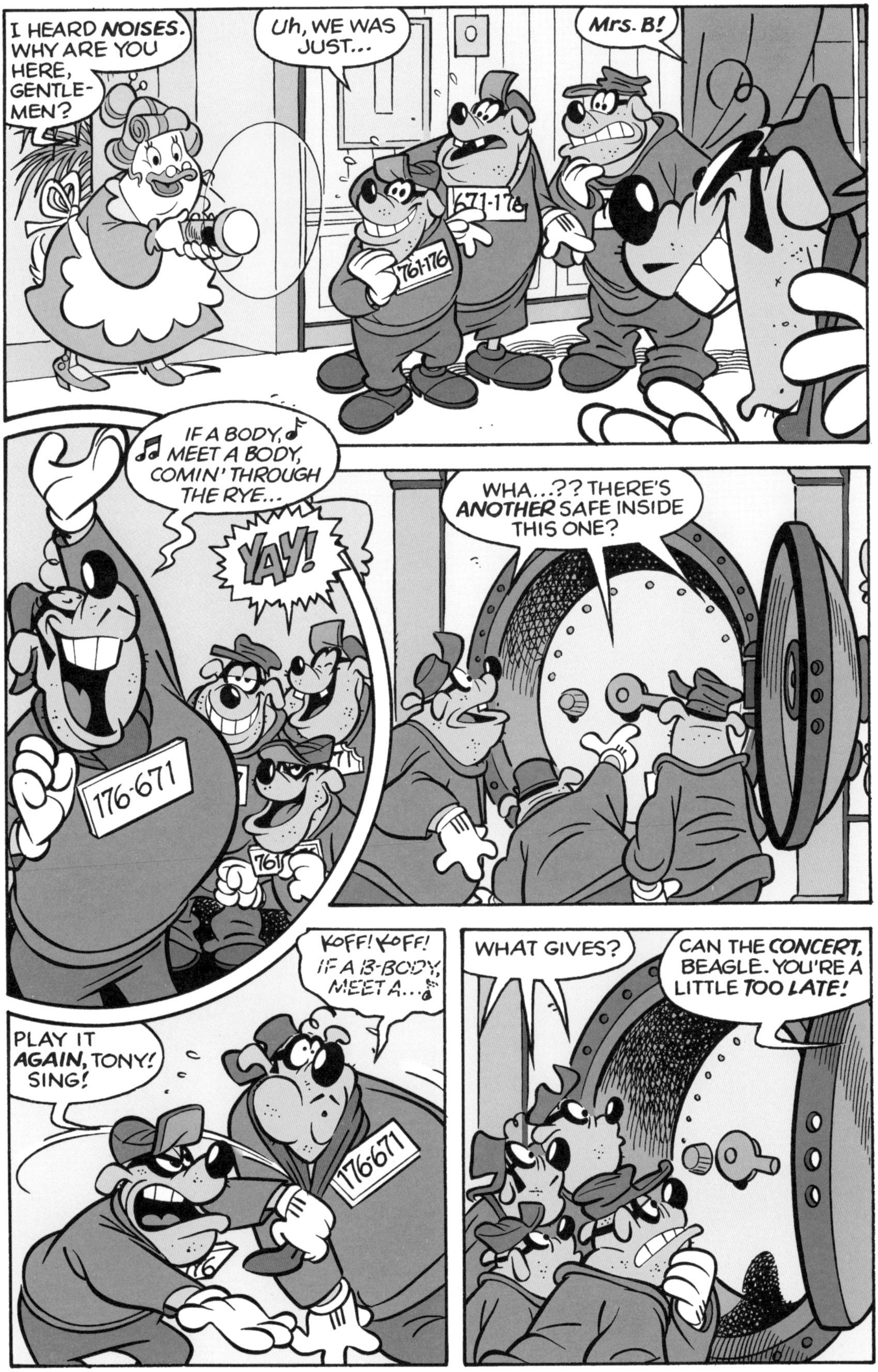

I HEARD NOISES. WHY ARE YOU HERE, GENTLEMEN?
Uh, WE WAS JUST...
Mrs. B!
671-176
761-176
IF A BODY, MEET A BODY, COMIN' THROUGH THE RYE...
YAY!
176-671
WHA...?? THERE'S ANOTHER SAFE INSIDE THIS ONE?
KOFF! KOFF! IF A B-BODY, MEET A...
PLAY IT AGAIN, TONY! SING!
176-671
WHAT GIVES?
CAN THE CONCERT, BEAGLE. YOU'RE A LITTLE TOO LATE!

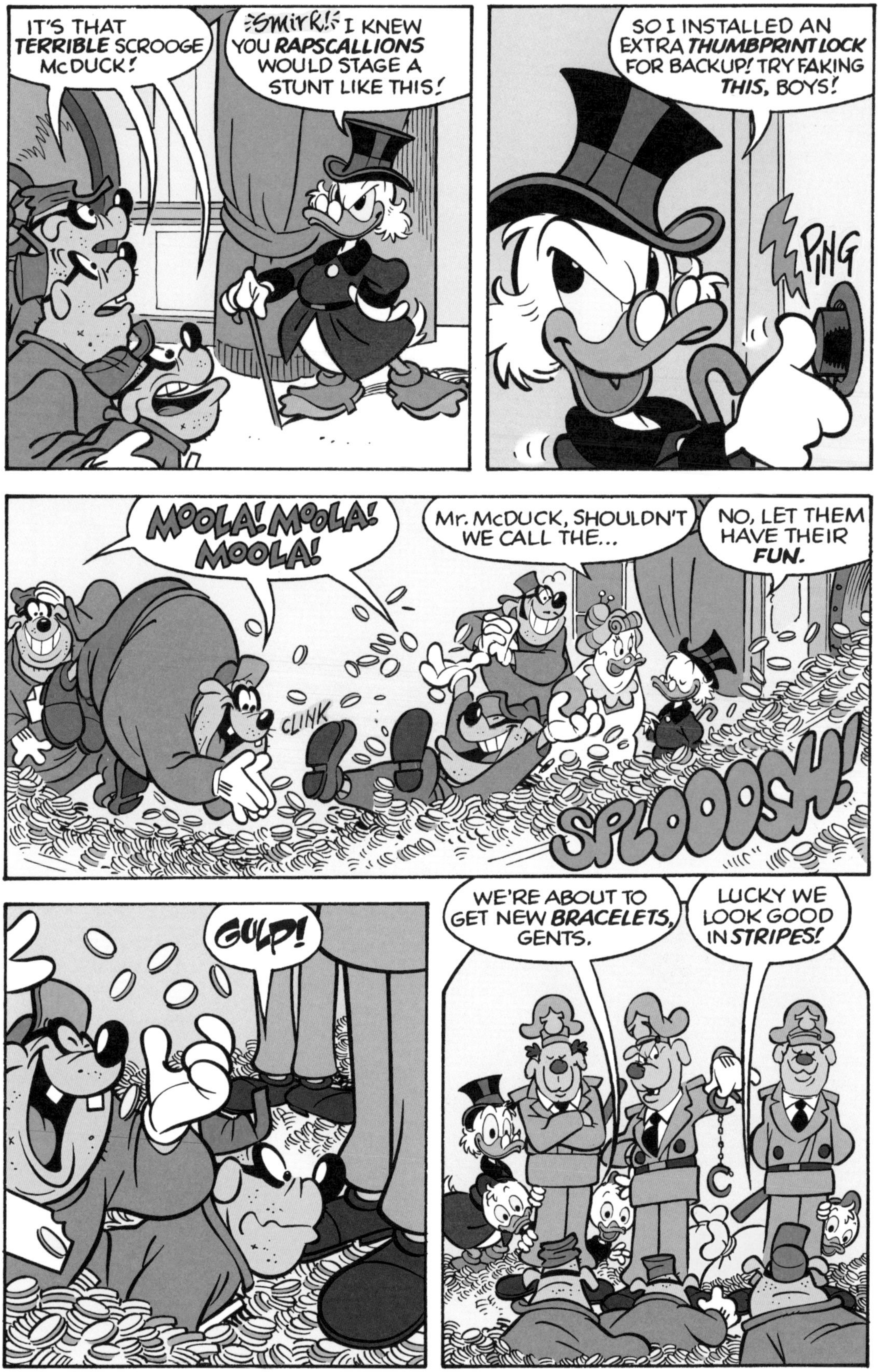
IT'S THAT TERRIBLE SCROOGE McDUCK!
SMIRK! I KNEW YOU RAPSCALLIONS WOULD STAGE A STUNT LIKE THIS!
SO I INSTALLED AN EXTRA THUMBPRINT LOCK FOR BACKUP! TRY FAKING THIS, BOYS!
PING
MOOLA! MOOLA! MOOLA!
CLINK
Mr. McDUCK, SHOULDN'T WE CALL THE...
NO, LET THEM HAVE THEIR FUN.
SPLOOOSH!
GULP!
WE'RE ABOUT TO GET NEW BRACELETS, GENTS.
LUCKY WE LOOK GOOD IN STRIPES!

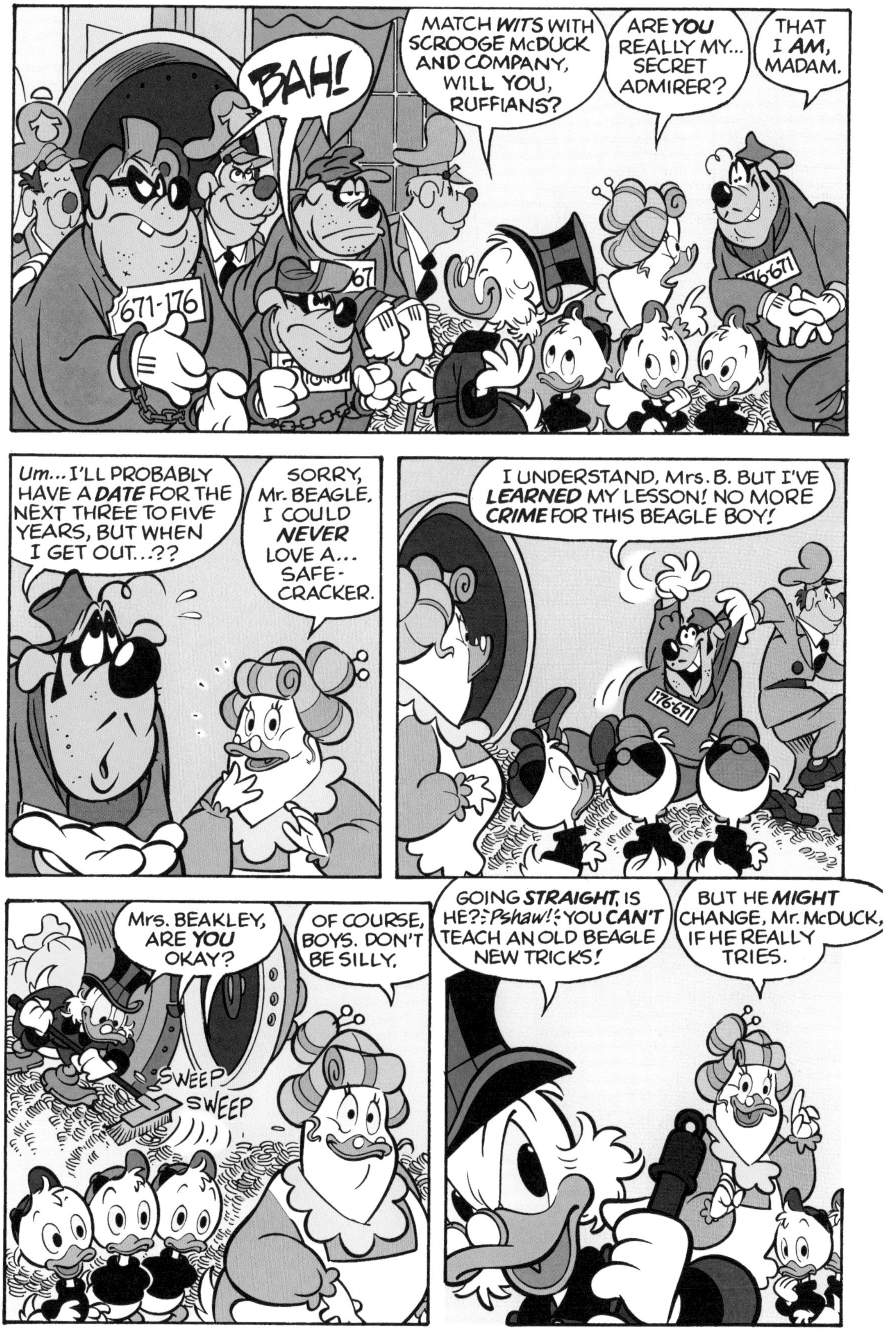
BAH!
MATCH WITS WITH SCROOGE McDUCK AND COMPANY, WILL YOU, RUFFIANS?
ARE YOU REALLY MY... SECRET ADMIRER?
THAT I AM, MADAM.
671-176
176-671
Um... I'LL PROBABLY HAVE A DATE FOR THE NEXT THREE TO FIVE YEARS, BUT WHEN I GET OUT...??
SORRY, Mr. BEAGLE. I COULD NEVER LOVE A... SAFE-CRACKER.
I UNDERSTAND, Mrs. B. BUT I'VE LEARNED MY LESSON! NO MORE CRIME FOR THIS BEAGLE BOY!
Mrs. BEAKLEY, ARE YOU OKAY?
OF COURSE, BOYS. DON'T BE SILLY.
SWEEP SWEEP
GOING STRAIGHT, IS HE?-Pshaw!- YOU CAN'T TEACH AN OLD BEAGLE NEW TRICKS!
BUT HE MIGHT CHANGE, Mr. McDUCK, IF HE REALLY TRIES.

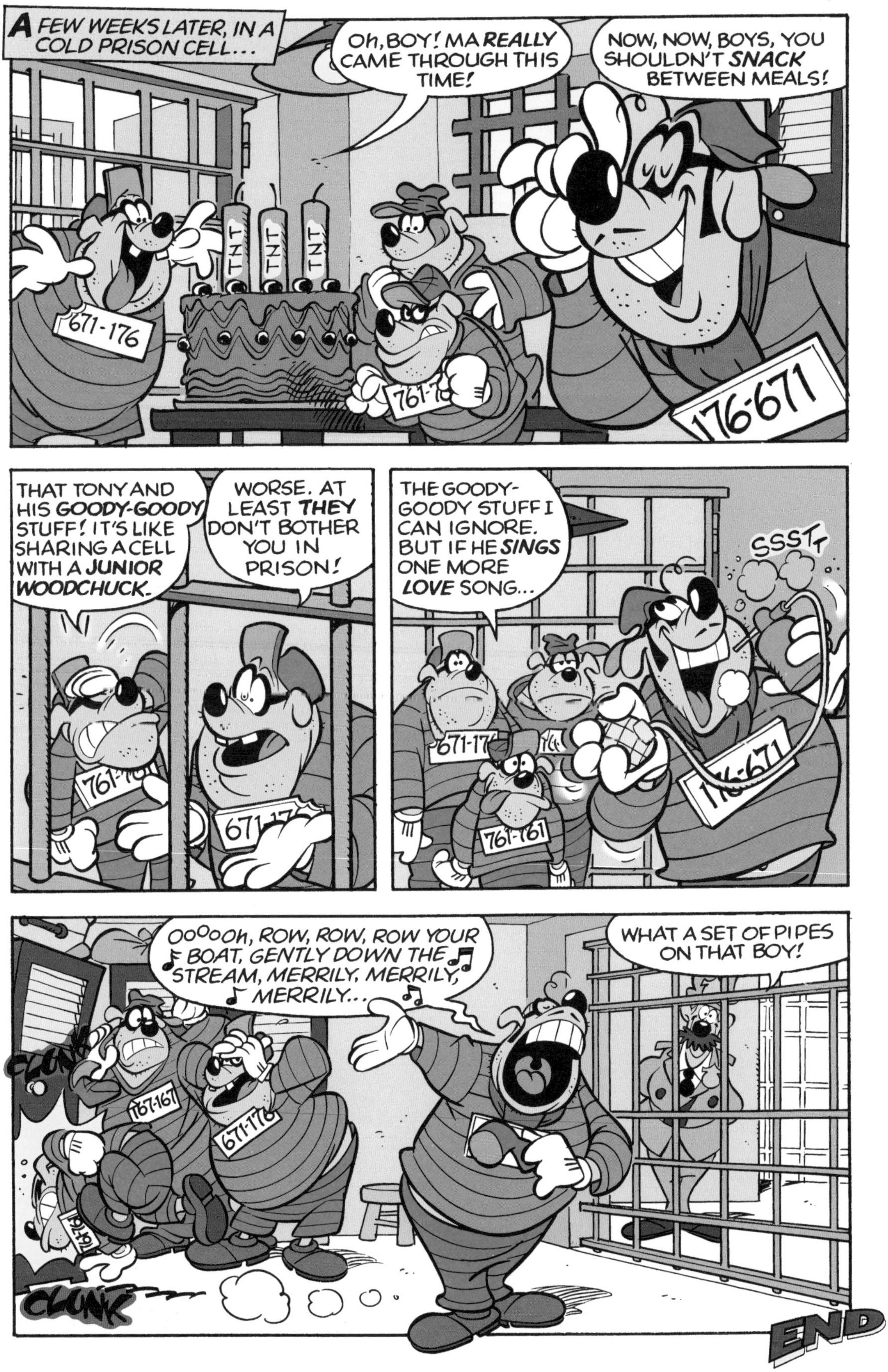

A FEW WEEKS LATER, IN A COLD PRISON CELL...
Oh, BOY! MA REALLY CAME THROUGH THIS TIME!
NOW, NOW, BOYS, YOU SHOULDN'T SNACK BETWEEN MEALS!
TNT
TNT
TNT
671-176
176-671
THAT TONY AND HIS GOODY-GOODY STUFF! IT'S LIKE SHARING A CELL WITH A JUNIOR WOODCHUCK.
WORSE. AT LEAST THEY DON'T BOTHER YOU IN PRISON!
THE GOODY-GOODY STUFF I CAN IGNORE. BUT IF HE SINGS ONE MORE LOVE SONG...
SSST
761-761
Oooooh, ROW, ROW, ROW YOUR BOAT, GENTLY DOWN THE STREAM, MERRILY, MERRILY, MERRILY...
WHAT A SET OF PIPES ON THAT BOY!
CLUNK
767-167
671-176
CLUNK
END